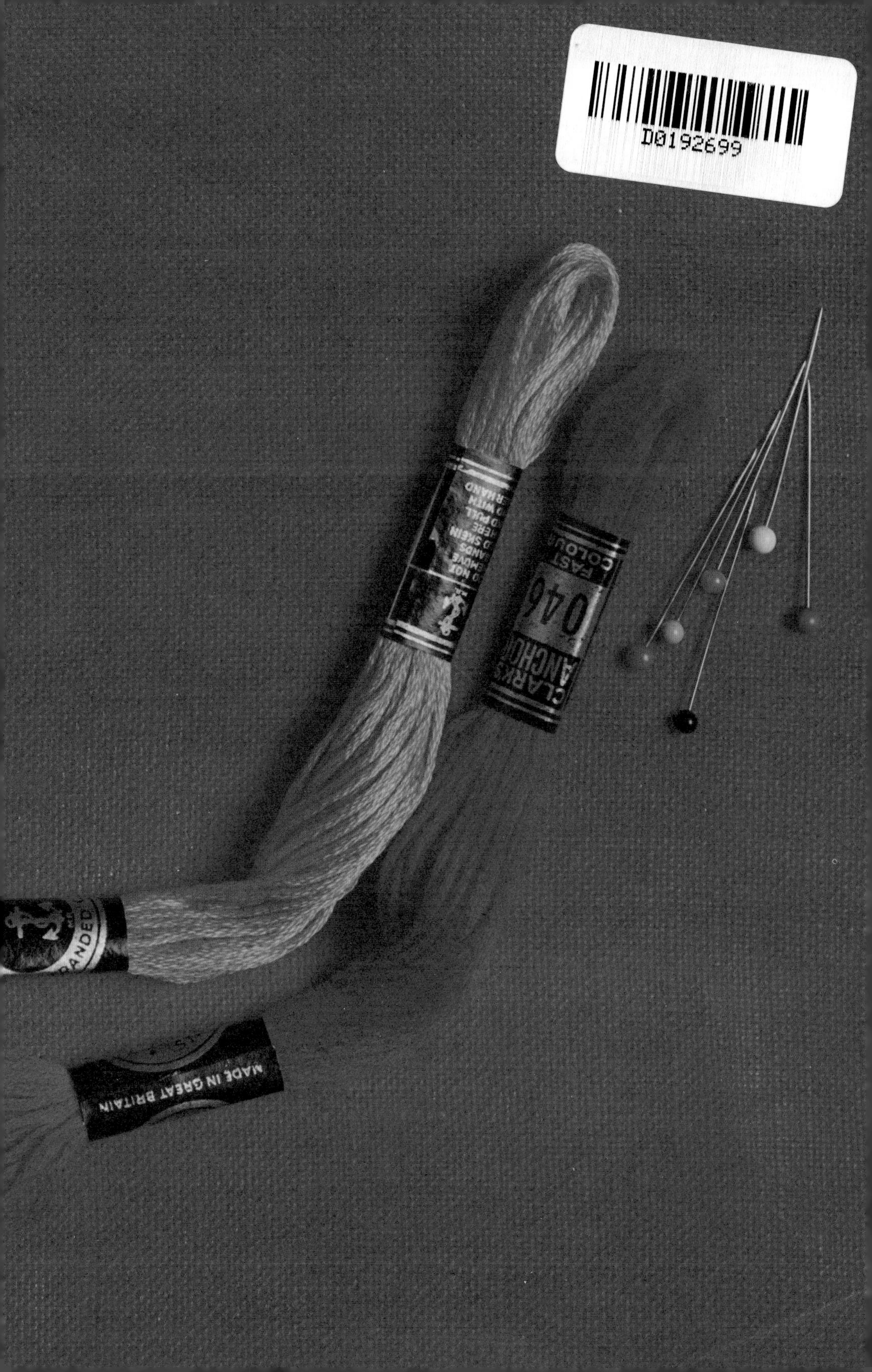

Creative
Crafts in Fabric
and Yarn

Creative Crafts in Fabric and Yarn

Galley Press

CREATIVE CRAFTS IN FABRIC AND YARN – this material was previously published as THE BASIC BOOK OF SEWING, KNITTING FOR FUN and MACRAME AND TATTING.

This edition published 1979 by
Galley Press
in association with Cathay Books
59 Grosvenor Street, London W1

© 1973, Hennerwood Publications
Limited

ISBN 0 904644 76 6

Produced by Mandarin Publishers
Limited
22a Westlands Road
Quarry Bay Hong Kong

Printed in Hong Kong

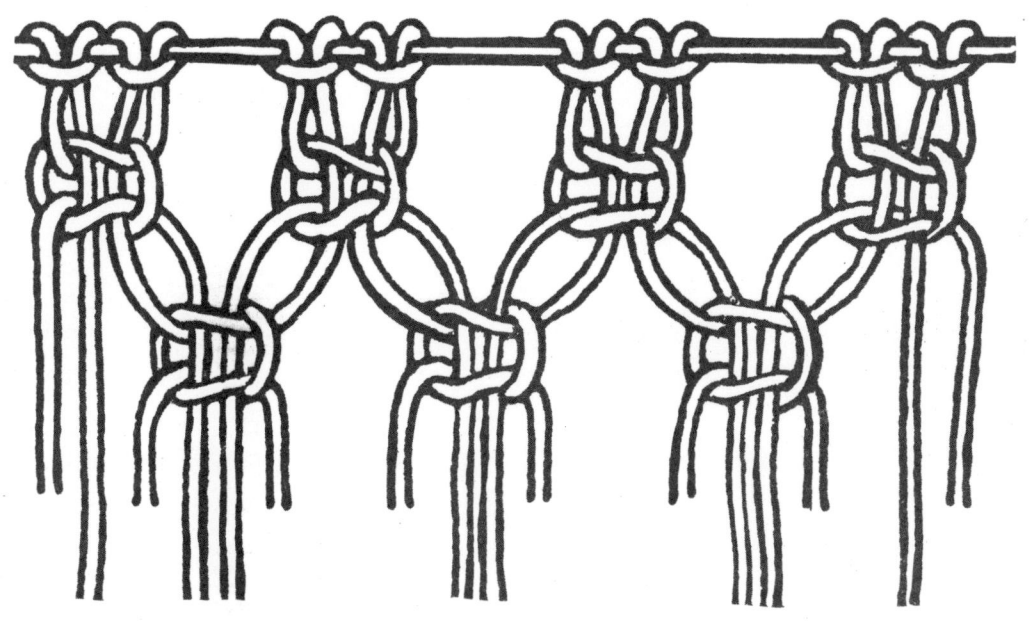

Acknowledgements

The Publishers would like to thank the following people and organisations for their assistance in the preparation of this book:

Photographers: Jason Biggs, John Gill, Alan Meek, John Webb.

Dressmaking diagrams on pages 121–168 by courtesy of McCall's Pattern Company.

Fabrics and haberdashery from John Lewis Partnership, Oxford Street, London W1.

Accessories and clothes from D. H. Evans Ltd., Oxford Street, London W1.

Macrame articles and materials by courtesy of Hobby Horse Limited, London.

Contents

Contents

Knitting

Knitting abbreviations

Abbreviations are used in knitting patterns to make instructions easier and less tedious to follow. Many of them are easily recognisable to most knitters. Make sure you do understand them all before you begin to knit. This will save you time and trouble once you have started.

K.,	*Knit*
p.,	*purl*
g.st.	*garter stitch.*
st.st.	*stocking stitch.*
st(s).	*stitch(es).*
inc.,	*increase.*
dec.,	*decrease.*
alt.,	*alternate.*
foll.,	*following.*
beg.,	*beginning.*
cont.,	*continue.*
patt.,	*pattern.*
tog.,	*together.*
p.u.k.,	*Pick up loop lying before*
next st.,	*and k. into back of it.*
rep.,	*repeat.*
rem.,	*remaining.*
p.s.s.o.,	*pass slipped st. over.*
sl.,	*slip.*
t.b.l.,	*through back of loop(s).*
d.m.st.,	*double moss stitch.*
m.st.,	*moss stitch.*
c.n.,	*cable needle.*
sl.1, k.1, p.s.s.o.,	*slip 1, knit 1, pass slipped stitch over.*
K.b.1 or P.b.1.,	*knit or purl into back of next st.*
T2F.,	*(Twist 2 Front) K. into front of 2nd st. on left hand needle, then k. first st. and sl. both from needle tog.*
T2B.,	*(Twist 2 Back) K. into back of 2nd st. on left hand needle, then into front of first st. and sl. both off tog.*
Cable 5.,	*Sl. next 2 sts. on to c.n. and leave at front, sl. next st. on to 2nd c.n., and leave at back, k. next 2 sts., then p.1 from back c.n., and k.2 from front c.n.*
C3R.,	*(Cross 3 right) Sl. next st. on to c.n. and leave at back, k.2, then p.1 from c.n.*
C3L.,	*(Cross 3 Left) Sl. next 2 sts. on to c.n. and leave at front, p.1, then k.2 from c.n.*
DC9.,	*(Double cable 9) Sl. next 3 sts. on to c.n. and leave at back, k.1, then k.3 from c.n., k.1, sl. next st. on to c.n., and leave at front, k.3, then k.1 from c.n.*

K.1B.	*Knit next st. but insert needle into st. in row below, allowing st. above to drop from needle.*
y.fwd.	*yarn forward.*
y.r.n.	*yarn round needle.*
y.o.n.	*yarn over needle.*
w.fwd.	*wool forward.*
w.o.n.	*wool over needle.*
w.r.n.	*wool round needle.*
w.b.	*wool back.*
K.f.b. or p.f.b.,	*K. or P. into front and back of next st.*
3-in-1.,	*K.1, p.1, k.1 all into next st.*
C6B or C6F.,	*(Cable 5 Back or cable 6 Front) Sl. next 3 sts. on to c.n., and leave at back, or front, k.3, then k.3 from c.n.*
TR.,	*(Twist Right) Sl. next 2 sts. on to c.n. leave at back, k.1, then k.2 from c.n.*
T.L.,	*(Twist Left) Sl. next st. on to c.n., leave at front, k.2, then k.1 from c.n. These twists are used in the Lobster claw and honeycomb patterns.*
C2B.,	*(Cable 2 back) Sl. next st. on to c.n., and leave at back, k.b.1., p.1 from c.n.*
C2F.,	*(Cable 2 front) Sl. next st. on to c.n., and leave at front, p.1, then k.b.1 from c.n.*
C4B.,	*(Cable 4 back) Sl. next 2 sts. on to c.n., leave at back, k.2, then k.2 from c.n.*
C4F.,	*(Cable 4 front) As C4B but leave 2 sts. on c.n. at front.*
CP7.,	*(Claw Patt. 7) Sl. next 2 sts. on to c.n., leave at back, k.1, then k.2 from c.n., k. next st., then sl. foll. st. on to c.n., leave at front, k.2, then k.1 from c.n.*
Cross 5.,	*S. next 3 sts. on to c.n., leave at back, k.2, now pass the p. st. from other end of c.n. back on to left hand needle, bring c.n. to front, p.1 from left hand needle and lastly, k.2 from c.n.*
M.B.,	*(Make Bobble) Into next st., work k.1, (w.fwd., k.1) twice, turn and p. these 5 sts., turn, k.5, turn p.5, turn. Now sl. 2nd, 3rd and 4th sts. over 1st and off needle, then k. tog. the rem. 2 sts. t.b.l. On next row, k. the st. over bobble tightly.*
R.S.,	*(Rich Stitch) As given in pattern concerned.*
C6R.,	*(Cable 6 right) Sl. next 4 sts. on to c.n., leave at back, k.2, sl.2 p. sts. from c.n. to left hand needle, bring c.n. to front, p.2 from left hand needle, then k.2 from c.n.*
C6L.,	*(Cable 6 left) Sl. next 2 sts. on to c.n., leave at front, sl. next 2 sts. on to 2nd c.n., leave at back, k.2 from left hand needle, p.2 from back c.n., k.2 from front c.n.*
M.L.,	*(Make Loop) Insert point of right hand needle into next st. and wind yarn over point of needle and first finger of left hand twice, then over needle again, draw through three loops. Place these 3 loops back on left hand needle and k. tog. t.b.l.*
ins.,	*Inches.*

Comparative knitting needle sizes

English	000	00	0	1	2		3	4	5	6	7	8	9	10	11	12	13	14
American	15	13	12	11	10 1/2	10	9	8	7	6	5	4	3	2	1	0	00	

Knitting needle sizes are not yet uniform in all countries and it is not always easy to decide which size is required. This chart tells you how English and American sizes compare. The important thing in all patterns will be the tension at which the item should be knitted. It is essential to obtain the correct tension in order to make the size given. Change needles to obtain the correct tension, as knitters vary, some people knitting loosely and some tightly. In all patterns in this book, the English needle size is given first, followed by the equivalent American needle size, given in brackets.

Comparative wool chart

All items in the knitting section have been made up in specific yarns. The best results will always be obtained if the stated yarn is used.

When a particular yarn is not obtainable in any country, the following chart may be used as a guide to a second choice.

If it is essential to use a different yarn, it is most important to make a tension check, using a suitable needle size for the yarn involved. Yarns of the same thickness can vary in the number of yards there are in a ball, so the quantity of yarn required may vary if the yarn has to be changed.

United Kingdom	Australia	Canada	S. Africa	U.S.A.
EMU	All yarns mentioned are on sale in all above countries and in each case are sold under the EMU brand name.			
LISTER	Yarns should be readily available in all countries. In case of difficulty use:			
Lavenda Double Crepe	Standard D.K. in all cases			
Lavenda D.K.	Standard D.K. in all cases			
Prema Bulky Knitting	Standard Double Double Knitting in all cases			
Lavenda 4-ply	Standard 4-ply in all cases			
Aran Knitting Wool	Standard Triple Knitting in all cases			
Lavenda Double Six	Standard Triple Knitting in all cases			
LEE TARGET MOTORAVIA D.K.	Standard D.K. in all cases			

United Kingdom	Australia	Canada	S. Africa	U.S.A.
EMU MACHINE WASHABLE D.K.	Often available in all countries, in case of difficulty use Standard D.K. in all cases			
MAHONY	Should be readily available in all countries In U.S.A. Sold under the Bernat Label			
Blarney Bainin				Bernat Blarney Spun
Blarney Berella				Bernat Blarney Beralla
PATONS				
Trident D.K.	Standard D.K. in all cases			
Patons D.K.	Standard D.K. in all cases			
Limelight Double Crepe	Standard D.K. in all cases			
SIRDAR				
Candytwist	Standard Triple Knitting in all cases			
Pullman	Standard Double Double Knitting in all cases			
Sirdar D.K.	Standard D.K. in all cases			
Topline Nylon D.K.	Standard D.K. Nylon in all cases			
Talisman 4-ply	Standard 4-ply in all cases			
TWILLEY	All yarns should be available in all countries			
WENDY				
4-ply Nylonised	Standard 4-ply in all cases			
Wendy D.K.	Standard D.K. in all cases			
Tricel Nylon D.K.	Standard Tricel Nylon D.K. in all cases			
D.K. Nylonised	Standard D.K. in all cases			
Diabolo D.K.	Standard D.K. in all cases			

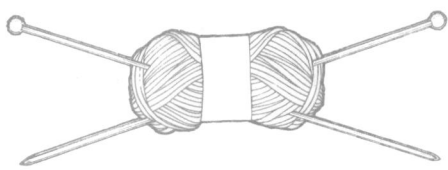

Trims and Finishes

Even though you make something from a pattern which many other people may be using, your own individual touch can be given, to make it quite different.

Your own choice of colour is only the beginning. After that, the plainest knitting can be trimmed very easily. Fringes, cords, tassels and pompons are simple to make. If Fair Isle knitting is difficult for you to do, patterns can be added to stocking stitch knitting by using Swiss darning. It is not a method to use for a very complicated, all-over pattern, but for borders and motifs it is ideal.

TO MAKE TASSELS

Take a piece of cardboard which is the length you wish to make the finished tassel. Wind yarn round until you have the required thickness. With a large eyed needle and matching yarn, secure the yarn to the loops at one end. Bind through the loops, fasten off and leave the end of yarn. This can join the tassel to the item to be trimmed.

With a length of matching yarn, bind round all threads about a quarter of the length from the top. Thread the yarn through needle and draw down to the lower end. Cut loops at lower end and trim evenly.

TO MAKE POMPONS

Cut two circles of firm cardboard. The diameter should be that required for the finished pompon. Cut a circle out of each piece of cardboard at centre and place the pieces together. Wind yarn through the centre hole and round both pieces of cardboard until the centre hole is completely filled.

Thread a large eyed needle with matching yarn. Cut the loops between the two circles of cardboard and separate a little. Bind yarn tightly between the circles in

the centre and tie firmly. Remove cardboard and trim pompon evenly.

TO MAKE TWISTED CORDS

Take several lengths of yarn. They should be three times the length required for the finished cord and about half as thick. Secure one end firmly and taking the other end, twist until it forms a firm, tight cord. Fold in half and allow the two halves to twist together from the centre. Tie a knot at each end and trim to make a tassel. For a two colour cord, the same method is used but it is best to use half the length in one colour and the second half in another. Tie in a knot at the centre. When the twisted strands run together, the colours will appear alternately in stripes.

TO MAKE FRINGES

The thickness of a fringe will depend on the number of strands used.

Cut strands of yarn a little more than twice the length of the required fringe. Take two or more strands, according to the thickness wanted in the finished fringe. Fold the strands in half and with a crochet hook, draw the fold through the edge to be trimmed. Then draw the ends through the fold and pull tight.

If a tasseled fringe is required, knot each piece a quarter of the length down from the top. Make sure the knots make a level line.

TO DO SWISS DARNING

Any cross stitch chart or one used for tapestry can be followed. You can work your own motifs and borders out on squared paper. If you do this, remember that the stitch will be a little wider than it is long, so the final result will be contracted in length. This will not effect the appearance of a balanced Fair Isle design but if you are using a flower or figure motif, they can appear rather squat and look less attractive.

When planning charts for figures, animals and flowers, I find it best to elongate the design a little, although it is easily enough regulated while working. The stitches are simple to put in and take out.

Swiss darning looks as if it has been knitted in but is added to stocking stitch afterwards and follows the path of the knitted stitch.

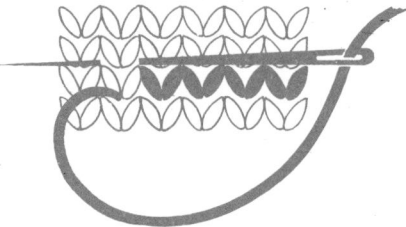

Thread a large eyed, blunt pointed needle with the required yarn in the same thickness as the original work. Insert the needle into the base of the stitch to be covered, from the back of the work. Pass the needle behind the two threads forming the stitch and down again into the base of the stitch from the front of the work. Continue in this way until the stitches for the pattern have been covered in the correct colours.

The Fair Isle mitts and the embroidered patches in the Hexagon patchwork bedspread were worked in this way. Charts are given for both on the appropriate pages.

TO DO GRAFTING

This is a method which can be used to join two sets of stitches. The finished result looks like a row of knitting and there is no ridge.

The toes of socks and stockings are usually finished in this way and the shoulders of sweaters can be grafted. The two sets of stitches should be equal in number.

Place the two sets of stitches on their own needles together with right sides outside. The points of the needles should be to the right hand side and the end of wool at the back needle at the right.

Thread yarn into a large eyed needle. Insert the needle purlwise through the loop of the first stitch on the front needle but do not slip the stitch off the needle. Insert the needle knitwise through the first stitch on the back needle, but do not slip off.

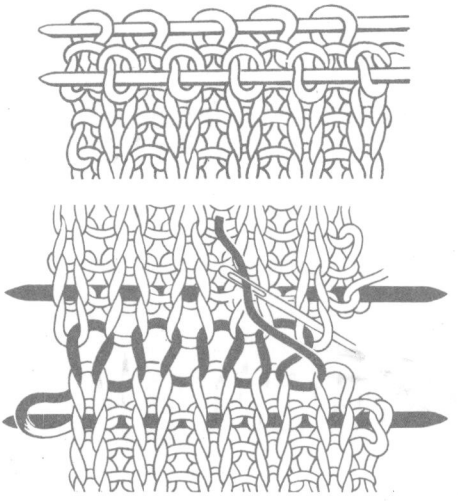

* Insert needle knitwise through first stitch on front needle and slip off needle, then purlwise through the second stitch on front needle, but do not slip off. Now insert wool needle purlwise through first stitch on back needle and slip off, then through second stitch on back needle, knitwise and do not slip off. Repeat from * until all stitches are worked off both knitting needles. Fasten off.

Attractive accessories

Hats and caps for fun and fashion,
gaily striped stockings for the young, but made in one
colour, all good and warm for country walkers
in winter.

Tiny slippers for a baby and a toddler and gloves and
mitts for summer and winter. These are the
small things to add a touch of colour
or warmth to life and yet so easy to make

Toddlers' slippers

for colour illustration, see page 19

Children's feet seem to grow so quickly, it is hard to keep up with them. Make the next size of slippers from just a little thick wool and keep those toddling feet warm

Materials: Two 50 gramme balls of Sirdar Pullman in White and 1 in Turquoise; a pair of No. 7(6) knitting needles.

Tension: 5 sts. to 1 inch.

Measnrements: Back of heel to toe: 5 ins.

Abbreviations: See Page 12

TO MAKE

With Turquoise, cast on 39 sts. and knit 1 row. Now work in patt.
1st row: K.1, s.k.p.o., * k.9, sl.2, k.1, p.s.s.o., rep. from * ending k.9, k.2 tog., k.1.
2nd row: K.1, * p.1, k.4, (k.1, w.r.n., k.1) all into next st., k.4, rep. from * to last 2 sts., p.1, k.1. Change to White.
3rd and 4th rows: As 1st and 2nd rows. Repeat these 4 rows once again then repeat rows 1 and 2. Change to white and knit 1 row. Work 5 rows k.1, p.1, rib. K. 1 row. Begin shaping.
1st row: K.19, p.u.k., k.1, p.u.k., k.19.
2nd and alt. rows: Knit.
3rd row: K.19, p.u.k., k.3, p.u.k., k.19.
5th row: K.19, p.u.k., k.5, p.u.k., k.19.
Continue to work in this way until 11 sts. are worked at centre for toe. Now work 10 rows in garter stitch. Dec. 1 st. at each end of next 2 rows. Cast off. Press. Join back and foot seam. Make another slipper to match.

Baby slippers

for colour illustrations, see page 19

However tiny you are you can always do with some slippers. This pair will be the neatest and sweetest you have made

Materials: 1 oz. Lister Lavenda Double Crepe;
a pair of No. 11(2) and a set of 4 No. 10(3) double pointed knitting needles.

Tension: 6½ sts. and 9 rows to 1 inch on No. 10(3) needles.

Measurements: Length of foot: 4 ins. To fit 2nd size.

Abbreviations: See Page 12

TO MAKE

With No. 11(2) needles, cast on 11 sts. for instep. Beg. with a k. row, work 4 rows st.st. Change to two No.10(3) needles and work a further 4 rows. Make a hem.
9th row: Fold work in half. With p. side inside, k. tog., 1 st. from needle and one from cast on edge to end of row. Beg. with a p. row, work 12 more rows st.st. Dec. 1 st. at each end of next row. K. 1 row, then dec. 1 st. at each end of next row. Break wool and leave these sts. on needle. With 3rd No. 10(3) needle, cast on 13 sts. then, with right side of work facing, pick up and knit 15 sts. along right-hand side of instep. With free needle, knit the 7 sts. from instep, then with 3rd needle, pick up and knit 15 sts. along other side of strip. Turn and cast on 13 sts. Work in rows, using 4 needles. Beg. with a k. row and work 5 rows reversed st.st. **Next row:** (Right side) K. tog. 1 st. from needle and 1 from cast on edge along 13 sts. Now k. tog. 1 st. from needle and one from back of pick-up sts. then continue to make hem round top of slipper to end of row. Beg. with a p. row, work 8 rows in st.st., working all sts. on to one needle on last row.
Foot shaping: Change to reversed st.st.
1st and alt. rows: S.k.p.o., k. to last 2 sts., k.2 tog.
2nd row: P.21, (p.2 tog., p.4) 3 times, p.2 tog., p.20. **4th row:** P.19, (p.2 tog., p.3) 3 times, p.2 tog., p.19.
6th row: P.17, (p.2 tog., p.2) 3 times, p.2 tog., p.18. **8th row:** P.15, (p.2 tog., p.1) 3 times, p.2 tog., p.17. Cast off.

TO MAKE UP

Fold cast off edge in half and join with flat seam. Join back seam. Press seams.

Big tammy

A big tammy is tops for fashion just now, but if you prefer the normal beret, then the instructions cater for that too

Materials: 3 ozs. Sirdar Double Knitting wool in Blue and 1 oz. each of Red and Brown; a pair each of Nos. 11(2) and 9(4) knitting needles.

Tension: 6 sts. and 8 rows to 1 inch on No. 9(4) needles.

Measurements: To fit an average head.

Abbreviations: See Page 12

TO MAKE

With No. 11(2) needles and Blue, cast on 106 sts. and work in k.1, p.1 rib for 1½ ins. Change to No. 9(4) needles and Brown and k.2 rows. Change to Blue. 1st inc. row: *K.6, p.u.k., rep. from * to last 4 sts., k.4. Purl 1 row.

Pattern Row: (right side) * W.r.n., sl.1, k.1, p.s.s.o., rep. from * to last st., k.1. Purl 1 row. Change to Red and knit 2 rows. Change to Blue and knit 1 row.

2nd inc. row: * P.5, p.u.k., rep. from * to last 3 sts., p.3. Now rep. patt. row, then purl 1 row. Change to Brown and knit 2 rows. Change to Blue and knit 1 row.

3rd inc. row: * P.6, p.u.k., rep. from * to last 3 sts., p.3. Rep. patt. row. Purl 1 row, change to red and knit 2 rows, change to Blue and knit 1 row. Cont. to keep striped patt. correct and work until 3 more increase rows have been worked. **Note:** For yellow beret, work 1 more decrease row only. Now decrease. Begin decreasing for yellow beret on 3rd dec. row.

1st dec. row: * P.8, p.2 tog., rep. from * to last 3 sts., p.3. Rep. patt. row, purl 1 row. Change colour and knit 2 rows, change colour and knit 1 row.

2nd dec. row: * P.7, p.2 tog., rep. from * to last 3 sts., p.3. Rep. patt. row, purl 1 row, change colour and knit 2 rows, change colour and knit 1 row.

3rd dec. row: * P.6, p.2 tog., rep. from * to last 3 sts., p.3. Rep. patt. row, purl 1 row, change colour and knit 2 rows, change colour and knit 1 row. Cont. to keep patt. correct and dec. in the same way, working 1 stitch less between decreases until row * P.1, p.2 tog., rep. from * to end has been worked. Rep. patt. row, purl 1 row, change colour and knit 1 row. Change colour. K.2 tog. to end of row. Next 2 rows, K.2 tog. to last st., k.1. Break wool, draw through rem. sts., secure firmly. Press lightly and join seam. Press seam. Trim with long tassel of remaining wool.

Striped cap with bobble

Football fan, rally driver, or student, for fishing, sailing or ski-ing, this is the cap so many people need, be they boy or girl

Materials: 2 ozs. Sirdar Double Knitting Wool in main colour and oddments in 3 contrasting colours; a pair of No. 8(5) knitting needles.

Tension: 6½ sts. and 8 rows to 1 inch over pattern.

Measurements: To fit an average head.

Abbreviations: See Page 12

TO MAKE
With Main colour, cast on 142 sts.
1st row: P.1, * k.2, p.1, rep. from
* to end. 2nd row: K.1, * p.2, k.1, rep. from * to end. **3rd row:** As 1st.
4th row: K. These 4 rows form the patt. Repeat them twice more. Change to first contrast and k.1 row. Beg. with 2nd row, work 7 rows of patt. Change to 2nd contrast and knit 1 row. Beg. with 2nd row, work 3 rows patt. Change to 3rd contrast and k. 1 row. Work 2nd patt. row. Change to main colour and k. 1 row. Cont. in patt. until work measures 5 ins. from beg. ending with a 4th row. Keeping patt. correct, **Shape Top:**
Next row: * Patt. 8, k.2 tog., rep. from * to last 2 sts. patt. 2. Next and every alt. row. Work to end.
Next row: * Patt. 7, k.2 tog., rep. from * to end.
Next dec. row: * Patt. 6, k.2 tog., rep. from * to end. Cont. to dec. on alt. rows in this way until 30 sts. remain.
Next row: K.2 tog., to end. Draw wool through rem. sts. and secure. Join seam. Trim top with pompon.

Stocking cap

Just a long straight piece of plain knitting with a tassel on the end. Arrange to suit yourself and the rest makes a scarf. You will find more than one way to wear it. Have fun trying

Materials: 5 ozs. Sirdar Talisman 4-ply in Peacock blue; 3 ozs. in Turquoise; 2 ozs. in orange and 1 in white;
a pair of No. 9(4) knitting needles.

Tension: 6½ sts. and 8½ rows to 1 inch.

Measurements: To fit an average head; Length: approx. 60 ins.

Abbreviations: See Page 12

TO MAKE
With Peacock, cast on 130 sts. and work in st.st. throughout. Work 28 rows. Now work in stripes as follows. * 6 rows turquoise, 2 rows white, 6 rows turquoise, 14 rows peacock, 6 rows orange, 2 white, 6 rows orange, 14 rows peacock. * Rep. from * to * until piece measures 60 ins. Cast off. Press lightly. Fold in half lengthwise, and join long seam neatly. Turn to right side and press with seam in centre of one side. Fold cast on edge to last row of 28 peacock rows and catch down. Gather cast off edge and secure firmly. Cut remaining wool into 4 inch lengths to make a tassel and sew to gathered end of cap.

Aran cap and mitts

for colour illustrations, see page 30

If you can't face a whole sweater in Aran stitches, go for small accessories like this and enjoy these traditional patterns

Materials: 4 balls of Mahony's Blarney Bainin; a pair each of Nos. 7(6) and 9(4) knitting needles, 2 cable needles.

Tension: 9 sts. and 13 rows to 2 ins. over st.st. on No. 7(6) needles.

Measurements: Cap: to fit an average head; Mitts: Round palm: 7½ ins.; length of hand excluding ribbing: 7½ ins.

Abbreviations: See Page 12

CAP

With No. 9(4) needles, cast on 93 sts., and work 9 rows k.1, p.1 rib. Change to No. 7(6) needles.

Next row: * P. twice into next st., p.1, rep. from * to last st. p. twice into last st. Now cont. in patt.

1st row: P.1, * k.6, (p.2, k.2) 3 times, p.2, rep. from * ending last rep. p.1.

2nd row: K.1, *(p.2, k.2) 3 times, p.6, k.2, rep. from * ending last rep. k.1.

3rd row: P.1, * C3L. C3R., p.2, C6R., p.2, k.2, p.2, rep. from * ending last rep. p.1.

4th row: As 2nd.

5th and 6th rows: As 1st and 2nd.

7th row: P.1, * C3R., C3L., p.2, k.2, p.2, C6L., p.2, rep. from * ending last rep. p.1. **8th row:** As 2nd. Rep. these 8 rows until work measures 5 ins. from beg. ending on wrong side.

Next row: P.1, * patt. 6, p.2 tog., patt. 10, p.2 tog., rep. from * ending last rep. p.1 instead of p.2 tog. Cont. in patt. as set with p.1 instead of p.2 between panels until work measures 6½ ins. from beg. ending on right side.

Next row: P.1, * p.2 tog., p.3, p.2 tog., p.2, rep. from * to end. Cont. in k.1, p.1 rib.

Shape Top: 1st and every alt. row: K.1, p.1, to last st., k.1.

2nd row: Rib 6, * p.3 tog., rib 11, rep. from * to last 9 sts., p.3 tog., rib 6.

4th row: Rib 5, * k.3 tog., rib 9, rep. from * to last 8 sts., k.3 tog., rib 5. Cont. to dec. in this way until

12th row: P.1, * k.3 tog., p.1, rep. from * to end. Break wool, draw through rem. sts., fasten off and secure. Press on wrong side with a warm iron over a damp cloth. Join back seam. Add pompon to top of cap.

28

MITTS

With No. 9(4) needles cast on 39 sts. and work 2 ins. in k.1, p.1 rib. Change to No. 7(6) needles and p. 1 row, increasing 3 times evenly across row. Cont. working 25 sts. for back of hand in patt. as for last part of cap with p.1 between panels and the rem. sts. in purl for palm thus:

1st row: P.1, k.6, p.1, (k.2, p.2) twice, k.2, p.1, k.6, p.17.

2nd row: K.17, p.6, k.1, (p.2, k.2) twice, p.2, k.1, p.6, k.1.

3rd row: P.1, C3L., C3R., p.1, C6R., p.2, k.2, p.1, C3L., C3R., p.17.

4th row: As 2nd. Cont. in patt. as set until work measures 4½ ins. from beg. ending on wrong side. ★★

Shape Thumb: Next row: Work across 31 sts., turn, cast on 3 sts.

Next row: K.9, turn, cast on 4 sts. Work 14 rows in purl fabric on these sts.

Next row: P.1, (p.2 tog., p.1) 4 times.

Next row: K. **Next row:** P.2 tog., 4 times, p.1. Break wool, draw through rem. sts. and fasten off securely. Join seam to base of thumb. With right side facing, rejoin wool at point of right hand needle and pick up 6 sts. along cast on thumb sts. Work to end of row. Work 3½ ins. on these sts. ending on wrong side.

Next row: K.1, (k.2 tog., k.1) 8 times, p.17. **Next row:** K.

Shape Top: 1st row: P.1, p.2 tog., p.11, p.2 tog., p.2, p.2 tog., p.11, p.2 tog., p.1. **2nd row:** K.

3rd row: P.1, p.2 tog., p.9, p.2 tog., p.2, p.2 tog., p.9, p.2 tog., p.1. Cont. to dec. in this way at each end and at each side of centre 2 sts. on every p. row until 14 sts. rem. ending with a dec. row. Divide sts. on to 2 needles and graft or cast off tog.

Left Hand:

Work ribbing as for right hand then reverse patt. and purl fabric thus:

1st patt. row: P.17, k.6, p.1, (k.2, p.2) twice, k.2, p.1, k.6, p.1. Cont. on sts. as now set to ★★.

Shape Thumb: Next row: P.17, turn and cast on 3 sts.

Next row: K.9, turn and cast on 4 sts. Complete thumb and rest of mitt as for right hand reversing shaping. Press lightly on wrong side with a damp cloth and hot iron. Join side seam. Press seams.

Striped stockings

for colour illustration, see page 31

Maybe too gaudy for some, but choose a bright colour if you prefer or play really safe and use straight stocking shades. Anyway, you will be warm in winter legwise

Materials: 3 balls of Sirdar Top Line Nylon D.K., in Blue; 2 balls in Red and yellow and 1 ball in Mulberry; a set of four double pointed needles No. 11(2)

Tension: 8 sts. to 1 inch

Measurements: Length of leg: $24\frac{1}{2}$ ins. Foot: 9 ins. Both adjustable.

Abbreviations: See Page 12

TO MAKE

With Blue, cast on 86 sts. 28 on 1st and 3rd needles and 30 on 2nd needle. Work in k.1, p.1 rib for 28 rounds. Cut blue and join red. **Next round:** K. Cont. in k.1, p.1 rib for a further 17 rounds.

1st dec. round: S.k.p.o., cont. in rib until 3 sts. rem. at end of round, k.2 tog., p.1.

Note: The last p. stitch is the centre back seam. Cont. in k.1, p.1 rib until 27 rounds of red have been worked. Cut red, join yellow. Knit 1 round. Cont. in rib keeping sts. correct over decreasings until 11 rounds have been worked from last dec. round.

2nd dec. round: S.k.p.o., p.1, k.1 rib until 4 sts. rem. k.1, k.2 tog., p.1. Cont. in rib until 27 rounds in yellow have been worked, still decreasing on every 12th round as before. Cut yellow and join Mulberry. Knit 1 round. Cont. in rib, decreasing on every 12th round and working 27 rounds in rib in each colour. Always work 1 knit round when changing colour. When 58 sts. are left on needles, work without further shaping until 27 rounds in 2nd stripe in Mulberry have been completed. Cut Mulberry. Arrange the sts. from 1st and 3rd needles on one needle, having the p. seam stitch in the centre with 14 sts. on each side. (29 sts.) Divide the instep sts. on two needles. Join Blue to beg. of 29 heel sts. and work 18 rows in st.st.

Turn Heel: K.17, s.k.p.o., k.1, turn.
2nd row: P.9, p.2 tog., p.1, turn.

3rd row: K.10, s.k.p.o., k.1, turn.
4th row: P.11, p.2 tog., p.1, turn.
5th row: K.12, s.k.p.o., k.1, turn.
6th row: P.13, p.2 tog., p.1, turn.
7th row: K.14, s.k.p.o., k.1, turn.
8th row: P.15, p.2 tog., p.1, turn.
9th row: K.16, s.k.p.o., k.1, turn.
10th row: P.19. **11th row:** K.19.

Now pick up and knit 12 sts. from left side of heel flap. With next needle, knit the 29 sts. from instep on to one needle, with next needle, pick up and knit 12 sts. from other side of heel flap. K. 9 sts. from 1st needle on to 3rd needle. (72 sts.) Now begin shaping.
1st round: 1st needle: K. to last 3 sts., k.2 tog., k.1. 2nd needle: K.1, p.1, to last st., k.1. 3rd needle: K.1, s.k.p.o., k. to end.
2nd round: 1st needle: Knit. 2nd needle: K.1, p.1, to last st., k.1. 3rd needle: Knit. Repeat last 2 rounds 6 times more. Now repeat 2nd round only until foot measures 7 ins. changing to Red after 28 rounds and working 18 rounds only in Red. Change to Yellow and work 5 rounds.
Shape Toe: 1st round: 1st needle: K. to last 3 sts., k.2 tog., k.1. 2nd needle: K.1, s.k.p.o., k. to last 3 sts., k.2 tog., k.1. 3rd needle: K.1, s.k.p.o., k. to end.
2nd round: Knit. Repeat last 2 rounds until 22 sts. remain.
Arrange remaining sts. evenly on 2 needles and graft the stitches. Fasten off. Make another stocking to match.

Made plain and decorated after with Swiss darning, see page 17. So easy you can make a pair in an evening. Embroider them to suit your fancy

Materials: 2 ozs. Sirdar Double Knitting Wool in white; scraps of Red, Black and Blue for Swiss darning; a pair of No. 10(3) and 8(5) knitting needles.

Tension: 5½ sts., and 7½ rows to 1 inch over stocking stitch.

Measurements: Length: 10 ins., round hand: 8 ins.

Abbreviations: See Page 12

TO MAKE
With No. 10(3) needles and white wool cast on 40 sts. work 6 rows of k.2, p.2 rib. Change to red and work 6 rows. Change to white and work 12 rows. Change to No. 8(5) needles and st.st. Work 4 rows. Increase 1 st. at end of last row.

Shape for thumb: 1st row: K.20,
p.u.k., k.1, p.u.k., k. to end.
2nd and alt. rows: Purl.
3rd row: K.20, p.u.k., k.3, p.u.k., k. to
end.
5th row: K.20, p.u.k., k.5, p.u.k., k. to
end. Cont. to increase in this way on all
knit rows until there are 53 sts. on needle,
ending with a p. row.
Thumb: 1st row: K.33, turn. **2nd row:**
P.13, turn and cast on 2 sts.
3rd row: K.15. **4th row:** P.15. Repeat
these 2 rows twice more.
Shape Top of Thumb: K.1, k.2 tog.,
k. to last 3 sts., k.2 tog., k.1.
Next row: Purl. Repeat these 2 rows
twice more. Break wool, thread through
remaining sts. and fasten off securely.
Hand: Return to remaining sts. and with
right side facing, join wool to sts. on
left hand needle. Knit to end.
Next row: P.20, cast on 2 sts., purl across
other set of sts. Work 3 ins. in st.st. on
these sts.
Shape Top: 1st row: *K.1, k.2 tog.,
k.15, k.2 tog., k.1, rep. from * to end.
2nd and alt. rows: Purl.
3rd row: * K.1, k.2 tog., k.13, k.2 tog.,
k.1, rep. from * to end.
5th row: * K.1, k.2 tog., k.11, k.2 tog.,
k.1, rep. from * to end.
7th row: * K.1, k.2 tog., k.9, k.2 tog.,
k.1, rep. from * to end. **8th row:** * P.1,
p.2 tog., p.7, p.2 tog., p.1, rep. from * to
end. Cast off. Make another mitt to match.

TO MAKE UP

Press pieces. Embroider back of each hand
with Swiss darning, following chart 2
Begin with 1 row of 1 stitch red, 1 white.
next row 1 stitch white, 1 red. Then
repeat these 2 rows using black in place of
red and repeat them using red again.
Continue with diamond pattern on back
only. Press on wrong side. Join side and
thumb seams. Press seams.

× Red
╱ Blue
• Black

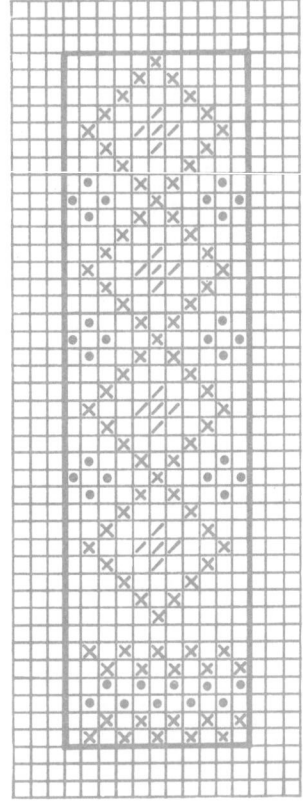

Summer gloves on two needles

Made in cool cotton for the summer, slightly starched for a crisper look. You can forget the frill, make a longer rib and they would make good riding or driving gloves

Materials: 2 balls of Twilley's Stalite; a pair each of Nos. 11(2) and 12(1) knitting needles.

Tension: 7 sts. and 9 rows to 1 inch over st.st.

Measurements: To fit an average hand.

Abbreviations: See Page 12

TO MAKE

With No. 11(2) needles, cast on 58 sts., inserting point of right hand needle into each preceeding loop.
1st row: K.1B., * p.2, k.1B., rep. from * to end.
2nd row: P.1, * k.1B., k.1, p.1, rep. from * to end. Repeat these 2 rows 4 times.
Next row: K.1B., * drop next st. off needle, p.1, k.1B., rep. from * to end. (39 sts.) Change to No. 12(1) needles.
1st row: P.1, * k.1B., p.1, rep. from * to end.
2nd row: K.1B., * p.1, k.1B., rep. from * to end. Rep. these 2 rows twice more. Allow the dropped sts. from last row of frill stitch to run down to cast on edge. Change to No. 11(2) needles. Work in pattern and begin to shape the thumb.
1st row: P.2, * p.u.k., p.7, rep. from * to last 2 sts., p.u.k., p.2. (45 sts.)
1st pattern row: K.1, * p.u.k., k.1, slip made st. over knit st., k.1, rep. from * to end. **2nd row:** Purl. These 2 rows form the pattern.
To Shape Thumb: 1st row: Patt. 21 k. twice into next st., k.1, k. twice into next st., patt. 21.
2nd and alt. rows: Purl.
3rd row: Patt. 21, k.5, patt. 21.

5th row: Patt. 21, k. twice into next st., k.3, k. twice into next st., patt. 21.
7th row: Patt. 21, k.7, patt. 21.
8th row: Purl. Cont. to increase in this way, keeping thumb sts. in st. st., until there are 53 sts. on needle, ending with a p. row.
Next row: Patt. 21, k. to last 21 sts., turn and cast on 2 sts. Leave remaining sts. on a stitch holder.
Next row: P.13, turn and cast on 2 sts., leave remaining sts. on a stitch holder.
Next row: Knit.
Next row: Purl. Work 2¼ ins. in patt. on these 15 sts., ending with a p. row.
Shape Top: K.1, * k.2 tog., rep. from * to end. **Next row:** Purl.
Next row: K.2 tog., to end of row. Cut yarn, draw through rem. sts., and fasten off securely. Join seam. With right side of work facing, rejoin yarn to base of thumb. Pick up and knit 5 sts. from base of thumb, then pattern across sts. from 1st stitch holder. **Next row:** Purl. (47 sts.) Rep. patt. rows for 1¾ ins., ending with a p. row.
1st finger: Patt. 29, turn and cast on 1 st. **Next row:** P.12, turn and cast on 1 st.
Next row: K.2, * p.u.k., k.1, slip made st. over the knit st., k.1, rep. from * to last st., k.1. **Next row:** Purl. Rep. these 2 patt. rows for 2½ ins., ending with a patt. row.
Shape Top: * P.1, p.2 tog., rep. from * to last st., p.1. **Next row:** Knit.
Next row: P.2 tog., to last st., p.1. Fasten off and join seam.
2nd finger: With right side facing, join yarn to base of 1st finger, pick up and knit 2 sts. from base, patt. 6 sts., turn and cast on 1 st.
Next row: P.15, turn and cast on 1 st. Work 3 ins. on these sts. in patt. Shape Top and finish as for first finger.
3rd finger: With right side facing, pick up and knit 2 sts. from base of 2nd

finger, patt. 5 sts., turn and cast on 1 st.
Next row: P.13, turn and cast on 1 st.
Work 2½ ins. in patt. on these sts.,
finish as before.
4th finger: With right side facing, pick

up 2 sts. from base of 3rd finger. Patt.
across sts. on left hand needle, turn and
purl across all sts. Work 2 ins. on these
sts. and finish as before. Join final seams.
Make another glove in the same way.

Fun Fashion

Fashion has always been interesting and never
such fun as it is today. If time is spent knitting
something smart, it must last a little while, so I have
come to terms, just a little, with that fact
of life. If something is fun to wear,
it must quite certainly be comfortable first.
Even if it is eye catching and head turning,
you must be able to put it on and forget about it.
I hope you will like this bright
collection and that the men folk will
enjoy the two included for them

Tartan tabard

for colour illustrations, see page 39

Wear it over a cat suit if you have the nerve, but it would look just as good over slacks

Materials: 12 ozs. Sirdar Double Crepe in Black; 7 ozs. in yellow and 6 ozs. in red; a pair each of Nos. 8(5) and 9(4) knitting needles; a stitch holder.

Tension: 15 sts. and 13 rows to 2 ins.

Measurements: To fit Bust 32 to 34 ins. Length: 31 ins.

Abbreviations: See Page 12. Also for this design only Black., A; Yellow., B; Red., C.

TO MAKE

With No. 8(5) needles, and Black cast on 103 sts. Work in st.st. in the foll. tartan pattern.

1st row: * K.1C, 5B., 6A., 2C., 1A., 1C., rep. from * to last 7 sts., 1C., 5B., 1A.
2nd row: * P.2B., 2A., 1B., 2C., 1B., 2A., 2C., 4A., rep. from * to last 7 sts., 2B., 2A., 1B., 2C.
3rd row: * K.1B., 2C., 3A., 2B., 2A., 2C., 2A., 2B., rep. from * to last 7 sts., 1B., 2C., 3A., 1B.
4th row: * P.3A., 2C., 1A., 4B., 2A., 2C., 2B., rep. from * to last 7 sts., 3A., 2C., 1A., 1B.
5th row: * K.3A., 2C., 3A., 2B., 2A., 4B., rep. from * to last 7 sts., 3A., 2C., 2A.
6th row: * P.1A., 2C., 5A., 6B., 2C., rep. from * to last 7 sts., 1A., 2C., 4A.
7th row: * K.5A., 3C., 2A., 4B., 2A., rep. from * to last 7 sts., 5A., 2C.
8th row: * P.2C., 8A., 4B., 1A., 1C., rep. from * to last 7 sts., 2C., 5A.
9th row: * K.4A., 2C., 1A., 2C., 5B., 2A., rep. from * to last 7 sts., 4A., 2C., 1A.
10th row: * P.2A., 2C., 4A., 2B., 2A., 1B., 2C., 1B., rep. from * to last 7 sts., 2A., 2C., 3A.
11th row: * K.2A., 2C., 2A., 3B., 2C., 3A., 2B., rep. from * to last 7 sts., 2A., 2C., 2A., 1B.
12th row: * P.2B., 2A., 2C., 2B., 3A., 2C., 1A., 2B., rep. from * to last 7 sts., 2B., 2A., 2C., 1B.
13th row: * K.2B., 2A., 4B., 3A., 2C., 3A., rep. from * to last 7 sts., 2B., 2A., 3B.
14th row: * P.6B., 2C., 1A., 2C., 5A., rep. from * to last 7 sts., 6B., 1C.
15th row: * K.2A., 4B., 7A., 3C., rep. from * to last 7 sts., 2A., 4B., 1A.
16th row: * P.2A., 4B., 1A., 3C., 6A., rep. from * to last 7 sts., 2A., 4B., 1A.
These 16 rows form the pattern and are repeated. Cont. straight until work measures 27 ins. from beg., ending with a p. row. **Next row:** K.29, place rem. sts. on stitch holder.

Shape Neck: Cast off 3 sts. at beg. of next row and cont. to cast off 3 more sts. at this edge once more. Work straight on rem. 23 sts. until measurement is 30 ins. from beg., ending with a k. row. Place these sts. on a spare needle and return to rem. sts. Join wool to centre edge. Cast off first 45 sts. then work on rem. sts. to match other side, ending with same patt. row as other shoulder.
Next row: P.23, cast on 57 sts. for back of neck, p. across rem. 23 sts. from spare needle. Cont. straight on all sts. until measurement is 29 ins. from cast on sts. at back of neck. Cast off.
Border: With No. 9(4) needles, and Black, cast on 13 sts.
1st row: K.2 tog., k. to last st., k. twice into this st.
2nd row: P. Repeat these 2 rows until border is long enough to fit all round edge of tabard. Cast off. Make a similar bias binding to go round neck.

TO MAKE UP

Press on wrong side with a hot iron over a damp cloth. Back stitch the bias binding all round tabard, fold inside in half, to wrong side of work and catch into place. Sew binding to neck in same way. Press edges.

Man's aran jerkin

for colour illustration, see page 43

For the man who likes something with a bit of style. Super Aran stitches make a jerkin to wear with flair

Materials: 11(12,13) balls of Mahony's Blarney Bainin;
an extra ball if belt is made;
a pair each of Nos. 7(6) and 9(4) knitting needles;
2 cable needles;
6 buttons;
a buckle for belt;
1½ yds. of 1½ inch facing ribbon.

Tension: 5 sts. and 6½ rows to 1 inch over double moss stitch.

Measurements: Chest: 38(41,44) ins.
Length: 28½ ins.

Abbreviations: See Page 12

BACK

With No. 9(4) needles, cast on 115(123, 131) sts. and work 2 rows k.1, p.1 rib. Change to No. 7(6) needles and purl 1 row. Now cont. in patt.
1st row: (K.1, p.1) 4(4,6) times, k.1,
* p.2(3,3), k.b.1., p.2(3,3), T2F., p.5, cable 5, p.5, T2B., p.2(3,3), k.b.1., p.2 (3,3)*, T2F., p.1, k.9, p.1, T2B., p.1, (k.1, p.1) 3 times, k.1, p.1, T2F., p.1, k.9, p.1, T2B., rep. from * to *, (k.1, p.1), 4(4,6) times, k.1.
2nd row: (P.1, k.1) 4(4,6) times, p.1,
*k.2(3,3), p.b.1, k.2(3,3), p.2, k.5, p.2,

k.1, p.2, k.5, p.2, k.2(3,3), p.b.1., k.2(3,3),
* p.2, k.1, p.9, k.1, p.2, k.1, (p.1, k.1) 3 times, p.1, k.1, p.2, k.1, p.9, k.1, p.2, rep. from * to *(p.1, k.1) 4(4,6) times, p.1.
3rd row: (P.1, k.1) 4(4,6) times, p.1,
* p.2(3,3), k.b.1, p.2(3,3), T2F., p.4, C3R., k.1, C3L., p.4, T2B., p.2(3,3), k.b.1., p.2(3,3), * T2F., p.1, DC9., p.1, T2B., p.1, (p.1, k.1) 3 times, p.1, (for double moss stitch), p.1, T2F., p.1, DC9., p.1, T2B., rep. from * to *, (p.1, k.1) 4(4,6) times, p.1.
4th row: (K.1, p.1) 4(4,6) times, k.1,
* k.2(3,3), p.b.1, k.2(3,3), p.2, k.4, p.2, k.1, p.1, k.1, p.2, k.4, p.2, k.2(3,3), p.b.1, k.2(3,3) *, p.2, k.1, p.9, k.1, p.2, k.1, (k.1, p.1) 3 times, k.1, (for double moss stitch), k.1, p.2, k.1, p.9, k.1, p.2, rep. from * to *, (k.1, p.1) 4(4,6) times, k.1.
These 4 rows complete the patt. of the twisted rib, lobster claw and double moss stitch panels. Keeping these correct, cont. on the diamond panels of 15 sts. thus:-
5th row: P.3, C3R., k.1, p.1, k.1, C3L., p.3.
6th row: K.3, p.2, (k.1, p.1) twice, k.1, p.2, k.3.
7th row: P.2, C3R., d.m.st.5, C3L., p.2.
8th row: K.2, p.2, d.m.st.7, p.2, k.2.
9th row: P.1, C3R., d.m.st.7, C3L., p.1.
10th row: K.1, p.2, d.m.st.9, p.2, k.1.
11th row: P.1, C3L., d.m.st.7, C3R., P.1.
12th row: K.2, p.2, d.m.st. 7, p.2, k.2.
13th row: P.2, C3L., d.m.st.5, C3R., p.2.
14th row: K.3, p.2, d.m.st.5, p.2, k.3.
15th row: P.3, C3L., d.m.st.3, C3R., p.3.
16th row: K.4, p.2, d.m.st.3, p.2, k.4.
17th row: P.4, C3L., p.1, C3R., p.4.
18th row: K.5, p.2, k.1, p.2, k.5.
These 18 rows complete the diamond patt. Beginning again at 1st row of diamond, but noting that the next row will be the 3rd of lobster claw, cont. in patt. until 8 rows of 7th diamond have been worked. **
Shape Armholes: Cast off 5(7,9) sts. at beg. of next 2 rows, then dec. 1 st. at each end of the next 5 rows. Now dec.

1 st. at each end of the next 6(6,7) right side rows. Cont. without further shaping on 83(87,89) sts. with an extra p. st. outside diamond on 3rd size, until 2nd row of 11th diamond has been worked.
Shape Shoulders: Cast off 7 sts. at beg. of next 4 rows and 8(9,10) sts. on foll. 2 rows. Cast off rem. sts.

LEFT FRONT

With No. 9(4) needles, cast on 63(67,71) sts. and work as for Back to end of ribbing. Purl 1 row. Cont. in patt. as for right hand side of Back but with 9 sts. at front edge in double moss stitch thus:-
1st row: (K.1, p.1) 4(4,6) times, k.1, rep. from * to * of 1st patt. row, T2F., p.1, k.9, p.1, T2B., p.1, (k.1, p.1) 4 times, k.1. Cont. in patt. as set for 5 more rows.
Next row: Work to last 7 sts., cast off 3, double moss stitch to end. In next row, cast on sts. over those cast off in previous row. Cont. in patt. for 28 rows, then make another buttonhole in next 2 rows. Make 5 more buttonholes with 28 rows between and cont. until work matches Back to **.
Shape Armhole: Cast off 5(7,9) sts. at beg. of next row then dec. 1 st. at same edge on every row 5 times. Then on right side rows only 6(6,7) times. Cont. without further shaping on 47(49,50) sts. until the 16th row of the 9th diamond has been worked. (2 rows after last buttonhole)
Shape Neck: Next row: Patt. 22(23, 24), turn. Leave rem. sts. on spare needle and cont. in patt. until 2nd row of 11th diamond has been worked.
Shape Shoulder: Cast off 7 sts. at beg. of next 2 rows beg. at armhole edge, then 8(9,10) sts. at same edge on next row.

RIGHT FRONT

Work to match Left Front reversing front border thus:
1st patt. row: (K.1, p.1) 4 times, k.1, p.1, T2F., p.1, k.9, p.1, T2B., rep. from * to* of 1st patt. row of Back, (k.1, p.1) .. 4(4,6) times, k.1. Cont. to match with Left Front, omitting buttonholes and working an extra row to end at side edge before shaping armhole, until 16th row of 9th diamond has been worked.
Shape Neck: With No. 9(4) needle, k.25 (26,26) and leave on spare needle. Change to No. 7(6) needles and cont. to match Left Front, but working 1 extra row before shaping shoulder.

NECK AND ARMHOLE BORDERS

Pin out and press on wrong side with hot iron and a damp cloth. Join shoulders. Slip the sts. of Right Front neck on to a No. 9(4) needle, then on to the same needle, pick up and knit 21 sts. up side of neck, 39(41,41) sts. across Back of Neck, 21 sts. down other side of neck and k. sts. from spare needle. Work 2 rows k.1, p.1 rib. Cast off in rib, taking 2 tog., each side of each front corner while casting off. Work armhole borders to match, picking up and knitting 123(127,131) sts. round each armhole and working 4 rows in rib.

BELT

With No. 9(4) needles, cast on 13 sts.
1st row: Sl.1, (k.1, p.1) to last 2 sts., k.2.
2nd row: Sl.1, (p.1, k.1) to end. Rep. these 2 rows for required length, ending with 2nd row. Now dec. 1 st. at each end of every row until 3 sts. remain. P.3 tog., fasten off.

TO MAKE UP

Join side seams. Face front borders with ribbon, cutting and neatening buttonholes. Sew on buttons. Add buckle to belt. Make 2 crochet chain loops and add to sides of jerkin to hold belt. Make another to slip over belt. Press seams.

Blue and yellow pinafore dress

for colour illustration, see page 46

Checked in two colours to wear over shirts or sweaters. The matching sweater on page 60 uses one of the colours only

Materials: Dress: 9(10,11) ozs., yellow and 6(7,8) ozs. blue Wendy 4-ply Nylonised; 3 ozs. Blue Wendy D.K. Nylonised;
a pair each of Nos. 10(3) and 11(2) knitting needles;
a No. 4.00 m.m crochet hook;
a belt buckle.
Sweater: 14(15,16) ozs. Yellow 4 ply. Nylonised.

Tension: $7\frac{1}{2}$ sts. and 11 rows to 1 inch over pattern.

Measurements: Bust: 34(36,38); Hips: 36(38,40) ins.
Dress length: 36 ins., plus fringe;
Sweater length: 24 ins.; Sleeve seam: $17\frac{1}{2}$ ins.

Abbreviations: See Page 12

DRESS BACK

With No. 11(2) needles and yellow, cast on 149(157,165) sts. and beg. with a k. row, work 8 rows st.st. Join on Blue K.2 rows. Change to No. 10(3) needles and beg. patt.
1st row: K. **2nd row:** P. Change to yellow.
3rd and 5th rows: * Sl.1 purlwise, k.3, rep. from * to last st., sl.1 purlwise.
4th and 6th rows: * Sl.1, p.3 yellow, rep. from * to last st., sl.1. Change to Blue. K. 1 row then p. 1 row.
9th and 11th rows: Change to yellow. K.2 yellow, * sl.1 purlwise, k.3 yellow, rep. from * to last 3 sts., sl.1 purlwise, k.2. yellow
10th and 12th rows: P.2 yellow, * sl.1, p.3, yellow, rep. from * to last 3 sts., sl.1, p.2. yellow. These 12 rows form the

pattern and are repeated throughout. Cont. in patt. until Back measures 3 ins. from hemline. Now dec. 1 st. at each end of next and every foll. 10th row until 131(139,147) sts. rem. Then dec. at each end of every foll. 8th row until 101 (109,117) sts. are on needle. (Waist) Now inc. 1 st. at each end of every foll. 6th row until there are 125(133,141) sts. on needle. When Back measures 27 ins. from beg.
Shape Armholes: With right side facing, cast off 7(8,9) sts. at beg. of next 2 rows. Then k.2 tog., at each end of next and every alt. row until 97(103,109) sts. remain. Cont without further shaping until Back measures 36 ins. from hemline.
Shape Shoulders: Cast off 7(7,9) sts. at beg. of next 2 rows and 7(8,8) sts. at beg. of foll. 4 rows. Leave rem. sts. on a spare needle.

FRONT

Work as for Back until waist is reached, then inc. as for Back until there are 121(129,137) sts. on needle.
Divide for centre neck: Work to centre st., cast off centre stitch, turn and complete this side first.
Cont. to inc. at side edge as before until 12 increasings have been completed. Work without further shaping at this edge and dec. 1 st. at neck edge on every 4th row. When work measures the same as Back to armhole, ending at side edge, beg. shaping.
Shape Armholes: Cast off 7(8,9) sts. at beg. of next row. Then k.2 tog., at armhole edge on alt. rows 7 times.
At the same time, cont. to dec. at neck edge as before until 21(23,25) sts. rem. ending at side edge.
Shape Shoulders: Cast off 7(7,9) sts. at beg. of next row and 7(8,8) at beg. of foll. 2 alt. rows.

Poncho in squares

for colour illustration, see page 10

Rejoin yarn to centre and work to match other side.

Press work carefully.

Join left shoulder seam and press. With No. 11(2) needles and blue, cast on 60(62,64) sts. With right side facing, pick up and knit 70(72,74) sts. from right side of V-neck. Beg. with a p. row, work 3 rows st.st., purl 2 rows and work 2 rows st.st. Cast off loosely.

With right side facing and No. 11(2) needles, pick up and knit 125(129,133) sts. from back of neck and left side of V-neck. Work to match other half. Join right shoulder seam and press. Turn neck facing to wrong side on purl hemline and slip stitch. Join edges of crossover binding very neatly and catch down to form mock crossover.

Armhole Binding: With Blue and No. 11(2) needles, pick up and knit 148 sts. round armhole. Work as for front facing.

TO MAKE UP

Join side seams. Turn in and slip stitch armhole facings. Press seams. Turn up hem.

Fringe: With crochet hook and D.K. yarn join to side edge of lower edge through blue line at hem edge. Make 42 chain, work 1 double crochet into 3rd k. st. along hem. Cont. in this way all round hemline. Fasten off.

Belt: With Blue and No. 10(3) needles, and D.K. yarn, cast on 8 sts. and work 30 ins. in g. st. Cast off. Add buckle. Make belt loops in crochet chain and add to waist line at side edges.

If you can knit a square you can make this gay poncho. As easy as pie and all you need will be odd ounces and as many colours as you like to use

The Poncho takes 24 squares, made in the same way and to the same tension as those for the bedspread on page 113. It measures 25 inches square, excluding the fringe.

TO MAKE

Make 4 strips each with 5 squares and join the remaining 4 squares together in pairs.

Join two strips of five squares matching corners carefully, then join a pair of two squares to each side of one edge, leaving one square free in the centre. Join the other two strips of five squares together in the same way and add to the other side of the centre pairs, still leaving a free square in the centre for neck. With right side facing, with No. 9(4) needles, pick up and knit across one edge of neck. Work 4 rows k.1, p.1 rib, decreasing 1 st. at each end on 2nd and 4th rows. Cast off in rib. Work other three sides to match. Join corners of neck ribbing. Press Poncho on wrong side. Add fringes all round lower edge.

Long skirt and shawl

for colour illustration, see page 47

You'll never be cold shouldered in this brightly striped shawl, with the skirt added it makes a gorgeously warm set for evenings at home

Materials: 18(18,19) balls of Wendy Tricel/Nylon D.K. in main colour and 5 balls in first contrast and 3 in 2nd; a No. 7(6) and 8(5) circular needle 30 ins. long and a No. 9(4) circular needle 24 inches long;
waist length of elastic for skirt.
For shawl: 12 balls of 1st; 5 balls 2nd and 3 balls 3rd contrast.

Tension: 6 sts. and 7 rows to 1 inch, on No. 7(6) needles.

Measurements: Waist: 26(28,30) ins. Hip: 36(38,40) ins.; Length of skirt: 40 ins.

Abbreviations: See Page 12

Note on shawl: As shaping is worked by turning before the end of every row, always knit into the back of last st., before turning and slip first st., pulling yarn tight to avoid holes.

SHAWL

With No. 9(4) circular needle and 1st colour, cast on 480 sts. Knit 1 row.
2nd row: K.479, turn. **3rd row:** k.478, turn. Beg. shaping. **1st row:** K.237, sl.1, k.1, p.s.s.o., k.2 tog., k.236, turn. **2nd row:** Sl.1, p.473, turn. **3rd row:** K.235, sl.1, k.1, p.s.s.o., k.2 tog., k.234, turn. **4th row:** Sl.1, p.469, turn. Cont. to work in this way, decreasing 2 sts. at centre of every k. row and leaving 1 stitch extra at end of every row until 24 rows have been completed. Change to 2nd colour and work 16 rows in same way. Change to 3rd colour and work 2 rows, then 2 rows 2nd colour, 2 rows 3rd, 2 rows 2nd, 12 rows 3rd. Change to 1st colour and repeat the striped sequence but leaving 2 sts. less on every row. Change to 1st colour and cont. in this leaving 3 sts. less on every row. Last 2 rows will be worked thus: Sl.1, sl.1, k.1, p.s.s.o., k.2 tog., turn. **Next row:** Sl.1, p.1, turn. Break yarn and slip sts. from right hand needle on to left hand. With No. 8(5) circular needle, and 1st colour, knit into back of all sts. across all sts. Work 3 rows in g.st. Cast off with No. 7(6) needle.
Trim pointed edge with fringe.

SKIRT

With No. 7(6) needle, cast on 384 sts. with first colour. Work 4 rows g.st. Join into ring and begin chevrons.
1st round: * K.1, k.2 tog., k.13, p.u.k., and knit into back of it, k.1, p.u.k., k.13, sl.1, k.1, p.s.s.o., rep. from * to end.
2nd round: K. These 2 rounds form the chevron. When 24 rounds have been worked, change to 2nd colour and work 16 rounds. Change to 3rd colour and work 2 rounds, then 2 rounds 2nd, 2 rounds 3rd, 2 rounds 2nd, and 12 rounds 3rd. Change to No. 8(5) needles and repeat these stripes once, beg. with 1st colour. Change to No. 9(4) needles and 1st colour again

Red fringed dress

for colour illustration, see page 51

and work 4 rounds. This completes chevron patt. Still with 1st colour,
Begin shaping:
Next round: K.14, * sl.1, k.1, p.s.s.o., k.1, k.2 tog., k.27, rep. from * ending last rep. with sl.1, k.1, p.s.s.o., k.1, k.2 tog., k.13. Now work 14(17,20) rounds in st.st., (Every round K.)
Next round: K.13, * sl.1, k.1, p.s.s.o., k.1, k.2 tog., k.25, rep. from * ending last rep. sl.1, k.1, p.s.s.o., k.1, k.2 tog., k.12. Work 14(17,20) rounds st.st.
Work 2 further dec. rounds on next and foll. 15th(18th, 21st) rounds. Then on 19th(23rd, 25th) rounds., until 9(8,7) decreases in all have been worked. There will be 2 sts. less between decs. on each succeeding round. Cont. without further shaping until skirt measures 40 ins., or desired length from point of chevron. Cast off.

TO MAKE UP
Join side edges. Join waist elastic into a ring and set to waist on wrong side with casing stitch.

Tailored to fit with slimming darts. The fringes add the final touch to a very plain dress which you will find easy to make

Materials: 31(33,35) ozs. Wendy Double Knitting Nylonised and three 50 gramme balls of Wendy Diabolo Double Double Knitting to match; 1 pair each of Nos. 9(4) and 10(3) knitting needles; a 22 inch zip fastener; a medium sized crochet hook.

Tension: 6 sts. and 8 rows to 1 inch on No. 9(4) needles.

Measurements: Bust: 34(36, 38) ins. Hip' 36(38,40) ins. Length: 41(41¼, 41½) ins. Sleeve:17 ins.

Abbreviations: See Page 12

THE DRESS
Worked in 1 piece to the armholes.
With No. 9(4) needles and D.K., cast on 272(284,296) sts. and work 6 rows k.1, p.1 rib, knitting into back of all k. sts. on right side rows.
Next row: K.5, p.1, k. to last 6 sts., p.1, k.5. **Next row:** P. Rep. last 2 rows 10 times more.
Next row: K.5, p.1, k.28(30,32), * k.2 tog., k.1, (mark the last st.) sl.1, k.1, p.s.s.o., * k.61(63,65), rep. from * to * k.62(66,70), rep. from * to * k.61(63,65), rep. from * to *, k.28(30,32), rep. from * to *, p.1, k.5. Keeping the 2 p. sts. in line, work 21 rows. **Next row:** Dec. at each side of the marked sts. as for first row. Cont. to decrease, working 19 rows between each set of decreasing until 224(236,248) sts. remain.
Cast off 3 sts. at beg. of next 2 rows. Work 11 rows, then dec. as before. Work 13 rows between each of the next 2 dec. rows.

Work 7 rows between each of the next 2 dec. rows. Work 5 rows between each dec. row until 154(166,178) sts. rem. Work 9 rows straight.

Now make 1 at each side of marked sts. on next and every foll. 4th row until there are 210(222,234) sts. remaining. Cont. without further shaping until work measures 8 ins. from the beginning of the increase, ending after a p. row.

Divide for Armholes: Next row: Work 48(50,52) sts., cast off 9(11,13), k.96(100,104), cast off 9(11,13), work 48(50,52). Working on the last set of sts., dec. 1 st. at armhole edge on next 7 rows. Cont. without further shaping until armhole measures 5(5¼,5½) ins., ending at front edge.

Shape Neck: Cast off 5(6,7) sts. at beg. of next row, then dec. 1 st. on every row at the neck edge until 23(24,25) sts. remain. Cont. without further shaping until armhole measures 6¾(7,7¼) ins., ending at shoulder edge.

Shape Shoulder: Cast off 7(8,8) sts. at beg. of next row, then cast off 8 sts. at beg. of next alt. row then, 8(8,9) sts. at beg. of foll. alt. row. Return to centre sts. and work Back. Dec. 1 st. at each end of next 7 k. rows. Cont. without further shaping until armhole measures the same as the front. Shape shoulders to match front, then cast off remaining sts.

SLEEVES

With No. 10(3) needles, cast on 44 (48,52) sts. and work 2½ ins. in twisted rib. Change to No. 9(4) needles and st.st. Inc. 1 st. at each end of next and every foll. 6th row until there are 80(84,88) sts. on needle. Cont. straight until sleeve measures 17 ins. from beg., ending with a p. row.

Shape Top: Cast off 5(6,7) sts. at beg. of next 2 rows, then dec. 1 st. at each end of next 12(8,4) rows. Now dec. 1 st. at each end of next and every foll. alt. row until 38 sts. remain.

Dec. 1 st. at each end of next 4 rows. Cast

off 3 sts. at beg. of next 4 rows. Cast off rem. sts.

Front Borders:
With right side of work facing and with No. 10(3) needles, pick up and knit 234(236,238) sts. along line of p. sts. at front edge. Work 4 rows in twisted rib. Cast off in rib. Work other side to match.

Neckband:
With right side facing and No. 10(3) needles, pick up and knit 108(110,112) sts. round neck. Work 3 ins. twisted rib. Cast off in rib.

Pockets:
Cast on 39(41,43) sts. and beg. with a p. row work 15 rows in st. st.

Next row: K.17(18,19), k.2 tog., k.1, (mark the last st.) sl.1, k.1, p.s.s.o., k.17(18,19). Work 5 rows. Rep. last 6 rows and dec. on each side of marked st. 3 times more. Work 4 rows. Beg. with a k. row to reverse work, work 4 more rows. Now inc. 1 st. at each side of marked st. Work 5 rows. Cast off. Make another pocket to match.

Fringes:
Using Diabolo double and with crochet hook, make 19 chain. Change to single yarn and make 24 chain. *Slip stitch into first of the 24 sts. and last of double yarn chain. Slip stitch into next double yarn chain, make 24 chain and repeat from * to end. Make two for wrists.

For pockets, work in same way using 13 chain in double yarn as base. For Shoulders work on a base of 21 double yarn chain.

TO MAKE UP

Press pieces. Turn hem of pockets to wrong side and catch down. Sew fringes to edges of pockets. Turn neck band in half to wrong side and catch down. Set zip into front edges, beg. at top, then join centre seam to bottom of hem. Join shoulder and sleeve seams and set in sleeves. Add fringes to shoulders, wrists and side of sleeves. Add pockets to fronts. Press sleeve and shoulder seams.

Man's longline sweater

for colour illustration, see page 54

Random yarn makes an interesting sweater for the man who likes a classic. With a wide leather belt it will please the less conventional dresser

Materials: 14(15,16) 50 gramme balls of Patons Double Knitting Wool; a pair each of Nos. 12(1), 9(4), and 7(6) knitting needles; a set of 4 double pointed needles No. 10(3); 1 button.

Tension: 16 sts. and 14 rows to 2 ins. measured slightly stretched over rib pattern on No. 7(6) needles.

Measurements: Chest: 38(40,42) ins. Length: 27(27½, 28) ins. Sleeve: 18 ins.

Abbreviations: See Page 12

FRONT

With No. 12(1) needles, cast on 161 (169,177) sts. Change to No. 9(4) needles. Work in rib thus:
1st row: (right side) P.1, (k.1 t.b.l., p.1) to end. **2nd row:** K.1, (p.1, k.1 t.b.l.) to end. Rep. these 2 rows throughout. Work until Front measures 4 ins. from beg. Change to No. 7(6) needles. Cont. in patt. until Front measures 17 ins. from beg., ending with wrong side row.
Shape Armholes: Cast off 5 sts. at beg. of next 4 rows, then dec. 1 st. at each end of next 7(9,11) rows and then of foll. 3 alt. rows. Cont. without further shaping until Front measures 7(7½,8) ins. from beg. of armhole shaping, ending with a wrong side row.
Shape Neck: Rib 44(46,48) turn. Work another 17 rows on these sts. for left shoulder, decreasing 1 st. at neck edge on next and foll. alt. rows until 36(38,40) sts. remain.
Shape Shoulder: Cast off 12 sts. at beg. of next and foll. alt. row then 12(14,16)

sts. at beg. of next alt. row. Slip centre 33 sts. on to a spare needle. Rejoin yarn to remaining sts. and complete to match first side, reversing shapings.

BACK

Work as for Front, omitting front division for neck and working straight after completion of armhole shaping. When Back measures the same as Front to beg. of Shoulder shaping, cast off 12 sts. at beg. of next 4 rows and 12(14,16) sts. at beg. of foll. 2 rows. Leave remaining sts. on a spare needle.

SLEEVES

With No. 9(4) needles, cast on 54(56,58) sts. and work in rib patt. as for main part. When Sleeve measures 3 ins., inc. 27(29,31) sts. evenly across next row. Change to No. 7(6) needles. Inc. 1 st. at each end of every 4th row until there are 125(133,137) sts. Cont. without further shaping until sleeve measures 18 ins.
Shape Top: Cast off 5 sts. at beg. of next 4 rows, then 2 sts. at beg. of foll. 28(30,30) rows. Now cast off 4 sts. at beg. of next 2 rows. Cast off rem. sts.

NECKBAND

Join shoulder seams. With right side facing and set of double pointed needles, rejoin yarn and leaving first 16 sts. on spare needle at front, knit across remaining 17 sts. Cont. to pick up and knit sts. round neck, including 16 sts. from spare needle. Turn and cast on 10 sts. Work 3 rows in twisted rib pattern.
Next row: (Buttonhole row) Patt. to last 7 sts., y.r.n., twice, k.2 tog., patt. to end. Rib 3 more rows, dropping extra loop at buttonhole on next row. Cast off in rib.

TO MAKE UP

Do not press. Join side and sleeve seams. Set in sleeves. Sew button to neckband at side front, to match buttonhole.

Rainbow striped shortie

for colour illustration, see page 55

Make it in rainbow colours for effect or choose the prettiest colours from your odd ounce box

Materials: 2 ozs. Lister Lavenda 4-ply in Main (1st) colour and 1 oz. each in 4 other colours; a pair each of Nos. 10(3) and 11(2) knitting needles.

Tension: 7 sts. and 9 rows to 1 inch on No. 10(3) needles.

Measurements: Bust: 32(34, 36) ins.; Length: 18(18½, 18½) ins.; Sleeve: 4½ ins.

Abbreviations: See Page 12

BACK AND FRONT ALIKE

With No. 11(2) needles, cast on 98 (104,112) sts. in main (1st) colour and work 10 rows k.1, p.1 rib. Change to No. 10(3) needles and st.st. Work 2 rows in each of the 5 colours, beg. with 2nd colour. Cont. in stripes and inc. 1 st. at each end of every 10th row until there are 112(118,126) sts. on needle. Cont. without further shaping until 90 rows have been worked, thus ending with the 2nd row in main (1st) colour.

Shape Armholes: Cast off 5(6,7) sts. at beg. of next 2 rows, then dec. 1 st. at each end of next and foll. 2 alt. rows. (96, 100, 106) sts. Cont. in stripes for a further 17 rows, thus ending with 2 rows in 3rd colour.

Shape Neck: K.38(40,42) sts., turn. Leave rem. sts. on a spare needle Dec. 1 st. at neck edge on next and alt. rows until 20(22,24) sts. rem. Cont. until armhole measures 7¾(8,8¼) ins. from beg. of armhole shaping ending at armhole edge.

Shape Shoulder: Cast off 10(11,12) sts. at beg. of next and foll. alt. rows. Return to rem. sts. and slip centre 20(20,22) sts. on to a spare needle. Rejoin wool to remaining sts. and complete to match other side.

SLEEVES

With No. 11(2) needles and main(1st) colour, cast on 88(94,100) sts. and work 10 rows in k.1, p.1 rib. Change to No. 10 (3) needles and st. st. in stripes as for main part. Work 40 rows, thus ending with 2nd row of main(1st) colour.

Shape Top: Cast off 5(6,7) sts. at beg. of next 2 rows. Then cast off 3 sts. at beg. of foll. 4 rows and 2 sts. at beg. of next 4 rows. Now dec. 1 st. at each end of alt. rows until 24 sts. remain. Cast off.

NECKBAND

Press pieces and join one shoulder. With main colour and No. 11(2) needles, and with right side facing, pick up and knit 100(104,108) sts. round neck. Work 8 rows in k.1, p.1 rib. Cast off in rib.

TO MAKE UP

Join second shoulder. Set in sleeves, matching stripes from underarm. Join side and sleeve seams. Press seams.

Striped sleeveless shortie

for colour illustration, see page 58

Zig-zag stripes make a cute top for summer days. Apart from the main colour, odd ounces will make the coloured stripes

Materials: 6(6,7,7,8) balls of Twilley's Cortina in White; 1 ball each in Rose, Mulberry, Blue and Purple;
a pair each of Nos. 10(3) and 12(1) knitting needles.

Tension: 8 sts. and 10 rows to 1 inch.

Measurements: Bust: 30(32,34,36,38) ins. Length from shoulder: $17(17\frac{1}{2},17\frac{1}{2},18,18)$ ins.

Abbreviations: See Page 12

BACK

With No. 12(1) needles and white, cast on 131(139,147,155,163) sts. and work in k.1, p.1 rib for 7 ins. Change to No. 10(3) needles and work in pattern.

1st row: With Rose, k.2, * p.u.k., k.2, sl.1, k.2 tog., p.s.s.o., k.2, p.u.k., k.1, rep. from * to last st., k.1. **2nd row:** K.1, p. to last st., k.1. **3rd and 4th rows:** With white as 1st and 2nd. **5th and 6th rows:** With Mulberry as 1st and 2nd. **7th and 8th rows:** With White as 1st and 2nd. **9th and 10th rows:** With Blue as 1st and 2nd.

11th and 12th rows: With White as 1st and 2nd.

13th and 14th rows: With Purple as 1st and 2nd.

15th and 16th rows: With White as 1st and 2nd. These 16 rows form the striped pattern sequence. Repeat them until work measures 11 ins. from beg., ending with wrong side.

To Shape Armholes: Cast off 8(9,10, 11,12) sts. at beg. of next 2 rows, then dec. 1 st. at each end of next 10 rows. Now dec. 1 st. at each end of foll. 4(5,6,7,8) alt. rows. Cont. on rem. sts. until work measures $17(17\frac{1}{2},17\frac{1}{2},18,18)$ ins. from beg., ending with a wrong side row.

Shape Shoulders and neck: Cast off 7(8,8,9,9) patt. until there are 18(18,20,20, 22) sts. on right hand needle. Turn. Leave rem. sts. on a spare needle.
Next row: K.2 tog., work to end.
Next row: Cast off 7(8,8,9,9) sts., work to last 2 sts., k.2 tog.
Next row: K.2 tog., work to end. Cast off rem. sts. With right side of work facing, join on wool and cast off 37(39,39,41,41) sts. for back of neck, patt. to end.
Next row: Cast off 7(8,8,9,9) work to end. Now complete to match first side.

FRONT
Work as for Back until Front measures 10 rows less than back to armhole, ending with a wrong side row. Divide for U-neck.
Next row: Patt. 52(55,59,62,66) sts., turn. Leave rem. sts. on a spare needle. Dec. 1 st. at neck edge on next 8 rows. Work 1 row straight. Work 2 rows here when completing second side.
Shape Armhole: Cast off 8(9,10,11,12) sts. at beg. of next row, then dec. 1 st. at armhole edge on next 10 rows. Now dec. 1 st. at armhole edge on foll. 4(5,6,7,8) alt. rows. Cont. on rem. sts. until Front measures the same as Back to shoulder, ending at armhole edge.

Shape Shoulder: Cast off 7(8,8,9,9) sts. at beg. of next and foll. alt. row. Work 1 row and cast off rem. sts. With right side of work facing, rejoin wool to inner edge of sts. on spare needle. Cast off next 27(29,29,31,31) sts., patt. to end. Complete to match first side noting the exception.
Borders: With right side of work facing, join on White and with No. 12(1) needle, pick up and knit 45(47,47,49,49) sts. round back of neck. Work 6 rows in g.st. Cast off. With right side of work facing and with White, pick up and knit 64(68,68, 72,72) sts. along left side of front neck, 27(29,29,31,31) from cast off group and 64(68,68,72,72) along right side of front neck. Work 6 rows in g.st., cast off.
Armhole Borders: Join shoulder seams. Pick up and knit 118(126,128,136,138) sts. in same way, round armhole. Work 6 rows g.st. Cast off. Work both armholes to match.

TO MAKE UP
Press work lightly on wrong side with a warm iron and a damp cloth. Join side seams. Press seams.

Pink mohair jumper

for colour illustration, see page 59

Made in a gossamer yarn as light as a feather and as warm as a kiss. Really feminine with a fragile look

Materials: 4(5,5,6,6) balls of Twilley's Mohair in Pink and 1 ball in contrast; a pair of No. 9(4) knitting needles; crochet hook No. 2.50 m.m.

Tension: 7½ sts. and 10 rows to 1 in.

Measurements: Bust: 32(34,36,38,40) ins. Length: 20 ins.

Abbreviations: See Page 12

BACK

With two strands of mohair, cast on 112(120,128,136,144) sts. Change to single yarn and knitting into back of every st. work in g.st. Inc. 1 st. at each end of every 13th row until there are 132(140, 148,156,164) sts. on needle. Cont. straight until Back measures 13 ins. from beg.
Shape Armholes: Cast off 8(9,10,11,12) sts. at beg. of next 2 rows. Then dec. 1 st. at each end of next 14(15,16,17,18) rows. Work straight until armhole measures 7(7,7,7½,7½) ins. from beg. of shaping.
Shape Shoulders: Cast off 7 sts. at beg. of next 4 rows. Cast off rem. sts.

FRONT

Work as for Back until Front measures 4 rows less than Back before armhole shaping.
Shape Neck: Work across 51(55,59,63,67) sts., turn and complete this side first.
★★ Cast off 3 sts. at neck edge on alt. row, then cast off 2 sts. at this edge on next alt. row. Then dec. 1 st. at this edge of foll. 10(12,14,16,18) rows. **At the same time,** when front matches Back to armhole, beg. armhole shaping.
Armhole Shaping: Cast off 8(9,10,11,12) sts. at side edge, then dec. at this edge

1 st. on foll. 14(15,16,17,18) rows. Work straight until armhole matches Back to shoulder.
Shape Shoulder: Cast off 7 sts. at beg. of next 2 rows at armhole edge.★★ Rejoin yarn at inner edge and cast off centre 30 sts. Work to end. Now work from ★★ to ★★ reversing shapings.

THE BRAID

With No. 2.50 crochet hook and single yarn, make 8 chain, using contrast.
1st row: Miss 1st chain, 1 d.c. into 2nd chain. Work 1 d.c. into each chain to end. 1 chain, turn.
2nd row: As first row, working last double crochet into turning chain. 1 chain, turn. Repeat 2nd row 4 times.
7th row: Work as for 2nd row for 3 double crochet. Join in main colour. Work bobble into 4th st. thus: 3 chain, yarn over hook, and draw loop through 3 times, wool over hook and draw through all loops on hook, 1 chain, 1 slip st. into same st. Drop main and leave at back of work, with contrast, work to end of row as before. Repeat 2nd to 7th rows until braid fits round armhole edge. Make another piece to match. Make a strip to fit front and back neck edges.

TO MAKE UP

Press pieces lightly. Sew braid to neck and armhole edges. Press seams.

Yellow sweater

Skinny rib you'll find useful, see it teamed with the matching pinafore dress on page 46

Materials: See Pinafore dress on page 44.

BACK
With No. 11(2) needles and yellow, cast on 126(134,142) sts. and work in k.2, p.2 rib throughout.
1st row: K.2, p.2, to last 2 sts., k.2.
2nd row: P.2, k.2, to last 2 sts., p.2. Cont. thus until Back measures 16 ins. from beg.
Shape Armholes: Cast off 4(5,6) sts. at beg. of next 2 rows, then k.2 tog., at each end of next and every alt. row until 104 (108,112) sts. remain. Work without further shaping until Back measures 23¼ ins. from beg.
Shape Shoulder and Neck: Cast off 8 sts., rib 24(26,27) turn, k.2 tog., and work to end of row.
Next row: Cast off 7(8,8) sts., work to

end. **Next row:** K.2 tog., at neck edge, work to end. Rep. these 2 rows. Cast off rem. sts. Place centre 40(40,42) sts. on a needle for neck. Rejoin wool to rem. sts. and complete to match other side.

FRONT
Work as for Back until Armhole measures 5½ ins. **Next row:** Rib 32(34,36) sts. turn. Now dec. 1 st. at neck edge on every row until 29(31,32) sts. remain. Cont. without further shaping until work matches back to shoulder, ending at side edge.
Shape Shoulder: Cast off 8 sts. at beg. of next row and 7(8,8) sts. on foll. 2 alt. rows. Work 1 row and cast off rem. sts. Return to sts. for other side and work to match.

SLEEVES
Cast on 50(54,54) sts. and work in rib as for Back for 20 rows. Now inc. 1 st. at each end of next and every foll. 8th row until there are 90(94,98) sts. on needle, taking increased sts. into rib pattern. Cont. without further shaping until sleeve measures 17½ ins.
Shape Top: Cast off 4(5,6) sts. at beg. of next 2 rows, then dec. 1 st. at each end of next and every foll. alt. row until 44(46,48) sts. rem. Now dec. 1 st. at each end of every row until 26 sts. rem. Cast off in rib.

ROLL COLLAR
Join left shoulder seam. Pick up and knit 136(140,140) sts. round neck. Work in k.2, p.2 rib for 6 ins. Cast off in rib.

TO MAKE UP
Do not Press. Join right shoulder seam and seam of roll collar. Set in sleeves. Join side and sleeve seams.

Chosen for Children

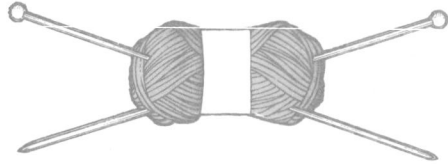

Special designs, each with a particular use in mind. Plain or pretty, all will find a welcome with the mother of small folk as a change from the usual knitting for children

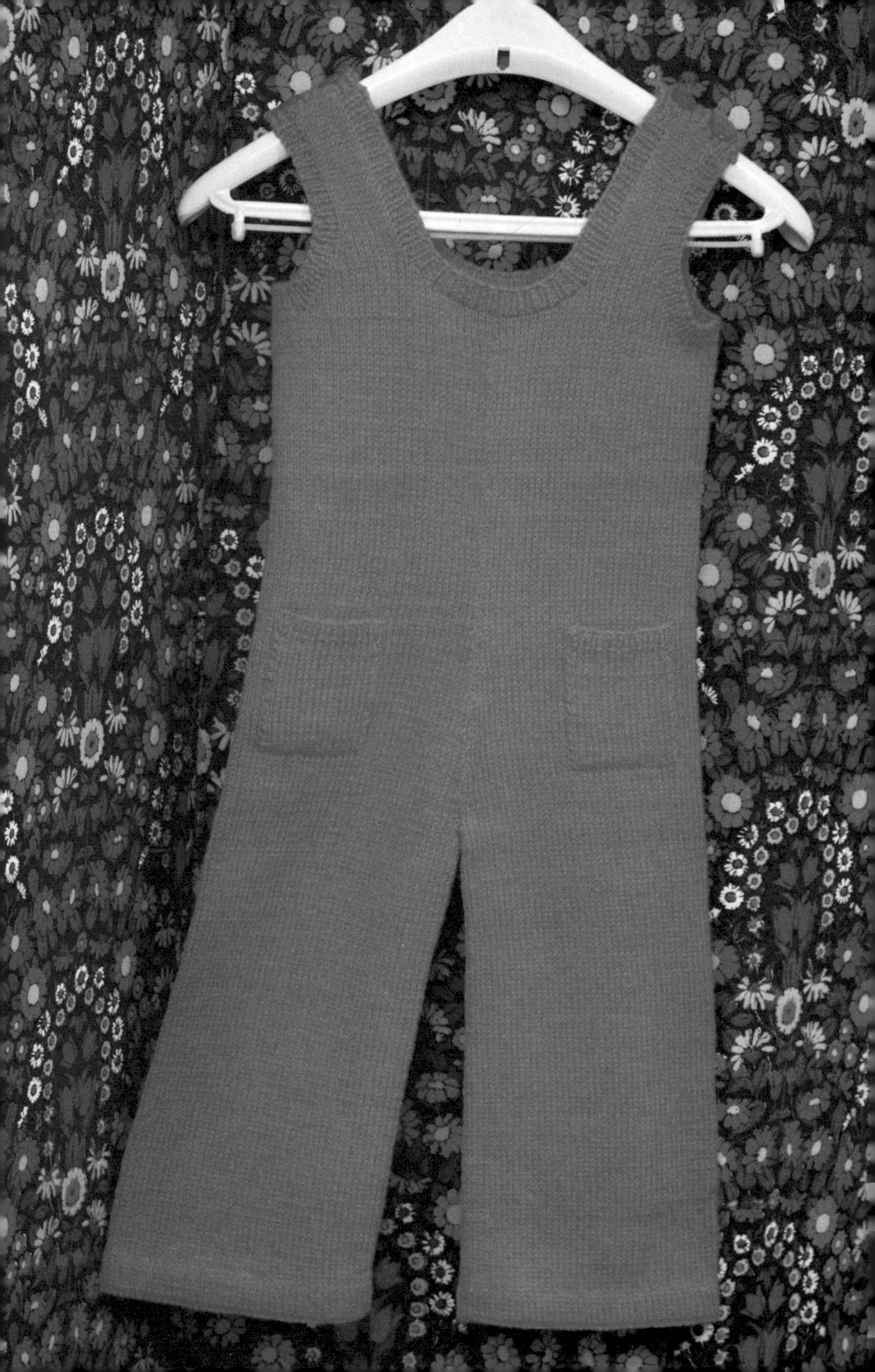

Child's Dungarees

for colour illustration, see page 63

Tough and cheerful for playtime, to wear with a variety of shirts and sweaters. Instructions are given for three sizes

Materials: 6(7,8) 50 gramme balls of Patons Trident Double Knitting; a pair each of Nos. 10(3) and 8(5) knitting needles; 4 buttons

Tension: 11 sts. and 15 rows to 2 ins. over st.st. on No. 8(5) needles.

Measurements: Chest: 22(24,26) ins. Leg seam: $12\frac{1}{2}(14,15\frac{1}{2})$ ins.; Centre Front seam: $11\frac{1}{2}(13\frac{1}{2},15\frac{1}{2})$ ins.

Abbreviations: See Page 12

Note: Instructions for the larger sizes are given in brackets. Where one figure only is given, this applies to all sizes.

RIGHT LEG

With No. 10(3) needles, cast on 80(86,92) sts. and work 7 rows st.st., beg. with a k. row. Knit next row to mark hemline. Change to No.8(5) needles and beg. with a k. row, cont. in st.st. until piece measures $12\frac{1}{2}(14,15\frac{1}{2})$ ins. from hemline, ending with a p. row. Place a marker at each end of last row and then shape as follows:

Cast off 2 sts. at beg. of next 2 rows, then dec. 1 st. at each end of 5th and every foll. 6th row until there are 64(70,76) sts. Cont. without further shaping until work measures $7\frac{1}{2}(8\frac{1}{2},9\frac{1}{2})$ ins. from markers, ending with a k. row.

Shape Back: 1st row: P.32(35, 38), turn. **2nd and every alt. row:** K. **3rd row:** P.24(27,29) turn. **5th row:** P.16(19,20) turn. **7th row:** P.8(11,11) turn. **9th row:** P. across all sts. Cont. without further shaping until work measures 11(13,15) ins. from markers, measuring at short edge of work, ending with a p. row.

Divide for Armhole: Next row: K.26 (29,32) turn and leave rem. sts. on a spare needle. **Next row:** P. Now dec. 1 st. at end of next row. Work 1 row straight.

Shape front neck and cont. to shape armhole: Next row: Cast off 7(8,9) sts., k. to last 2 sts. k.2 tog. Now dec. 1 st. at neck edge on every row and **at the same time** dec. 1 st. at armhole edge on every foll. alt. row until 11(13,15) sts. rem. Cont. to dec. at armhole edge, keeping neck edge straight, until 10 sts. rem. Work without further shaping until piece measures 16(18½,21) ins. from markers, measured at short edge of work, ending with a p. row. Leave these sts. on a spare needle. With right side facing, rejoin wool to sts. on first spare needle, cast off 12 and knit to end. Now work to match other side reversing shapings.

LEFT LEG

As for right leg, reversing all shapings.

POCKETS

With No. 8(5) needles, cast on 15(17,19) sts. and work as folls. K. 1 row.
Next row: K.1, p. to last st., k.1. Rep. last 2 rows for 22(24,26) rows. Change to No. 10(3) needles and work in k.1, p.1 rib for 4 rows. Cast off. Make another pocket to match.

TO MAKE UP

Press pieces lightly with a cool iron and a dry cloth. Sew pocket to each side of front. Join leg and front and back seams. With No. 10(3) needles and with right side facing, pick up and knit 68(74,80) sts. round each armhole. Work 4 rows k.1, p.1 rib. Cast off in rib.
Pick up and knit 66(76,86) sts. round Front neck border and work 5 rows k.1, p.1 rib. Cast off in rib. Work Back neck border to match.
Pick up and knit 4 sts. from rib at back shoulder, 10 sts. from spare needle, inc. 1 st. at centre and pick up and knit 4 sts. from other rib.
Next row: *P.1, k.1, to last st. p.1.
Next row: *K.1, p.1, to last st., k.1. Work 3 more rows in rib and cast off in rib.
Work front shoulders to match, making buttonholes on 2nd and 3rd rows as folls:
2nd row: Rib 4, cast off 2, rib to last 6 sts., cast off 2, rib to end. **3rd row:** In rib, casting 2 sts. on over those cast off in previous row.
Fold hems of legs to wrong side and catch neatly into position. Press seams and add buttons to shoulders.

Toddler's Poncho and pants

Pretty lace stitch in three colours makes the pointed poncho. Make the pants to pick up the main colour, for the smartest babes in town

Materials: Poncho: 2 balls of Mahony's Blarney Berella Baby Quickerknit in White, 3 balls in pink and 2 balls of blue;
Pants: 4 balls of blue for pants only;
a pair each of Nos. 9(4), 10(3), and 11(2) knitting needles;
a set of 4 double pointed needles Nos. 9(4) and 10(3);
Elastic for waist.

Tension: 7 sts. to 1 inch over st.st., and 6 sts. to 1 inch over pattern on No. 9(4) needles.

Measurements: Poncho: Centre front seam: 15 ins.;
Pants: Waist to crutch: 8½ ins.; Inside leg seam: 10¼ ins., with ribbing turned up.

Abbreviations: See Page 12

THE PONCHO

With No. 9(4) needles and white, cast on 191 sts. **1st row:** (wrong side) P.
2nd row: K.1, sl.1, k.1, p.s.s.o., p. to last 3 sts., k.2 tog., k.1. Rep. 1st and 2nd rows twice. Change to pink. **7th row:** P.
8th row: K.1, sl.1, k.2 tog., p.s.s.o., * y.fwd., k.3, y.fwd., sl.1, k.2 tog., p.s.s.o., rep. from * to last 7 sts., y.fwd., k.3, y.fwd., k.3 tog., k.1.
9th row and 11th row: P.
10th row: K.1, sl.1, k.1, p.s.s.o., * y.fwd., sl.1, k.2 tog., p.s.s.o., y.fwd., k.3, rep. from * to last 6 sts., y.fwd., sl.1, k.2 tog., p.s.s.o., y.fwd., k.2 tog., k.1.
12th row: K.1, sl.1, k.1, p.s.s.o., k.2 * y.fwd., sl.1, k.2 tog., p.s.s.o., y.fwd., k.3, rep. from * to last 8 sts., y.fwd., sl.1, k.2 tog., p.s.s.o., y.fwd., k.2, k.2 tog., k.1.
13th to 18th rows: As rows 7 to 12. Change to white. Rep. these 18 rows but use blue and pink in turn for 12 rows of lace patt., until 5 patts. and 6 rows of 6th patt. have been worked. Change to No.10 (3) needles and cont. to 18th row of 7th patt.
Next row: Still with pink, (p.2 tog., p.2) 15 times, p.2 tog., p.1, p.2 tog. Leave these sts. on a spare needle and make another piece to match. Now arrange all the sts. from both pieces on three No. 10 (3) needles, and with right side facing, and still with pink, knit 1 round and then work in k.2, p.2 rib for 1½ ins. Change to set of No. 9(4) needles and work a further 2½ ins. Cast off loosely in rib. Press lightly and join seams very neatly.

PANTS
Right Leg

With No. 11(2) needles and blue, cast on 81 sts. and work 14 rows in k.1, p.1 rib. Change to No. 9(4) needles and work 1 more row in rib. Purl 1 row then shape thus:
1st row: K.10, turn. **2nd and every**

Pram cover

wrong side row: Sl.1, p. to end.
3rd row: K.18, turn. **5th row:** K.26,
turn. **7th row:** K.34, turn. **9th row:**
K.42, turn. **10th row:** Sl.1, p.41. Cont.
in st.st. and inc. 1 st. at longer edge on
foll. 7th and every foll. 8th row until there
are 87 sts. Cont. without further shaping
until short edge measures 9 ins. ending
with a p. row.
Shape Leg: Cast off 3 sts. at beg. of next
2 rows, then dec. 1 st. at each end of next
5 rows. Now dec. 1 st. at each end of next
3 k. rows and then at each end of every
foll. 4th row 3 times. Cont. without
further shaping until leg measures 8½
ins. ending with a p. row. Change to No.
11(2) needles. **Next row:** (K.2 tog., k.2)
14 times, k.2 tog., k.1. Now work 3½ ins.
in k.2 p.2 rib. Cast off loosely in rib.
Work Left Leg to match reversing all
shapings.

TO MAKE UP

Press pieces lightly on wrong side. Join
front and back seams. Join inside leg seam
using flat seam for ribbing. Turn waist
ribbing in half to wrong side and catch
down. Insert elastic. Turn up ankle
ribbing. Press seams.

A very quick and easy gift to make for the
newcomer to your own family or for any
pram riding baby

Materials: Six 2 ozs. balls of Lister
Prema Bulky Knitting;
a pair of No. 5 knitting needles;
4 yds. of Blanket ribbon;
matching sewing silk.

Tension: 3 sts. to 1 inch.

Measurements: 18 by 24 ins. excluding
ribbon frill.

Abbreviations: See Page 12

TO MAKE

Cast on 57 sts. and knit 1 row. Now work
in pattern.
1st row: Slip 1, * k.1, k. into st. of row
below, rep. from * to last 2 sts. k.2.
2nd row: Slip 1, * k.1 into st. of row
below, k.1, rep. from * to end. These 2
rows form the pattern and are repeated.
Work in pattern until piece measures 24
ins. from beginning. Cast off loosely.

TO MAKE UP

Do not press. Open blanket ribbon out to
single thickness. Mark the centre of
length. Join into a circle. Mark a point
half way between the join and the marked
centre point on each side. Gather between
these points, gathering each single
thickness of ribbon. Pin evenly round
cover, folding the ribbon in half and
sewing each edge neatly to each side of
cover.

Sleeping bag for a baby

So many parents go camping and sailing, taking Junior too. Here's the ideal garment to keep a travelling child warm and cosy

Materials: Nine 50 gramme balls of Sirdar Candytwist;
a pair each of Nos. 8(5) and 10(3) knitting needles;
a 22 inch zip fastener;
a length of shirring elastic.

Tension: 9½ sts. to 2 ins. on No. 8(5) needles.

Measurements: Chest: 30 ins.; Length: at centre back 25 ins.; Sleeve: 8 ins.

Abbreviations: See Page 12

BACK AND FRONT

Working in one piece up to the armholes, with No. 8(5) needles, cast on 142 sts.
1st row: K.12, * (p.1, sl.2 purlwise with y.fwd.) 4 times, p.1, * k.92, rep. from * to * once, k.12.
2nd row: K.12, p.13, k.92, p.13, k.12.
3rd and 4th rows: As 1st and 2nd.
5th row: K. **6th row:** As 2nd. Rep. these 6 rows until work measures 18 ins.
Divide for Armholes: Next row: Patt. 33, cast off 4, k.68 including st. left on needle after casting off, cast off 4, patt. 33. Work on group of sts. for left front. K.12, p.13, k. to end.
1st row: K.2 tog., patt. to end.
2nd row: K.12, p.13, k. to end.
3rd row: Patt. to end. **4th row:** As 2nd. Rep. 1st and 2nd rows until 19 sts. remain, ending at neck edge.
Next row: Cast off 5, work to end. Still dec. at armhole edge as before and dec. 1 st. at neck edge. Work 1 row. Rep. last 2 rows until 5 sts. remain. Now dec. at armhole edge only until 2 sts. remain. Fasten off. Rejoin yarn to remaining sts.

for Back and with wrong side facing, k. to end.
Next row: K. 2 tog., k. to last 2 sts., k.2 tog. **Next row:** K. Repeat last 2 rows until 20 sts. remain. Cast off. Rejoin yarn to remaining sts. for Right Front and with wrong side facing, complete to match Left Front, reversing all shapings.

SLEEVES

With No. 10(3) needles, cast on 38 sts. and work in single rib for 4 rows. Change to No. 8(5) needles and cont. in g.st. Inc. 1 st. at each end of 7th and every foll. 8th row until there are 52 sts. on needle. Work without further shaping until sleeve measures 7½ ins. from beg.
Shape Top: Cast off 2 sts. at beg. of next 2 rows. **Next row:** K.2 tog., k. to last 2 sts., k.2 tog. **Next 3 rows:** K. Rep. last 4 rows once more, then 1st and 2nd rows until 4 sts. remain. Cast off.

HOOD

With No. 10(3) cast on 84 sts. and work in single rib for 15 rows. Change to No. 8(5) needles and cont. in g.st. until work measures 6½ ins.
Next row: K.1, k.2 tog., * k.2, k.2 tog., rep. from * to last st., k.1.
Next row: Cast off 23, k.17, cast off 23. Rejoin yarn to remaining sts. and cont. in g.st. Dec. 1 st. at each end of every 14th row until 13 sts. remain. Cont. without further shaping until work measures 5 ins. Cast off.

BOTTOM GUSSET

With No. 8(5) needles, cast on 40 sts. and knit 2 rows. Cont. in g.st. and cast on 4 sts. at beg. of next 2 rows. Then cast on 2 sts. at beg. of foll. 2 rows. Now inc. 1 st. at beg. of next 10 rows. Work 5 rows without further shaping. Now dec. 1 st. at beg. of

next 10 rows, cast off 2 sts. at beg. of foll.
2 rows and cast off 4 sts. at beg. of next 2
rows. Knit 2 rows. Cast off.

TO MAKE UP

Join sleeve and raglan seams. With wrong
side of sleeve facing, thread shirring
elastic through first 4 rows at lower edge of
sleeve. Set in zip fastener. Set Hood to
neck and set gusset into lower edge.

Baby's carrying cape

Smarter than a shawl and ideal for the Babe in arms. Simple stocking stitch in pink is striped with pattern in white

Materials: 5 balls of Mahony's Blarney Berella Baby Quickerknit in main colour and 2 balls in contrast;
a pair each of Nos. 8(5) and 10(3) knitting needles;
3 buttons;
1 yd. of 1 inch facing ribbon;
1 yd. of narrow ribbon for neck tie.

Tension: 6¼ sts. and 8 rows to 1 inch on No. 8(5) needles.

Measurements: Length from Neck: 21½ ins. All round lower edge: 42 ins.

Abbreviations: See Page 12

TO MAKE

With No. 8(5) needles and main colour, cast on 278 sts. and p. 5 rows. Change to No. 10(3) needles and contrast.
1st row: (wrong side) P.
2nd row: K.1, then k.2 tog., to last st., k.1.
3rd row: K.1, * p.u.k. winding yarn twice round needle, k.1 winding yarn twice round needle, rep. from * to last st. k.1. **Note** Do not work into thread before last st.
4th row: K. dropping extra loops. Change to No. 8(5) needles and main colour. **5th row:** P.
6th row: P.4, k. to last 4 sts., p.4.
7th to 18th rows: Rep. 5th and 6th rows 6 times. Change to No. 10(3) needles and contrast. These 18 rows form the pattern. Rep. them once more then rows 1 to 17 again.
Next row: P.4, k.2, (k.2 tog., k.10, k.2 tog.) 19 times, k.2, p.4. Work 35 rows of pattern on these sts.
Next row: P.4, k.2, (k.2 tog., k.8, k.2

tog.) 19 times, k.2, p.4. Work 35 rows of patt. on these sts.
Next row: P.4, k.2, (k.2 tog., k.6, k.2 tog.) 19 times, k.2, p.4. Work 17 rows of patt. on these sts.
Next row: P.4, k.1, (k.2 tog., k.4, k.2 tog.) 19 times, k.1, p.4. Work 5 rows of patt. on these sts. Cont. in k.2, p.2 rib keeping garter st. borders. Make buttonhole in 4th row thus: Work to last 4 sts., y.r.n., p.2 tog., p.2. Work 8 rows in rib with garter st. borders.
Next row: P.4, (k.2, p.2 tog.) to last 6 sts., k.2, p.4.
Next row: P.4, (p.2, k.1) to last 6 sts., p.2, y.r.n., p.2 tog., p.2. Work 6 more rows with centre sts. in k.2, p.1 rib.
Next row: P.4, (k.2 tog., p.1) to last 6 sts., k.2 tog., p.4. Change to No. 10(3) needles and work 2 rows with centre sts. in p.1, k.1 rib. Make a buttonhole on next row then work 6 more rows.
Next row: P.4, (y.o.n., k.2 tog., k.1, y. fwd., k.2 tog., p.1) 10 times, p.3. Work 3 more rows with centre sts. in rib as before but inc. 1 st. in centre of last row
Next row: Cast off 8, k.7, (including st. on needle), (inc. into next st., k.2) 6 times, inc. into next st., turn. Change to No. 8(5) needles and work on these sts. for one side of hood. **1st row:** P. **2nd row:** P.4, k. to end. Rep. these 2 rows once. * Now beg. with 1st row, work in patt. as for main part but with border at front edge only. Inc. 1 st. at other edge on 2nd and 11th rows of each st.st. band until 36 rows have been worked from *. Work 7 rows without further shaping, then dec. 1 st. at shaped edge on alt. rows 3 times, then on every row 4 times. Cast off rem. sts. Rejoin yarn to rem. sts. at centre.
1st row: (With right side facing) Inc. into 1st stitch, (k.2, inc. into next st.) 6 times, k.7, cast off 8 sts. Break yarn and rejoin at needle point. Complete to match first side of hood, reversing border and shaping.

TO MAKE UP

Press lightly with a dry cloth and a warm iron. Face front edges neatly with ribbon as far as base of yoke. Add buttons. Join back and top seam of hood. Thread ribbon through holes at neck and tie in a bow.

It's in the bag

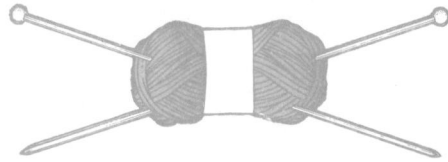

One needs a bag for so many things. All these are easy and one can be made in less than an evening. Most of them would take only two evenings to complete. From a washable shopping bag to one for the evening, take one to the beach or carry your playing cards in it, make one to match a summer outfit, all of them have that certain flair to make them different

Striped summer handbag

Two straight pieces and easy knitting. You could make more than one and have them to match your summer wardrobe

Materials: 2 balls each of Twilley's Lysbet in Mauve and Purple; a pair of No. 10(3) knitting needles; a pair of circular handles 5 ins. diameter; lining material to match.

Tension: 7 sts. and 9 rows to 1 inch.

Measurements: Width: 13 ins., **Depth:** 10 ins.

Abbreviations: See Page 12

TO MAKE

With Mauve, cast on 80 sts. and work $1\frac{1}{4}$ ins. Change to purple and work $1\frac{1}{4}$ ins. Cont. in this way until 4 purple and 5 mauve stripes have been worked. Cast off. Make another piece to match. Press lightly with a cool iron over a dry cloth. Cut lining to match. Join seams of lining and knitted pieces, leaving one wide edge open for top. Insert lining. Begin $1\frac{1}{2}$ ins. from one side and insert a handle, sewing knitted piece over handle to lining. Insert second handle in same way. Neatly join lining and knitted edges at sides. Trim lower corners with a tassel.

Shopping bag

That old string bag, you remember, you used it to cart the vegetables home and it wore out. Make another, it's easy and washable

Materials: 2 balls of Twilley's Stalite cotton No. 3;
a pair each of Nos. 12(1) and 9(4) knitting needles.

Tension: 6½ sts. and 8½ rows to 1 inch on No. 9(4) needles.

Measurements: Width: 18 ins. all round;

Length: 13 ins.

Abbreviations: See Page 12

TO MAKE

With No. 12(1) needles, cast on 9 sts. and knit 1 row.
1st inc. row: * (K.1, p.u.k.) twice, k.1, rep. from * twice more.
Next row: Knit. (15 sts.)
2nd inc. row: * (K.1, p.u.k.) 4 times, k.1, rep. from * twice more.
Next row: Knit. (27 sts.)
3rd inc. row: * (K.1, p.u.k.) 8 times, k.1, rep. from * twice more.
Next row: Knit. (51 sts.)
4th inc. row: * (K.1, p.u.k.) 16 times, k.1, rep. from * twice more.
Next row: Knit (99 sts.) Change to No. 9 (4) needles and pattern.
1st row: K.1, * y.r.n., k.2 tog., rep. from * to end. **2nd row:** Knit. Rep. these 2 rows for a further 12 ins. Change to g. st. Knit 6 rows. Cast off. Press lightly. Join seam. Make a twisted cord and thread through first row of holes below garter stitch border.

Yellow tote bag

You see them around all over the place, so you really should have one. This is another two row pattern and one for which you can change the colour on every two rows, so odd balls will make a very cheerful bag, and cost you nothing

Materials: Two 50 gramme balls of Paton's Double Knitting Wool in Yellow, gold and orange;
a pair of No. 9(4) knitting needles;
4 brass rings;
lining material to match.

Tension: 6 sts. and 8 rows to 1 inch over pattern.

Measurements: Width: 12 ins., Depth: 15 ins.

Abbreviations: See Page 12

TO MAKE

With Yellow, cast on 72 sts. and work 2 ins. in garter stitch. Now begin pattern.
1st row: (Wrong side) Purl.
2nd row: K.2, * w.r.n., k.3, pass first of 3 knit sts. over 2nd and 3rd sts., rep. from * to last st. k.1. Change to gold. **3rd row:** Purl.
4th row: K.1, * k.3, pass first of 3 knit sts. over 2nd and 3rd sts., w.r.n., rep. from * to last 2 sts., k.2. Change to orange and repeat pattern, using each colour in turn for 2 rows. Continue until piece measures 30 ins., ending with yellow. Now work a further 2 ins. in garter stitch and cast off.

TO MAKE UP

Press piece on wrong side lightly. Cut lining material to match, less the 2 ins. of garter stitch at each end. Fold lining in half and join both long sides, leaving one narrow end open. Join seams of knitted piece in same way. Insert lining and turn the 2 ins. of garter stitch inside over the edge of lining and sew neatly into place. Make a thick twisted cord 72 inches long. Sew two brass rings to each side of top about 2 ins. from each end. Thread cord through rings and tie in a knot to form double handle.

Orange and white beach bag

In thick cotton and a simple two row pattern which makes the points at top and bottom. You will find many uses for this bag

Materials: 3 balls of Twilley's Knitcot in White and 2 balls Tango; a pair of No. 9(4) knitting needles; a pair of handles approx. 10 ins. wide; 3/4 yd. of 1 in. wide binding; towel lining.

Tension: 6¼ sts. and 6 rows to 1 inch over pattern.

Measurements: Width: 13 ins.; Length: 14 ins.

Abbreviations: See Page 12

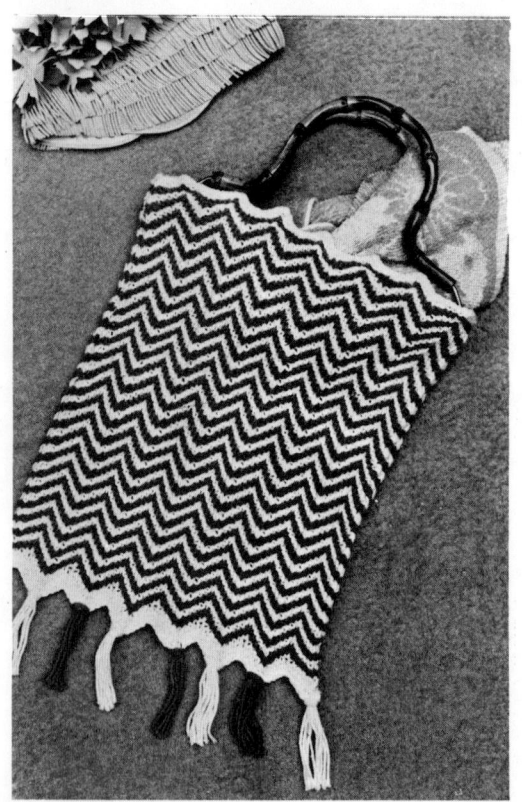

TO MAKE

With White, cast on 87 sts. and work in patt. as follows.

1st row: (Right side) K.1, sl.1, k.1, p.s.s.o., * k.9, sl.2, k.1, p.2 s.s.o., rep. from * to last 12 sts., k.9, k.2 tog., k.1.

2nd row: K.1, * p.1, k.4, (k.1, y.o.n., k.1) all into next st., k.4, rep. from * to last 2 sts., p.1, k.1. Change to Tango. **3rd and 4th rows:** As 1st and 2nd rows.

Repeat these 4 rows, changing colour on right side rows, working 2 rows in each colour in turn until piece measures 14 ins., ending with white and 2nd row. Cast off loosely. Make another piece.

TO MAKE UP

Press pieces lightly. Cut two pieces of lining to match. Join three sides leaving one narrow end open. Join seams of knitted pieces in same way, leaving cast off edges open for top. Insert lining. Join one edge of binding to top of bag at lower edge of points. Insert frame of handle under binding and sew other edge of binding to lining. Complete other side, inserting second handle. Trim points at bottom of bag with alternate tassels of white and tango.

Evening bag

Knit a bit of glamour to carry those bits
and pieces you must have with you, even
on the best occasions. It is very easy,
fringes make the magic

Materials: 3 ozs. Twilley's Goldfingering
in Silver and 1 oz. each in Copper and
Pewter;
a pair of No. 11(2) knitting needles;
a medium sized crochet hook for fringing.

Tension: 7 sts. and 14 rows to 1 inch.

Measurements: Width: 7 ins. Depth: 9
ins.

Abbreviations: See Page 12

TO MAKE
With No.11(2) needles and Silver, cast on
50 sts. and work 18 ins. garter stitch. Cast
off.
Strap: Cast on 4 sts. in silver and work
34 ins. g. st. Cast off.

TO MAKE UP
Do not press. Fold main part in half and
join sides, Sew ends of strap to each side.
To Fringe: With silver, cut 6 strands
each 16 ins. long, fold in half and with
crochet hook, knot through every 3rd
stitch round top of bag. With Copper,
fringe in same way into every 3rd stitch
round centre. With Pewter, fringe round
lower edge into every 3rd stitch. Trim
fringes neatly.

Toy cupboard

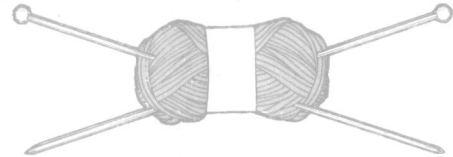

Soft toys quickly become constant companions for a small child. In order to make sure they will last as long as the love of their owner, do make certain that the pieces are all very well and firmly stuffed. Stitch pieces together firmly and take a little time to make them as nearly indestructible as possible. Never use buttons or eyes with pins or anything a small child can detach and swallow. A toy will then be a joy and never a sorrow to anyone.

Since a poncho is still so popular, every smart doll should have one too. This one is very simple to make

Pink elephant

for colour illustration, see page 83

A fat and cuddly elephant for a change.
She might have come straight from
Toyland Zoo

Materials: Ten 25 gramme balls of
Machine Washable Emu Double Knitting
Wool;
scraps of felt for ears, eyes, feet and
flower;
washable stuffing;
a pair of No. 10(3) knitting needles.

Tension: 7 sts. and 8 rows to 1 inch.

Measurements: Height: 9 ins.; Length:
17 ins.

Abbreviations: See Page 12

TO MAKE
1st Side:
Cast on 8 sts. and work 2 rows st.st.
Cast on 5 sts. at beg. of next 4 rows.
7th row: Cast on 34 sts., k. to end.
8th row: Purl. **9th row:** Cast on 3 sts.
at beg. of row, k. to last st., k. twice into
last st. **10th row:** P. twice into first and
last sts. **11th row:** As 9th. **12th row:** P.
to last st., p. twice into last st. Repeat last
4 rows once more.
17th row: K. twice into 1st and last st.
18th row: As 12th. Repeat last 2 rows
twice more. **23rd row:** K. twice into
1st st., k. to end. **24th row:** As 12th.
25th row: As 17th. **26th row:** Purl.
27th row: As 23rd. **28th row:** Purl.
Repeat last 4 rows once more.
33rd row: As 17th. **34th row:** P. twice
into 1st st., p. to end. **35th row:** K. to
last st., k. twice into last st.
36th row: P. Repeat last 4 rows once
more. (109) sts.
41st row: As 35th. **42nd row:** As 34th.
43rd row: As 35th. **44th row:** Purl.
45th row: K.98, turn, leaving 14 sts.
on spare needle. Work 3 rows st.st.
49th row: K.80, cast off 3 sts., k.8 turn.
Leave last 7 sts. on needle. **50th row:**

Working on the 8 sts. p.2 tog. at each end
of row. **51st row:** K.2 tog. at each end of
row. Cast off last 4 sts. Rejoin wool at
inner edge of the 7 sts. Cast off 2, k.5.
Next row: P.3, p.2 tog.
Next row: K.2 tog., k.2. **Next row:** P.1,
p.2 tog. Cast off last 2 sts.
Rejoin wool at inner edge of the 80 sts.
Next row: P.2 tog., p. to end.
Next row: K. Repeat last 2 rows 3 times
more. (76) sts. Work 13 rows st.st. ★
Next row: K.50, k.2 tog., k. to end. Leave
50 sts. on a spare needle.
Next row: P. to last 2 sts., p.2 tog.
Next row: K.2 tog., k. to end. Repeat
last 2 rows once more.
Next row: P. to last 2 sts., p.2 tog.
Work 16 rows st.st. Cast off last 20 sts.
With wrong side facing, rejoin wool to
inner edge of 50 sts. on spare needle. Cast
off 25 sts., p. to end. **Next row:** K. to
last 2 sts., k.2 tog.
Next row: P.2 tog., p. to end. Repeat
last 2 rows once more. K. to last 2 sts. k.2
tog. Work 16 rows st.st. Cast off last 20
sts. ★
Rejoin wool to inner edge of 14 sts. with
right side facing.
1st row: Cast off 5, k. to last st., k. twice
into last st.
2nd row: Cast on 2 sts., p. to last 2 sts.,
p.2 tog. **3rd row:** Cast off 2 sts., k. to last
st., k. twice into last st. **4th row:** As 2nd.
Repeat last 2 rows 3 times more. Now dec.
1 st. at each end of next 4 rows.
Next row: K.2 tog., k.1. Cast off. Make
another side to match reversing shaping.
Underside:
Cast on 36 sts. Work 2 rows st.st. Cast on
10 sts. at beg. of next 4 rows. Work 8 rows
st.st. Cont. as for first side from ★ to ★
Make another piece to match.
Rear section: Cast on 8 sts. Work 16
rows st.st. **17th row:** K. twice into 1st
stitch, k. to end.
18th row: P. to last st., p. twice into last
st. Repeat last 2 rows twice more. (14 sts.)
Cast on 14 sts. at beg. of next row. Do not

Little lamb

for colour illustration, see page 87

knit across row. Break wool. Now cast on 8 sts. on the same needle holding the 28 sts. Work 16 rows st.st. on 8 sts. **17th row:** K. to last st., k. twice into last st. **18th row:** P. twice into 1st stitch, p. to end. Repeat last 2 rows twice more. (14 sts.) All 42 sts. should now be on the same needle. Two legs with 14 cast on sts. in centre. Work 8 rows st.st. * **Next row:** K.2 tog., at each end of row. **Next row:** P. Repeat last 2 rows 3 times more. Take 2 tog. at each end of next 3 rows. **Next row:** P. Repeat last 4 rows 3 times more. Take 2 tog. at each end of next 4 rows. Cast off last 2 sts.

Chest:
Work as for rear section from beg. to *
Take 2 tog. at each end of next 3 rows.
Next row: P. Repeat last 4 rows 3 times more. Take 2 tog. at each end of next row. Work 2 rows st.st. Repeat last 3 rows. Take 2 tog. at each end of next row. Next row: P. Work 20 rows st.st. Cast off last 12 sts.

Trunk Under-section:
Cast on 12 sts. and work 4 rows st.st.
Next row: K.2 tog., at each end. Work 5 rows st.st. Repeat last 6 rows twice more. Inc. 1 st. into first st. of next 4 rows. Work 1 row. Cast off 10 sts.

TO MAKE UP

Press all pieces carefully. Join side sections together starting at trunk and ending approx. 5 ins. beyond cast on edge. Set rear section into back neatly. Set in trunk under-section and sew in chest section. Join 2 under sections, leaving 4 ins. open on straight edge for stuffing. Sew to sides of elephant, matching legs, etc.
Cut two ears in felt and sew to head. Make eyes from felt scraps and add to face. Cut 4 circles of felt and sew to bottom of feet and a small circle to end of trunk. Stuff firmly and close opening. Make a tail in plaited wool and attach to back. Embroider toes on feet. Add a flower to mouth.

A very attractive toy to find a place in any child's heart

Materials: 10 ozs. Emu Machine Washable Double Knitting Wool in white; 2 ozs. in Black; washable stuffing; strip of ribbon or felt for collar; 3 bells; scraps of felt or embroidery wool for features; a pair of No. 10(3) knitting needles.

Tension: 6 sts. and 8 rows to 1 inch over st.st.

Measurements: Height: approx. 13 ins.

Abbreviations: See Page 12

TO MAKE
Side of Body:
Beg. with front leg, cast on 14 sts. in Black wool. Work 8 rows st.st.
9th row: Change to white and knit.
10th row: K.1, k.1 winding wool twice round needle and first finger, then round needle only, draw loops through, slipping original st. off left hand needle. Holding loops at back of work, slip loops back on to left hand needle and knit them together through back of loops. Repeat these loop sts. to last st., k.1. Repeat last 2 rows until 42nd row has been worked. Leave sts. on a spare needle. For Back leg work as for front leg until 30th row has been completed.
31st row: Inc. 1 st. at end of row. Work 3 rows straight.
35th row: K.2 tog. at beg. of row and inc. 1 st. at end. **36 and 38th row:** Loop Row.
37th and 39th rows: As 35th row.
Work 3 rows straight.
43rd row: K.2 tog., k. to end of row, turn and cast on 10 sts., then knit across the 14 sts. on spare needle. Cont. to work 44th and every even row in loop stitch.

45th row: Inc. 1 st. into first st. work to end.

47th row: Inc. into last st.

49th row: As 45th row. (41 sts.)

50th row: Loop st. Repeat 9th and 10th rows 3 times.

57th row: K.2 tog., work to end. Dec. in same way on odd rows 3 times more.

65th row: K.2 tog. at each end. **67th row:** As 57th. Dec. at each end of next odd row.

71st row: Cast off 18 sts. at beg. of row. (14 sts.)

73rd row: As 57th. **75th row:** As 57th. Cast off.

Making another piece to match but reversing shapings and work the back leg first. 43rd row will read: Knit to end of row, turn and cast on 10 sts., knit across back leg sts. to last 2 sts., k.2 tog.

Underbody (first side)

Work as for first body side but in st.st. only. Work to completion of 44th row (38 sts.)

45th row: Cast off 6 sts., work to end.

47th row: Cast off 6 sts. work to end, increase at end of row. **49th row:** As 45th.

51st row: As 45th. **53rd row:** Cast off 7 sts. at beg. of row, work to end.

55th row: Cast off.

Work 2nd side to match reversing shapings, as for second body side but in st.st. to end of 42nd row.

43rd row: Knit to end of row, turn and cast on 10 sts., knit across back leg sts., to last 2 sts., k.2 tog.

44th row: Cast off 6 sts. at beg. of row.

46th row: As 44th.

48th row: Cast off 6 sts., work to last st., inc. into last st.

50th row: As 44th. **52nd row:** Cast off 7 sts. at beg. of row. Cast off.

TO MAKE UP BODY

Join two under body pieces along upper cast off edge. Place the joined pieces between sides of body, matching the legs and seam into place. Seam body sides together above front and back legs along back but leave cast off edge open. Stuff evenly and firmly.

Tail:

With White wool, cast on 8 sts.

1st row: Knit. **2nd row:** Loop st. Cont. in this way and inc. 1 st. at each end of next row, then work straight until 26 rows have been worked. Cast off and make another piece to match, but in st.st. for under side of tail.

Join pieces together, leaving cast off edge open. Turn to right side, join open end and stitch firmly to back.

Side of Head:

With White wool, cast on 18 sts. Work 6 rows st.st.

7th row: Inc. into 1st stitch, knit to end, turn and cast on 3 sts.

8th row: P. to last 8 sts., loop st. 7, k.1.

9th row: Inc. 1 st. at each end of row.

10th row: Inc. into first st., p. to last 8 sts., loop st. 7, k.1.

11th row: As 9th. **12th row:** As 10th.

13th row: K. **14th row:** P. to last 8 sts., loop st. 7, k.1. **15th row:** K.

16th row: P. to last 7 sts., loop st. 6, k.1. **17th row:** K.

18th row: P. to last 6 sts., loop st. 5, k.1. **19th row:** K.

20th row: P. to last 5 sts., loop st. 4, k.1. **21st row:** K. **22nd row:** As 20th.

23rd row: Inc. 1 st. at beg. of row. (29 sts.)

24th row: As 20th. **25th row:** K.2 tog., at end of row. (Tie in a coloured marker to first st.)

26th row: P.2 tog., p. to last 5 sts., loop st. 4, k.1. **27th row:** K.2 tog., at end of row.

28th row: P.2 tog., work to last 5 sts., loop st. 4, k.1. **29th row:** K. **30th row:** P. to last 5 sts., loop st. 4, k.1. **31st row:** K. Repeat last 2 rows three times.

38th row: As 30th row. **39th row:** K.2 tog. at each end of row. **40th row:** As

Harry hedgehog

for colour illustration, see page 83

30th. **41st row:** As 39th. **42nd row:** As 30th. **43rd row:** K.2 tog., across row to last st., k.1. **44th row:** As 30th. Cast off. Make another piece to match, reversing shapings and loops will be at beg. of rows.
Head Gusset.
With White wool, cast on 4 sts. and work 6 rows in st.st. **7th row:** Inc. 1 st. at each end of knit row.
8th row: P. **9th row:** As 7th. **10th row:** P. **11th row:** As 7th. **12th row:** P. **13th row:** As 7th. (12 sts.) **14th row:** K.1, loop st. to last st., k.1. **15th row:** K. Repeat these 2 rows to end of 50th row. **51st row:** K.2 tog., at each end of next and alt. rows until 2 sts. remain. Cast off.

TO MAKE UP HEAD

Place the head gusset between sides of head, placing cast on edge of gusset level with the coloured marker on head sides. Seam gusset into place. Then seam head sides together from side to side, above and below gusset leaving cast on edge of head sides open. Stuff firmly and carefully. Stitch head very firmly to body.
Muzzle:
With Black wool, cast on 12 sts. and work in st.st.
1st row: P. **2nd row:** Inc. 1 st. at each end of next row. Repeat these 2 rows until there are 20 sts. on needle. Cont. in st.st. until 13 rows have been completed from beg.
14th row: K.2 tog., at each end of this and every foll. alt. row until 12 sts. remain. Cast off. Run a thread of wool round edge of muzzle, pull up slightly and stuff slightly. Sew to head at nose, over base of gusset. Embroider features or cut out in scraps of felt and sew to face.
Ears:
With black wool, make 4 pieces as for tail. 2 in st.st. for inner ear and 2 in loop st. Join the pieces together and attach to head. Join three bells to collar and fit round neck.

Harry's happy in the garden and he could be made in an evening, ready to greet a new owner in the morning

Materials One 50 gramme ball of Patons Double Knitting Wool;
a pair of No. 9(4) knitting needles·
scraps of Red and White wool for features;
stuffing.

Measurements: Length: 7 ins.

Abbreviations: See Page 12

BODY AND HEAD

Cast on 25 sts.
1st row: (Right side) Purl.
2nd row: *K.1, M.L., rep. from * to last st. k.1. **3rd row:** Purl. **4th row:** M.L., * K.1, M.L., rep. from * to end. These 4 rows form the pattern. Continue until piece measures $4\frac{1}{2}$ ins. Change to garter stitch and work as follows:
1st row: K.2 tog., k. to last 2 sts., k.2 tog. **2nd row:** Knit. Rep. last 2 rows until 9 sts. remain, ending with 2nd row. Cast off.

UNDER BODY

Cast on 15 sts. and work 6 rows in loop pattern then work 35 rows in garter stitch.
Next row: K.2 tog., k. to last 2 sts., k.2 tog., **Next row:** Knit. Rep. these 2 rows until 7 sts. remain, ending with 2nd row. Cast off.

FEET

Cast on 12 sts. and work 6 rows garter stitch. **Next row:** K.2 tog. to end. Break wool, thread through remaining sts., draw up and secure. Fold piece in half and join seam. Make three more to match.

TO MAKE

Join body and under body together, leaving an opening for stuffing. Stuff firmly and shape head carefully. Sew up opening. Sew feet to under body. Embroider white eyes and red mouth.

Mick monkey

for colour illustration, see page 83

Cute little chap from the jungle to make mostly in garter stitch, with very little shaping

Materials: Three 50 gramme balls of Patons Limelight Double Crepe in Brown and 1 in fawn;
a pair of No. 8(5) knitting needles;
stuffing;
a scrap of white wool for features.

Tension: 11 sts. to 2 ins. over st.st.

Measurements: Height: 21 ins. approx.

Abbreviations: See Page 12

BODY

With Brown cast on 10 sts. and work in garter stitch. Knit 1 row. Now cast on 4 sts. at beg. of next 4 rows. (26 sts.) Cont. on these sts. until piece measures 6 ins. from beg. Cast off 8 sts. at beg. of next 2 rows. Work 8 rows on remaining sts. Cast off. Make another piece to match.

LEGS

With Brown, cast on 24 sts. and work 100 rows in garter stitch, placing a marker at each end of 33rd and 67th rows. Cast off. Make another leg.

ARMS

With Brown, cast on 20 sts. and work 80 rows in garter stitch. Place a marker at each end of 31st and 51st rows. Cast off. Make another Arm.

HANDS

With Brown cast on 4 sts. and work in st.st., beg. with a k. row. Inc. 1 st. at each end of 2nd and every alt. row until there are 10 sts. Work 4 rows straight. Now dec. 1 st. at each end of every 3rd row until 6 sts. remain. Cast off. Make another piece in Brown and 2 pieces to match in fawn.

FEET

With Brown cast on 8 sts. and work in st.st., beg. with a k. row. Inc. 1 st. at each end of 2nd and every alt. row until there are 12 sts. Work 6 rows straight. Now dec. 1 st. at each end of every 3rd row until 8 sts. remain. Cast off. Make another piece in Brown and 2 pieces in fawn.

EARS

With Fawn, cast on 11 sts. and work in st.st., beg. with a k. row. Work 3 rows. Now dec. 1 st. at each end of next row. Rep. these 4 rows once more, Cast off. Make 3 more pieces.

BACK OF HEAD

With Brown, cast on 10 sts. and work 8 rows in garter stitch.
Next row: Inc. into 1st st., k. to end.
Next row: K. Rep. these 2 rows 3 times more. (14 sts.)
Next row: Inc. into 1st stitch, k. to last 2 sts., k.2 tog., **Next row:** K. Rep. these 2 rows 4 times in all. **Next row:** Inc. in 1st st. k. to end.
Next row: K. Rep. these 2 rows until there are 20 sts. Work 10 rows straight. Cast off 4 sts. at beg. (shaped edge) of next and foll. 3 alt. rows. Work 1 row straight. Cast off. Make another piece.

FRONT OF HEAD

With Fawn, cast on 24 sts. and work 8 rows in st.st., beg. with a k. row.
Next row: K.4, sl.1, k.1, p.s.s.o., k. to last 6 sts., k.2 tog., k. to end. **Next row:** Purl. Rep. these 2 rows 5 times in all. (14 sts.) Cast off. Make another piece to match.

Doll's poncho

TAIL

With Brown, cast on 12 sts. and work 3 ins. in garter stitch. Place a marker at each end of next row and work a further 3 ins. Place another marker and work another 3 ins, Cast off.

TO MAKE UP

With Brown, gather slightly between markers on legs, arms and tail. Fold each piece in half lengthwise and join seam firmly, leaving ends open. Turn to right side and stuff firmly. Close ends. Take care to retain curves while stuffing these parts. For hands and feet, take a brown and fawn piece and place together. Join firmly, leaving cast-on edge open. Turn to right side and stuff firmly. Close opening. For Ears, finish as for hands and feet, using 2 pieces of fawn together. With curves of legs and arms facing outwards, join hands and feet with fawn sides facing outwards. Embroider fingers and toes in Brown.

Join two body pieces together firmly, and stuff but leave neck open. Join arms, legs and tail to body. Join shaped edges of two pieces for back of head and join two pieces for face in same way, leaving cast-on edge open. Place a little stuffing in back and front of head and sew into position, matching centre seam. Continue to stuff head through neck, placing extra stuffing round mouth. Join ears to head, gathering cast-on edges slightly. When head and body are both firmly stuffed, join head to body. Embroider eyes, nose and mouth in Brown and White.

A fashionable cover-up for that doll who never has a thing to wear. Made in the time it takes you to knit up two ounces of double knitting wool

Materials: 2 ozs. Sirdar Double Knitting Wool in Main colour; 1 oz. contrast; a pair of No. 8(5) knitting needles; a medium sized crochet hook.

Tension: $5\frac{1}{2}$ sts. and $7\frac{1}{2}$ rows to 1 inch.

Measurements: To fit a 16 inch doll.

Abbreviations: See Page 12

TO MAKE

With main colour, cast on 60 sts. Knit 1 row and purl 1 row. Cont. in st.st. and dec. 1 st. at each end of every k. row until 22 sts. remain. Leave these sts. on a spare needle and make another piece to match. Now, with right side facing and contrast colour, knit across both sets of sts. Work 12 rows k.1, p.1 rib. Cast off. Press and join seams. With the crochet hook, and contrast wool, work 2 rows double crochet round lower edge. Embroider flowers in lazy daisy stitch round bottom. Trim with fringe through the last row of double crochet, using main and contrast wool together.

Charlie crocodile

for colour illustration, see page 83

He's too friendly to have crawled out of a swamp and will make a new friend for all the other jungle toys

Materials: 2 ozs. Twilley's Bubbly in green and yellow and 1 oz. orange; a pair of No. 10(3) knitting needles; scraps of felt for features; stuffing.

Tension: 5 sts., and 8 rows to 1 inch.

Measurements: Length: 14 ins.

Abbreviations: See Page 12

TO MAKE
Back:
Using yarn double and with green, cast on 8 sts. Working in st.st., inc. 1 st., at each end of every alt. row until there are 26 sts. on needle. Cont. without further shaping until piece measures 9 ins. from beg. Now dec. 1 st. at each end of next and every foll. 4th row until 2 sts. remain. Fasten off.
Front: As for Back using yellow double, but inc. only to 20 sts. then work without further shaping to 8½ ins. Dec. 1 st. at each end of next and every foll. 6th row until 2 sts. remain. Fasten off.
Mouth: Using orange double, cast on 6 sts. Work in st.st. and inc. 1 st. at each end of every alt. row until there are 22 sts. on needle. Cont. without further shaping until piece measures 4 ins. from beg., ending with a p. row. **Next row:** K.2, (k.2 tog., k.3) 4 times. Cont. without further shaping until piece measures 6½ ins. Now dec. 1 st. at each end of next and every alt. row until 6 sts. remain. Cast off.

Legs: Using 2 strands of green, cast on 6 sts. and work in st.st., Inc. 1 st. at each end of 2nd and 3rd rows. Cont. without further shaping until piece measures 2 ins. ending with a p. row. **Next row:** Cast on 6 sts., knit to end. Work 9 rows st.st., beg. with a p. row. Now dec. 1 st. at each end of next and beg. of foll. row. Cast off. Make another piece to match in green and two in yellow. Then work 2 in green and 2 in yellow but ending with a k. row before casting on 6 sts. Cont. to work to match in reverse.

TO MAKE UP
Join leg pieces matching pairs of green and yellow, leaving top of leg open. Stuff. Sew mouth to cast on ends of back and front. The wider end of mouth to back for 4 ins, then the narrower end to front for 4 ins. Join remaining edges of back and front, leaving 5 inches open at each side. Stuff body. Insert legs and join remaining side seams. Cut 4 lengths of white felt to make teeth and add to mouth. Cut two circles of black and white for eyes. Sew eyes to head.

Hula doll

for colour illustration, see page 83

With Jungle toys about there must be a lady in a grass skirt somewhere. She could have flowers in her hair and bead bangles and necklace, but not for a child still at the stage of swallowing small objects

Materials: One 50 gramme ball of Patons Double Knitting Wool in Brown; 1 ball of Limelight Double Crepe in Nectarine; 1 ball in Capstan in Gold and Emerald; 1 ball Doublet in Black; a pair of No. 9(4) knitting needles; a No. 4.50 mm crochet hook; kapok for stuffing.

Tension: 5½ sts. and 7½ rows to 1 inch in Double knitting.

Measurements: Height: 15 ins.

Abbreviations: See Page 12

BODY AND LEGS

Cast on 7 sts. in Brown and work in st.st. for 40 rows. Break yarn. Make another piece to match. Knit across first 7 sts., cast on 3 sts., and work across second set of 7 sts. Work 35 rows on these 17 sts. Cast off. Make another piece in the same way. Join the two pieces together, leaving neck open. Stuff firmly and sew up neck opening.

ARMS

Cast on 12 sts. in brown and work 32 rows in st.st. Cast off. Make another piece to match. Join the long edges of each piece, stuff firmly and sew to body.

HANDS

Cast on 14 sts. in Brown and work 14 rows in st.st. Cast off. Make another piece to match. Join seams and stuff firmly and sew to arms.

HEAD

Make two pieces, one in Brown and one in Black for back of head.
Cast on 8 sts. and work in st.st. Inc. 1 st. at each end of 3rd and foll. alt. rows until there are 28 sts. Work 15 rows straight.
Next row: K.2 tog. along row. Work 1 row
Next row: K.2 tog. along row. Cast off.
Join the two pieces together leaving cast on edges open for neck. Stuff firmly and sew to body.

FEET

Cast on 26 sts. in Brown and work 8 rows in st.st. Cast off. Join bottom and side seams. Place legs inside this casing at the back. Stuff and sew up the front seams. Sew the top of the sides and back to legs.

GRASS SKIRT

With Green wool, crochet a 6 inch chain. Work in slip stitch along the chain. Fasten around waist. Make 22 chains in Green and 22 in gold in double crochet each 5 ins. long. Take one strand in each colour in turn and attach to waistband, working all round waist.

NECK GARLAND

Cast on 46 sts. in Nectarine and make a loop row thus:
Insert needle into first st. Wind yarn over point of needle and first two fingers of left hand 3 times, then over needle again. Draw the loop through the st. and place loops back on left hand needle. Knit the 3 loops together through back of loops. Cont. in this way to end of row. Cast off.
For ankles and wrists, make a garland for each by casting on 12 sts. in Nectarine and working a row of loop st. as for neck garland.

Fasten garlands round neck, ankles and wrists.

For the Flower make by casting on 30 sts. in Nectarine and working 1 loop row but winding the yarn round 3 fingers instead of two. Cast off. Gather into a flower shape and sew to side front of head.

HAIR

Cut Black yarn into 40 lengths each 18 ins. long. Divide into groups of 10. Fold in half and join 3 groups to the back of head at seam and one group over the top at centre front on the seam. Embroider features in Black and Nectarine.

Japanese doll

She is wearing her kimono in the colour picture opposite but she took it off for us to take the picture on page 97.

Materials: Two 2 oz. balls of Twilley's Stalite in Blue and 1 ball each in Gold, Black and green;
a pair of No. 12(1) knitting needles;
kapok for stuffing;
felt or wool for features, and flowers.

Tension: $7\frac{1}{2}$ sts. and 10 rows to 1 inch.

Measurements: Height: 16 ins.

Abbreviations: See Page 12

DOLL

Skirt: Make two pieces. With Blue, cast on 37 sts. and knit 4 rows. **Next row:** Knit.
Next row: K.3, p.31, k.3. Rep. last 2 rows until work measures $8\frac{1}{2}$ ins. from beg., ending with wrong side row.
Next row: K.1, (k.2 tog., k.1) 12 times.
Next row: Purl. Leave these two pieces on spare needle. (Each 25 sts.)
Main Part: * With Black cast on 13 sts. for base of left shoe. Work 8 rows st.st., increasing 1 st. at each end of first 2 rows and decreasing 1 st. at each end of last 2 rows. Cast off.
With Black, cast on 34 sts. for left shoe. Work 10 rows st.st. Beginning with a k. row, change to Gold and work 2 rows st.st. **Next row:** K.14, k.2 tog., k.2, k.2 tog., k.14. **Next row:** P.
Next row: K.13, k.2 tog., k.2, k.2 tog., k.13. **Next row:** Purl.
Next row: K.12, k.2 tog., k.2, k.2 tog., k.12. **Next row:** Purl.
Next row: K.2 tog., k.9, k.2 tog., k.2, k.2 tog., k.9, k.2 tog. (24 sts.) Cont. without further shaping until work measures 8 ins. from cast-on edge, ending

with a p. row. * Leave these sts. on a spare needle and rep. from * to * for right shoe, foot and leg. Change to Blue.
Next row: K.12, and leave these 12 sts. on a spare needle, k.12, cast on 1 then knit first 12 sts. from left leg, turn and leave rem. 12 sts. on a spare needle. Work on 25 sts. for Back of body. ** Work $1\frac{3}{4}$ ins. st.st., ending with a p. row. **Next row:** Place 25 sts. of one piece of skirt in front of sts. on needle, then knit both lots of sts. together, taking 1 st. from each needle together across the row. Work $1\frac{1}{4}$ ins. in st.st. beg. with a p. row. Cont. in st.st. and cast off 2 sts. at beg. of next 2 rows then dec. 1 st. at each end of every 3rd row until 9 sts. rem., ending with a k. row. Knit 3 rows.
Change to gold for head. **Next row:** k. twice into every st. to end of row. Cont. in st.st. and inc. 1 st. at each end of every alt. row until there are 28 sts. on needle. Cont. without further shaping until head measures $2\frac{1}{2}$ ins. from beg. Now dec. 1 st. at each end of next and every alt. row until 16 sts. rem. Cast off. Return to rem. sts. and with right side facing, and Blue, knit 12 sts. from left leg, cast on 1, k.12 sts. from right leg and complete front as for back from **.

Arms:

With Gold, cast on 7 sts. and work 2 rows st.st., beg. with a k. row.
Next row: K.1, (inc. into next st.) 6 times. Work 3 rows st.st., beg. with a p. row. **Next row:** K.1, (inc. into next st., k.1) 6 times. (19 sts.) Cont. in st.st., beg. with a p. row until arm measures $4\frac{3}{4}$ ins. from cast on edge, ending with a k. row.
Next row: P.3, (inc. into next st., p.2) 5 times, p.1. Change to Blue and knit 4 rows. Now work in st.st., beg. with a k. row. Cast off 2 sts., at beg. of next 2 rows and then dec. 1 st. at each end of every alt. row until 4 sts. rem. Knit 1 row. Next row: (k.2 tog.) twice. Knit 1 row and cast off.

TO MAKE UP

Join leg seams. Sew bases into shoes. Join shaped top edges of arms to back and front, then join side and arm seams. Join head seams, leaving an opening at top to allow stuffing. Stuff firmly and join opening. Join the side seams of skirt, leaving 4 ins. open at lower edge for slits. With a quarter of remaining black yarn, wind an even hank 6 ins. in circumference using a small book or box which measures 6 ins. round. Slip hank off and wind a length of Black round the centre of hank to make the top knot. Wind the remaining Black into a hank 16 ins. in circumference. Slip off and place the yarn around the head. Arrange evenly over centre of head and sew neatly working from front to back. Twist the remainder into a bun and secure to back of head. Add top knot to top of head. Make flowers from scraps of felt and sew to hair. Cut features from scraps of felt and add to face, or embroider with scraps of yarn.

KIMONO

Main Part:

With Blue, cast on 133 sts. ** Knit 3 rows. Join in Green.

Next row: K.3 Blue, knit with Green to last 3 sts., join second ball of Blue, k.3 Blue. **Next row:** K.3 Blue, p. with Green to last 3 sts., k.3 Blue. Work 2 more rows in st.st. in Green, keeping 3 sts. at each end in Blue g.st. ** Now work in pattern.

1st row: (wrong side) With Blue, K.6, * insert needle through next st., 4 rows below (in first Green row) and knit through the st., drawing up a long loop, knit the next st. on needle still, then take the loop over this st., k.3, rep. from * to last 3 sts., k.3.

2nd row: With Blue, K.3, p. to last 3 sts., k.3. **3rd row:** With Blue, Knit.

4th row: As 2nd. **5th row:** K.3 Blue, k.1 Green, * with Green, insert needle through next st., 4 rows below (first Blue row) and knit through it, drawing up a long loop, knit next st. Still on needle then take loop over this st., k.3 Green, rep. from * to last 5 sts., with Green, insert needle through next st. 4 rows below as before, k.1 Green, 3 Blue. **6th row:** K.3 Blue, purl with Green to last 3 sts., k.3 Blue.

7th row: K.3 Blue, k. with Green to last 3 sts., k.3 Blue. **8th row:** As 6th. These 8 rows form the pattern.

Cont. in pattern until work measures 4¾ ins. from beg. ending with a 2nd or 6th patt. row.

Next row: With Blue, K.6, (k.1, k.2 tog.) to last 7 sts., k.7. Now rep. from ** to ** again, then work first 5 rows of pattern.

Divide for Armhole: K.3 Blue, with Green, p.19, cast off 7, p.35, cast off 7, p. 19, k.3 Blue. Work on last set of sts. for left front.

Keeping 3 sts. at front edge in Blue g.st., Work 1 row. **Next row:** Patt. to last 5 sts., p.2 tog., k.3 Blue. Now dec. in this way on every alt. row inside front border until 10 sts. remain. Cont. without further shaping in patt. with front border as before until work measures 9½ ins. from cast on edge, ending at armhole.

Cast off 7 sts. at beg. of next row. Work 1½ ins. g.st. in Blue on rem. 3 sts. Rejoin yarn to centre 35 sts. for Back. Cont. in pattern excluding Blue g.st. borders until work measures 9½ ins. from cast-on edge. Cast off 7 sts. at beg. of next 2 rows. Cast off rem. sts.

Rejoin yarn to rem. 22 sts. for right front. Keeping 3 sts. at front edge in Blue g.st., as before, work 1 row pattern. **Next row:** K.3 Blue, p.2 tog., patt. to end. Dec. in this way inside front border on every alt. row and complete to match left front.

Sleeves:

With Blue, cast on 51 sts. and knit 3 rows. Join in Green and work 4 rows st.st., beg. with a k. row. Now work in pattern.

1st row: (wrong side) With Blue, k.3,

* insert needle into next st. 4 rows below as on main part, k.3, rep. from * to end. Work 3 rows st.st. in Blue, beg. with a p. row.

5th row: With Green, K.1, * insert needle into next st. 4 rows below as before, k.3, rep. from * to end, ending k.1. Work 3 rows st.st. in Green beg., with a p. row. These 8 rows form the pattern. Cont. until work measures 3½ ins. from cast-on edge.

To Shape Top: Cont. in patt. and cast off 4 sts. at beg. of next 10 rows. Cast off rem. sts.

Waistband and Bow:
With Blue, cast on 32 sts. for waistband. Work 8 ins. in st.st. Cast off. cast on 18 sts. for bow. **1st row:** K.

2nd row: K.4, p.10, k.4. Rep. last 2 rows for 10 ins. Cast off.

TO MAKE UP

Join sleeve and shoulder seams. Set in sleeves. Fold waistband in half and join sides. Turn to right side and join ends. Fold bow with ends at centre back and stitch lightly. Gather centre of bow and sew to one end of waistband. Sew three press fasteners to ends of waistband and fasten at centre back of kimono. Press seams and edges.

Home comforts

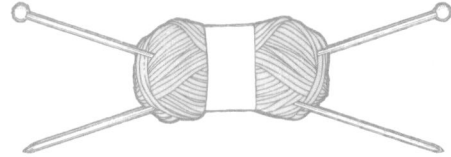

A collection of exciting items to make, most of them just a
straight piece of knitting. It is what you do with the piece that
matters, and the colours you choose to enhance your home.
The Aran cushions and lampshades are very effective and an
unusual use for these traditional stitches. Tea, coffee and egg
cosies are always useful and a hand knitted bedspread will last
a lifetime. The cheerful cushions will do good service in garden
or playroom, or for sheer comfort by the fire. The simple bath
mat, so quick to make, would also be as good as a bedside rug

Oblong cushion and tall lampshade

Really smart to bring a touch of real craftsmanship to the things you can make for your home. Cream Aran wool was used and is most effective. In the lampshade, when the light is on, the result is even better

Materials: Six 2 oz. balls of Lister Aran Knitting Wool for cushion and 4 balls for lampshade;
a pair each of Nos. 7(6) and 9(4) knitting needles;
a cable needle;
a lampshade frame 19 ins. in circumferance and $13\frac{1}{2}$ ins. deep;
cushion pad to fit;
a No. 4.00 m.m. crochet hook.

Tension: 5 sts. and 7 rows to 1 inch.

Measurements: Cushion: 12 by 18 ins. Lampshade as size of frame given.

Abbreviations: See Page 12

CUSHION
With No. 9(4) needles, cast on 90 sts. and knit 1 row.
Next row: K.3, *(p.f.b., p.2) 3 times, (k.1, p.1, 3-in-1, p.1, k.1, p.1) twice, k.1, p.1, 3-in-1, k.1, rep. from * twice more, (p.f.b., p.2) 3 times, k.3. (120 sts.) Change to No. 7(6) needles and patt.
1st row: K.2, p.1, * k.12, p.22, rep. from * twice more, k.12, p.1, k.2.
2nd row: K.3, * p.12, k.1, (3-in-1, p.3 tog.) 5 times, k.1, rep. from * twice more, p.12, k.3.
3rd row: As 1st. **4th row:** K.3, * p.12, k.1, (p.3 tog., 3-in-1) 5 times, k.1, rep. from * twice more, p.12, k.3.
5th row: K.2, p.1, * C6B., C6F., p.22, rep. from * twice more, C6B., C6F., p.1, k.2. **6th row:** As 2nd.
7th row: As 1st. **8th row:** As 4th

9th row: As 1st. **10th row:** As 2nd.
11th row: As 5th. **12th row:** As 4th.
13th to 20th row: Rep. from 1st to 4th rows inclusive twice. **21st row:** K.2, p.1, * C6F., C6B., p.22, rep. from * twice more, C6F., C6B., p.1, k.2.
22nd row: As 2nd. **23rd row:** As 1st.
24th row: As 4th. **25th row:** As 1st.
26th row: As 2nd. **27th row:** As 21st.
28th row: As 4th. These 28 rows form one pattern. Cont. until 6th patt. is completed, then work first 3 rows again. Change to No. 9(4) needles.
Next row: K.3, *(p.2 tog., p.2) 3 times, (k.1, p.3 tog., k.1, p.1, k.1, p.1) twice, k.1, p.3 tog., k.2., rep. from * twice more, (p.2 tog., p.2) 3 times, k.3. Cast off tightly.

TO MAKE UP
Fold work in half and join three sides. Insert cushion pad. Work 1 row double crochet through two thicknesses along one end, turn with 1 chain. Now make fringe thus: With a piece of cardboard $1\frac{3}{4}$ ins. wide, hold card above work, insert hook into first double crochet, wind wool round card and then over hook and draw loop through, complete the double crochet. Cont. to end of row, slipping some loops off card as work progresses. Work other side to match.

LAMPSHADE
With No. 9(4) needles, cast on 95 sts. and work 2 rows g.st.
Next row: K.1, *(k.1, p.1, 3-in-1, p.1, k.1, p.1) twice, k.2, (p.f.b., p.2) 3 times, rep. from * to last 2 sts., k.2. (123 sts.) Change to No. 7(6) needles and patt.
1st row: K.1, p.1, * k.12, p.18, rep. from * to last st., k.1.
2nd row: K.1, * k.1, (3-in-1, p.3 tog.) 4 times, k.1, p.12, rep. from * to last 2 sts., k.2. **3rd row:** As 1st.
4th row: K.1, * k.1, (p.3 tog., 3-in-1) 4

times, k.1, p.12, rep. from * to last 2 sts., k.2. **5th row:** K.1, p.1, * C6B., C6F., p.18, rep. from * to last st., k.1. Cont. in this way, working in these positions as on the cushion until 3 patterns have been completed. Repeat first 3 rows again. Change to No. 9(4) needles.

Next row: K.1, * (k.1, p.3 tog., k.1, p.1, k.1, p.1) twice, k.2, (p.2 tog., p.2) 3 times, rep. from * to last 2 sts., k.2. Work 2 rows in g.st. Cast off tightly.

TO MAKE UP

Join side edges. Fit over lampshade frame. Work 1 row double crochet all round top and bottom edges, taking in the edge of frame.

Bedspread and cushion in squares

Make use of all those odd ounces or plan to a careful colour scheme and buy the wool bit by bit. You will have a bedspread to last a lifetime and a cheerful cushion to stand up to hard use

Materials: The bedspread and cushion are made in Double knitting wool on No. 10(3) needles.

Tension: 6 sts. and 8 rows to 1 inch over stocking stitch.

Measurements: The squares are 5 inches square and approx. 3 squares can be made from 1 oz. of wool. The bedspread measures 90 inches by 60 ins. excluding the fringe. The fringe used approx. 7 ozs. of wool in odd balls.

Note: To obtain these measurements any stitch may be used and it is essential to obtain the correct tension for the stitches given in this pattern. It is wise to work a tension square when undertaking any knitting. Collect 5 inch tension squares every time you use the same thickness of wool, until enough have been collected. In this way, both variety in stitch and colour will be achieved. In the centre of the bedspread there is a panel of 24 two and three colour squares. These use up the oddments of wool one collects. They are all in star stitch, which was also used for a cushion, and a bag.

STITCHES USED
Star Stitch

With No. 10(3) needles and first colour, cast on 33 sts.

1st row: (wrong side) Purl.
2nd row: K.2, * w.r.n., k.3, pass first of the 3 knit sts. over 2nd and 3rd sts., rep. from * to last st., k.1. **3rd row:** With second colour, P.
4th row: K.1, * k.3, pass the first of 3 knit sts. over 2nd and 3rd sts., w.r.n., rep. from * to last 2 sts., k.2. Rep. rows 1 to 4 for 5 ins.
Any number of colours may be used, changing colour on odd rows.

Moss Knit Rib

Cast on 32 sts.
1st row: * K.3, p.1, rep. from * to end.
2nd row: * K.2, p.1, k.1, rep. from * to end. Rep. these 2 rows for 5 ins.

Crossed Rib

Cast on 33 sts.
1st row: *(P.1, k.1) twice, rep. from * to last st., p.1.
2nd row: *(K.1, p.1) twice, rep. from * to last st., k.1. **3rd row:** As 1st.
4th row: As 2nd.
5th row: * P.1, cross 2R by knitting the 3rd st., p. 2nd st., and k. first st., then let all 3 drop from left hand needle. Rep. from * to last st., p.1.
6th row: As 2nd. Rep. these 6 rows for 5 ins.

Laburnham Stitch

Cast on 32 sts.

1st row: P.2, * w.fwd., sl.1 purlwise, w.b., k.2 tog., p.s.s.o., w.r.n., p.2, rep. from * to end.

2nd row: * K.2, p. into front and back of next st., p.1, rep. from * to last 2 sts., k.2.

3rd row: P.2, * k.3, p.2, rep. from * to end.

4th row: * K.2, p.3, rep. from * to last 2 sts., k.2.

Rep. these 4 rows for 5 ins.

Campanular Stitch

Cast on 32 sts.,

1st row: K.1, * k.3, p.2, rep. from * to last st., k.1.

2nd row: K.1, * k.2, p.3, rep. from * to last st., k.1.

3rd row: As 1st. **4th row:** As 2nd

5th row: K.1, * w.r.n., sl.1, k.2 tog., p.s.s.o., w.r.n., p.2, rep. from * to last st., k.1. **6th row:** As 2nd. Rep. these 6 rows for 5 ins.

Alternating Link Stitch

1st row: Cast on 32 sts. * P.5, k.1, p.1, rep. from * to last 4 sts., p.4.

2nd and 4th rows: K.4, * k.1, p.1, k.5, rep. from * to end.

3rd row: * P.5, k.1, p.1, rep. from * to last 4 sts., p.4.

5th and 7th rows: * P.4, k.1, p.1, k.1, rep. from * to last 4 sts., p.4.

6th row: * K.4, p.1, k.1, p.1, rep. from * to last 4 sts., k.4.

8th row: As 2nd.

Rep. these 8 rows for 5 ins.

TO MAKE UP BEDSPREAD

Pin out squares and press. Join in strips of 12 squares. Join strips together matching corners carefully. Press seams. Add fringing.

CUSHION

Join squares together in strips of 3. Join three strips together for each side of cushion. Press pieces. Cut lining to match and make up cushion pad. Join three sides of knitted pieces and insert cushion pad. Close fourth side. Make a thick twisted cord using two colours and sew round edge of cushion.

This will make a cushion 15 inches square.

Hexagon patchwork bedspread and cushion

The beauty of patchwork is that you can make the pieces when and where you like. They are small to carry and can be put together when you have time. See page 16 for how to do Swiss darning.

Materials: Both bedspread and cushion are made in Twilley's Afghan wool in five colours.
No. 10(3) knitting needles.
Lining and stuffing for cushion.

Tension: 6 sts. and 8 rows to 1 inch.

Measuresments: Each six sided patch is 6 inches wide and 6 ins. long. The finished bedspread measures 75 ins. long and 62 ins. wide.

Abbreviations: See Page 12

Note: This design requires 48 yellow patches, and 48 in rust, 30 brown, 24 white, 16 green in garter stitch. 12 white patches in stocking stitch and 2 in brown for the embroidered patches and 2 half patches in each colour in garter stitch. Assorted colours could be used and the patches arranged in any design to please the owner. 1 oz. makes 4 patches.

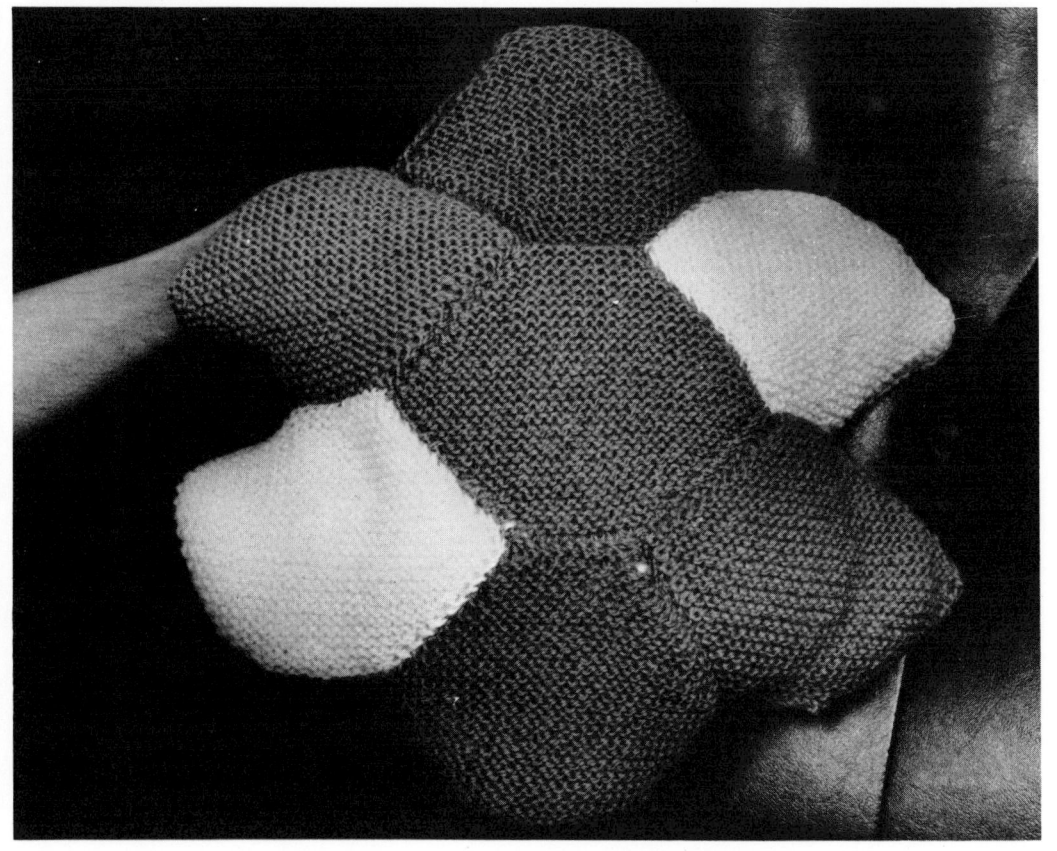

TO MAKE
Garter Stitch Patch
Cast on 12 sts. and k. 1 row.
2nd row: K.1, p.u.k., k.10, p.u.k., k.1.
3rd and all alt. rows: K.
4th row: K.1, p.u.k., k.12, p.u.k., k.1.
6th row: K.1, p.u.k., k.14, p.u.k., k.1.
Cont. to inc. in this way until there are 36 sts. on needle. Knit 1 row then dec. 1 st. at each end of every alt. row until 12 sts. remain. Cast off.
Stocking stitch Patch
Cast on 12 sts. and k. 1 row.
2nd row: As for garter st. patch.
3rd and alt. rows: K.2, p. to last 2 sts., k.2.
Continue to inc. to 36 sts. and dec. back to 12 sts. as for garter stitch patch. Cast off.

Half Patches
Cast on 36 sts. and work decrease half of garter stitch patch.

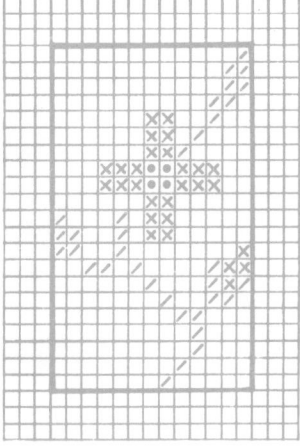

✕ Rust or Yellow
╱ Green
• Brown or Rust

TO MAKE UP
Press pieces. Whatever design is followed, the end result is neatest if the patches are joined first in strips and then the strips joined together.

Make 4 strips of 12 patches in yellow; 4 strips of 12 patches in rust; 2 strips of 12 patches in brown and 2 strips the same in white, garter stitch.

Embroider white stocking stitch patches and two brown with flower motif, follow Chart using oddments of wool. For centre panel make one strip of 12 patches thus: * 2 green, 1 white embroidered, 1 green, 1 white embroidered, rep. from * 2 green. Make another strip to match. The centre strip is made thus: 2 brown garter st., 1 white embroidered, 1 brown garter st., 1 white embroidered, 1 brown embroidered, 1 brown garter st., 1 embroidered brown, 1 white embroidered, 1 brown garter st., 1 white embroidered, 1 brown garter st.

Join strips in this order, starting with yellow, rust, yellow, brown, white, rust, green and white embroidered, the centre strip of brown and white. Then continue to match other side. Add small tassels to points along the sides and add half patches where required at top and bottom. Press.

Take 14 patches for cushion. Make one strip of three patches, joining cast on edges to cast off edges. Join two patches by cast on edges and fit in to one side of strip of three. Make other side to match. Make another piece in the same way.

Cut lining material from paper pattern made from completed knitted piece. Make two pieces and join carefully, leaving small part open for stuffing. Stuff, taking care to keep shape of points. Close opening. Make up knitted pieces, leaving opening to insert pad. Insert pad and close opening.

Striped cushion

Straight knitting again and three toning colours, but again, the choice is yours.

Materials: 5 ozs. Lee Target Motoravia Double Knitting Wool in Brown and 2 ozs. each in cream and gold; a pair of No. 7(6) knitting needles; lining and stuffing.

Tension: 5¼ sts. and 7 rows to 1 inch.

Measurements: Approx. 15 ins. wide by 22 ins. long.

Abbreviations: See Page 12

TO MAKE

With Brown, cast on 72 sts. and work in st.st. throughout. Work in stripes. * 14 rows Brown, 1 inch each in cream, gold and cream. * Rep. from * to * then repeat 14 rows Brown. Cast off. Make another piece to match. Cut lining to match. Join 3 sides and stuff. Close 4th side. Make up knitted pieces to match, taking care to match stripes. Insert the cushion and close 4th side. Fringe short ends with remaining wool, using 4 strands each 4 ins. long for each tassel.

Square cushion and large lampshade

Just a different shape for both and different stitches too. If you make them as gifts, you will find it hard to part with them

Materials: Eight 2 oz. balls of Lister Aran knitting wool for cushion cover and 6 balls for the lampshade;
a pair each of Nos. 7(6) and 9(4) knitting needles;
a cable needle;
a No. 4.00 m.m crochet hook;
a lampshade frame 9 ins. deep by 44 ins. circumference;
$2\frac{1}{2}$ yds. wool braid to match;
$\frac{1}{2}$ yd. press stud tape.

Tension: 5 sts. and 7 rows to 1 inch over st.st. on No. 7(6) needles.

Measurements: Cushion cover: 17 ins. square.;
Lampshade as size of frame.

Abbreviations: See Page 12

CUSHION COVER

With No. 9(4) needles, cast on 101 sts. and knit 1 row.
Next row: K.3, * p.1, (p.f.b., p.1) twice, k.f.b., (p.2, p.f.b.) 7 times, p.4, k.f.b., (p.1, p.f.b.) twice, p.1, * k.8, p.2, k.1, p.2, k.8, rep. from * to *, k.3. (127 sts.)
Change to No. 7(6) needles and patt.
1st row: K.2, p.1, * k.7, p.2, k.32, p.2, k.7, * p.8, cross 5, p.8, rep. from * to *, p.1, k.2.
2nd row: K.3, * p.7, k.2, p.32, k.2, p.7, *, k.8, p.2, k.1, p.2, k.8, rep. from * to *, k.3. **3rd row:** K.2, p.1, *CP7, p.2, (C4B, C4F) 4 times, p.2, CP7, * p.7, C3R, p.1, C3L, p.7, rep. from * to *, p.1, k.2.
4th row: K.3, * p.7, k.2, p.32, k.2, p.7, * k.7, p.2, k.3, p.2, k.7, rep. from * to *, k.3. **5th row:** K.2, p.1, * k.7, p.2, k.32, p.2, k.7, * p.6, C3R, p.3, C3L, p.6, rep. from * to * p.1, k.2.
6th row: K.3, * p.7, k.2, p.32, k.2, p.7, * k.6, p.2, k.5, p.2, k.6, rep. from * to * k.3. **7th row:** K.2, p.1, * CP7, p.2, (C4F, C4B) 4 times, p.2, CP7 *, p.5, C3R, p.2, MB, p.2, C3L, p.5, rep. from * to *, p.1, k.2.
8th row: K.3, * p.7, k.2, p.32, k.2, p.7, * k.5, p.2, k.7, p.2, k.5., rep. from * to *, k.3. These 8 rows complete the patt. for double honeycomb and claw patt. panels. Cont. to keep these correct and at the same time, cont. with diamond panel in the centre.
9th row: K.2, p.1, patt. 50, p.4, C3R, p.7, C3L, p.4, patt. 50, p.1, k.2.
10th row: K.3, patt. 50, k.4, p.2, k.9, p.2, k.4, patt. 50, k.3.
11th row: K.2, p.1, patt. 50, p.3, C3R, p.2, MB, p.3, MB, p.2, C3L, p.3, patt. 50, p.1, k.2.
12th row: K.3, patt. 50, k.3, p.2, k.11, p.2, k.3, patt. 50, k.3.
13th row: K.2, p.1, patt. 50, p.2, C3R, p.11, C3L, p.2, patt. 50, p.1, k.2.
14th row: K.3, patt. 50, k.2, p.2, k.13, p.2, k.2, patt. 50, k.3. **15th row:** K.2, p.1,

patt. 50, p.2, k.2, p.2, MB, p.7, MB, p.2, k.2, p.2, patt. 50, p.1, k.2.

16th row: As 14th. **17th row:** K.2, p.1, patt. 50, p.2, C3L, p.11, C3R, p.2, patt. 50, p.1, k.2. **18th row:** As 12th.

19th row: K.2, p.1, patt. 50, p.3, C3L, p.2, MB, p.3, MB, p.2, C3R, p.3, patt. 50, p.1, k.2. **20th row:** As 10th.

21st row: K.2, p.1, patt. 50, p.4, C3L, p.7, C3R, p.4, patt. 50, p.1, k.2.

22nd row: As 8th. **23rd row:** K.2, p.1, patt. 50, p.5, C3L, p.2, MB, p.2, C3R, p.5, patt. 50, p.1, k.2.

24th row: As 6th. **25th row:** K.2, p.1, patt. 50, p.6, C3L, p.3, C3R, p.6, patt. 50, p.1, k.2. **26th row:** As 4th

27th row: K.2, p.1, patt. 50, p.7, C3L, p.1, C3R, p.7, patt. 50, p.1, k.2.

28th row: As 2nd. These 28 rows form patt. for diamond panel. Cont. until 8 complete patts. have been worked in this panel. Work 1st and 2nd rows again. Change to No. 9(4) needles.

Next row: K.2, p.1, * k.1, (k.2 tog., k.1) twice, p.2 tog., (k.2, k.2 tog.) 7 times, k.4, p.2 tog., (k.1, k.2 tog.) twice, k.1, * p.8, k.2, p.1, k.2, p.8, rep. from * to * p.1, k.2. Cast off.

TO MAKE UP

Fold work in half with wrong side out and join cast on and cast off edge, Press seam. Turn right side out. Along one side edge, work a row of double crochet through both thicknesses. Work a row of double crochet round the 2 sides of other edge. Sew press stud tape to opening. Insert cushion and fasten.

LAMPSHADE

With No. 9(4) needles, cast on 131 sts. and work 3 rows g.st.

Next row: K.1, * k.8, p.2, k.1, p.2, k.8, (p.1, p.f.b.) twice, p.1, k.f.b., (p.2, p.f.b.,) 9 times, p.4, k.f.b., (p.1, p.f.b.) twice, p.1, rep. from * once, k.2. (161 sts.) Change to No. 7(6) needles and patt.

1st row: K.1, p.1, * k.7, p.2, k.40, p.2, k.7, p.8, cross 5, p.8, rep. from * once, k.1.

2nd row: K.1, * k.8, p.2, k.1, p.2, k.8, p.7, k.2, p.40, k.2, p.7, rep. from * once, k.2. **3rd row:** K.1, p.1, * CP7, p.2, (C4B, C4F) 5 times, p.2, CP7, p.7, C3R, p.1, C3L, p.7, rep. from * once, k.1. Cont. in patt. as now set working 40 sts. in double honeycomb and other panels as on cushion, until 58 rows have been worked in patt. Change to No. 9(4) needles.

Next row: K.1, p.1, * k.1, (k.2 tog., k.1) twice, p.2 tog., (k.2, k.2 tog.) 9 times, k.4, p.2 tog., (k.1, k.2 tog.) twice, k.1, p.8, k.2, p.1, k.2, p.8, rep. from * once, k.1. Change to g.st., and work 3 rows. Cast off. Make another piece to match.

TO MAKE UP

Place pieces together and join into a circle. Press seams. Fit over frame, placing seams over 2 of side supports. Catch the seams to supports. Fold g.st. edges over top and bottom of frame and catch down firmly, so that cover is stretched over frame slightly. Sew braid to top and bottom.

Fringed cushion in star stitch

Just two squares in a pretty stitch. Three colours were used for this one, but you could use as many colours as you like, changing every two rows

Materials 2 ozs. each of Lee Target Motoravia Double Knitting Wool in White, mauve and blue;
a pair of No. 9(4) knitting needles, lining material;
stuffing.

Tension: 6 sts. and 6 rows to 1 inch over pattern.

Measurements: 12 inch square.

Abbreviations: See Page 12

With Mauve, cast on 72 sts. and work in Star stitch for 12½ ins.

1st row: (wrong side) Purl.
2nd row: K.2, * w.r.n., k.3, pass first of 3 knit sts. over 2nd and 3rd sts., rep. from * to last st., k.1. Change to White.
3rd row: Purl.
4th row: K.1, * k.3, pass first of 3 knit sts. over 2nd and 3rd sts., w.r.n., rep. from * to last 2 sts., k.2. Change to Blue and work 1st and 2nd rows again.
Continue to work in patt. in this way, working 2 rows in each colour in turn. When work measures 12½ ins. Cast off. Make another piece to match.

TO MAKE UP
Cut two pieces of lining to match and join three seams. Stuff and close fourth side. Join knitted pieces in same way. Insert cushion into knitted cover and join fourth seam of cover. Fringe all round with remaining wool.

Tea, coffee and egg cosies

Matching set of cosies in traditional Aran stitches. Use them to keep things warm for breakfast or make them for a friend

Materials: 5 ozs. Lister Lavenda Double Knitting Wool for Tea or Coffee Cosy and 2 ozs. for a pair of Egg Cosies; a pair each of Nos. 9(4), and 11(2) knitting needles; a cable needle; a No. 3.50 m.m. crochet hook; 1 yd. single sided quilted fabric to line Tea and Coffee cosies; sewing silk.

Tension: 6½ sts. and 9 rows to 1 inch.

Measurements: Tea cosy: Width: 13 ins.; depth: 9 ins.; Coffee cosy: Width: 10 ins.; depth: 13 ins.; egg cosies: Depth: 5 ins.

Abbreviations: See Page 12

TEA COSY

Front: With No. 11(2) needles, cast on 87 sts. and work in rib.
1st row: K.2, * p.1, k.1, rep. from * to last st., k.1.
2nd row: K.1, * p.1, k.1, rep. from * to end. Rep. these 2 rows twice more, then 1st row again.
Next row: K.f.b., k.14, * p.1, (p.f.b., p.1) twice, k.f.b., (p.2, p.f.b.) 5 times, p.4, k.f.b., rep. from * once, p.1, (p.f.b., p.1) twice, k.14, k.f.b. Change to No. 9(4) needles. Now begin pattern.
1st row: (K.1 t.b.l., p.1) 8 times, * k.7, p.2, (TR., TL.) 4 times, p.2, rep. from * once, k.7, (p.1, k.1 t.b.l.,) 8 times.
2nd row: K.16, * p.7, k.2, p.24, k.2, rep. from * once, p.7, k.16.
3rd row: (K.1 t.b.l., p.1) 8 times, * TR., k.1, TL., p.2, (TL., TR.) 4 times, p.2., rep. from * once, TR., k.1, TL., (p.1, k.1 t.b.l.) 8 times.
4th row: As 2nd. These 4 rows form one pattern. Cont. until work measures 5 ins. from beg. Now dec. 1 st. at each end of next row, then work 3 rows straight. Rep. last 4 rows 3 times more. Dec. 1 st. at each end of next row then work 1 row straight. Rep. last 2 rows 3 times more. Cast off 2 sts. at beg. of next 4 rows. Now cast off 3 sts. at beg. of next 4 rows and then cast off 6 sts. at beg. of next 4 rows. Now cast off tightly over the honeycomb panels.
Back: Work as for Front.

TO MAKE UP

Fold quilting in half with wadding inside and cut a section for Back in double thickness and one to match for Front. Join double sections together round side and top edges through four thicknesses. Join the knitted sections and insert lining. Turn ½ inch in all round lower edges and slip stitch to wrong side of first pattern row, leaving ribbing free.

COFFEE COSY

Front: With No. 11(2) needles, cast on 65 sts. and work 7 rows in rib as for Tea Cosy. **Next row:** K.f.b., k.16, rep. from * in same row as for tea cosy once, p.1, (p.f.b., p.1) twice, k.16, k.f.b. Change to No. 9(4) needles and pattern.

1st row: (K.1 t.b.l., p.1) 9 times, k.7, p.2, (TR., TL.) 4 times, p.2, k.7, (p.1, k.1, t.b.l.) 9 times

2nd row: K.18, p.7, k.2, p.24, k.2, p.7, k.18.

3rd row: (K.1 t.b.l., p.1) 9 times, TR., k.1, TL., p.2, (TL.,TR.) 4 times, p.2, TR., k.1, TL., (p.1, k.1 t.b.l.) 9 times.

4th row: As 2nd. These 4 rows form the pattern. Cont. in pattern until work measures 10 ins. from beg. Dec. 1 st. at each end of next row, then work 3 rows straight. Rep. last 4 rows once. Dec. 1 st. at each end of next row, then work 1 row straight. Rep. last 2 rows twice more. Cast off 2 sts. at beg. of next 6 rows, then cast off 4 sts. at beg. of next 2 rows, then 6 sts. at beg. of next 2 rows. Cast off rem. sts. tightly over honeycomb panels.

Back: Work as for Front. Make up as for Tea Cosy.

EGG COSY

With No. 11(2) needles, cast on 55 sts. and work in rib as for tea cosy for 5 rows. **Next row:** K.f.b., k.10, p.1, (p.f.b., p.1) twice, k.23, p.1, (p.f.b., p.1) twice, k.10, k.f.b., Change to No. 9(4) needles and pattern.

1st row: (K.1 t.b.l., p.1) 6 times, k.7, (p.1, k.1 t.b.l.) 11 times, p.1, k.7, (p.1, k.1 t.b.l.) 6 times.

2nd row: K.12, p.7, k.23, p.7, k.12. Cont. to keep panels of 12 sts. at each end of row and 23 sts. at centre in Rice stitch as on these 2 rows.

3rd row: RS.12, TR., k.1, TL., RS.23, TR., k.1, TL., RS.12.

4th row: As 2nd. Rep. these 4 rows 4 times more, then 1st, 2nd and 3rd rows again.

Next row: K.10, k.2 tog., p.7, k.2 tog. t.b.l., k.19, k.2 tog., p.7, k.2 tog. t.b.l., k.10.

Next row: RS.9, p.2 tog. t.b.l., k.7, p.2 tog., RS.17, p.2 tog. t.b.l., k.7, p.2 tog., RS.9.

Next row: K.8, k.2 tog., p.7, k.2 tog. t.b.l., k.15, k.2 tog., p.7, k.2 tog. t.b.l., k.8. Cont. to dec. in same positions on next 5 rows, keeping claw pattern correct.

Next row: K.1, (w.fwd., k.2 tog.) 14 times. Change to No. 11(2) needles and beg. with 1st row, work 4 rows in rib. Cast off in rib.

Join sides and press seam. With double wool, make a length of crochet chain about 14 ins. long. Thread through holes at top and draw up and tie in a bow.

Bath mat

Big needles and thick yarn make a quick job of this mat. It's easy too, so any beginner can manage it

Materials: 5 hanks of Twilley's 747 Orlon Sayelle; a pair of $\frac{1}{2}$ inch Whizz pins; a crochet hook No. 4.50.

Tension: 3 sts. to 2 ins.

Measurements: 31 by 20 ins., excluding fringe.

Abbreviations: See Page 12

TO MAKE
Cast on 30 sts. loosely. K.2 rows.
3rd row: Sl.1, * K.1, k.1b. rep. from * to last st., k.1.
4th row: Sl.1, * k. the slip thread of previous row with the st. above it, k.1, rep. from * to last st., k.1.
5th row: Sl.1, * k.1 b., k.1, rep. from * to last st., k.1.
6th row: Sl.1, * K.1, k. the slip thread of the previous row with the st. above it, rep. from * to last st., k.1. Cont. in patt. from 3rd row until work measures 30 ins. from beg. Then slipping the first st. on each row. K. 2 rows. Cast off loosely.
Fringe the narrow ends.

Sewing

The pleasures of sewing

This chapter is planned to introduce you to sewing. It is not a *complete* course in the craft – that would take several volumes – but all the basic knowhow and techniques you need to be able to make simple garments are explained here. You are shown how to pin out a pattern properly and the right way to cut out is described (usually a most frightening step for a beginner, but once you know how, you will never be afraid).

The following sections take the beginner dressmaker through all the stages of putting a garment together and all are explained in the simplest possible way. There is even a section on those decorative touches which can add distinction to hand-made things.

If you have never sewn before, it is suggested that you read these sections very carefully indeed, perhaps reading them twice over before starting your first garment. Once you have got the principles well in your mind, you will be so much more confident and your first project is more likely to be a success.

When you have read the sections on techniques carefully, you will be ready to try making some of the clothes in the Pattern Book. The patterns in this section

are given as graph patterns but do not be afraid of them – they are very easy to work with once you know how.

Graph patterns are simply full-sized garment patterns scaled down to the size of a page. They are designed in exactly the same way as the paper patterns one buys – the only difference is that the graph pattern is a kind of small master plan from which you draw up your own pattern. The advantage of graph patterns is that one can easily make alterations for size or even for style while one is drawing the pattern out and, if the alterations are actually marked onto the graph itself, the alterations are there to remind you when the pattern is wanted again at a later date. Instructions are given for drawing up graph patterns. Start with one of the simpler outlines, such as the man's apron or the pinafore dress and in almost no time at all, you'll be quite at ease with graph patterns.

All the designs in the pattern book have been especially chosen for beginners, but more experienced dressmakers will enjoy them too. The clothes are simple and all use the basic sewing techniques; their charm and attractiveness lies in the finish and the choice of fabrics.

Choosing styles, measuring and altering

Choosing the right style

Although the simple styles given as graph patterns later in this chapter are intended to start you off on dressmaking, sooner or later you are going to use a commercial paper pattern. Choosing the right style for your figure type is one of the most

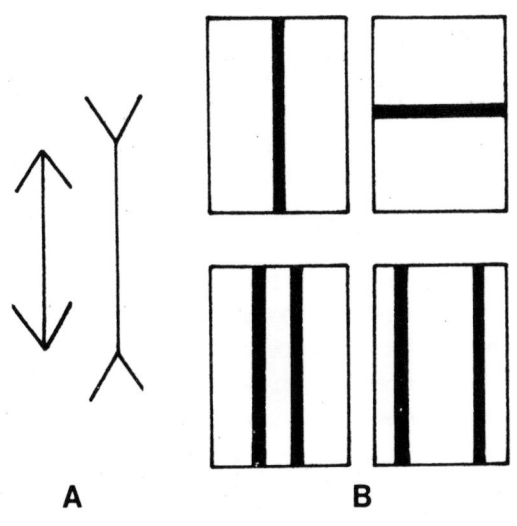

A **B**

A change in line direction can alter the length of a line or size of an area

important parts of learning to make your own clothes. Too often, a dressmaker chooses a style because she likes it in the catalogue, without really considering whether it will suit her or not and then she is disappointed in the final result. The design of a pattern and the fabric itself can flatter you into looking exactly how you want to look. You can look taller, shorter or slimmer. The right style can add roundness exactly where your figure needs it or can distract the eye away from those areas where you wish you were slimmer. The trick is to fool the eye and the rules are simple. Study the geometric diagrams given here and note how the direction of the arrow heads can make the vertical lines seem longer or shorter (A). Look at the boxed vertical and horizontal lines (B). The dimensions of the boxes are exactly the same in each case but see how the vertical line makes the box appear taller.

How to look taller

The rules of fooling the eye are simple: to create the illusion of looking taller, the eye has to be carried up and down the figure. In garment design, this can be achieved by long pleats, long seams and long sleeves. If the eye is stopped at any point, such as by a wide contrasting colour belt, then the effect becomes shorter. Sheath-shaped dresses, straight front fastenings, Princess lines and long, tight sleeves will all help to give a tall look. Necklines also need to be vertical in effect – V-necklines are good and so are open collars. Round or square necklines stop the eye and so shorten the look of the neck.

The width of stripes and the spaces between can make a figure look taller or shorter

How to look shorter

To create a wider or more rounded effect on a figure, the design of the garment should encourage the eye to move from side to side or diagonally rather than up and down. In this case, stopping the eye helps the effect and is achieved by designs which have a break at the hipline, either by a seam or by a change in colour, by big patch pockets, and by full sleeves. Jackets and tunics which cut across the hipline help to make the figure look shorter and large collars can shorten the length between shoulder and waist.

Figure faults and solving them

Almost everyone has a figure fault which they would like to correct. By choosing the right style of pattern and, to a certain extent, the right fabric, most figure faults can be camouflaged by dressmaking. A collar line, for instance, which draws attention to a pretty face or a shapely bust is obviously going to mean less attention for over-sized hips! The chart on the following page, worked out by a well-known paper pattern company, gives some useful solutions for common figure faults. Bear them in mind when you are choosing your first commercial paper pattern.

Matching colours to styles

Colours of fabrics can appear to correct figure faults too. Black, as everyone knows, makes one's measurements appear smaller but it also tends to outline the shape. If the outline isn't quite perfect, choose dark grey or brown instead – they are just as slimming but the effect tends to blend you into the background more. This general rule applies to any figure area which is out of proportion to the rest of the body – wearing light or bright contrasts of colour tends to emphasise a fault. Those people with short, plump figures should go for one-colour outfits and choose soft fabrics rather than crisp ones. If prints are worn, clearly-defined patterns should be avoided.
Tall, heavily built women also look

For accuracy, get someone to help with measuring

FIGURE FLAW	SUITABLE SOLUTIONS
Hip Heavy	Create interest at neck and shoulder line. Broaden shoulder Line.
Small Bust	Softly draped bodices, collars, decorative bodice details.
Large Bust	Soft draping, simple necklines, surplice closings, long or $\frac{3}{4}$ sleeves.
Thick Rib Cage	Boxy jackets, bloused bodices, soft draping and overblouses.
Short-Waisted	Low waisted designs, hip length jackets and overblouses. Smooth, uninterrupted lines.
Long-Waisted	Wide sashes, set-in midriffs, contrasting belts, tunics, peplums, long jackets.
Round shoulders	Place shoulder seam back of its normal position. Use set-in sleeves. Blouse with soft fullness at back. Collar to fill hollow at back. Collared boleros and jackets.
Narrow Shoulders	Set-in sleeves narrowly padded.
Short Neck	Collarless style, V- or U-shaped necklines, standaway collars.
Long Neck	Turtle and mandarin necklines, large collars, high chokers.
Prominent Abdomen	Pleats or shirring at sides of a skirt, creating a straight front panel. Boxy hip length jackets, vertical lines.
Prominent Derrière	Hip length boxy jackets, box pleated flared skirts, shirred waistlines.

better in soft fabrics and should avoid large patterns and shiny surfaced materials.

The tall, thin type of figure can wear bright colours as these tend to add fullness to a shape and colour contrasts should be worn at the waistline or hips – such as belts – to make the figure seem more shapely.

Measuring up

After deciding on the style of garment you're going to make, the next point to aim for is perfect fit. All paper patterns are made to standard measurements and, because there are variations in figure types, to different sizes within the figure types. Even

YOUR PERSONAL MEASUREMENTS CHART

			inches
1	**BUST**	Measure over fullest part of bust and around back	
2	**WAIST**	On natural waistline	
3	**HIPS**	Measure over highest part of buttocks and the thickest part of the thighs	
4	**SHOULDER**	Measure from the base of neck	
5	**ACROSS BACK**	From armhole seam to armhole seam	
6	**BACK LENGTH**	From nape to waist	
7	**CENTRE FRONT**	From base of front neck to waist	
8	**FRONT WIDTH**	From armhole seam to seam, taken between shoulder and bustline	
9	**BUST POINT**	From centre shoulder to highest point of bust	
10	**ARMHOLE**	Over shoulder, around underarm and back to shoulder, taken with arm against body	
11	**SIDE SEAM**	From under armhole to waist	
12	**UNDERARM SLEEVE**	From lowest point of armhole to wrist with arm extended	
13	**OUTSIDE SLEEVE**	From halfway between shoulder and underarm, over bent elbow to wrist	
14	**CENTRE BACK, FULL LENGTH**	From nape, to waist to hem	
15	**SKIRT LENGTH**	From waist line, over hip bone to hem	
16	**DEPTH OF CRUTCH**	(for trousers) From centre front waistline, through crutch to centre back waist	
17	**INSIDE LEG**	With legs apart, measure from inside crutch to ankle bone	

though you might have exactly the same bust, waist and hips measurement as your friend, this doesn't mean that your figure shape is the same; the waist and bust positions may be entirely different. The leading commercial paper pattern companies produce charts in their pattern books to help the home dressmaker to choose the correct paper pattern for her size and shape. By checking your own measurements against those on the charts, you will be able to select the pattern with the best possible fit for you.

The graph patterns in this chapter are given in size 12 – that is bust 34 inches, waist 25–26 inches and hips 36 inches. You will be shown how to adapt the graphs to fit you own measurements. First of all however, you need to know exactly what your measurements are. Enlist the help of a friend or your husband to help you take them accurately.

Measuring children

One rarely needs to make children's clothes as closely fitting as adults' so fewer measurements are needed. The length of back, from neck to waist, back waist to hem, shoulder to wrist, chest, waist, inside leg and round the neck will suffice. One further measurement is essential if the child tends to have a pot belly – and most do when small – and that is the measurement from the base of the front neck to the hem, taken over the stomach.

Take measurements over a close-fitting sweater or slip. Pin a length of tape around the waist first – this helps to achieve exact bodice length measurements.

Adapting paper patterns to fit

Some people's measurements vary slightly from the average and it may be necessary to alter paper patterns to achieve an even better fit. Alterations are made on the paper pattern itself and commercial paper patterns are usually marked with lines where alterations to depth and width can be made.

To alter a pattern piece, cut through the paper with scissors and spread the pieces the amount to be altered. Tape a strip of tissue paper between the spread pieces and redraw any lines or markings to keep the original shape of the pattern.

To shorten pattern pieces, crease the paper across the guide lines given, pleating up the amount to be taken out. Pin and then redraw the lines to retain the original shape of the pattern.

The Pattern Book

The graph patterns in the Pattern Book are given only in size 12, to make it easier for beginners to draft patterns. However, it is a simple matter to alter patterns to sizes 10, 14 and in some cases to size 16 by adding to and subtracting from the overall width of the pattern.

Altering skirts

Draw the pattern pieces out on squared paper as instructed and then

Children's dresses (patterns, pages 208 and 212)

126

redraw the side seams to the new measurements. To decrease a hipline one size (2 inches), divide the amount by four and take an equal amount off each side seam allowance ($\frac{1}{2}$ inch), front and back pieces. Adjust the

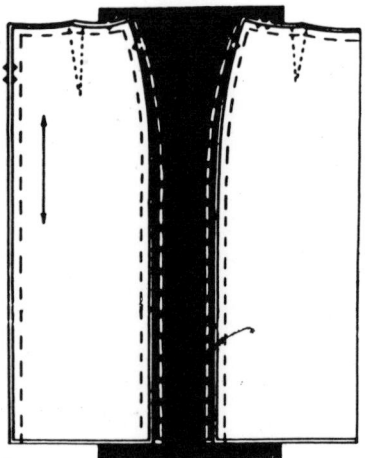

Method for increasing the hipline of a skirt pattern

waist measurement to size and taper the line off to the hem.

To increase the hip measurements by one size (2 inches), divide the total amount to be added by four and add equally to the seam allowances, front and back pieces.

Altering bodices

It is trickier to alter the size of bodice pieces by this method because alterations to the side seams affect the size of the armholes and this in

turn means altering the crown of the sleeve – a difficult exercise for a beginner.

A simpler method for achieving a straightforward increase or decrease in width is to cut the pattern from just below the shoulder line to the waist on both sides of the bodice and then across the bodice. Cut and spread the pieces for the increase in size required. Pleat and pin for a decrease in size.

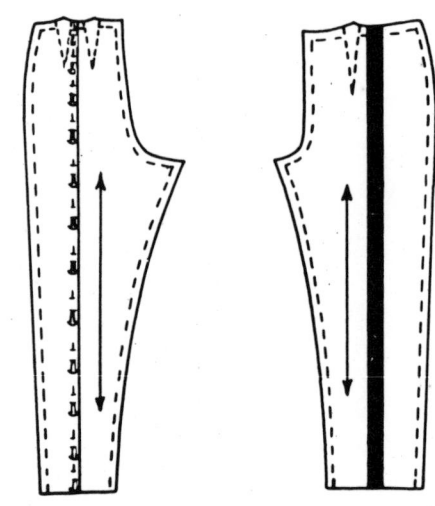

Trouser patterns are altered by slashing the length of the pattern piece

Many of the patterns in the Pattern Book can be adapted in this way and where this is possible, the patterns are marked with a dotted line to show the best place to cut and spread or pleat.

Fabrics and linings

All about fabrics

The next important subject in dressmaking is the fabric. There are some important things to know about the structure of fabric and some words and phrases which you need to be familiar with because they keep occurring in dressmaking instructions.

Grain and bias

All woven fabrics, whether made of natural fibres such as cotton, wool or linen or man-made fibre, are composed of two sets of threads that run at right angles to each other. The lengthwise threads (the warp), are called the *lengthwise grain* and the selvedge is the lengthwise finished edge on each side of the fabric.
The crosswise threads are called *the weft* and are referred to as the *crosswise grain*.
Bias refers to the diagonal of the fabric and *true bias* is the term used for the edge formed when the fabric is folded diagonally so that the crosswise threads run in the same direction as the lengthwise threads. Pattern pieces are usually marked with a heavy line with an arrowhead at each end to indicate that the pattern is to be placed to the lengthwise grain of the fabric. Some pieces – facings, collars and cuffs for instance – might be indicated to be cut on the bias to take advantage of the stretch in the fabric.

Napped or pile fabrics

Sometimes you will see that commercial pattern fabric requirements give a different quantity for fabrics 'with nap' and 'without nap'.
'With nap', in dressmaking, means a fabric with a pile (or nap), such as velvet, or with shading or with a one way design.
'Without nap' of course, means a fabric without a pile or nap and with a design which can be used any way round.

Choosing fabrics

Commercial paper patterns usually give the home dressmaker a good selection of fabrics to choose from when making up their designs. It is wiser to stick to their choice of fabrics unless you are very experienced because the weight and weave of the material are important if perfect fit and hang are to be achieved.
If the design is unsuitable for a

oneway or definite pattern, such as stripes, the fabric suggestions will tell you so.

A beginner might be tempted to use a very cheap fabric for her first attempt at dressmaking. It is understandable that she does not want to risk waste but it is unwise to do this. Cheap fabrics hardly ever make up into good-looking garments, but if you buy the best fabric you can afford, your time and effort in dressmaking are unlikely to be wasted. Good fabrics are often much easier to work with.

Fibres and finishes

Over the past twenty years, great advances have been made by fibre manufacturers, spinners, weavers and knitters in producing easy-care fabrics of every kind and in achieving special finishes.

It is important to be able to recognise a man-made fibre and to know its qualities. It is perhaps even more important to be able to recognise a special finish on a fabric and to know whether it is easy to handle in dressmaking and whether it should be washed or dry-cleaned.

Ask the shop assistant for all the information she can give you about a fabric before you buy it; will it wash, does it need ironing, will it dry-clean? There is not much point in making up an every-day dress in a white linen-type rayon if it is going to spend most of the time at the dry-cleaners!

Always test a fabric for crease-resisting qualities before deciding upon it. Crush a corner in your hand – if the creases stay – do not buy it!

Problem fabrics

Although most fabrics are very easy to handle and present no problems to the home dressmaker, there are a few fabrics which require a little expertise in both cutting out and stitching. Beginners are advised to choose firm cotton and woollen fabrics to start with and then they'll be ready to handle other fabrics when they have become more experienced. Knitted fabrics or jersey fabrics for instance are sometimes supplied in tubular form and can be tricky to handle. They are inclined to stretch out of shape as soon as the pieces are cut out and require immediate stay-stitching all round each garment piece.

Fabric quantities

Commercial paper patterns give the quantity of fabric needed in a variety of widths. This is because some weaves and knits are made narrower or wider than is usual. Do not be tempted to economize on the quantity of fabric recommended. The fabric layouts are worked out very carefully for the most economical use of the material and if you should find yourself with a good-sized piece of fabric left over, you can always make a matching cap or beret with it.

Unwrap and shake out your fabric as soon as you get it home or the folds may set into creases which are difficult to remove.

If there are creases in the fabric, press them out before pinning out the paper pattern, taking care to press under a dry cloth.

Linings, underlinings, interlinings and interfacings

All of these terms refer to dressmaking techniques for shaping garments and it is as well to know exactly what they all mean before you begin dressmaking. Each one uses different types of material; some will prevent loosely woven fabrics from sagging, others will give greater crease-resistance and extra firmness to pockets and necklines, while others will enable a detail, like a dramatic collar, to be become firm and stand away from the garment.

Linings

The back of the paper pattern envelope will tell you whether your garment requires lining. Linings are made up separately from the garment and inside out, being attached to the garment from a main seam, such as a shoulder seam. Linings shape a garment, improve its wearability and

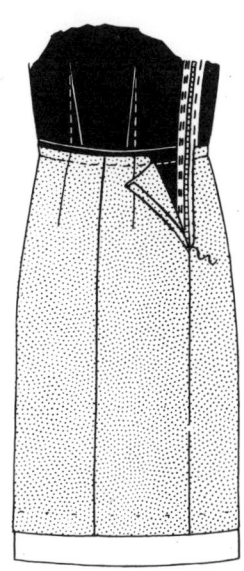

Linings are constructed separately

help to make the inside of a dress or suit look more attractive and well finished.

Underlinings

An underlining has a similar use to a lining but is never used where the fabric is to be draped. It provides backing for a section or sections of a garment where extra body is required.

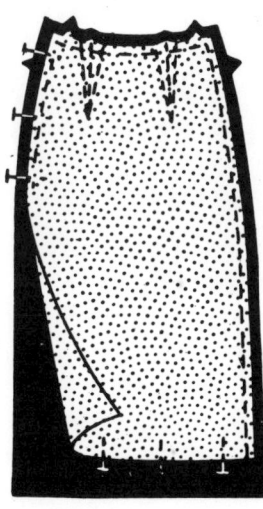

Underlinings are made up with the fabric

The underlining is cut out as soon as the garment piece has been cut out and the two pieces are made up together as one. All lining fabrics should be chosen to match the top fabric in both colour and quality. The lining, after all, takes a lot of the wear!

Interlining

This means a fluffy fabric lining, used in tailoring where both shaping and extra warmth are required. Interlining is used between the lining and the fabric, is sometimes made up separately and is catch-stitched to the garment before the lining is stitched in.

Interfacing

Interfacing is an extra layer of fabric between the facing and the garment itself and its purpose is to give

Interfacing is placed between facing and outer fabric

firmness to one part of the garment and to give a clean edge. It is used to reinforce such areas as a front fastening where there are buttons and buttonholes or between layers of top fabric for collars and cuffs. Interfacing fabrics must be carefully chosen because it is important that they should strengthen without changing the character of the top fabric.

As a general rule, choose a fabric such as fine lawn or cotton for interfacing light-weight wools and for heavier knits, such as those made of synthetic fibres, choose a non-woven interfacing in a weight to match the top fabric. Cotton organdie is ideal for interfacing fine fabrics or, if the fabric isn't patterned, an extra layer of the actual top fabric works very well.

The non-woven interfacings such as Vilene are economical to use because they haven't a grain and they are washable, but they have one disadvantage in that they have no stretch and so will not make softly moulded collars and cuffs. One type, made from Terylene ('bias facing') has a little more stretch to it and can be used fairly successfully for collars and cuffs.

Tools and equipment

Dressmaking, like every other craft, is so much easier if you have the right tools for the job. A sewing machine is the main piece of equipment needed and a tremendous advantage to the home dressmaker, helping her to achieve a professional finish. However, lovely clothes *can* be made without a sewing machine, so do not be discouraged if you do not have one. Machines with a swing needle are very efficient, enabling jersey and knitted fabrics to be sewn with ease, but straight stitch machines can cope with most fabrics if the tension, stitch length and thread are carefully chosen. Good machine sewing is the perfect union of thread and fabric, based on the correct thread, the proper needle size, the right tension and the appropriate number of stitches to the inch. Study the manufacturer's instruction book carefully – it pays to understand your sewing machine.

Stocking a work basket

Workbaskets are hardly ever large enough to take all the odds and ends a dressmaker needs but if cotton reels and lengths of elastic, tape and ribbons can be kept separately, it does help to keep things tidy. Store these items in glass jars where you can see what you want at a glance or ask a handyman to make you a little cabinet of drawers. Buttons, hooks and eyes and press studs can be kept in the drawers too.

Keep an eye on haberdashery and notion counters for dressmakers' aids. Lots of clever items can be found to include in your workbasket. Apart from the contents of your workbasket, you will need certain tools. Those listed here are not essential for beginners but they do make the job easier and more fun and are worth considering.

For measuring and pattern making

Ruler. You will need a long flexible ruler, for pattern making, preferably 36 inches long but a 12-inch one will do. A flexible *plastic rule* which bends easily is useful for drawing curves, but not essential.

Tape measure. Choose one made of glass fibre and with metal ends because this type does not stretch. If possible, have one that is marked with both inches and centimeters.

Squared paper. Squared paper can be obtained from stationery shops and from the dressmaking department of some large stores. It comes in sheets measuring 30 inches by 20 inches and is marked into 1 inch, $\frac{1}{2}$ inch and $\frac{1}{4}$ inch squares. It is used for drafting graph patterns and two or three sheets are required for a dress or suit. Sheets are joined together with Sellotape. Brown paper can be used for drafting patterns if squared paper is not easily available but the inch squares have to be drawn out on it very accurately.

Tracing paper. After the graph pattern has been drawn up onto the squared paper, thus making a master pattern, the paper pattern itself is traced off, using tracing paper. This gives you a more flexible pattern and one which is easier to pin – and you can keep the master pattern intact for using again.

For cutting

A pair of scissors should be kept especially for cutting paper. Tie a piece of coloured thread to the handles to keep them separate.

Dressmaking shears. These have long cutting blades and bent handles. They are more accurate in use than ordinary scissors as they lift the fabric less.

Pinking shears. These have notched blades and are used to trim seams on garments made of firmly woven fabrics to prevent fraying.

A small pair of scissors with sharp points should also be included in basic equipment. These are useful for jobs like cutting buttonholes and snipping into seams.

For marking

Tailor's chalk. This comes in white and in colours, in flat cakes or in pencil form. It is used for making pattern markings on smooth fabrics. It is particularly useful for marking alterations on the wrong side of the garment during fitting.

Dressmaker's carbon paper. This is available in sheets and in white, orange or black. To use it, a sheet is placed face downwards on the fabric under the paper pattern and another sheet face upwards under the bottom layer of fabric. The pattern markings are then traced through the paper either by using a *tracing wheel* or with a blunt pencil and ruler.

It is important to work on a flat, hard surface when using dressmaker's carbon paper or there may be distortion in reproduction.

For sewing

Needles. There are several different kinds of needles but for hand sewing a 'sharps' No. 7 is the best. 'Betweens', which are shorter, are used for fine sewing and size No. 8 is ideal; 'straws' are good for tacking jobs.

Sewing machine needles should be selected for thread and fabric following the guide given in the manufacturer's instruction book.

Threads. Pure silk is the best thread for sewing natural fabric but it is expensive and becoming difficult to obtain. Mercerized cotton, available in a wide range of colours, can be used instead.

Modern sewing machines stitch better with a fine gauge thread and Coats' Drima, available in slim spools and in a wide range of colours is ideal for synthetic fabrics and natural fibre fabrics alike. Drima is, however, very strong and should not be used for basting.

Basting thread is available on large-sized reels and machine embroidery thread, No. 30, is good for machine-made buttonholes and for zig-zag seam neatening.

Silk buttonhole twist is used for handworked buttonholes.

Button thread is used for sewing buttons on to heavier garments.

Pins. Choose dressmaker's pins and have a lot of them. Glass-headed dressmaker's pins are very sharp and slightly longer and look very pretty in use. They are easier to pick up too! **A magnet** is a great help for picking up loose pins and needles and for a quick tidy-up after a dressmaking session.

A quick **unpicking tool** is an invaluable aid for ripping seams and for lifting out tacking threads.

Dressmaker's dummy

A dressmaker's dummy or dress stand is by no means essential to dressmaking but it can be useful for fitting if you have nobody to help at this stage. It can also be a great help when putting in linings or placing pockets. Choose one which stands very firmly on its base; some types look very smart and efficient but simply have not the weight to take a garment without falling over. Try to select one with a fabric surface into which you can stick pins.

Press as you go

The golden rule of dressmaking, as any professional will tell you, is to press every seam as it is completed. Get into the habit of pressing at every single stage and you stand a good chance of having a garment which looks really professional.

Always press on the wrong side of the fabric and use a slightly dampened cloth. Always leave the fabric on the ironing board for a minute or two to allow the steam to cool out of it before going on.

The technique of pressing. Pressing is a quite different technique from ironing. Ironing is a smoothing movement, pressing is lifting the iron and putting it down again firmly, using the other hand to control the fabric.

Equipment for pressing

Ironing board. An ordinary ironing board will do and if possible, have a sleeve board as well that will stand on a table, for pressing small areas. The table will support the weight of the garment.

Seam roll. Make one from a 12-inch length of wood, such as a broom handle, and pad it with flannelette sheeting. Use this under seams as a pressing aid.

Tailor's ham. This is useful for pressing darts and is made with two oval pieces of cotton sheeting, about 15 inches by 10. The oval should have a narrow end, rather like the shape of an egg. Stitch the two pieces together and stuff with sawdust if possible or with scraps of fabric; the ham must be really firmly packed. The surface should be completely smooth and it may be necessary to make one or two small darts in the fabric to achieve this.

Pressing mitt. This can be purchased from haberdashery shops; it is quite useful for pressing rounded areas of garments but is not essential equipment.

Pressing cloth. Butter muslin makes the best pressing cloth. Lay it on the fabric before applying the iron, so that you press through it.

Point presser. This is a useful piece of equipment for pushing out collar points or the corners of pocket flaps. Wind a strip of soft fabric round the end of a large-sized knitting needle so that it is not too sharp.

Techniques and stitches

Dressmaking is a skill and to become really expert requires an extensive knowledge of the techniques involved and a great deal of practise. However, even a beginner can learn to make simply designed clothes if she has a good working knowledge of the basic sewing techniques.

The techniques on the following pages are planned to take a beginner-dressmaker through the various stages of putting a garment together, from pinning out the pattern on the fabric to making a perfect hem. You might wish to practise some of the more tricky techniques, such as bound buttonholes, on scraps of fabric first before attempting them on a garment.

Have all your equipment to hand before you start a dressmaking project. Most important of all, put the ironing board up and have the iron and pressing materials ready for work. A good dressmaker keeps her ironing board up all the time her sewing machine is in use. Pressing at every stage is absolutely essential for a good finish to a garment.

Laying out the pattern

Ideally, a large table should be used for cutting out but if this is not possible, use the floor, preferably an area without carpet.

Follow the fabric layout given with your paper pattern and fold the fabric as shown. Lay out the entire paper pattern on the fabric before attempting to cut out a single piece and take careful note of those pieces which are to be placed along the fold of the fabric. Place each piece of pattern so that the grain line (the heavy line with an arrow head at each end), follows the lengthwise grain or bias of the fabric.

Some pattern pieces will say 'cut 2' which you will do automatically as you cut from the folded double thickness of fabric. Where the pieces indicate that you are to 'cut 1', cut from a single thickness.

Pinning out

Do not cut out anything until you are absolutely sure that every piece of pattern is placed on the fabric correctly. First, place pins at each end of, and in the centre of, the grain lines. Next, pin pieces which are placed along the fold of the fabric. Place pins within the seam allowance at right angles to the cut edges, points towards the edge, but not so that the shears will touch the points.

Space pins about 6 inches apart and take up only a few threads of fabric so that the fabric lies as flat as possible.

Cutting out

Now comes the stage that every beginner dreads – actually cutting into the fabric. You have nothing to fear if you have pinned out every piece correctly, so check once more. A danger is where patterns show sleeves to be cut separately from single thicknesses of fabric, for economy. In these instances, you will see that on the fabric layout one sleeve is shaded to indicate that the pattern is placed printed side down for the second sleeve. If you miss this point, you will finish up with two sleeves for the right armhole and none for the left and you will have wasted your fabric.

Use bent-handled dressmaker's shears for cutting out because they lift the fabric less and give more accurate cutting out. Use long, steady cuts and if you can learn to cut without completely closing the blades you will get an even edge rather than a ragged one. Cut right on the cutting line and cut outwards round notches rather than inwards. Snip into selvedges if they show signs of pulling.

After cutting out all the pieces, leave the paper patterns pinned to the fabric ready for marking. Cut the remaining fabric up and keep the largest pieces for bias strips, covering buttons, making belts or, if there is enough, making caps and berets.

Marking

There are several methods of transferring the construction markings from the paper pattern to the fabric but the most reliable method is tailor's tacking. It might not seem the quickest method and many authorities recommend other ways as being easier. Tailor's tacks can, however, be made quite quickly, they can be used on any kind of fabric and they are a very accurate method of marking.

Tailor's tacks

Using doubled thread in a contrasting colour to that of the fabric, take a small stitch, at the point to be marked, through both fabric and pattern paper, leaving an inch of thread end. Take a second stitch in the same place leaving a small loop. The two layers of fabric are pulled gently apart and the threads cut between the layers leaving a tuft marking the position of the symbol. Markings which are close together can be marked without cutting the thread providing that enough thread is left between each tailor's tack.

Basting

Basting marks (see p. 139) are used along grain lines in those instances. where it is important to keep to the grain of a fabric, such as garments cut on the cross; they can also be used for marking buttonholes and placing pleats and trimmings.

Tracing wheel and carbon

This method of marking works on most fabrics but it cannot be used on sheer fabrics where the marks would show through the completed garment, or on heavily napped fabrics where the marks would not show at all. Use

only dressmaker's carbon paper and test the colour first on a scrap of the fabric to make sure that the marks show clearly. Place the carbon paper under the paper pattern, face down on the fabric and run the wheel along the lines to be marked, using the straight edge of a ruler as a guide. Mark circular symbols with two short crossed lines.

Tailor's chalk and pins

A tailor's chalk pencil is used as it can be sharpened to a good point. Place pins through the fabric and paper pattern at the points to be marked. Remove the paper pattern carefully and mark the position of the pins with tailor's chalk.

Stay-stitching

Patterns sometimes indicate that a row of stay-stitching be worked on a single thickness of fabric close to the seamline – necklines and shoulder seams are often stitched in this way. Stay-stitching helps to prevent edges stretching before the pieces are sewn together and on garments made of jersey fabrics this is often essential. A matching thread is used in the machine and a setting of 12 stitches to the inch. Stay-stitching is worked $\frac{1}{8}$ inch from the seamline ($\frac{1}{2}$ inch from the edge on $\frac{5}{8}$ inch seams). If the fabric is of a type that slips when being machined, baste tissue paper to it before stay-stitching.

Once the construction marks have been transferred from the pattern to

Preparing to sew

the fabric, the paper pattern can be unpinned. Cut any interfacings at this stage.

Basting

Basting or, as it is sometimes called, tacking, is used to hold two pieces of fabric together temporarily for fitting and for sewing. Basting is best done by hand and in a contrasting thread. There are four types of basting stitches:

Even basting. Even basting is used on seams where there is likely to be some strain. To work: Stitches should be made about $\frac{1}{4}$ inch long on both sides of the fabric.

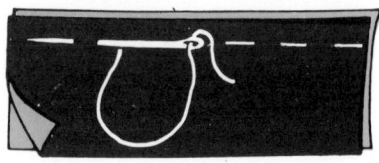

Uneven basting. A $\frac{1}{2}$ inch stitch is made on the upper side of the fabric and about $\frac{1}{8}$ inch on the underside. Uneven basting is used for marking or as a guideline for stitching.

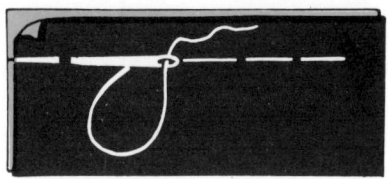

Diagonal basting. This is a useful stitch for keeping several layers of fabric together. To work: Sew at right angles to the fabric edge, a diagonal stitch appearing on the upper side of the fabric and a short vertical one on the wrong side.

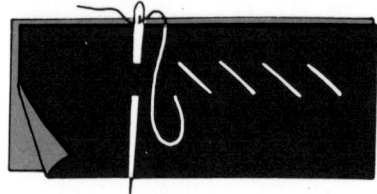

Slip basting. Slip basting is most useful where stripes or plaids need to be matched. To work: turn under the seam allowance on one side and press flat. Place this over the other section, right side up, and match the seam line. Take a small stitch on the seam line of the undersection, bring the needle through the seamline of the top section. Stitches should be kept to about $\frac{1}{4}$ inch in length and none should show on the right side of the fabric.

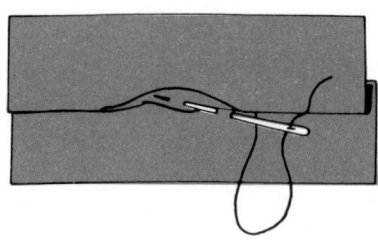

Stitches in dressmaking

Although most dressmaking sewing is done on a sewing machine, there are occasions when hand sewing is necessary, such as putting in zips and finishing hems. The diagrams given are for right-handed people, but if you are left-handed you can convert them to your way of working simply by holding a small hand mirror against the page. All permanent hand sewing should be started and ended with a back stitch (see below). Never use a knot.

Running stitch. This is the simplest of all hand sewing stitches and is used for gathering, for tucking and for mending jobs. To work, pass the needle in and out through the fabric, taking four or more stitches at a time before pulling the thread through. The stitches should be very small and neat.

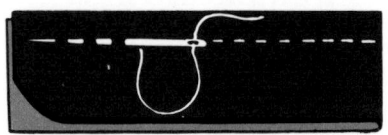

Back stitch. Properly done, back stitching resembles machine stitching on the right side but the stitches overlap on the wrong side. All hand sewing stitches should begin and end with one or two back stitches; back stitching is also used where particularly strong hand sewing is required.

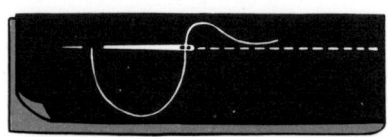

To work, bring the needle through from the wrong side of the fabric. Take a stitch *back* $\frac{1}{8}$ inch from where the needle came through and then bring the needle through $\frac{1}{8}$ inch in front. Continue in the same way.

Pick stitch. This is worked in a similar way to back stitch except that the needle picks up only two or three threads going back and comes out

$\frac{1}{4}$ inch ahead. Pick stitch is used for such jobs as inserting a zip fastener by hand.

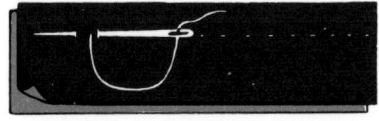

Slip stitch. Slip stitch is useful where an invisible finish is needed. To work, pick up one thread of the under section and then take $\frac{1}{8}$ inch stitch through the fold of the top fabric. Pick up the next stitch immediately below in the undersection.

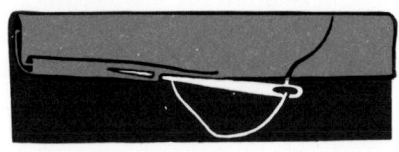

Hemming stitch. Once a much loved stitch in delicate hand sewing, hemming stitch is now used for such jobs as applying the facing to the backs of buttonholes. To work, pick up one thread of the garment and then pass the needle through the folded edge of the hem.

Invisible stitch. This is sometimes called French stitch, perhaps because it is used extensively in tailoring and haute couture clothes. It is used for attaching facings and interfacings and for finishing hems.

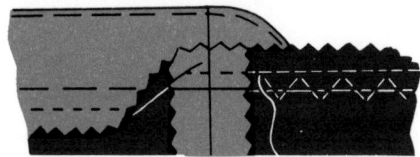

To work, turn the hem or facing back on the garment. Working from right to left pick up a thread of the garment and then pick up a thread from *under* the hem or facing above, working diagonally. The stitches should fall between the two layers of fabric.

Stitch a neat seam

Unless otherwise marked, all the seam allowances both in commercial paper patterns and graph patterns are $\frac{5}{8}$ inch. The method of sewing used for a seam is determined both by the fabric and by the position of the seam on the garment.

Plain seam. This seam is the most commonly used for joining sections of a garment together. The machine stitch is set to the number of stitches to an inch recommended by the manufacturer for that particular fabric. Pin the two pieces of fabric together and baste along the seam

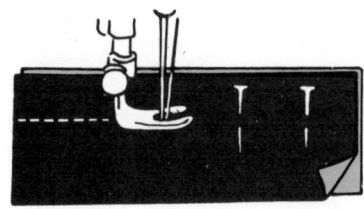

Machining a plain seam over pin basting

line. Machine stitch on the seam line, following the direction given in the pattern. Finish off at both ends either by tying a double knot in the two threads, by making a double back stitch or, if the machine has one,

by operating a forward and reverse motion.

Zigzag seams. Zigzag seams can only be worked on sewing machines with a swing needle but they are particularly good for seams on knitted fabrics where some 'give' is required. A narrow, closely spaced zigzag stitch should be used. Zigzag stitching can also be used effectively on seams of garments made of sheer fabrics. The fabric is placed right sides facing, with a fine cord placed along the stitching line. Narrow zigzag stitches are worked along the seam line, over the cord. The seam is then trimmed back close to the stitching and the garment turned to the right side and pressed.

French seam. This is a beautiful seam for sheer fabrics or for fine

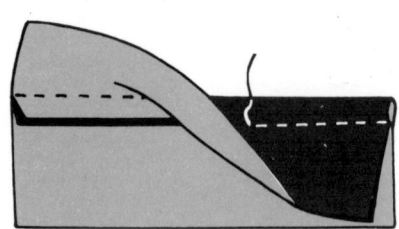

French seam

Stitching a seam (Photograph by Bernina Sewing Machines)

fabrics which are likely to fray. Pin the fabric wrong sides facing and stitch $\frac{3}{8}$ inch from the edge. Press the seam open. Turn the garment to the other side and press flat along the seam line. Stitch $\frac{1}{4}$ inch from the folded edge, thus encasing the raw edges.

Flat fell seam. This seam is used mostly on pyjamas, shirts and children's trousers, sometimes on adults' trousers and jeans. Make a plain seam first with wrong sides of fabric facing. Press the seam open.

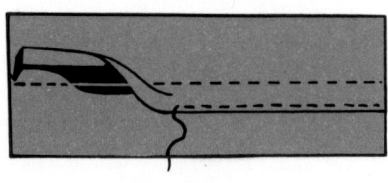

Flat-fell seam

Trim one seam allowance to $\frac{1}{8}$ inch. Turn under the raw edge of the other seam allowance. Press it down over the trimmed edge and top-stitch down to the garment, close to the folded edge.

Useful hints on seams

Grading. Sometimes pattern instructions will suggest 'grading' a seam to reduce bulk. This is usually done where there are more than two layers of fabric, such as an interfaced collar. Grading means cutting the seam allowance to different widths to reduce the thickness of a seam. The seam allowance nearest to the outside fabric is trimmed least while the

interfacing fabric is trimmed as close to the stitching line as possible.

Grading seams

Clipping curves. Pattern instructions will tell you to clip curved seams such as those in necklines. This is to make the curve lie flat. Use a sharply pointed pair of scissors and, for an inward curve (see diagram a) clip into the seam

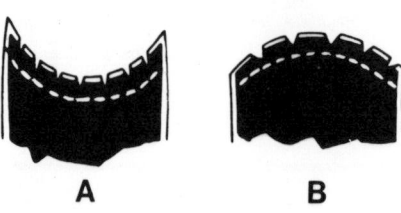

Clipping inward and outward curves

allowance towards the stitching line, stopping about $\frac{1}{8}$ inch from it. Clip at about $\frac{1}{2}$-inch intervals, closer if the curve is pronounced. On an outward curve (see diagram b), cut notches in the fabric to the line of stitching.

Seam finishes

Most fabrics fray to some degree

during wear and the raw edges of seams need to be finished off neatly. There are several methods of doing this.

Pinked edge. Pinked edges, cut with pinking shears, should only be used on fabrics which will not fray; it is not recommended as a method for seam finishing in good dressmaking.

Zigzag finish. Fabrics which are inclined to fray can be finished off with zigzag machine stitching. Press the seam open and machine stitch

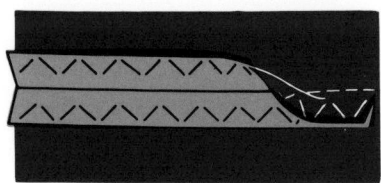

Zigzagged edge

with a medium zigzag close to the raw edge. It is inadvisable to finish underarm seams with zigzag stitching, as it is inclined to be uncomfortable in wear.

Double stitched seam. This is a sturdy finish for seams of garments which are going to be frequently in

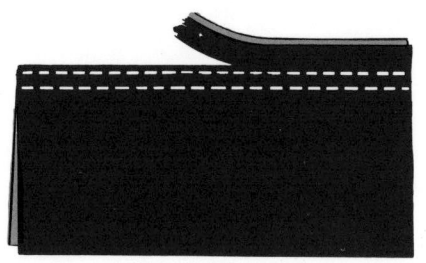

Double-stitched seam

the wash. Stitch a second row about $\frac{1}{4}$ inch away from the original seam line. Trim the fabric away close to the second line of stitching.

Overcasting. Fabrics which fray excessively can have seams overcast by hand. Press the seam open and work a row of machine stitching $\frac{1}{8}$ inch from the raw edges. Working

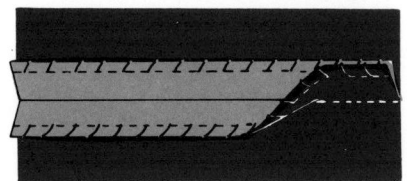

Overcast edge

from left to right, work overcasting over the cut edge and through the machine stitching.

Turned and stitched edges. This is the neatest finish of all and looks very good on the inside of a finished garment. Press the seam open and

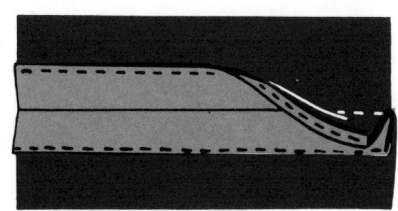

Turned and stitched edge

make a row of machine stitching $\frac{1}{8}$ inch from the raw edges. Turn under a hem along the stitched line and stitch again, close to the folded edge.

Bound edges. This is the most suitable seam finish for loosely woven fabrics. Encase each raw edge with commercial bias binding.

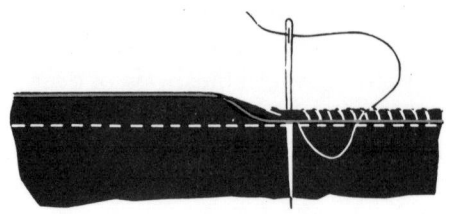

Rolled edge

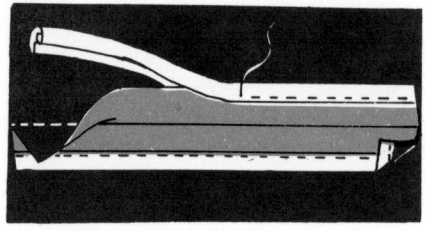

Bound edge

Rolled edges. This is a pretty finish for sheer fabrics, and is especially suitable for lingerie. Press the seam flat and trim back to $\frac{3}{8}$ inch. Using the thumb and forefinger, roll the seam allowance to the stitching line and sew over the rolled edge close to the stitching line.

Darts

Making perfect darts

Darts, as you will see from paper patterns, are used for shaping pieces of fabric to the curves of the body. They are usually used under the armhole, running from the side seams for bust shaping, from the shoulder seams and from the waistline, shaping both the waistline and the upper hip area.

Darts are marked with lines and a series of dots on commercial paper patterns and in outline on graph patterns.

Simple darts. Whether the dart to be sewn is a simple triangular dart or a curved dart, the sewing technique is the same.

Fold the dart along the centre, right sides of fabric facing. Pin and then baste firmly (see page 139). Stitch from the widest end towards the point, with the last three stitches on the fold. Secure the ends with forward and reverse machine stitching or tie off the ends tightly. It is *important* to make the last stitches on the fold, to achieve a smooth flow into the fabric and not make an ugly point. Press the dart flat and then press it towards one side. Darts in heavy fabrics can be slashed to within ½ inch of the point after stitching. Press open and

oversew the raw edges to prevent fraying.

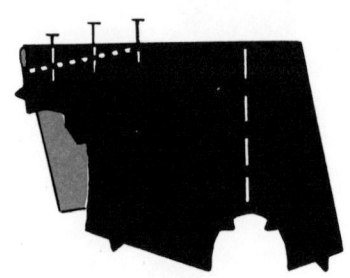

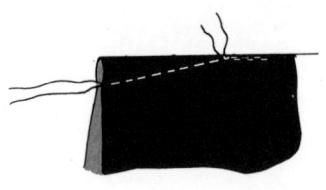

Three stages of making a dart

Bias binding

Necklines and armholes can be given a quick finish with a bound edging made of bias-cut self fabric. Commercially produced cotton bias bindings, available in different widths and colours, are used for finishing off curved seams and make very pretty trims for collar and cuff edgings and for children's clothes.

Cutting bias binding

Bias binding is cut on the true bias of the fabric. To find the true bias, fold the fabric diagonally so that the crosswise grain is parallel to the lengthwise grain. The folded edge is the true bias. Cut along the fold and measure the width of bias binding required from the cut edge. Cut strips diagonally as required.

Joining strips. Place two strips of binding together, right sides facing and at right angles to each other,

Applying binding. Bias binding is cut to twice the width of the finished binding plus seam allowances. Thus, if the finished bound edge is to show $\frac{1}{2}$ inch of binding, cut twice this plus two seam allowances – $2\frac{1}{4}$ inches.

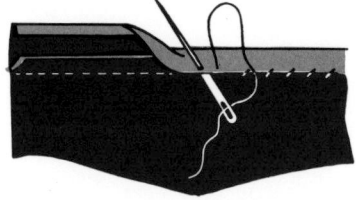

Applying bias binding

Mark the centre of the binding along the length with basting stitches (see page 139). Pin the binding to the garment, right sides facing, so that the marked centre will lie on the raw edge of the garment when the binding is folded over. Baste and then stitch the binding to the garment along the seam line. Turn the binding

Cutting and joining a bias strip

with corners overlapping so that the raw edges will line up with each other after joining. Stitch, then press open the seam and trim away the points that extend over the edges. Always stretch bias binding slightly before using it.

over the raw edge of the garment, turn under the binding seam allowance and hem by hand to the stitching line.

Binding can also be worked from the wrong side of the garment first and then top-stitched on the right side.

Facings

In a well-made garment, every raw edge has to be finished off neatly and facings are one of the techniques used for finishing. Facings are used for the inside fronts of blouses and jackets and for finishing off necklines and armholes. Sometimes, jacket front facings are cut in one with the section of garment and if a heavy fabric is being used the facing is simply folded back and hemmed down on the inside. In some cases however, the pattern instructions may indicate that an *interfacing* is to be cut from part of the facing pattern and used between the top fabric and the facing for greater firmness.

Neckline facings are cut separately from the garment section and are sometimes interfaced. Most paper patterns will instruct that the interfacing should be cut from the facing pattern piece, then machine stitched to the facing along the seam line. In the days before non-woven interfacing fabrics, interfacing was cut to within the seam line and attached to the facing with catch-stitches. This meant that the edges of interfaced pieces were less bulky and cleaner in line. Nowadays, all pattern instructions give the method illustrated here.

Applying facings

Pin and baste the facing to the garment edge, right sides together. Match notches carefully. Stitch the facing down, sewing on the seam line. Grade the seam and clip the curve (see page 144). Press the seam towards the facing. Understitch the facing (see diagram b) to prevent it from rolling to the outside. Turn facing to inside. Neck facings are catch-stitched to the shoulder seams.

Armhole facings are worked in exactly the same way. Catch-stitch to both shoulder and underarm seams.

1 Front and back neck facings joined at seams

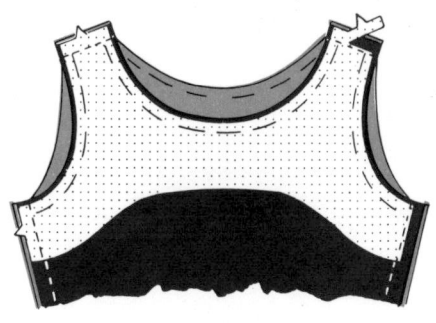

Facing cut in one with garment

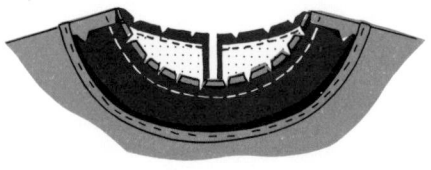

2 Facing stitched to neck edge with seam graded and clipped

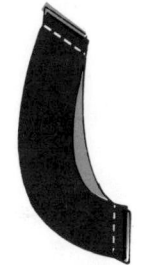

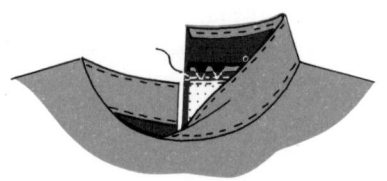

3 Facing understitched to prevent it from rolling

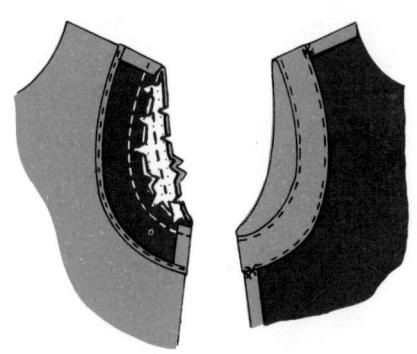

Three stages of applying armhole facing

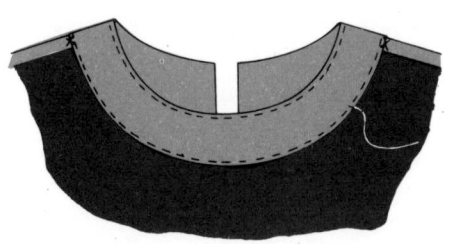

4 Sew facing to interfacing and catchstitch to shoulder seams

Collars and Cuffs

There are three types of collar for which you need to know the basic sewing techniques – the Peter Pan, the convertible shirt collar and the Mandarin or bias-cut collar.
All three types are interfaced.

Peter Pan collar

To make up. Pin and baste the interfacing fabric to the wrong side of the undercollar. Stitch both upper and lower sections of the collar together, leaving the neck edge open.

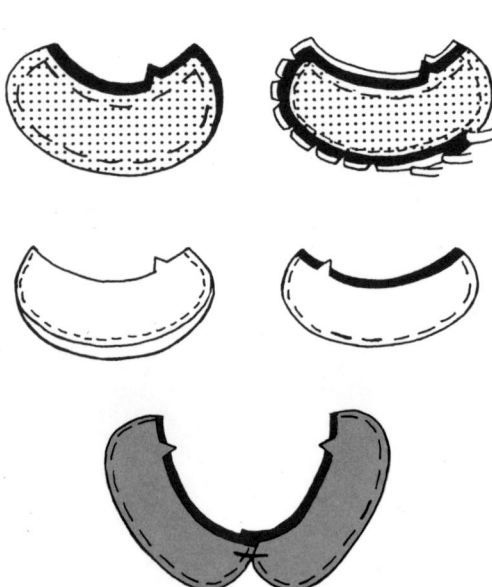

The Peter Pan collar

Turn collar to the right side. Pin and tack the undercollar to the neck edge, right sides of fabric facing. Stitch along neck seam line. Grade seams and clip into curve (see page 144). Turn under the seam allowance on the upper collar and baste then stitch invisibly to the inside neck along the stitched seam line.

Shirt or convertible collar

To make up. In some patterns, the collar and undercollar are cut in one piece but in shaped collars the collar is cut in two pieces, an upper and a lower piece with interfacing between. Make up the collar leaving the neck edge open. Pin and baste the collar to the neck edge. Stitch the front facing to the back facing piece at the shoulder seams. Pin the facing to the neck edge over the collar, right sides together. Baste and then stitch the entire neck edge. Trim interfacing, grade seam allowances and clip into curve (see page 144). Turn facing to the inside, press and catch-stitch to the shoulder seam allowances, leaving the facing free of the garment everywhere else.

Mandarin or bias-cut collar

This type of collar is interfaced with a

1 Interfacing hemmed to fold line of bodice and stitched to shoulder seams.

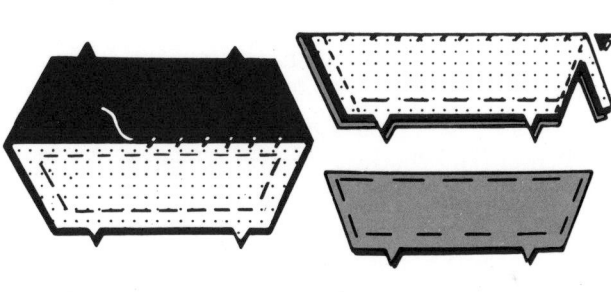

2 Making up the collar

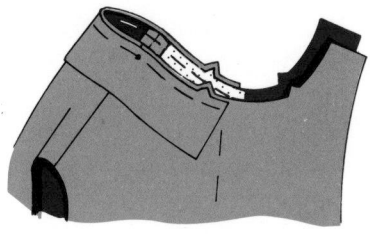

3 Collar basted to neck edge

4 Facing pinned to neck edge over collar

5 Grade seam allowances and clip seam

6 Catchstitch facing to shoulder seam allowance

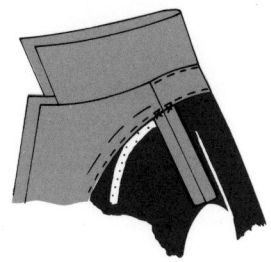

7 Trim interfacing to edge of facing

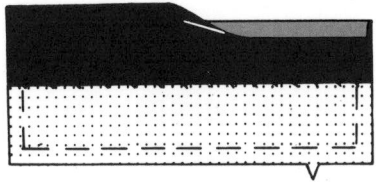

Mandarin or bias-cut collar: interfacing basted in position and seam allowance turned under

firm woven fabric cut with the grain the same way as the top fabric. A non-woven interfacing should not be used. Baste the interfacing to the wrong side of the collar piece. Stitch and then trim the interfacing close to the stitching. Press under the seam allowance on one long edge. Fold the collar in half and stitch both short ends. Turn collar to right side and with right sides facing, pin and tack the folded edge of the collar to the garment, matching notches. Make sure that the centre back edges are evenly matched. Stitch collar to neckline edge. Trim seam allowance of the garment to $\frac{1}{4}$ inch, and that of the collar to $\frac{3}{8}$ inch. Press the seam towards the collar. Turn the seam allowance on the other long edge of the collar under and slip-stitch to the inside of the garment.

Cuffs

There are many ways of finishing off the cuff edges of sleeves. The easiest is a simple bias binding or an applied self-fabric facing. The most difficult for a beginner to attempt is the button-fastened cuff on a gathered sleeve. The technique for this type of cuff is given here:

1. Reinforce the opening to be slashed or clipped on the lower sleeve edge with stay stitching or with facing.

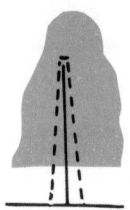

Reinforce slash with stay-stitching

2. Cut a strip of the same fabric the length of the entire slash and two inches wide. Open the slash and spread it until the stay stitching is in a straight line.

Open slash until stitching is straight and stitch fabric to opening

3. Pin the strip of fabric to the opening, right sides together. Stitch $\frac{1}{4}$ inch from the edge, tapering towards the end of the slash. Turn under the free edge of the strip and hem to the seamline.

Hem free edge of strip to seamline

4. Gather the sleeve edge as instructed.

Two rows of basting at lower edge of sleeve

5. Make up the cuff using the same method as that employed for the bias-cut collar.

A beautifully finished cuff

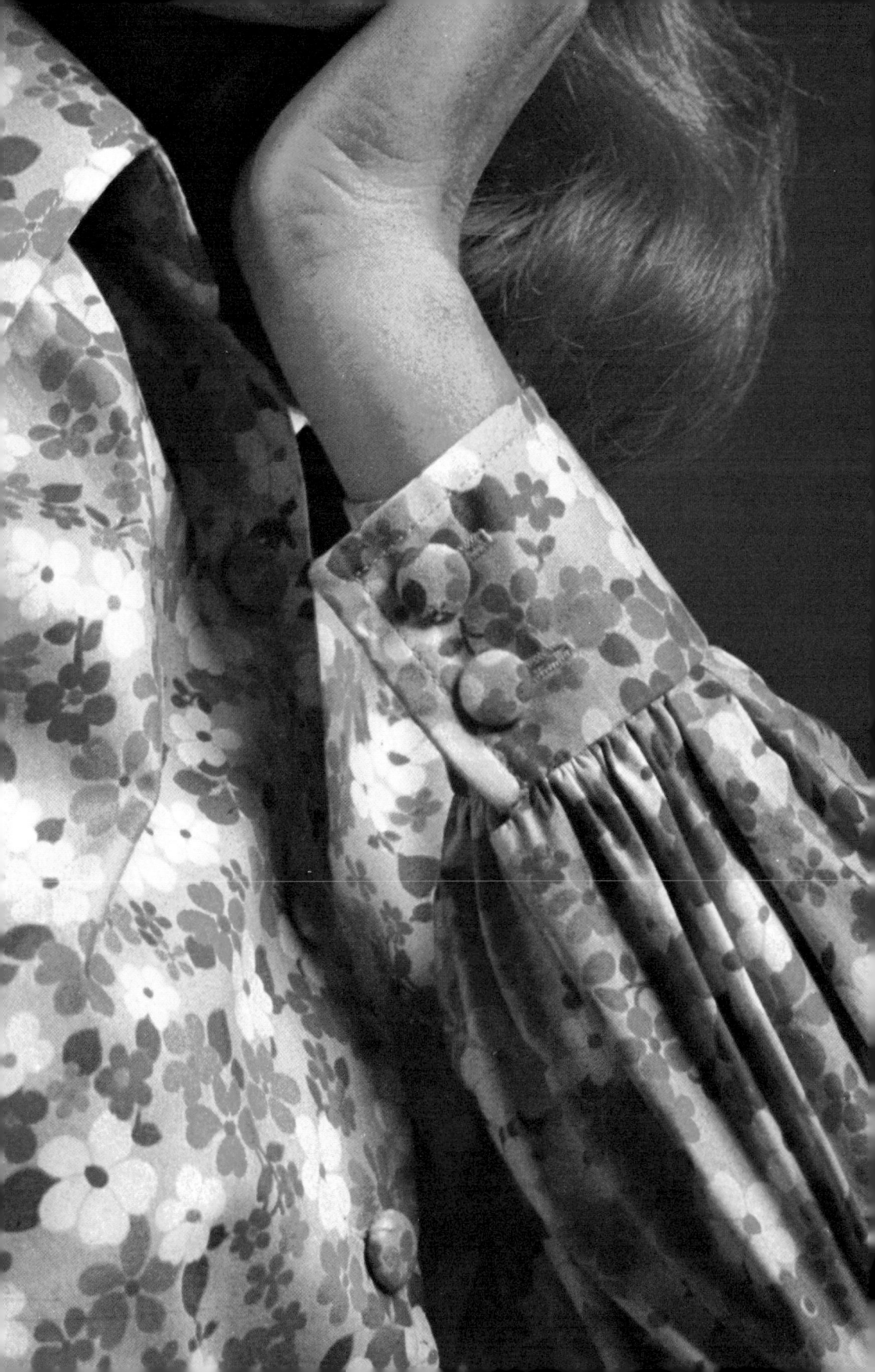

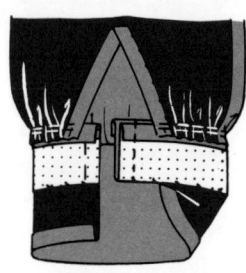

Pin notched edge to sleeve

Hem free edge over seam

6. Attach the cuff to the sleeve, working from the inside first and finishing on the right side with top stitching. Make buttonholes and attach buttons.

The one-piece quick cuff

This is a simple one-piece cuff which can be made for a long sleeve if a stretch fabric such as jersey is being used. Cut the cuff fabric to the measurement of the circumference of the clenched hand plus one inch and by twice the required depth. Right sides facing, join the narrow ends. Turn to the right side and fold double into a cuff. Slip onto the sleeve, raw edges together and right sides facing. Machine stitch $\frac{1}{2}$ inch from the edge. Trim the seam to $\frac{1}{4}$ inch and neaten with zigzag machine stitching. Fold down, the cuff with the seam allowance inside the sleeve.

Setting in sleeves

The traditional technique for sleeves, which used to be taught, involved shrinking the fabric of the head of the sleeve to fit the armhole. Now that so many dressmaking fabrics are pre-shrunk, this method does not work very well and the fullness at the top of the sleeve is 'eased' into the armhole.

Step-by-step guide to setting in a sleeve.

1. Turn the bodice section inside out. Turn the completed sleeve right side out. Slip the sleeve into the garment so that the raw edges of the sleeve and the armhole are matched together on the seamline. Put in a pin or two to hold the sleeve in position.

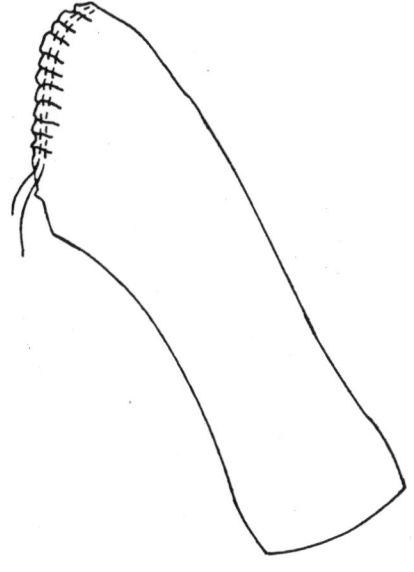

The sleeve made up and gathering stitches drawn up

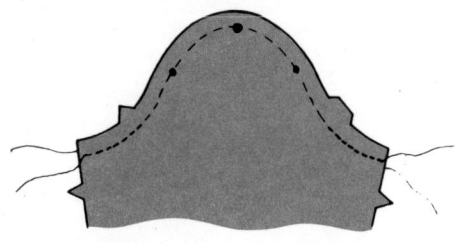

Gathering stitches run on seam line

2. Check to make absolutely sure that you have the right sleeve for the armhole. The back of the armhole is usually marked with two notches which correspond with two notches on the sleeve.

3. Pin and then baste the underarm section as far as the notches on front and back. There is not any ease on this part.

4. The head of the sleeve will have been gathered according to pattern instructions. Hold the bodice in the left hand with the inside of the sleeve towards you. Pin the centre of the sleeve head to the shoulder seam. Then proceed to put in pins, working to both left and right, placing pins across the seamline. Whilst holding the bodice and the sleeve in your left

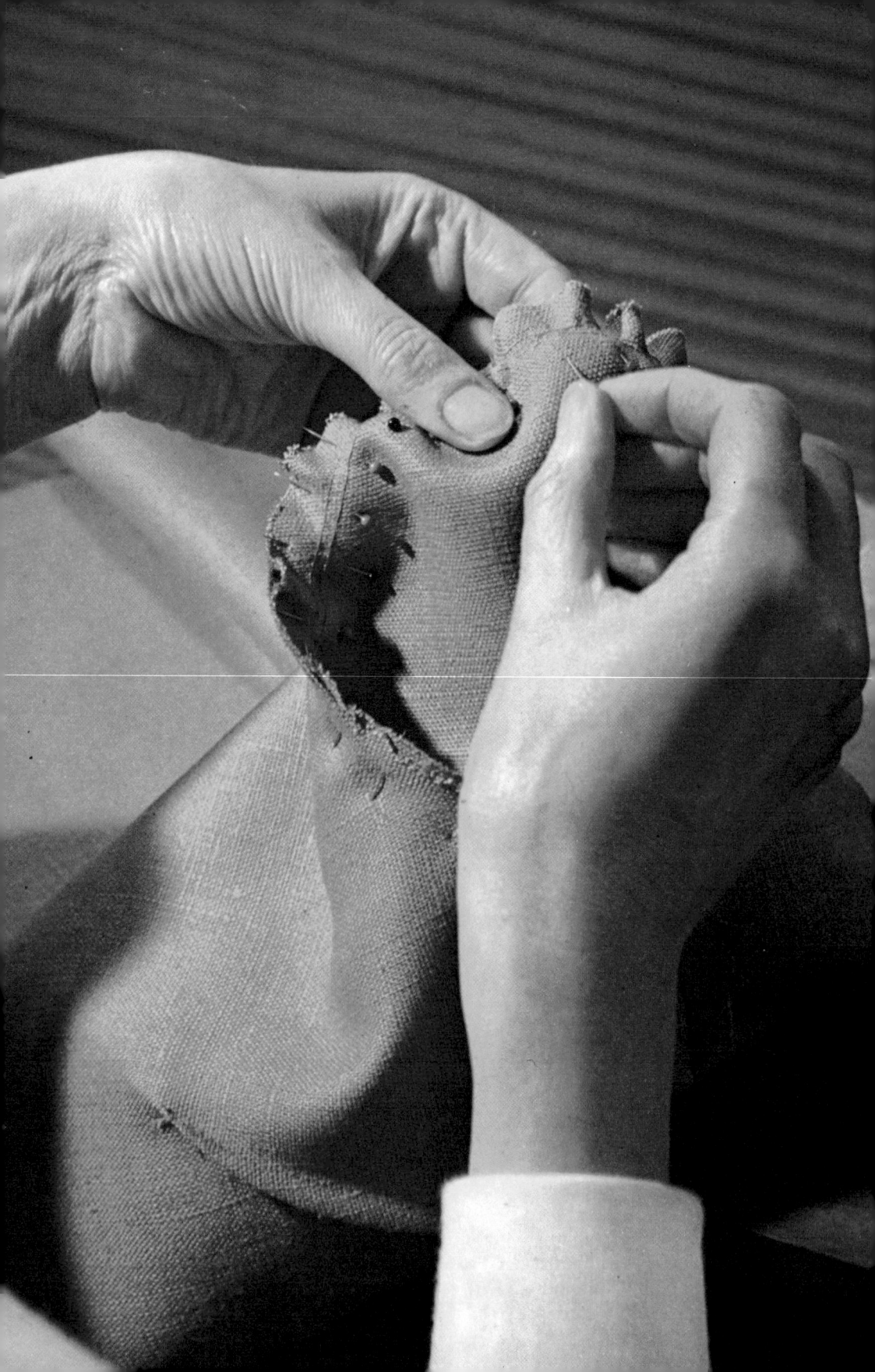

hand, your fingers will make a curved shape similar to the curve of a shoulder and this, you will find, makes it easier to place the pins so that the fullness is properly distributed. Use plenty of pins, as many as you need.

5. Baste all round the sleeve seam firmly and leave a few pins in position during machine stitching to make sure that the fabric does not slip.

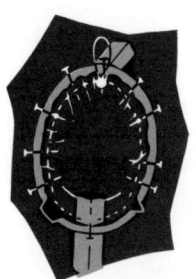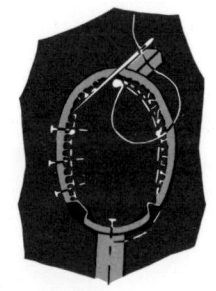

Sleeve pinned and basted into bodice

6. Pull the sleeve through the armhole and machine stitch, working from the sleeve side of the seam. Two rows of machining is advisable. Trim

the underarm seam allowance to $\frac{1}{4}$ inch and oversew to neaten.

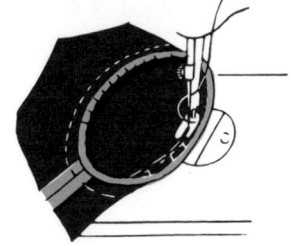

Machine stitch with sleeve uppermost

Two-piece set-in sleeve

The two-piece sleeve, featured on the Chanel-type suit, on page 115 is made up in two sections, both of which are shaped so that the finished sleeve fits without the use of darts. Join the two sections with plain seams and then insert the sleeve into the armhole in the same way as for a one-piece sleeve. Cuff edges are finished off in a suitable way, either with a single hem, a bias-cut facing or with bias binding cut from the same fabric.

Setting a sleeve into an armhole

Waistbands

The waistline of fitted skirts and trousers can be finished off in one of three simple ways – with a self-fabric waistband, with an interfaced facing or with a petersham band.
The waistband should lap front over back on a side closing and left over right on a back closing. After the zip has been inserted, close the waistband with two hooks and eyes or with a worked buttonhole and a button.

Self-fabric waistband
A waistband is usually cut along the lengthwise grain to prevent it from stretching. Interfacing is cut to half the depth of the band.
To make up. Turn under the seam allowance on the long edge of the waistband piece that has no notches. Pin and baste the interfacing to the

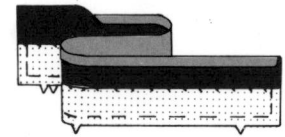

Interfacing hemmed to foldline

wrong side of the fabric, matching the notched edges and with the other edge of the interfacing along what will be the fold line.

Catch the interfacing to the fold line. Pin the notched edge of the waistband to the waist of the skirt, notches

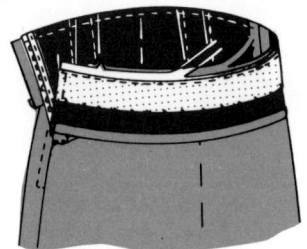

Stitch on seamline and grade seams

Stitch waistband ends, trim and grade seams

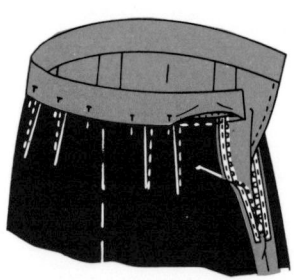

Lap free edge on waistband seam and pin

matching and right sides facing.
Baste while easing the waistband
onto the skirt. Stitch.
Trim interfacing close to stitching.
Grade seams.
Press seam towards waistband. Fold
the waistband, right sides facing and
stitch the short ends.
Turn to the right side and press.
Hem the folded edge of the waistband
to the seamline on the inside of the
skirt.

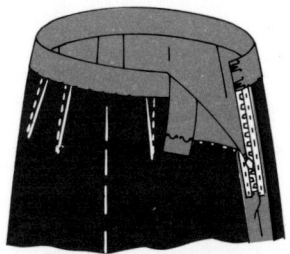

Hem waistband to seamline on inside

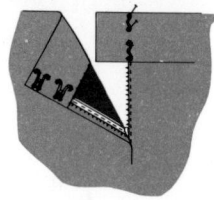

Hooks are sewn to the overlap of the closing

Faced waistband

Work following the same method
given for applying facings (see page
151).

Petersham bands

Cut petersham ribbon to the waist
measurement plus $2\frac{1}{2}$ inches.
Make a 1-inch hem on each of the
short ends.
Pin and baste the petersham to the
waistline on the right side of the
fabric, making a small pleat,
approximately $\frac{1}{8}$ inch at the side, the
centre front and centre back for ease.
The petersham should be standing up
above the skirt edge.
Stitch $\frac{1}{8}$ inch from the edge of the
ribbon. Turn the ribbon inside the
skirt and press. Sew hook and eye
fastenings to the hemmed ends.

Waist plackets

A placket is the opening in a seam
simply to allow one to get in and out
of a garment easily. Never alter the
recommended depth of a placket as
this could make the skirt difficult to
slide over the hips. Most plackets are
closed with a zip fastener but
occasionally a pattern will
recommend that hooks and eyes be
used.

Fastenings

The fastenings on your hand-made clothes – zips, buttons, buttonholes, press studs, hooks and eyes – must be beautifully done if the finished garments are to have the professional look which is the aim of every dressmaker. There are special techniques for sewing fastenings and you should learn these right from the start.

Zip fasteners

Zip fasteners are made both in nylon and metal and come in different weights for different types of clothes. They can be bought with an open end for the front of a jacket and a curved type is available for trouser fly fastenings. The leading brands mark their packets clearly with the type of garment for which the zip is intended. Zips are manufactured in a very wide range of colours but if an exact match is difficult to achieve, buy one that is near enough the right colour, and in a lighter tone rather than a dark tone.

Make sure that you buy a zip long enough for the opening and if necessary, make the opening longer to fit the nearest sized zip. The stop at the bottom of the zip should be exactly level with the bottom of the opening so that there is no strain on the lowest teeth of the zip when the garment is being put on and taken off. For back fastenings, the top of the zip should be about $\frac{1}{2}$ inch below the neck edge and a hook and eye should be sewn about it to take the strain off the top teeth.

Stitch the zip in by machine, if your machine has a zipper foot, otherwise Sew zips in by hand. Use pick stitch (see page 140) to do this and the stitches will be both strong and invisible. It is a wise precaution to neaten the turnings of the opening before putting the zip in because threads can very easily catch in zips and make them stick.

Follow the instructions on the packet for the best method of inserting a zip.

Three kinds of buttonholes are used in dressmaking – bound buttonholes, hand worked and eyelet buttonholes. A perfectly adequate buttonhole can be worked on swing needle sewing machines using the zigzag stitch and the machine manufacturer's handbook will give instructions for making this.

Bound buttonholes

Bound buttonholes must be made on interfaced areas of the garment.

Zip fasteners are both practical and decorative (Photograph by Lightning Zip Fasteners Ltd)

The method is as follows:

1. Cut a piece of fabric on the lengthwise grain 2 inches deep and to the width of the finished buttonhole plus $\frac{1}{2}$ inch.

2. Fold lengthwise and crease. Baste in position on the right side of fabric with the crease lying on the button-hole mark. Mark the width of the buttonhole along the crease with basting stitches.

3. Stitch with very small stitches round the marked line, $\frac{1}{8}$ inch away from it, along both sides and along each end.

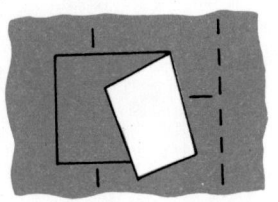 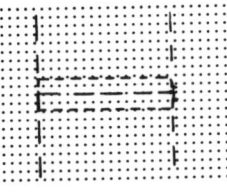

4. With sharp, pointed scissors, cut the fabric along the basted line to within $\frac{1}{8}$ inch of each end of the buttonhole and then into the corners.

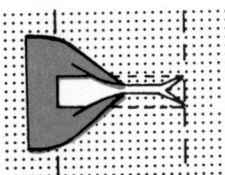 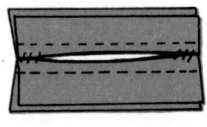

5. Turn the fabric through the slit to the wrong side (see diagram) to form a narrow binding on both edges of the

buttonhole and square the ends off neatly with a small pleat.

6. Baste flat and press.

7. Neaten by sewing all round the edge of the buttonhole on the right side, using pick stitches.

8. On the wrong side, baste the facing in position, cut a slit in the facing to correspond with the buttonhole, turn in the edges and hem neatly to the back of the buttonhole fabric.

Handworked buttonholes

Handworked buttonholes take rather a long time to do and need a great deal of patience but if you are making a garment from an expensive or a very lightweight fabric, then they are well worth the effort. They are also suitable for fabrics such as tweeds where bound buttonholes cannot be worked easily.

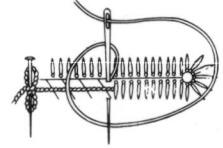 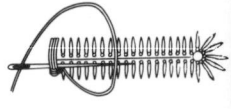

Two stages of the worked buttonhole

Handworked buttonholes are worked after the facing has been completed. Mark the position of the buttonhole and outline it with small stitches. Cut the slit through the fabric, interfacing and facing with a sharp, pointed pair of scissors.

Over-sew the cut edges immediately if the fabric frays easily. Work buttonhole stitch round the slit, starting from the square end. When you have stitched round the rounded end, using satin stitch on the curve instead of buttonhole stitch, finish by making three or four straight stitches across the square end and then buttonhole stitch across them.

Eyelet buttonholes

Cut a small circle with a stiletto and outline the circle with small running stitches. Work buttonhole stitch all round the edge closely.

Loop fastenings

Loop fastenings can be made of fabric or of thread, the former being a decorative form of fastening and the latter purely functional. Fabric loops are stitched into position before the facing is applied.

Thread loops

Use either buttonhole twist thread or pure silk.

To work: Sew two or three strands of thread through the fabric to the depth of the intended loop. Work over these threads with buttonhole stitch. If the loop is right on the edge of the garment and is to be used for a ball button, it helps to slip a matchstick under the threads while the buttonhole stitching is being worked.

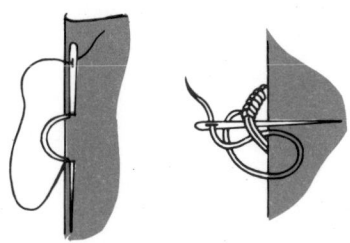

Thread loops

Fabric loops

Making the rouleau. Rouleau is the term given to a narrow tube of fabric. To make this, cut a strip of bias-cut fabric the width of the finished tube plus seam allowance. $1\frac{1}{4}$ inches is

usually enough. Fold in half lengthwise, right sides together and stitch leaving the ends open. Fasten a strong thread to one end of the tube at the seam. Using a bodkin or a large-eyed needle, and pushing it eye first through the tube, pull the thread through. This will turn the tube inside out. Do not press.

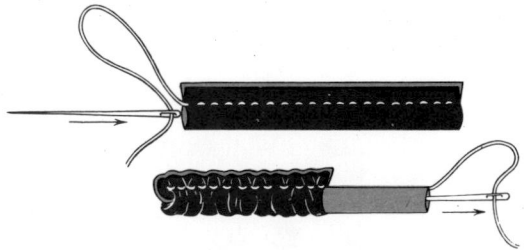

Making rouleau from bias strips

Making the loops. Cut the rouleau to the correct length to fit over the button plus seam allowances. Make the size and spacing of the loops on a piece of paper and sew the loops to the paper.

Stitch the loops, still on the paper, in position on the right side of the garment edge. Tear the paper away, apply the facing. Stitch the buttons to match the loops.

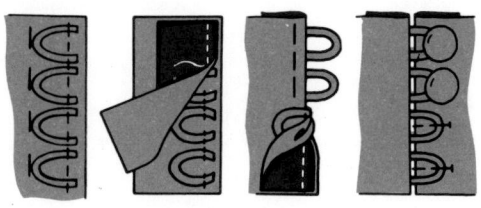

Stages of making loop fastenings

Snap fasteners

Snaps are used as fasteners where there is not likely to be very much strain but where a closure is needed. Stitch fasteners fairly close together,

about an inch apart if very small,
2 inches if they are fairly large. The
ball part of the fastener goes on to the
overlapping fabric.

To work. Fasten the thread to the
spot where the fastener is going to be
with a double back stitch. Hold the
fastener down with the left thumb
and stitch through each hole in turn
with four or five buttonhole stitches.

Take the thread under the snap to go
from one hole to the next. The
stitches should go through the fabric
and the interfacing but should not
show on the right side of the garment.
Sew the socket part of the fastener in
the same way.
For a couture finish, if the fasteners
are rather large, cover both parts

with circles of matching silk fabric
gathered round the edges before
sewing them on. The ball will break
through the silk and make a hole in
the socket the first time the fastener
is closed.

Hooks and eyes

Hooks and eyes are used mostly as a
waistband fastening.
The hook part is stitched to the
overlap about $\frac{1}{8}$ inch from the edge of
the opening and buttonhole stitches
are used to secure the fastener to the
fabric. Make stitches all round the

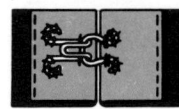 

holes of the hook and straight
stitches across the end under the
hook. Round eyes are stitched so
that they extend just beyond the edge
of the garment opening. Bar eyes are
placed about $\frac{1}{8}$ inch in from the edge.

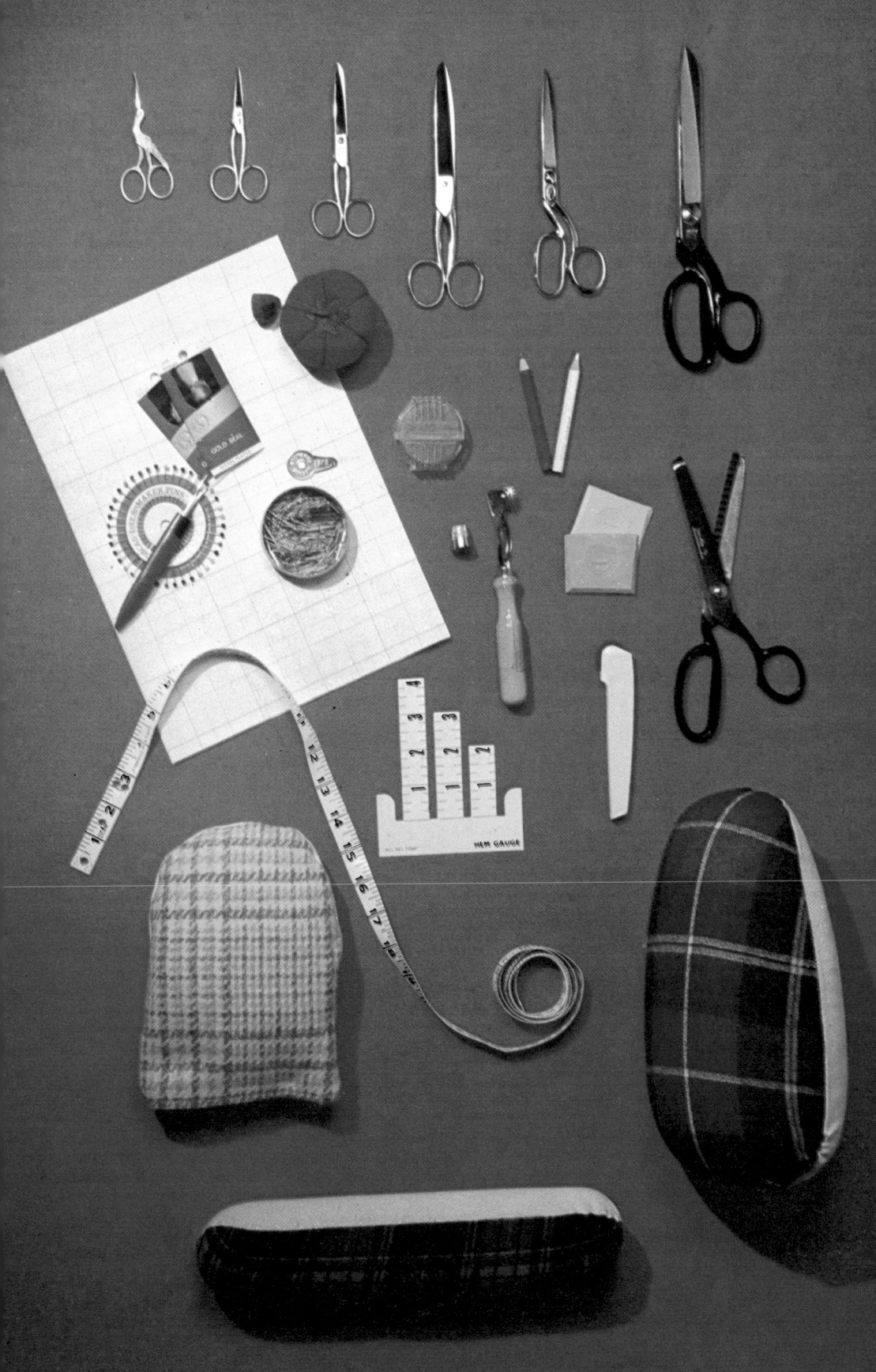

Perfect hems

The last perfect touch to an immaculately made garment is the hemline – and it is particularly important in those styles where the hemline area is the fashion point. Here are some basic rules for making hemlines:

1. Get someone else to measure while you are wearing the garment, measuring upwards from the floor.
2. Sew the garment working with it flat on the table so that the weight is supported.
3. Trim the raw edge if necessary to neaten before pinning up.
4. Pin evenly, placing pins at right angles to the hem. Never slant pins or the fabric may be pulled out of its true line. As you pin, the fabric will flute between the pins.
5. Baste about $2\frac{1}{2}$ inches from the folded edge and then press the fluted edge lightly with a damp cloth to shrink out the flutes. Do not press too hard or marks may be made through the fabric to the right side.
6. Baste again, $\frac{1}{2}$ inch down from the raw edge.
7. Hold the full depth of the hem in your hand and without creasing it

turn under a $\frac{1}{4}$ inch hem on the raw edge and stitch with invisible stitch (see page 141). Pick up only two or

Press along basted edge

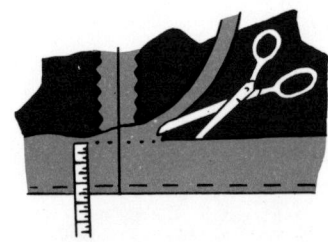

Trim hem to an even width

three threads from the skirt fabric and more fabric from the hem itself. Leave a loop every three or four stitches for ease.

8. Remove basting stitches and press again.

The pretty touch

Hand-made clothes can look delightful and rather expensive if you take the trouble to add decorative details. These can be as simple as neatly made loop fastenings or pretty buttons. Lace edgings and inserts give a charming feminine air to fragile clothes and pin tucks, worked on a baby's dress, are a lovely way to do fine needlework.

Braid and ribbon, stitched round the edges of a suit jacket or the hem of a full skirt add a distinctive touch. Ruffles, while requiring a little patience to make, lend a great deal of glamour to lingerie and nightdresses. Narrow ruffles, sewn in rows, look very dramatic on long, full sleeves.

Embroidery on clothes can convey any expression or mood. Small flower motifs, for instance, look pretty scattered across the bodice of a garment, while personal monograms and initials look smart on pockets, lapels and personal accessories. Formal cross-stitched designs look attractive down sleeves or in bands round skirt hems; children's clothes, as well as adults', can be decorated with bands of smocking.

Wool embroidery looks effective on fashion clothes, too. Big, bold flowers in brilliant colours worked on wool fabrics can look marvellous. The possibilities in embroidery are endless.

Embroidery should always be worked on garment sections before making them up.

Appliqué

To apply motifs to garments, trace off the design and transfer it to the contrasting fabric. Machine stitch round the outline of the motif. Cut out the shape allowing $\frac{1}{8}$ inch round the outside of the machine stitching. Turn this allowance under on the stitched line, press and baste to the garment. Hem or blanket stitch in position.

An alternative method for appliqué is worked on a swing needle sewing machine. Cut out the motif with a $\frac{1}{4}$-inch margin all round. Baste to the garment in position and machine stitch $\frac{1}{4}$ inch from the edge on the seamline. Trim the fabric off close to the machine stitching. Work close zigzag stitch all round, covering the raw edges.

Braids, ribbons and ric-rac

Braids and ribbons can be applied by hand or by machine. Narrow widths will need only one row of stitches down the centre while wider braids and ribbons will require stitching along both edges.

Ruffles

Ruffled edging can be purchased ready-made and this is simply stitched to the garment along the firm edge.

To make ruffles, allow fabric about twice to three times the finished length of the ruffle. Sheer or fine fabrics need more fullness than heavy ones. Bias-cut ruffles hang better but for an edging on skirts or aprons, the fabric can be cut to either lengthwise or crosswise grain.

Most sewing machines have an attachment for sewing a narrow hem on ruffles but if you prefer to do it by hand, roll and hem the edge. Divide and mark the hemmed fabric into quarters and gather evenly between the marks. This can be done either by hand or by machine, using a large-sized stitch. Stitch two rows and leave the ends of the threads free for adjustments to gathers.

To attach a ruffle

Faced ruffles. This method of application is used on faced edges such as collars or within a seam for an edging.
Draw up the ruffle. Pin the gathered edge to the edge of the garment, right sides facing. Match seamlines. Allow more fullness at corners. Baste. Pin facing right side down over the ruffle, matching seamlines. Baste and then stitch through all thicknesses. Trim corners, grade seams. Turn to the right side.

As a hem finish. Use this method of application where there is no facing such as on a hem.
Pin the edge of the ruffle to the garment edge, right sides facing, matching seamlines. Baste a strip of bias fabric right side down over the ruffle. Stitch on the seamline. Trim seam. Hem the other edge of the bias down to cover the raw edges of the garment and the ruffle.

Lace edgings

Lace edging should always be sewn on by hand for a delicate look. Use a sharp needle and fine thread. Place lace edge against the finished edge of the fabric, right sides facing and join the edges with oversewing or whipping stitch. Mitre the corners as illustrated by folding the lace down at the corner and cutting away the excess fabric. Sew the cut edges together with oversewing.

Lace insert

This is a very simple way of applying insert lace to a garment. Baste the lace, which has two straight edges, in position on the wrong side of the fabric. On the right side, cut away the fabric over the lace leaving $\frac{3}{8}$ inch on either side for turnings. Turn the

Flower-pretty embroidery; trace pattern on page 173 (Photograph by J & P Coats Ltd).

raw edges under to make narrow hems and machine stitch to the lace.

Embroidered bolero for a little girl

To work the embroidery on a bolero, trace off the design, which is given life-size. Trace the design down onto the fabric using dressmaker's carbon paper and reversing the tracing for the opposite side of the bolero.
Diagram 1 gives the key to stitches and colours of thread.
Materials required:
Child's bolero, made of a smooth fabric or of felt.
Clark's Anchor Stranded Cotton in the following colours and quantities:
Muscat Green 0280 2 skeins; Rose Madder 056 1 skein; Cyclamen 085, 088 1 skein each; Jade 0186, 0189 1 skein each; Muscat Green 0278 1 skein.
Crewel needle No. 8.
To work, use two strands of thread throughout. All parts of the design similar to numbered parts are worked in the same colour and stitch.
Press completed embroidery on the wrong side.

1 – 056		
2 – 085		
3 – 088		
4 – 0186	}	Satin Stitch
5 – 0189		
6 – 0278		
7 – 0280		
8 – 056		
9 – 085		
10 – 088	}	French Knots
11 – 0186		
12 – 0189		
13 – 0280		
14 – 0189		
15 – 0278	}	Stem Stitch
16 – 0280		
17 – 0186	}	Back Stitch
18 – 0189		
19 – 088 – Double Knot Stitch		
20 – 0189 – Buttonhole Stitch		

Diagram 1 – key to stitches and threads

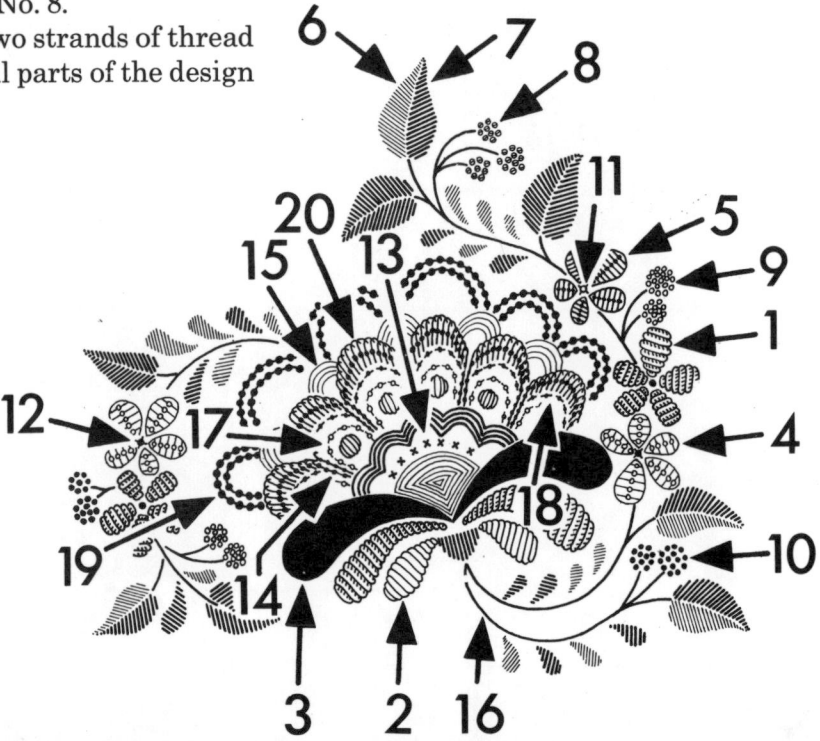

Trace pattern for the girl's bolero embroidery

Making a paper pattern

Here is a complete wardrobe of patterns for you to make up with the dressmaking know-how you have acquired. The patterns are given as graph patterns and these can seem rather strange at first. In fact, they are worked out in exactly the same way as commercial paper patterns but are scaled down to fit on to the page. The only difference is that a graph pattern is a plan from which you make your own paper pattern. Graph patterns can be very useful because while you are drawing out, minor alterations can be made to size, the style can be changed or fit can be improved. All the adults' graph patterns are given in one size only – size 12, 34 inch bust – to maintain clarity and to make them easier to understand. These and the children's patterns can be adapted to a size smaller and up to two sizes larger (see page 127).

1 Quick-make hostess apron
2 Apron for a man
3 Long gathered skirt
4 Sleeveless long evening dress
5 A-line button-through skirt
6 Short nightdress
7 Short housecoat
8 Angel top for a baby
9 Baby's sleeping bag
10 Trousers and waistcoat for a teenager
11 Top and trousers for a child
12 Pleated dress for a little girl
13 Short sleeved dress for a little girl
14 Baby's play trousers
15 Pinafore dress
16 Long-sleeved classic blouse
17 Chanel-type two piece suit
18 Trouser suit
19 Pleated skirt

To make a paper pattern from a graph pattern you will need the following materials and equipment.
Squared paper. This can be obtained from the dress fabric department of some large stores and is quite inexpensive. The sheets measure 30 inches by 20 inches, and they need to be joined together for patterns with several garment pieces.
If you cannot obtain squared paper, branches of chain stationers sell graph paper which will do just as well, but it is a little more expensive and the sheets are not as large.
Ruler. Ideally, one should use a yardstick measuring 36 inches long for pattern drafting but an ordinary 12-inch rule can be used, together with a tape measure.
Pencils. Medium-soft pencils, B or 2B are best. A black felt-tipped pen is

also required for strengthening the lines of the master pattern.

Eraser for correcting mistakes
Sellotape or Scotch tape for joining pattern sheets.
Scissors – a sharp pair kept especially for paper
Tracing paper. Buy a roll of tracing paper if you decide to keep your master pattern for re-use. Trace the pattern pieces off on to the tracing paper.

Drawing out the pattern

1. Check the scale given on the graph patterns. All those here are 1 inch to 1 square, which means that every square on the graph represents a 1 inch square on your squared paper. [The squared paper will be marked off into 1-inch squares with a heavy line.]
2. Number the graph pattern squares across the top and then down the side.
3. Draw out the area of the graph pattern on the squared paper and number in the same way.
4. You have now reproduced the area you are going to work in, scaled up from the graph pattern.

5. Draw the straight lines in first, for instance the line marked 'FOLD'. Look at the sample given here and you will see that in square 1 across and 2 down the line curves upwards.
6. Mark the places where the line of the pattern touches the lines of the graph as dots on your squared paper. When all the dots showing the outline of a piece have been marked, join them up. If the line looks a bit uneven, rub out and re-draw a smooth line.
7. Draw out all the pieces in the same way.
8. Mark in very carefully all the marks and words on the pattern pieces. You have now made your master pattern.

If you have decided to increase or decrease the size of the pattern this is the point at which it should be done. If the master pattern is to be kept for re-use, trace off all the pieces on to tracing paper and make sure that all words and markings are traced off also. If the master pattern is not intended to be kept, it is now cut out ready for pinning to the fabric.

A seam allowance of $\frac{5}{8}$ inch has been included on all patterns throughout the book.

NOTE: Dotted lines on the graph pattern indicate where patterns may be lengthened or shortened.

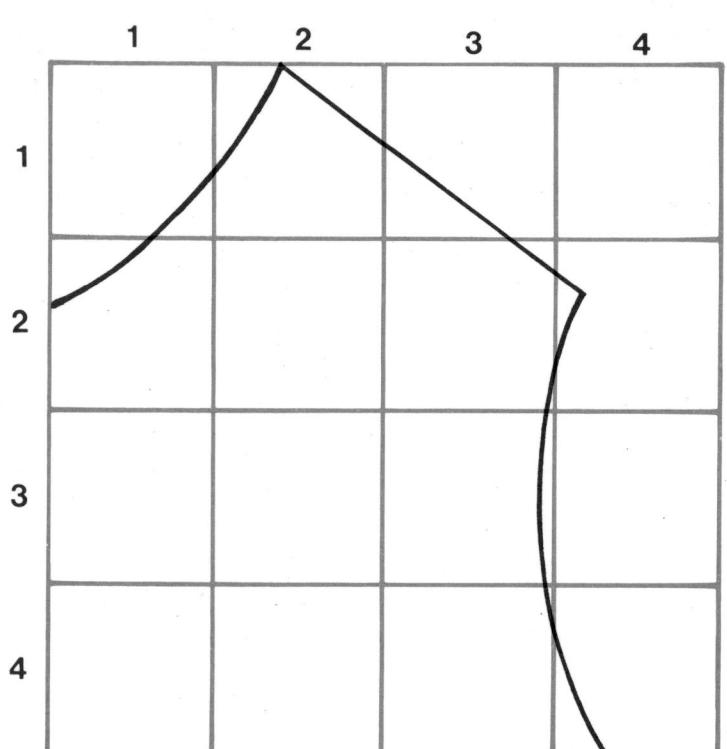

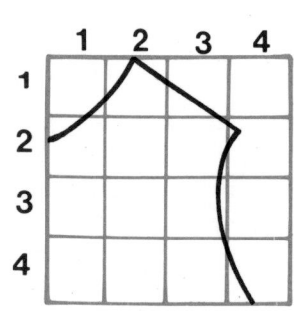

1. Mark numbers against the squares along one side and across the top of the graph pattern.

2. Tape dressmaker's squared paper together so that you have sufficient for the pattern. Number the pattern paper in the same way as the graph pattern.

3. Draw in any straight lines running vertically or horizontally first.

4. Following the graph pattern, mark dots on the lines of your pattern paper to correspond exactly with the places where the line of the pattern falls on the lines of the graph.

5. Join up the dots, following the curves of the pattern on the graph.

6. Write in all words and numerals; mark all balance marks.

Quick-make apron

No pattern is required for this apron – the pieces are simply cut to size.

Make it full-length for an apron glamorous enough to greet your guests in and add a 3-inch ruffle to the hem for a pretty look.

Materials required:

1 yard 36-inch wide fabric (for short version)
2½ yards will be required for a long apron.
Coats bias binding.
Coats Drima thread

Cutting directions

½ inch has been included for seam allowance.
Main section – 1 piece, 19 inches deep by 36 inches wide
Ties – 2 pieces, 4 inches deep by 38 inches wide.
Waistband – 1 piece, 5 inches deep by 20 inches wide.

To make up

1. Bind one long and two short edges of the main section.

2. Make two rows of gathering stitches along the seam line on the remaining edge of the main section.

3. Turn in the seam allowance on both short ends of the waistband and baste.

4. Place the gathered edge of the main section to the long edge of the waistband, matching seam lines, right sides together. Baste and stitch.

5. Fold the waistband and turn under the remaining raw edge. Baste to the seam line along the stitching.

6. Baste and stitch ¼-inch hems on the long edges and on one short end of both ties.

7. Insert the raw end of the ties into the open end of the waistband pleating to fit. Baste to secure.

8. Top-stitch the waistband all round, ⅛ inch from the edge, through all thicknesses of fabric.

For the longer version, cut the main piece 36 inches wide by 60 inches deep and do not bind the edges. Cut and join strips 4 inches deep to make a strip 90 inches wide for the ruffle. Turn a narrow hem on the two sides of the main section and make up and add the ruffle to the hem.

Apron for a man

Make this smart, hard-wearing apron for a domestically minded man and, if he is the type, add an appliqué motif to the pocket – a carrot shape, for instance, or a design of crossed spoons. In a plain fabric, the same pattern would make a gardening apron.

Materials required:
1¼ yards 36-inch wide fabric
Coats Drima thread.
Scraps of fabric for appliqué motif if required.

Cutting directions
Make a paper pattern from the graph pattern. ⅝ inch seam allowance included.
Pattern A – cut 1.
Pocket – 1 piece, 10 inches by 8½ inches.
Neckband – 1 piece, 2¼ inches by 21 inches.
Ties – 2 pieces, 2¼ inches by 30 inches

To make up
1. Fold the neckband in half lengthwise, right sides together. Baste and then stitch along the long edges. Turn to the right side.
2. Make up the ties in the same way, stitching along the long edges and one short end. Leave one short end of each tie open.
3. Turn a narrow hem on all sides of the main apron piece and machine stitch.
4. Turn a narrow hem on both ends of the neckband and press flat. Pin to the upper edge of the apron, at the corners so that the folded edge is about half an inch below the edge of the apron. Baste and then machine stitch the neckband to the apron.
5. Stitch ties to each side of the apron in the same way.
6. To neaten pocket edge, turn in ¼ inch on one short edge and stitch. Fold again 1½ inches to make a facing. Turn remaining edges to the wrong side, press and baste. Topstitch to apron.

Graph pattern for a man's apron

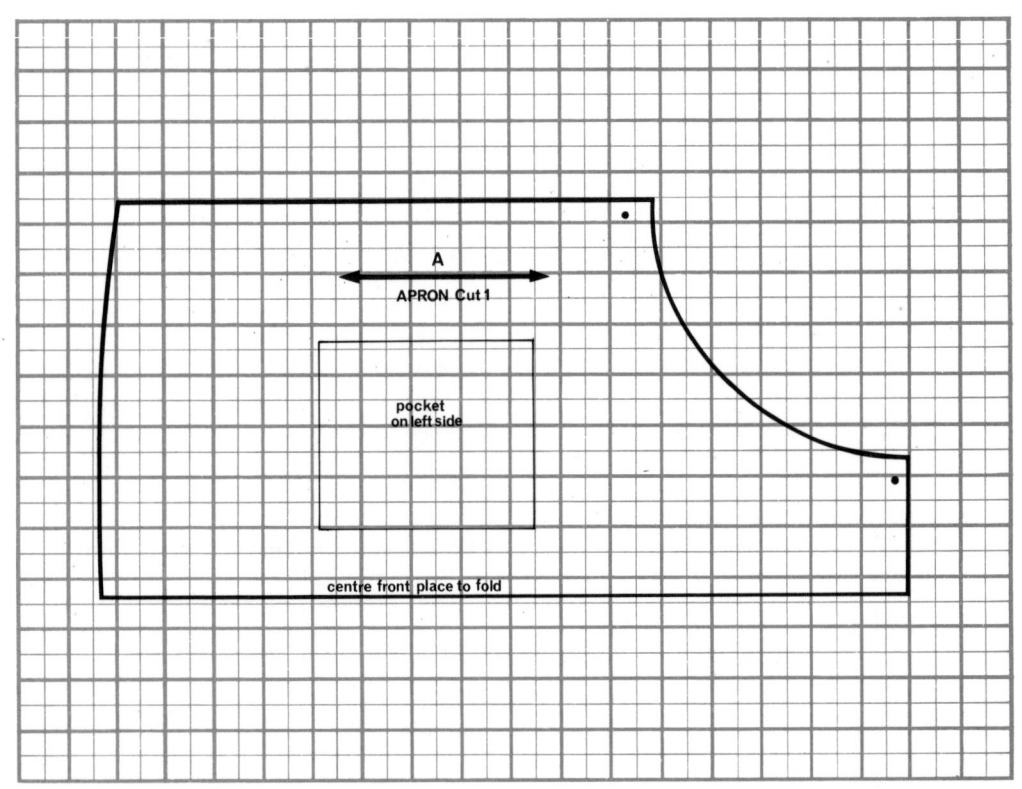

A
APRON Cut 1

pocket
on left side

centre front place to fold

1 square = 1 inch

Hostess skirt

Here is another simple garment that does not require a pattern to make it. The skirt can be made to fit any waist and hip measurement and the fabric quantities given here make a skirt $41\frac{1}{2}$ inches long from waist to hem. An alternative way to use the pattern might be to make the skirt up in a light summer fabric, cutting the length short to the knee, or in a plain fabric, trimming the hem with bands of ric-rac braid in bright, contrasting colours.

Materials required:

$1\frac{1}{3}$ yards of 54-inch wide fabric.
Interfacing for the waistband.
8-inch zip fastener.
2 hooks and eyes.
Coats Drima thread.

Cutting directions

$\frac{5}{8}$ inch has been included for seam allowance.
Skirt – 1 piece, 44 inches by 54 inches.

Waistband – 1 piece, $5\frac{3}{4}$ inches by the waist measurement plus $2\frac{3}{4}$ inches.
Waistband interlining – 1 piece $2\frac{7}{8}$ inches by the waist measurement plus $2\frac{3}{4}$ inches.

To make up

1. Fold skirt piece to make a piece 27 inches by 44 inches, baste and stitch the long edges together, leaving one end unstitched $8\frac{3}{4}$ inches for inserting the zip.
2. Insert the zip fastener. This is the Centre Back of the Skirt.
3. Make two rows of gathering stitches along the waistline seam line. Pull up the gathers to the waist measurement.
4. Make up the waistband with the interfacing and stitch to the waist of the Skirt.
5. Sew hooks and eyes to the waistband.
6. Make a hem on the lower edge. Give a final pressing and neaten all seams.

Hostess skirt

Evening dress

A sleeveless, high-necked dress which will have a favourite place in your wardrobe because it is a classic – and timeless. Make it up in any fabric which pleases you. The pattern will also adapt to make a sleeveless and very pretty blouse to wear under suits. Simply cut the pattern short 4 inches below the waist and use a shorter zip. The neckline can be given a different look by making up a soft bow and stitching it to the front of the collar or by cutting an extra length of fabric to make a scarf, stitching it to one side of the back fastening and allowing it to drape over one shoulder. The collar can be heavily beaded for a really glamorous look.

Materials required:

3¼ yards 45-inch wide fabric
Interfacing for collar.
22-inch zip fastener.
2 hooks and eyes.
Coats Drima thread.

Cutting directions

Make a paper pattern from the graph pattern, 1 square = 1 inch. ⅝ inch seam allowance has been included.

Long evening dress

Pattern A - Front cut 1 piece, facing cut off right side.
Pattern B – Back cut 2 facing cut off right side.
Pattern C – Armhole facing cut 2.
Pattern D – Collar cut 2, one from fabric, one from interfacing.

To make up

1. Baste and stitch darts on Front and Back.
2. Baste and stitch Centre Back seam, leaving 22 inches of seam unstitched for inserting zip fastener.
3. Join shoulder seams and right side seam.
4. Baste and stitch Back to Front at left seam to top of facing.
5. Insert zip fastener at Centre Back seam.
6. Make up and attach interfaced collar.
7. Sew hooks and eyes to fasten collar at back.
8. Baste and stitch armhole facings seams. Place facings to armholes, right sides facing, baste, stitch and trim. Turn to the inside of the dress. Catch facing to dress at shoulder and side seams.
9. Turn up and make the hem.
10. Turn side slit facings to the wrong side and sew lightly in position with catch-stitches.

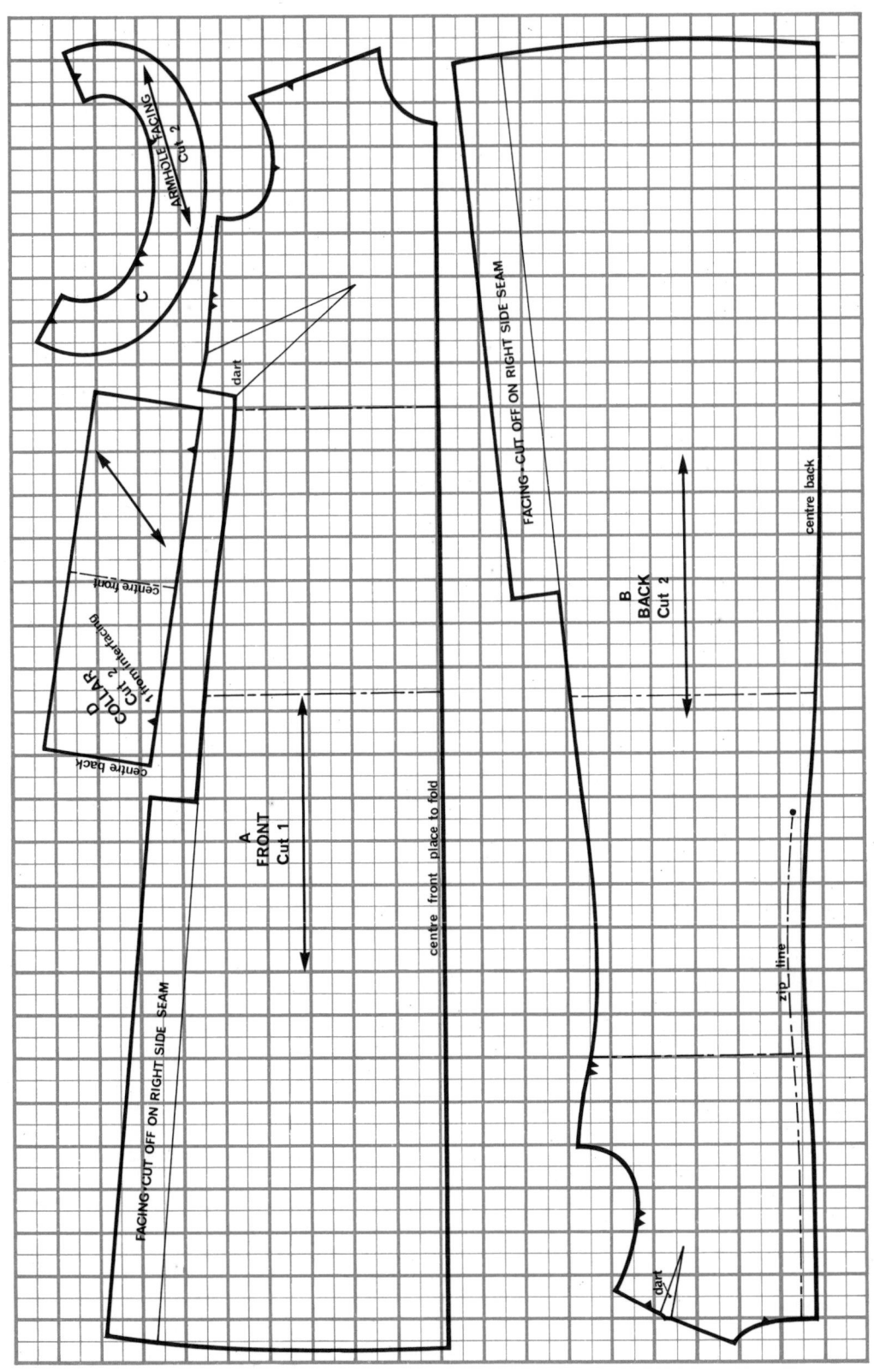

1 square = 1 inch

Simple skirt

A neat A-line skirt with a buttoned front fastening for casual wear, finished with contrast coloured top-stitching for fashion detail.

The buttonholes on the skirt illustrated were worked on a swing-needle sewing machine using the zigzag stitch, but if preferred, work bound buttonholes. The pattern can be adapted to a classic side-fastening skirt by omitting the front facings from the pattern and adding $\frac{5}{8}$ inch seam allowance to each side of centre front. Leave the left side seam open and insert a zip fastener. Make an interfaced waistband to finish.

Materials required:
$1\frac{5}{8}$ yards 54-inch wide fabric.
Interfacing for facings and waistband.
Seven 1-inch wide buttons.
Coats Drima thread.
Pearl Cotton No. 8 for top-stitching.

Cutting directions
Make a paper pattern from the graph pattern, 1 square = 1 inch. $\frac{5}{8}$ inch seam allowances have been included.
Pattern A – Front cut 2
Pattern B – Back cut 1
Pattern C – Front waist facing cut 4, (2 from interfacing)

Pattern D – Back waist facing cut 4, (2 from interfacing)
Front facings – cut 2 strips from interfacing, 2 inches by Centre Front measurement

To make up
1. Baste and stitch back and front darts.
2. Baste front interfacings to wrong side of front sections.
3. Baste and stitch Skirt Fronts and Skirt Backs at side seams.
4. Baste waist interfacings to waist facings.
5. Baste and stitch front facings to back waist facings at side seams.
6. Baste and stitch skirt waist facing to skirt front facings at side seams. Edge stitch remainder of inner edge of facing.
7. Turn facing to outside along fold line. Baste and stitch waist edge. Sew facing lightly to darts and seams.
8. Mitre corners at hem by bringing seam lines right sides together, baste and stitch. Trim seam and turn to the wrong side.
9. Make hem on lower edge.
Make buttonholes on right front of skirt. Sew buttons to correspond.
10. Top stitch $\frac{1}{4}$ inch from skirt edges by winding Pearl cotton No. 8 on bobbin of sewing machine. Thread machine with Drima thread and set machine for longest stitch. Machine from wrong side of fabric.

Graph pattern for A-line skirt

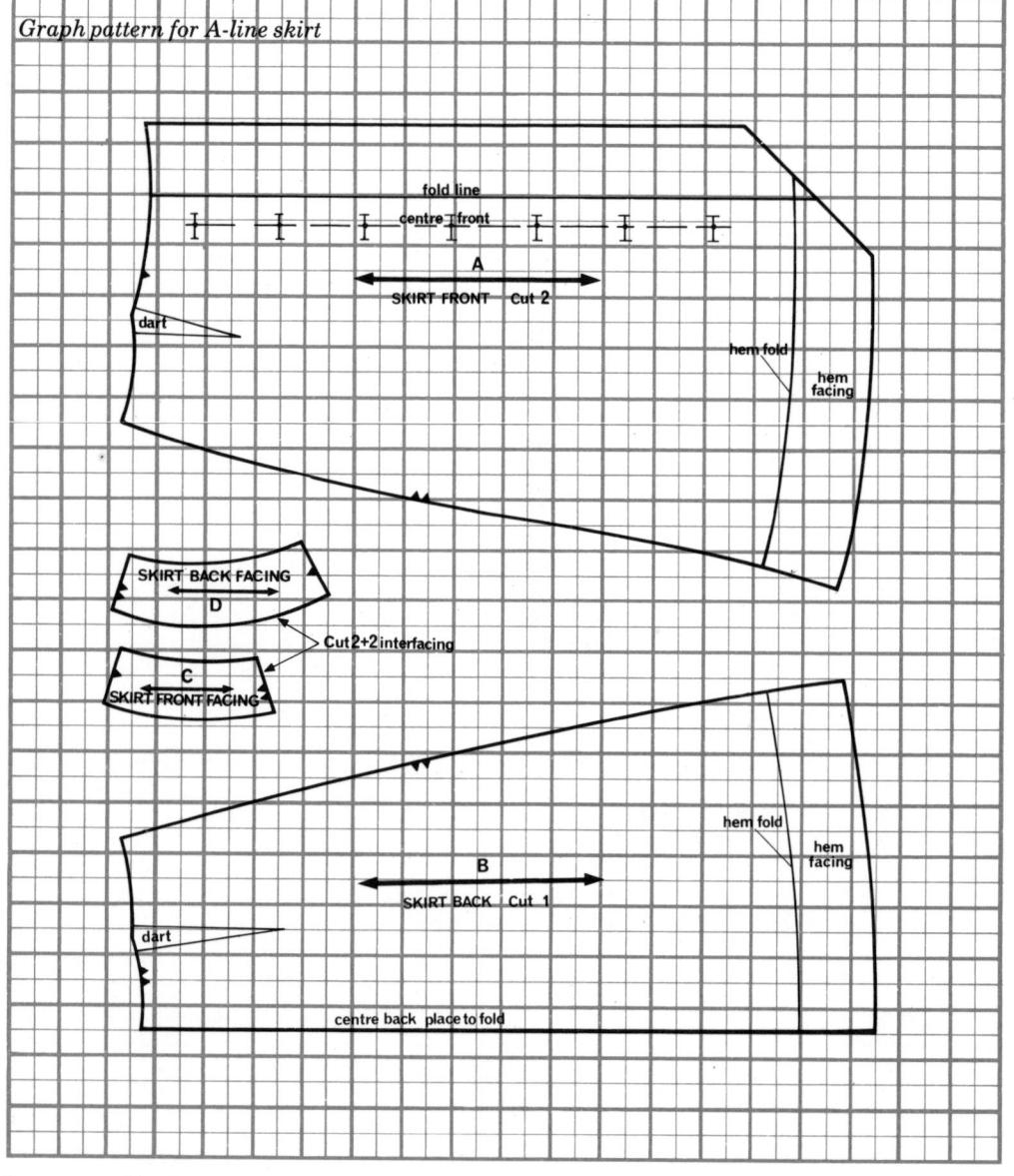

fold line

centre front

A

SKIRT FRONT   Cut 2

dart

hem fold

hem facing

SKIRT BACK FACING

D

Cut 2+2 interfacing

C

SKIRT FRONT FACING

hem fold

hem facing

B

SKIRT BACK   Cut 1

dart

centre back place to fold

1 square = 1 inch

Nightdress

A sweetly pretty nightdress to make from a very simple pattern. The nightdress illustrated was made up in broderie anglaise but an equally pretty effect would be achieved with flowered cotton lawn, dotted Swiss or two layers of Terylene organdie or chiffon. The pattern can be extended very easily to make a full-length nightdress and bias-cut ruffles could be added to the neckline and to the hem.

Materials required:

2¾ yards 45-inch wide fabric.
Coats Drima thread.
(allow 1 yard extra fabric for ruffles).

Cutting directions

Make a paper pattern from the graph pattern

1 square = 1 inch. ⅝ inch seam allowance has been included.
Pattern A – Front cut 1.
Pattern B – Back cut 1
Cut bias strip 1½ inches wide for neck binding, armhole binding and bow and join for length.

To make up

1. Gather neckline edge of Front piece as required.
2. Gather Back piece neckline in the centre for four inches.
3. Join shoulder seams and side seams.
4. Apply bias binding to the neckline, and the armholes.
5. Make rouleau for the front bow and stitch in position.
6. Make the hem.

189

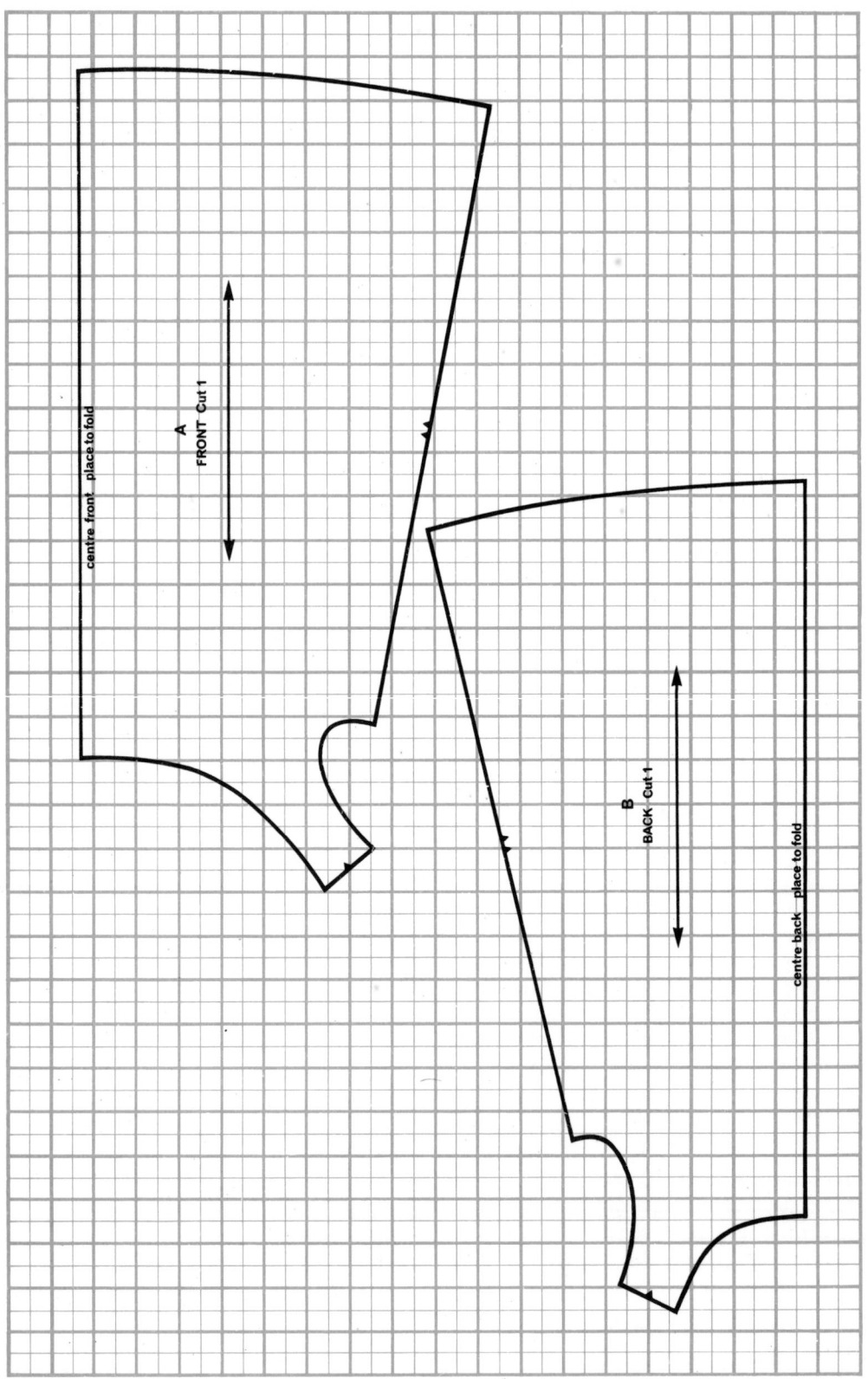

centre front · place to fold

A
FRONT Cut 1

B
BACK · Cut 1

centre back · place to fold

1 square = 1 inch

Housecoat

This easy-to-wear raglan-sleeved housecoat can be made up in the same fabric as the nightdress or, as shown, in a contrasting fabric. The pattern makes up equally well in winter-weight fabrics, such as Courtelle, which require no lining.

The housecoat can of course be cut as a full-length garment and if preferred the facings can be left off the pattern and seam allowances added to Centre Front pieces. A zip fastener closing can then be inserted, either from neckline to hem or simply from neckline to a given point. For this type of fastening, the zip should be open-ended.

Materials required:

4 yards 36-inch wide fabric.
$10 \times \frac{3}{4}$ inch buttons.
Gathered edging if required.
Coats Drima thread.

Cutting directions

Make a paper pattern from the graph pattern 1 square = 1 inch.
$\frac{5}{8}$ inch seam allowance has been included.
Pattern A – Front cut 2
Pattern B – Back cut 2.
Pattern C – Sleeve cut 2.
Pattern D – Back neck facing cut 1.

Pattern E – Pocket cut 2.

To make up

1. Baste and stitch Centre Back seam.
2. Baste and stitch front darts and sleeve shoulder darts.
3. Baste and join front to back at side seams.
4. Baste and stitch sleeve seams.
5. Stitch sleeves to main section. Clip curves so that they lie flat.
6. Stitch shoulder seams of back neck facing to front facing.
7. Fold back facing to outside on fold line. Stitch neck edge. Clip seams and turn to the wrong side. Catch facing to housecoat shoulder darts and sleeve seams.
8. Make hems on sleeves and lower edges.
9. Fold pocket pieces in half, right sides together on fold line. Baste and stitch leaving an opening for turning to right side.
10. Turn to right side and slipstitch opening.
11. Stitch trimming round front and neck edges.
12. Baste trimming to curved pocket edges. Stitch pockets to housecoat fronts.
13. Make buttonholes on right front. Sew buttons on left front to correspond.

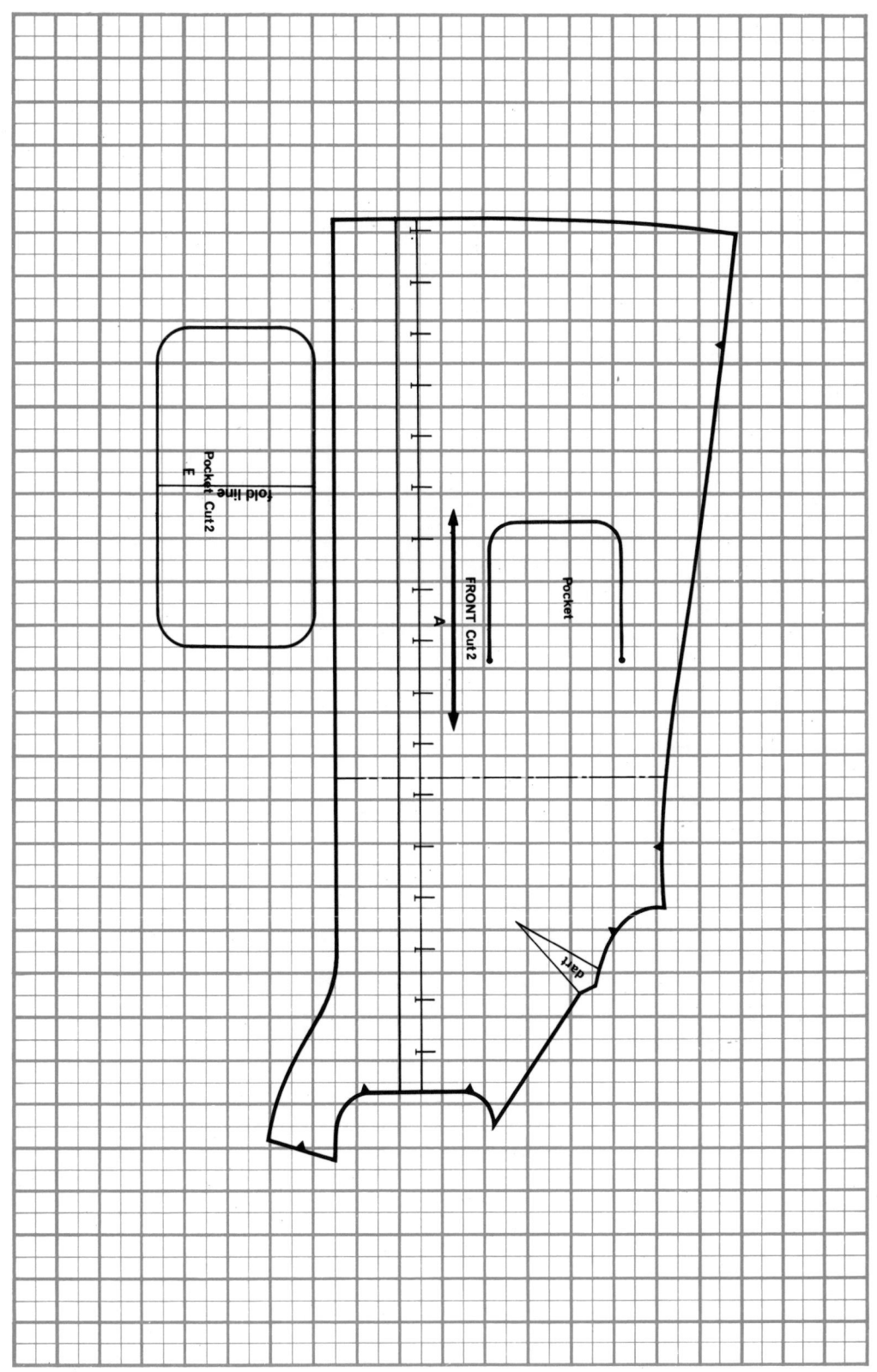

Pocket Cut 2
fold line
F

FRONT Cut 2
A
Pocket
dart

1 square = 1 inch

193

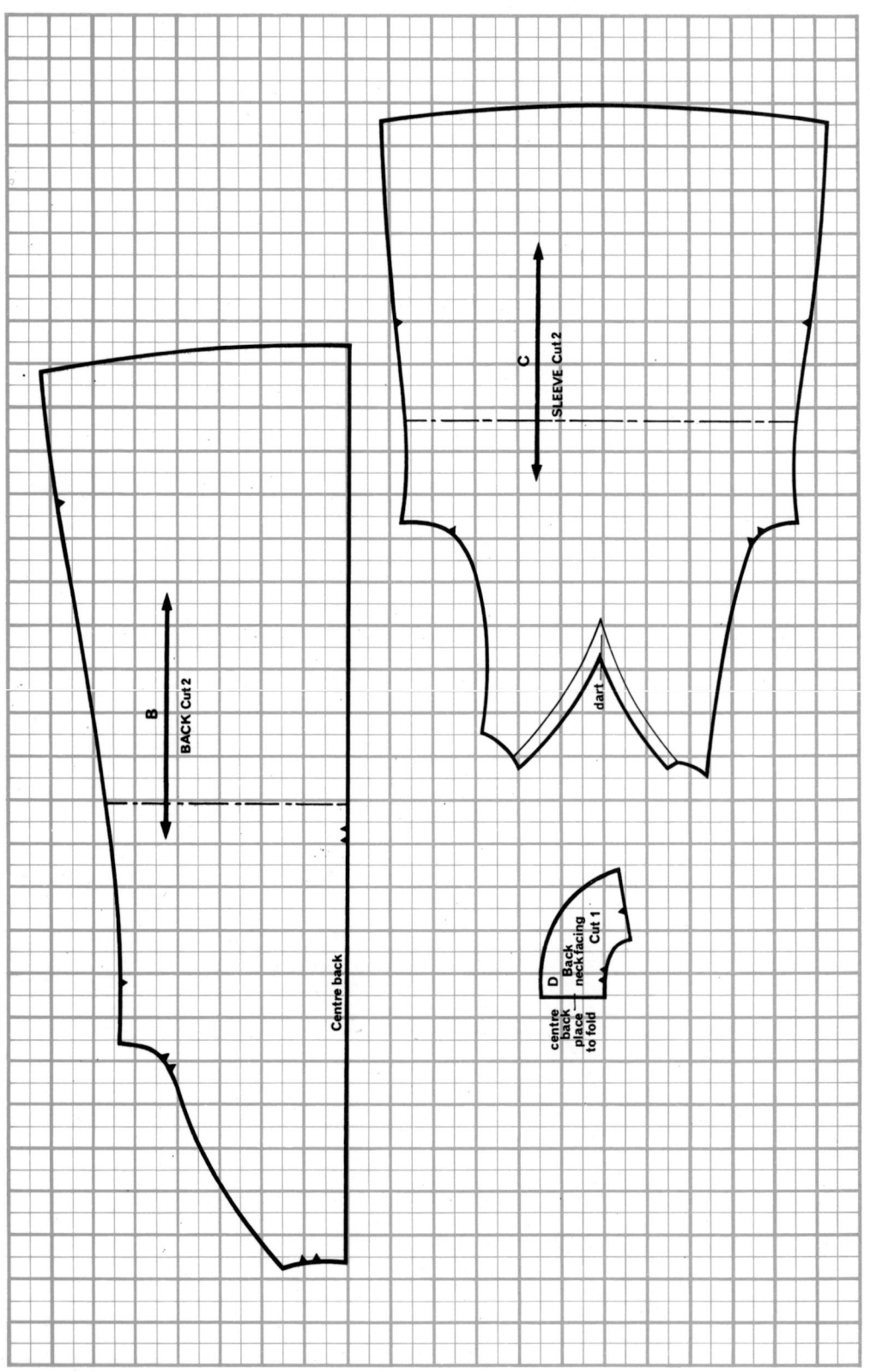

SLEEVE Cut 2

C

B

BACK Cut 2

Centre back

dart

D

Back neck facing

Cut 1

centre back place to fold

1 square = 1 inch

Baby's angel top

A pretty angel top for a six-month-old baby, to sew in light-weight fabrics. French seams would be ideal to give a flat neat seam finish but plain seams can be worked if you prefer.

Materials required:

1 yard 36-inch wide fabric.
$\frac{1}{4}$ yard narrow elastic.
Coats bias binding.
$3 \times \frac{1}{4}$-inch buttons.
Coats Drima thread.

Cutting directions

Make paper pattern from the graph pattern 1 square = 1 inch. $\frac{5}{8}$ inch seam allowances have been included.
Pattern A – Front skirt cut 1.
Pattern B – Back cut 1.
Pattern C – Yoke cut 2

To make up

Pattern D – Sleeve cut 2.
Cut bias strip for finishing off neck edge.
1. Gather yoke seam line on Front skirt between notches.

2. Place right side of one yoke section to wrong side of skirt, matching raw edges. Pull up gathers to fit. Baste.
3. Baste second yoke section, right sides together with raw edges even along gathered edge. Stitch all thicknesses of fabric. Baste yoke sections together.
4. Make a narrow hem on sleeve edges. Make wrist casings with bias binding on the wrong side of the fabric.
5. Cut elastic to baby's wrist measurement plus 1 inch. Insert through casings. Stitch ends to seam allowance of sleeve.
6. To make the back opening, slit from neck edge down the centre of the back skirt to the dot. Make a $\frac{1}{4}$-inch clip at the lower end of the slit. Turn in $\frac{1}{4}$-inch hems on slit edges and stitch.
7. Press stitched edges to inside along fold line and sew in place. Overlap right opening edge over left to form a pleat below the opening. Stitch through all thicknesses at end of slit.
8. Baste sleeves to front and back sections, right sides together. Stitch then clip curves.
9. Baste and stitch front to back along entire underarm and side seams.

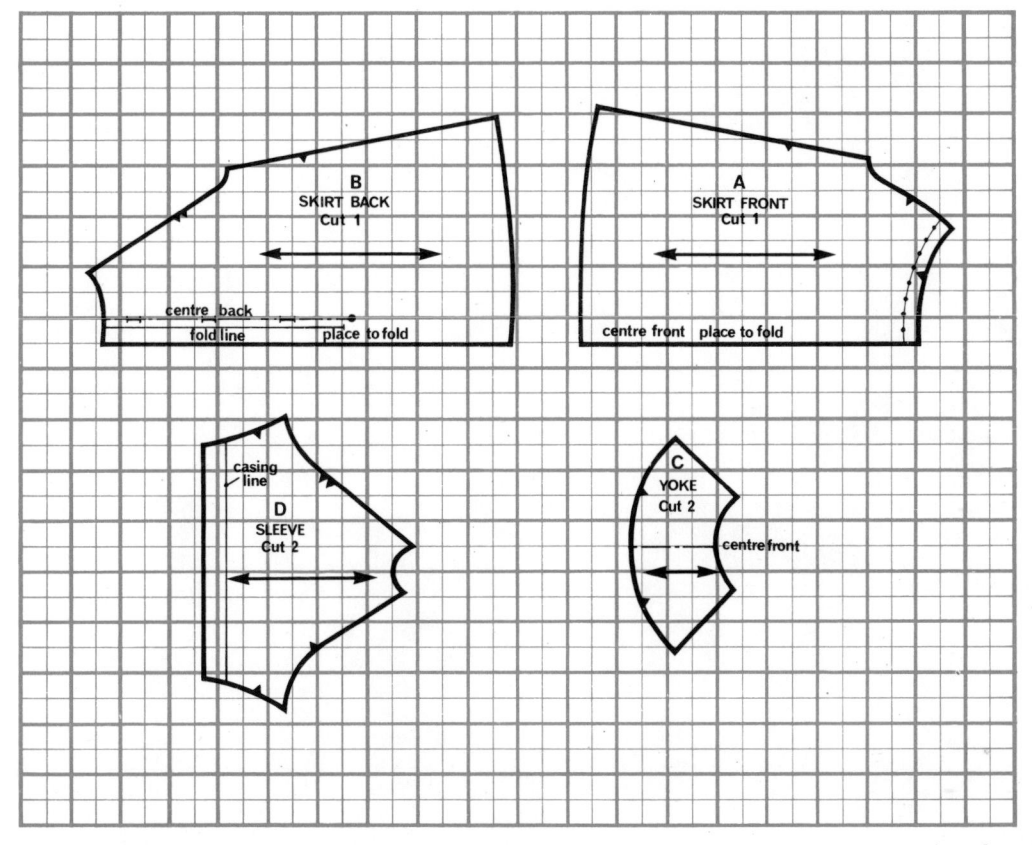

B
SKIRT BACK
Cut 1

centre back
fold line   place to fold

A
SKIRT FRONT
Cut 1

centre front   place to fold

casing
line
D
SLEEVE
Cut 2

C
YOKE
Cut 2

centre front

1 square = 1 inch

Angel top

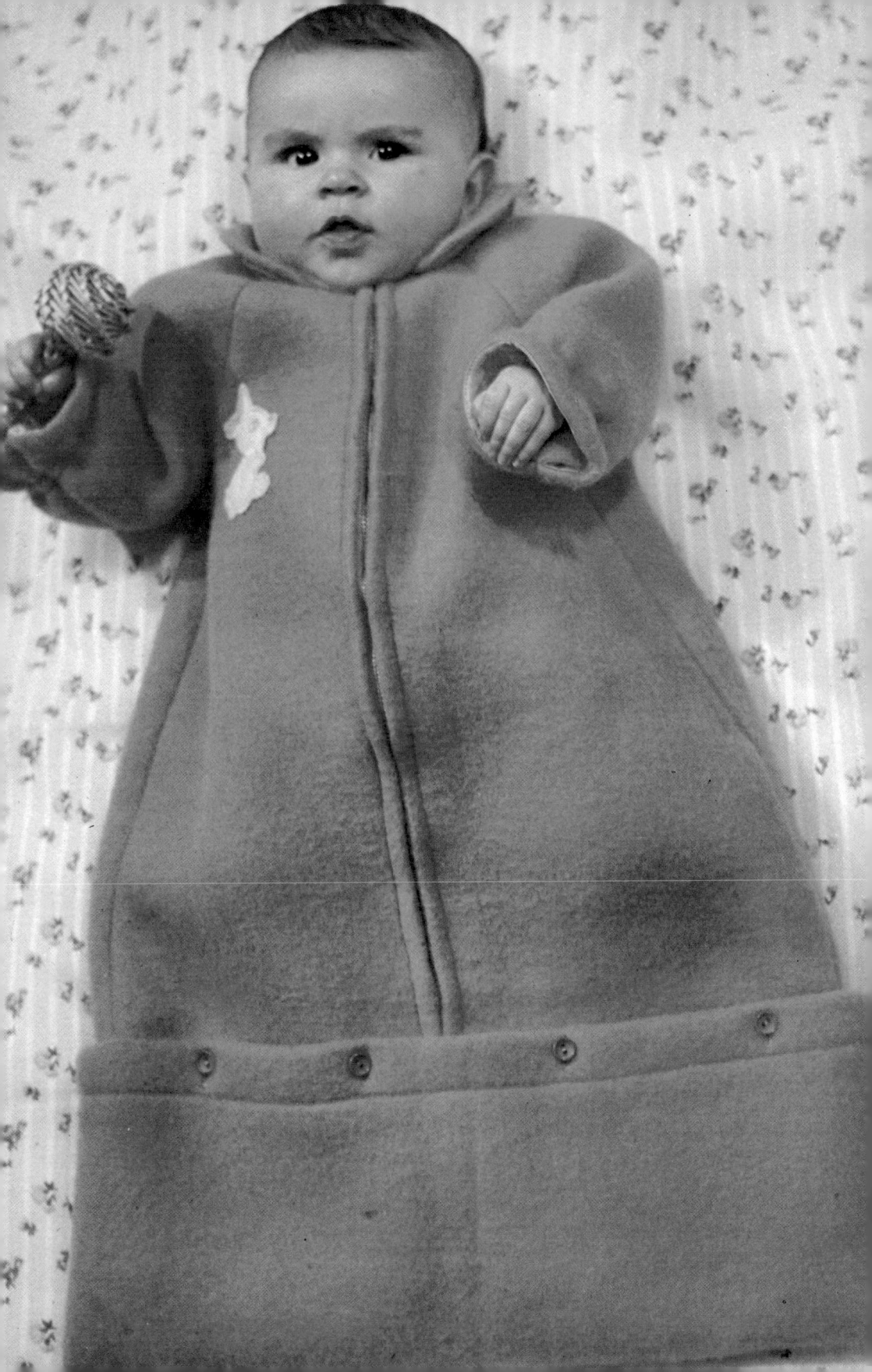

Snug sleeping bag

Made in brushed wool fabric, this cosy bag keeps a baby warm in his perambulator if he is inclined to kick the covers off and is an ideal travelling outfit. This size is for a six month old baby, with an approximate length of 24 inches.

Materials required:

1⅝ yards 36-inch wide fabric.
20 inch open end zip fastener.
8 × ½-inch buttons.
Coats Bias binding.
1 hook and eye.
¼-inch elastic for wrists.
Coats Drima thread.

Cutting directions

Make paper pattern from graph pattern
1 square = 1 inch. ⅝ inch seam allowance included.
Pattern A – Front cut 2.
Pattern B – Back cut 1.
Pattern C – Collar cut 2.
Pattern D – Sleeve cut 2.
Pattern E – Bag bottom cut 1.

To make up

1. Strengthen button positions by basting bias binding to the wrong sides of Front and Back section on button line.
2. Sew binding to wrong sides of sleeve pieces to make wrist casings.
3. Make narrow hems on sleeve edges.
4. Stitch sleeves to Front and Back sections, right sides facing.
5. Place collar section together right sides facing. Stitch the curved edge. Turn to right side. Top stitch ¼ inch from curved edge.
6. Join collar section to neck edge.
7. Insert zip fastener at Centre Front and continue machine stitching to lower edge of section.
8. Insert elastic through wrist casings. Stitch ends to sleeve.
9. Stitch entire underarm and side seams in one continuous seam.
10. Make a narrow hem on lower edge.
11. Fold bottom bag section in half, right sides facing. Baste and stitch short ends.
12. Make hems on long edges. Turn to right side.
13. Make 8 buttonholes, 4 on front, 4 on back. Sew buttons to correspond.

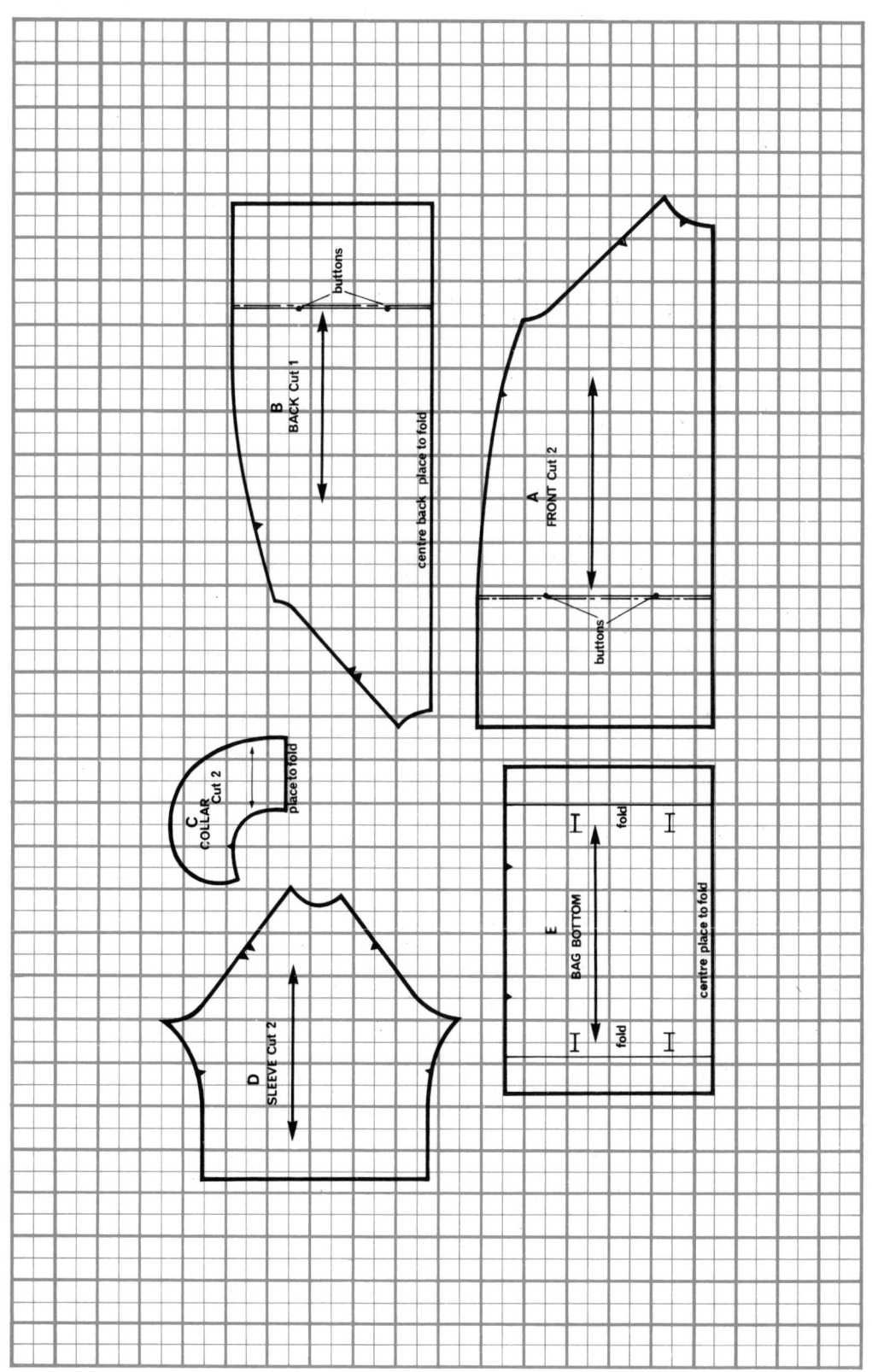

1 square = 1 inch

Teenager's suit

A very easy-to-make trouser and waistcoat outfit for girls aged 12 to 15 years.

The size of the graph pattern will fit bust 30 inches, waist 25½ inches and hips 32 inches, with the finished length of the trousers, from the waist, 36 inches. The pattern can be both lengthened and enlarged to fit older girls.

The suit shown has been made up in a hard-wearing denim fabric, but you can use almost any fabric from cotton velvet to seersucker and it will still look smart and be comfortable. Made in a plain fabric, the waistcoat lends itself well to all kinds of decoration, from appliqué motifs to embroidery in Raffene.

Materials required:

Trousers:

2¼ yards 36-inch wide fabric.
6-inch zip fastener.
Elastic, ¼ inch wide to fit back waist measurement plus 2 inches.
1 hook and bar fastener.
Coats Drima thread.

Waistcoat:

1¼ yards 36-inch wide fabric.
1¼ yards 36-inch wide lining fabric.
Coats Drima thread.

Cutting directions

Make a paper pattern from graph pattern 1 square = 1 inch. ⅝ inch seam allowance has been included.

Trousers
Pattern A – Front cut 2.
Pattern B – Back cut 2.
Pattern C – Front Facing cut 1

Waistcoat
Pattern D – Front cut 4, (2 from lining).
Pattern E – Back cut 2, (1 from lining).

To make up

Trousers
1. Baste and stitch darts on front sections.
2. Stitch Centre Front seam.
3. Stitch front facing to front waist edge, right sides together, turn to wrong side.
4. Baste and stitch Centre Back seam.
5. Fold back waist edge on fold line to inside. Baste and stitch a ½-inch casing. Insert elastic inside casing. Secure at both ends.
6. Join front section to back at side seams, making sure that front facing is not caught in the seam. Leave left side open for zip.
7. Insert zip fastener.
8. Turn down waist facing, turn in ends and sew to seams.
9. Sew hook and bar above zip fastener. Make hems on trouser ends.

Waistcoat
1. Stitch Front to Back at side seams.
2. Stitch front lining to back lining at side seams, leaving part of the seam unstitched for turning inside out.
3. Press shoulder seam allowance to the wrong side.
4. Place lining on outer fabric sections, right sides facing. Stitch all edges except the shoulder edges. Turn to right side through opening in side seam. Slipstitch seam closed.
5. Stitch shoulder seams of outer fabric section, right sides together. Trim seams. Slip seam allowance under lining. Slipstitch shoulder edges of lining together.

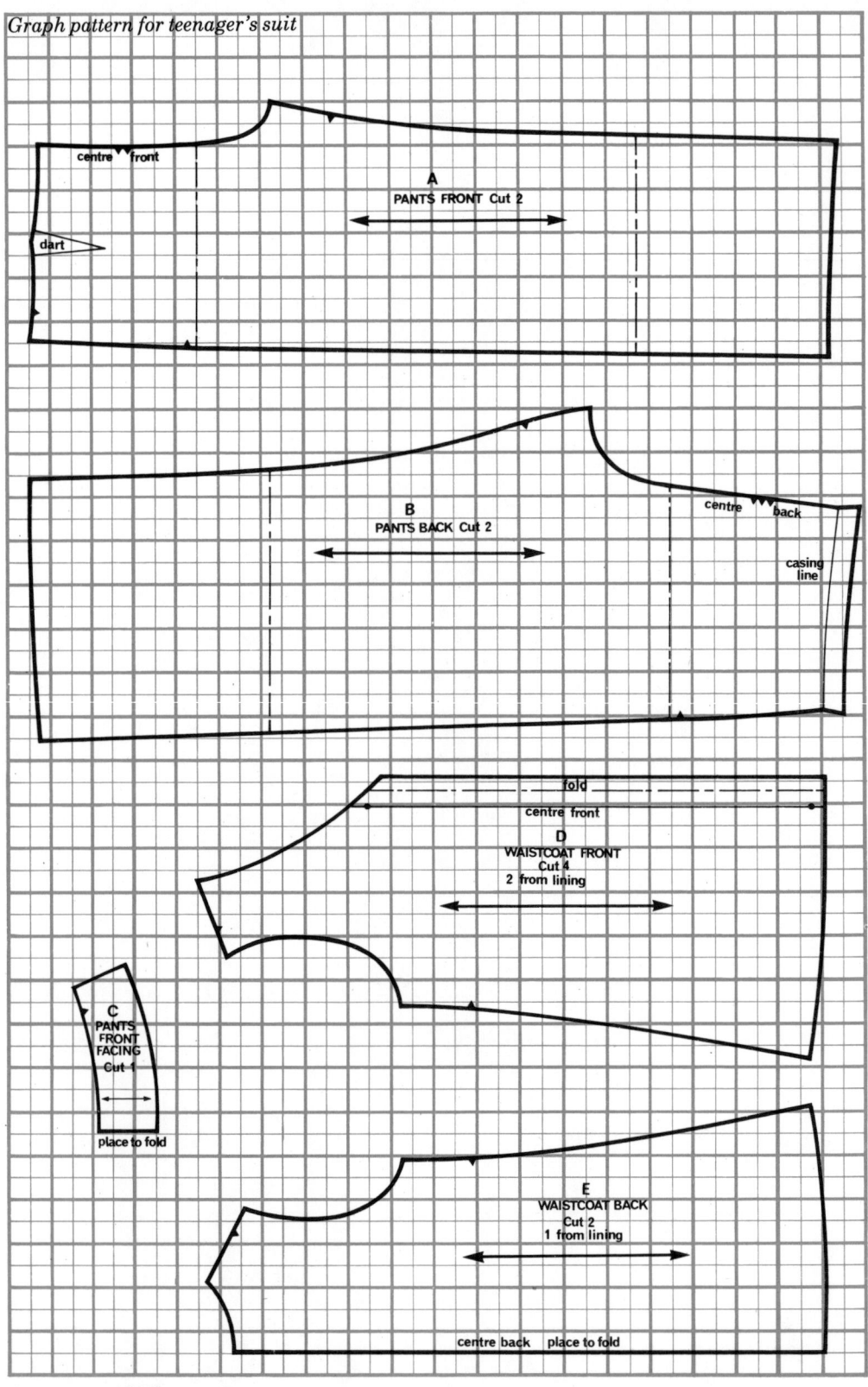

Graph pattern for teenager's suit

centre front

A
PANTS FRONT Cut 2

dart

B
PANTS BACK Cut 2

centre back

casing line

fold

centre front

D
WAISTCOAT FRONT
Cut 4
2 from lining

C
PANTS
FRONT
FACING
Cut 1

place to fold

E
WAISTCOAT BACK
Cut 2
1 from lining

centre back   place to fold

1 square = 1 inch

Child's trouser suit

This trouser suit is styled so that it can be worn either by a boy or a girl, depending on the fabric chosen. For a girl, the sleeves can be left out of the bodice and the armholes finished with bias-cut binding, to make a sleeveless summer suit.

Measurements

Chest 23 inches; Waist 21 inches; Top length from neck to hem 16 inches.
Trousers – finished length from waist $24\frac{1}{2}$ inches.

Materials required

Top
$1\frac{1}{8}$ yards 45-inch wide fabric.
$3 \times \frac{1}{2}$-inch buttons.
7-inch zip fastener.

Trousers
$1\frac{5}{8}$ yards 36-inch wide fabric
$\frac{5}{8}$ yard elastic $\frac{3}{4}$-inch wide.
Coats Drima thread.

Cutting directions

Make a paper pattern from the graph pattern 1 square = 1 inch. $\frac{5}{8}$ inch seam allowance included.

Trousers
Pattern A – Front cut 2.
Pattern B – Back cut 2.

Top
Pattern C – Front cut 1
Pattern D – Back cut 2.
Pattern E – Front cut 1.
Pattern F – Back facing cut 2.
Pattern G – Tab cut 1
Pattern H – Sleeve cut 2.

To make up

Top
1. Stitch Centre Back seam leaving opening for zip fastener.
2. Make up tab as follows: turn in seam allowance on two long sides and short straight edge. Press. Baste in place to top front neck edge, matching centres. Stitch in position.
3. Join Back to Front at shoulder seams.
4. Join front facing to back facing at shoulder seams.
5. Stitch facing to neck edge, right sides facing. Turn to inside and catch facing to shoulder seams.
6. Insert zip fastener at centre back seam; avoid catching neck facing.
7. Turn in neck facing short ends, stitch to zip tape.
8. Stitch sleeves in armholes at the sleeve crown.
9. Stitch sleeve seams and side seams in one continuous seam.
10. Hem sleeve edges.
11. Hem lower edge of top.
12. Sew buttons to front tab.

Trousers
1. Join one front section to one back section at side and inner leg seams.
2. Place one leg inside the other, right sides together. Stitch centre seam.
3. Stitch $1\frac{1}{2}$-inch casing at waist, leaving opening for inserting elastic.
4. Insert elastic, overlap ends, stitch securely by hand.
5. Close casing opening. Make hem on leg sections.

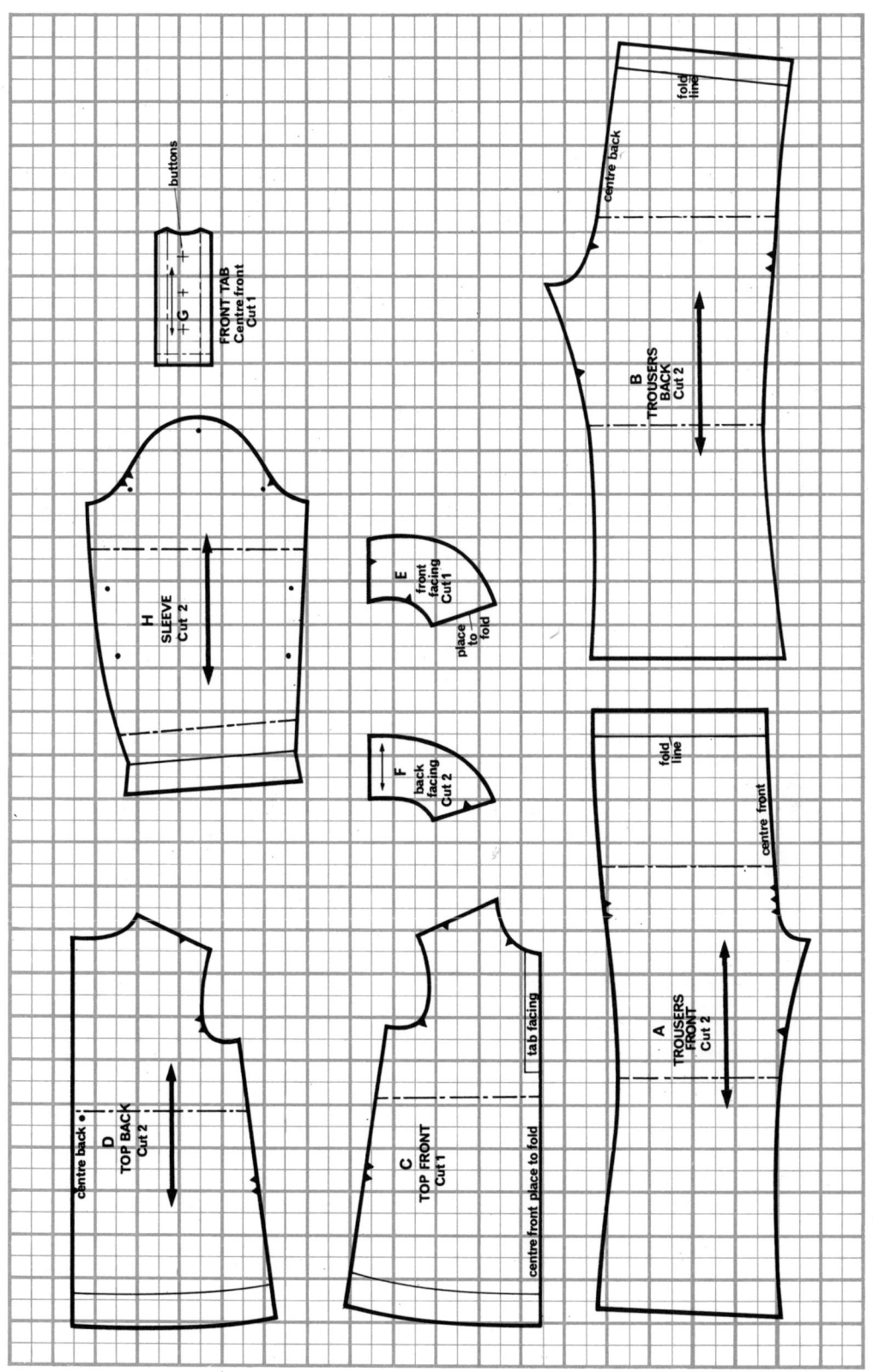

1 square = 1 inch

Pleated party dress

This pattern makes up well in cotton or light-weight wool fabrics for day wear but made with a full length skirt and in cotton voile, it is a perfect style for a bridesmaid's dress. The sleeves can be left out of the bodice for a sleeveless summer style.

Measurements

Chest 24 inches; Waist 21½ inches; Hips 25 inches; Finished length 22 inches.

Materials required:

1⅝ yards 36 inch wide fabric.
¼ yard fabric for yoke lining (this can be the same as the top fabric, in which case 2⅛ yards altogether is required).
14 inch zip fastener.
Coats Drima thread.

Cutting directions

Make paper pattern from graph pattern
1 square = 1 inch. ⅝ inch seam allowance included.
Pattern A – Front yoke cut 2 (1 for lining).
Pattern B – Back yoke cut 4 (2 for lining).
Pattern C – Front skirt cut 1.
Pattern D – Back skirt cut 2.
Pattern E – Sleeve cut 2.

French seams should be used, otherwise use plain seams.

To make up

1. Make pleats on Front Skirt section as follows: fold along solid lines and bring to meet the broken lines, working on the right side of the fabric. Press. Baste along top edge.
2. Join Front fabric Yoke section to Front Skirt, matching centres. Press seam upwards.
3. Stitch Centre Back seam of skirt leaving opening for zip fastener.
4. Make pleats on Back Skirt following the same method as for front.
5. Stitch Back Yoke fabric section to Back Skirt matching centres. Press seam upwards.
6. Join Front to Back at shoulder seams.
7. Join front lining yoke to back lining yoke at shoulder seams. Press seam allowance to wrong side at lower edges.
8. Place lining yoke to dress yoke right sides facing. Stitch Centre Back edges and neck edge. Clip curves, trim and turn to wrong side. Sew lining to yoke above machine stitching.
9. Insert zip fastener.
10. Join Front to Back at side seams. Stitch sleeve seams.
11. Make hems on sleeve edges.
13. Insert sleeves in bodice armholes.
14. Make hem on lower edge.

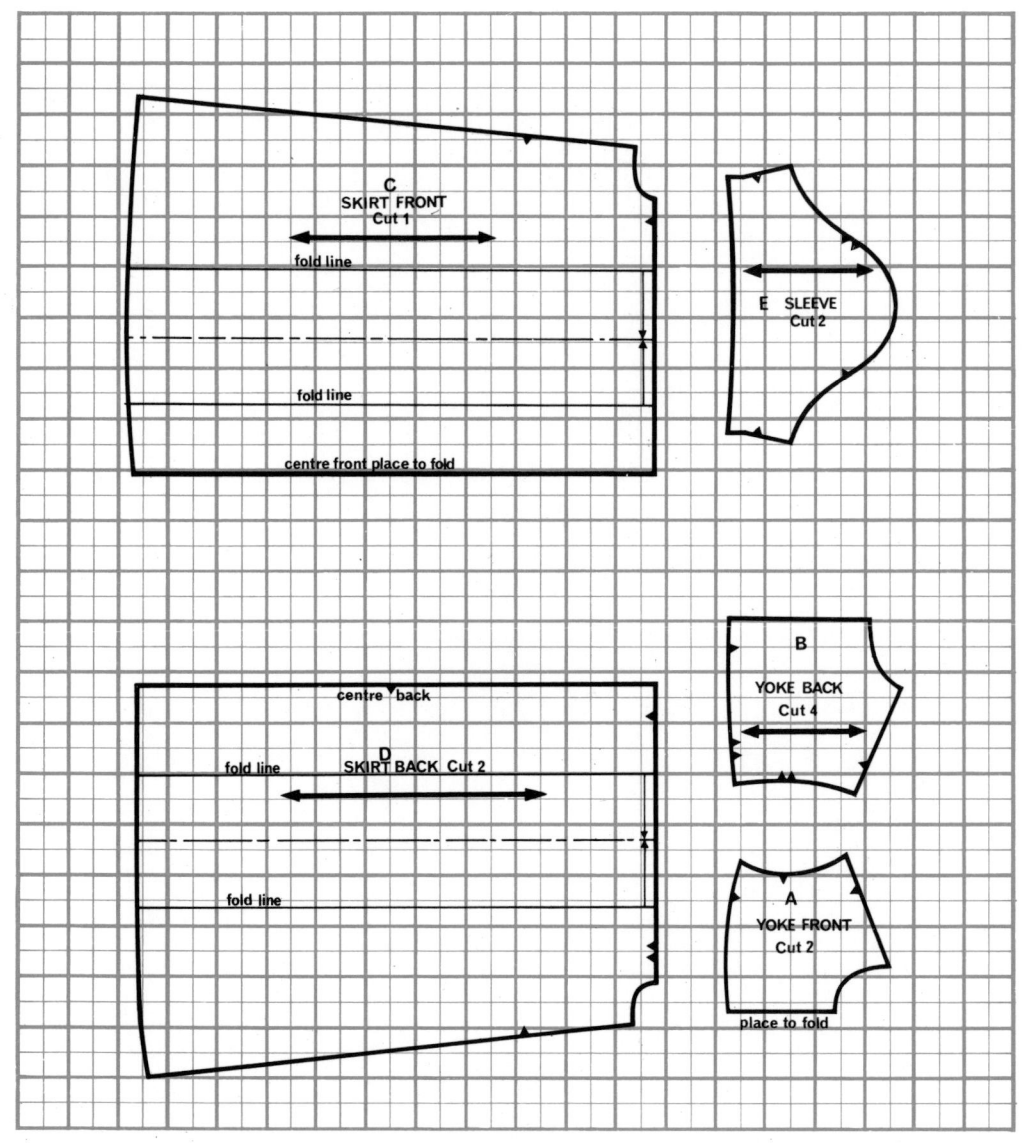

1 square = 1 inch

Child's pleated dress

Adaptable child's dress

A very straightforward dress like this can be made up in different colours and take a little girl through school days and holidays alike. The neckline can be finished off with bias-cut binding, with a narrow trimming or, if preferred, with a Peter Pan collar. Make the collar up in piqué and keep it as a detachable trim for a quick way of making the dress look different.

Measurements

Chest 23 inches; Waist 21 inches; Finished back length from neck to hem 20 inches.

Materials required:

1¼ yards 45-inch wide fabric.
12-inch zip fastener.
1⅛ yards trimming for version illustrated.
Coats Drima thread.

Cutting directions

Make paper pattern from graph pattern 1 square = 1 inch. ⅝ inch seam allowance. included.
Pattern A – Front bodice cut 1.
Pattern B – Back bodice cut 2.
Pattern C – Front neck facing cut 1.
Pattern D – Back neck facing cut 2.
Pattern E – Skirt Front cut 1.
Pattern F – Skirt back cut 2.
Pattern G – Sleeve cut 2.
Pattern H – Peter Pan collar cut 4.

To make up

1. Baste and stitch Back Bodice darts.
2. Stitch shoulder seams and side seams of Front bodice to Back bodice.
3. Stitch Centre Back seam of skirt leaving part of the seam open for inserting the zip.
4. Stitch side seams of Front skirt and Back skirt.
5. Pin bodice to skirt, right sides facing. Stitch side seams to join.
6. Insert zip fastener at Centre Back.
7. Join front neck facing to back neck facing at shoulder seams.
8. Place neck facing to neck edge, right sides together. Stitch, grade seams, clip curves, turn to inside. Catch facing to shoulder seams and to zip fastener tape.
9. Stitch sleeve seams.
10. Hem sleeve edges.
11. Insert sleeves in bodice.
Make skirt hem and stitch on trimming to cover seams if required. Make up Peter Pan collar as instructed on page 152.

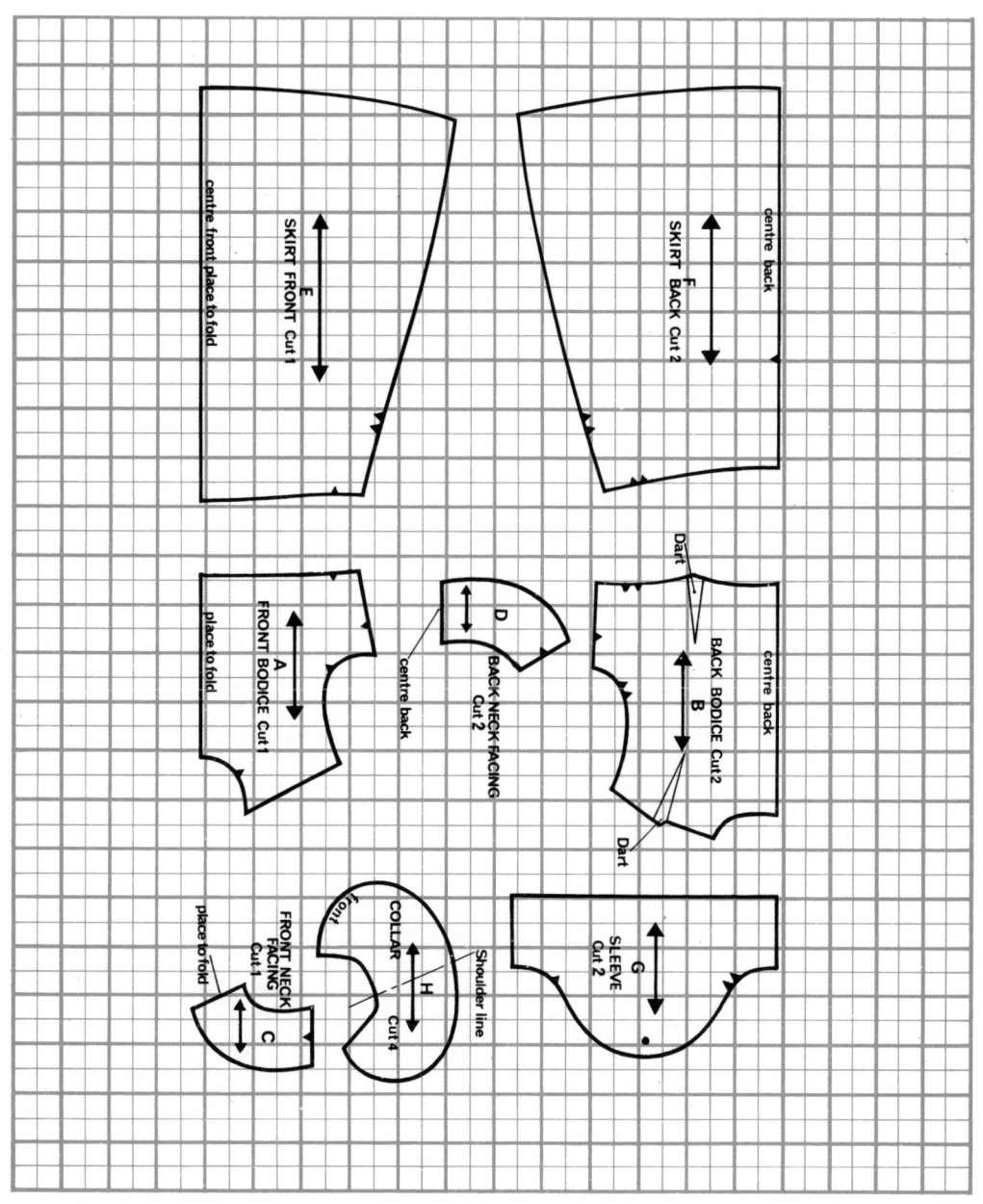

1 square = 1 inch

Toddler's dungarees

Dungarees, made in a hardwearing cotton needlecord keep a small child trim-looking, warm and comfortable. Make sure that you choose a non-shrink and washable fabric and make the play trousers for either a boy or a girl.

Measurements

Chest 21 inches; Waist 20 inches.

Materials required

$1\frac{1}{8}$ yards 36-inch wide fabric.
$4 \times \frac{1}{2}$-inch buttons.
12 inches $\frac{3}{4}$-inch wide elastic.
Coats Drima thread.

Cutting directions

Make a paper pattern from graph pattern 1 square = 1 inch. $\frac{5}{8}$ inch seam allowance has been included.
Pattern A – Front cut 2.
Pattern B – Back cut 2.
Pattern C – Bib cut 2.
Pattern D – Front waistband cut 1.
Pattern E – Suspender strap cut 2.
Pattern F – Pocket cut 2.

To make up

1. Join Centre Front seam.
2. Neaten pocket facing; turn under $\frac{1}{4}$ inch on upper edge and top stitch. Turn upper edge of pocket to right side along fold line and baste to make facing. Stitch along facing at side edges. Turn facing to wrong side. Press under remaining raw edges to wrong side.
3. Stitch pockets in place on front.
4. Stitch bib sections together, right sides facing, leaving one long edge open to turn. Trim seams and corners. Turn to right side.
5. Baste bib to wrong side of Front.
6. Join Centre Back seam of trousers.
7. Stitch Front to Back at side seams. Clip seam allowance to dot. Press seam open below clips and towards fronts above clip.
8. Stitch inner leg seams.
9. Stitch hem at waist back to form 1-inch casing for elastic.
10. Insert elastic and adjust to fit. Stitch elastic to trousers through all thicknesses of fabric.
11. On Front waistband, press seam allowance to wrong side on long unnotched edge and short ends.
12. Baste wrong side of trousers front to right side of band. Stitch and press seam upwards.
13. Turn band to outside, baste pressed edges over seams. Topstitch all edges of the band.
14. Fold suspender straps in half lengthwise, right sides facing. Baste and stitch taking $\frac{3}{8}$-inch seams and leaving opening for turning. Turn to right side and slipstitch to close.
15. Make a buttonhole at the shaped end of both suspender straps. Sew a button to the square end of both suspender straps.
16. Sew two buttons to inside of back top edge of trousers as marked on pattern.
17. Make buttonholes in bib at each top corner.
18. Make hem on trouser edges.

214

Graph pattern for toddler's dungarees

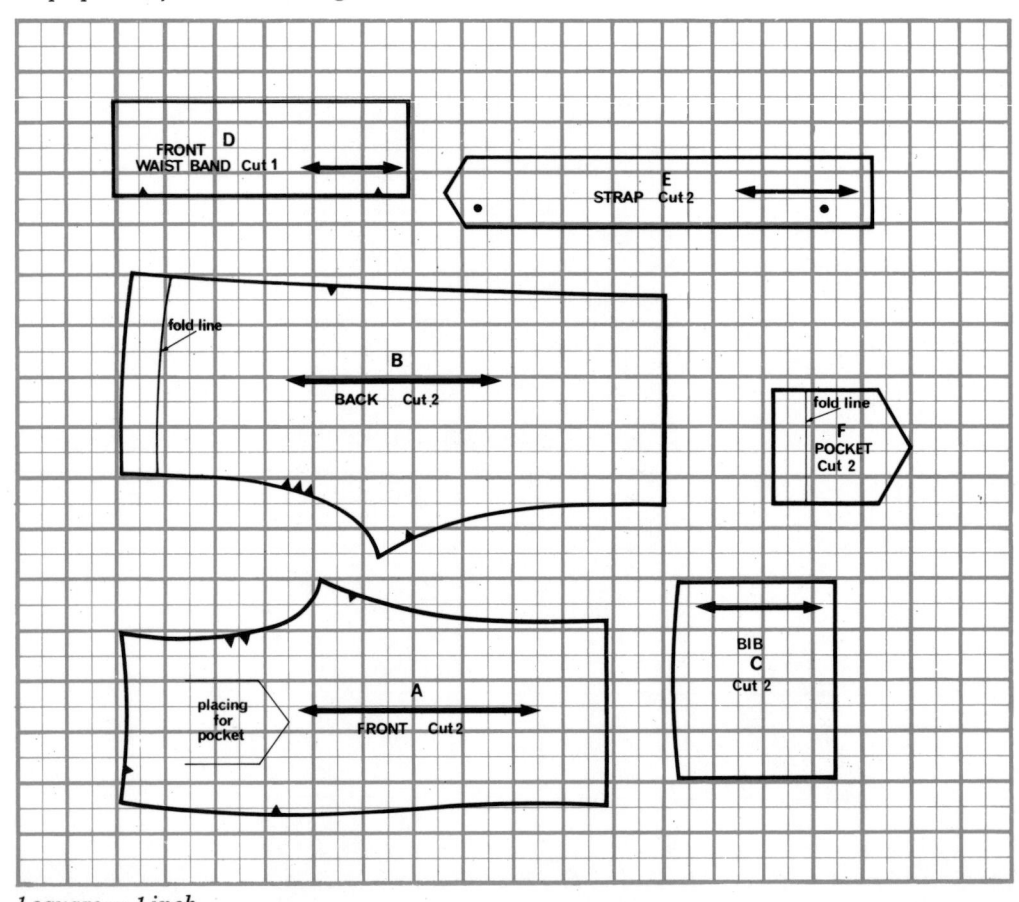

FRONT
WAIST BAND **D** Cut 1

E
STRAP Cut 2

fold line

B
BACK   Cut 2

fold line
F
POCKET
Cut 2

placing
for
pocket

A
FRONT   Cut 2

BIB
C
Cut 2

1 square = 1 inch

Pinafore dress

This is a very easy dress to make and is so simply designed that the style can be made up in a variety of fabrics for different occasions. For an alternative way with the pattern, cut the dress short at the hipline to make a useful jerkin to wear over trousers. Leave the last four inches of the side seams unstitched for greater ease of movement and catch-stitch the seam allowances back. Finish the hem off in the usual way.

Materials required:

1⅝ yards 54 inch wide fabric.
18 inch zip fastener.
1 hook and eye.
Coats Drima thread

Cutting directions

Make a paper pattern from the graph pattern, 1 square = 1 inch. ⅝ inch seam allowance has been included.
Pattern A – Front cut 2 pieces
Pattern B – Back cut 1 piece.
Pattern C – Armhole facing cut 2 pieces.
Pattern D – Front neck facing cut 2 pieces.
Pattern E – Back neck facing cut 1 piece.

To make up

1. Stitch darts on front and back sections.
2. Baste and stitch Centre Front seam leaving 18 inches below the spot open for the insertion of the zip fastener.
3. Join dress shoulder seams.
4. Join Back and Front facing on shoulder seams.
5. Baste and stitch facing to neckline and front edges of dress, taking $\frac{1}{4}$ inch seam on the front edge.
6. Insert zip fastener at Centre Front. Sew hook and eye above zip to secure.
7. Baste and stitch side seams.
8. Stitch short ends of armhole facings.
9. Place facings in corresponding armhole right sides facing. Baste and stitch. Turn facings to the inside of the garment and catch to seams at shoulder and underarm. Finish hem.

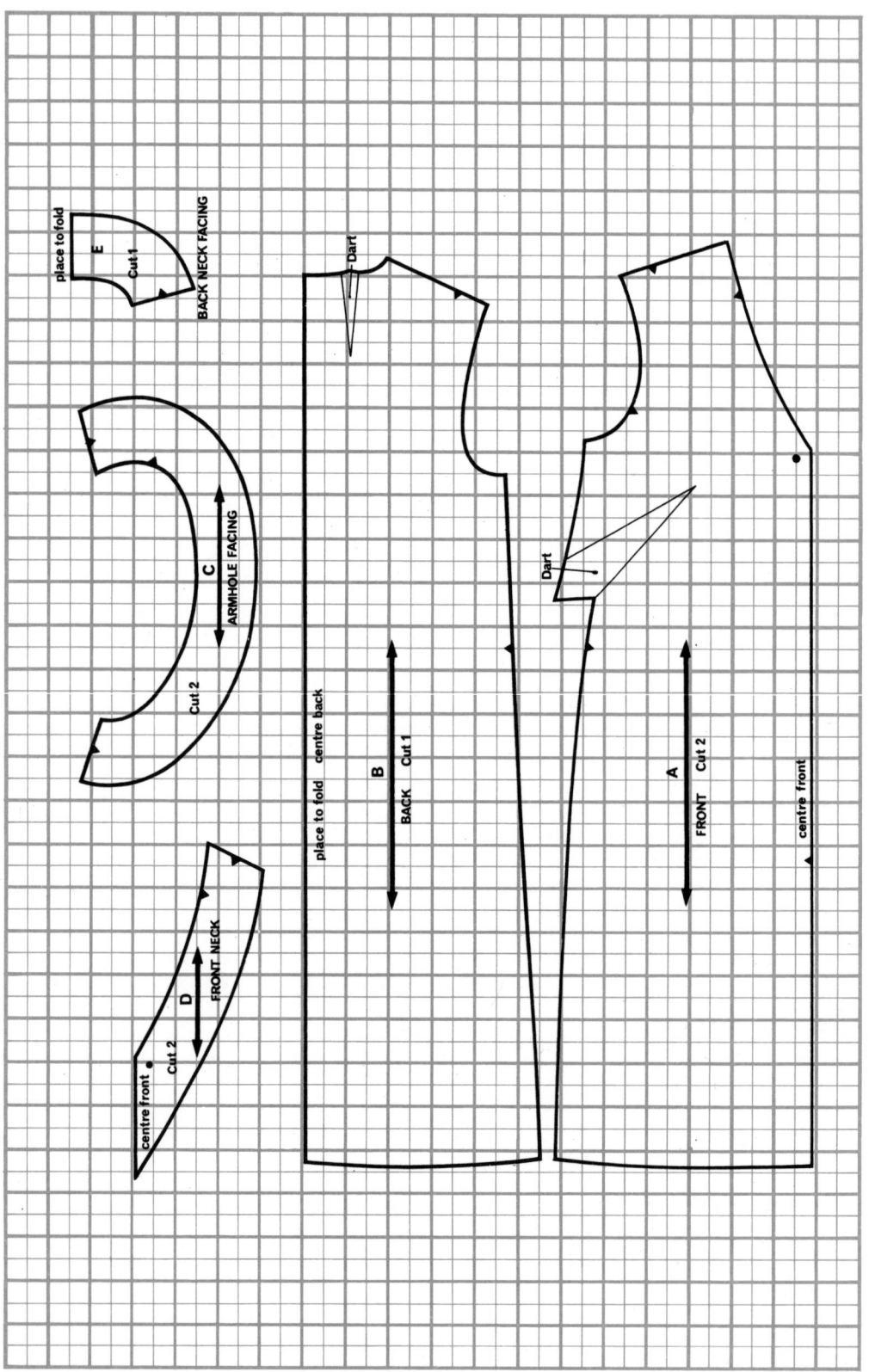

place to fold

E Cut 1

BACK NECK FACING

ARMHOLE FACING

C Cut 2

Dart

place to fold   centre back

B BACK Cut 1

Dart

A FRONT Cut 2

centre front

centre front   Cut 2   D   FRONT NECK

1 square = 1 inch

Shirt-style blouse

Make this classically styled blouse with the convertible collar to wear under the pinafore dress, with a skirt or tucked into trousers. As an adaptation, the waist could be extended to make a full length dress, to be worn with a belt.

Materials required:

3 yards 36 inch wide fabric.
Interfacing for collar and cuffs.
10 $\frac{5}{8}$-inch buttons.
Coats Drima thread.

Cutting directions

Make a paper pattern from the graph pattern 1 square = 1 inch.
$\frac{5}{8}$ inch seam allowances have been included.
Pattern A – Front cut 2.
Pattern B – Back cut 1.
Pattern C – Collar cut 3 (1 from interfacing).
Pattern D – Cuff cut 6 (2 from interfacing).
Pattern E – Sleeve cut 2.

To make up

1. Stitch darts on Back section.

2. Make two rows of gathering stitches between notches on Front shoulder edge.
3. Pull up gathers on Front shoulder sections to fit Back shoulder sections. Stitch Back to Front at shoulders.
4. Join Front to Back at side seams.
5. Fold Front facing Back to wrong side. Baste.
6. Make up interfaced collar and stitch to neckline.
7. Stitch fabric facing to sleeve edges on right side of fabric extending over dots.
Clip into edge to dots and turn facing to the wrong side.
8. Stitch sleeve seams.
9. Gather sleeve heads.
10. Make up cuffs and attach to sleeves. Make buttonholes on cuffs and sew on buttons to correspond.
11. Insert sleeves in blouse armholes.
12. Hem lower edge of blouse.
13. Top-stitch collar and cuff edges if desired.
14. Make 6 buttonholes on right Front of blouse and stitch buttons to correspond.

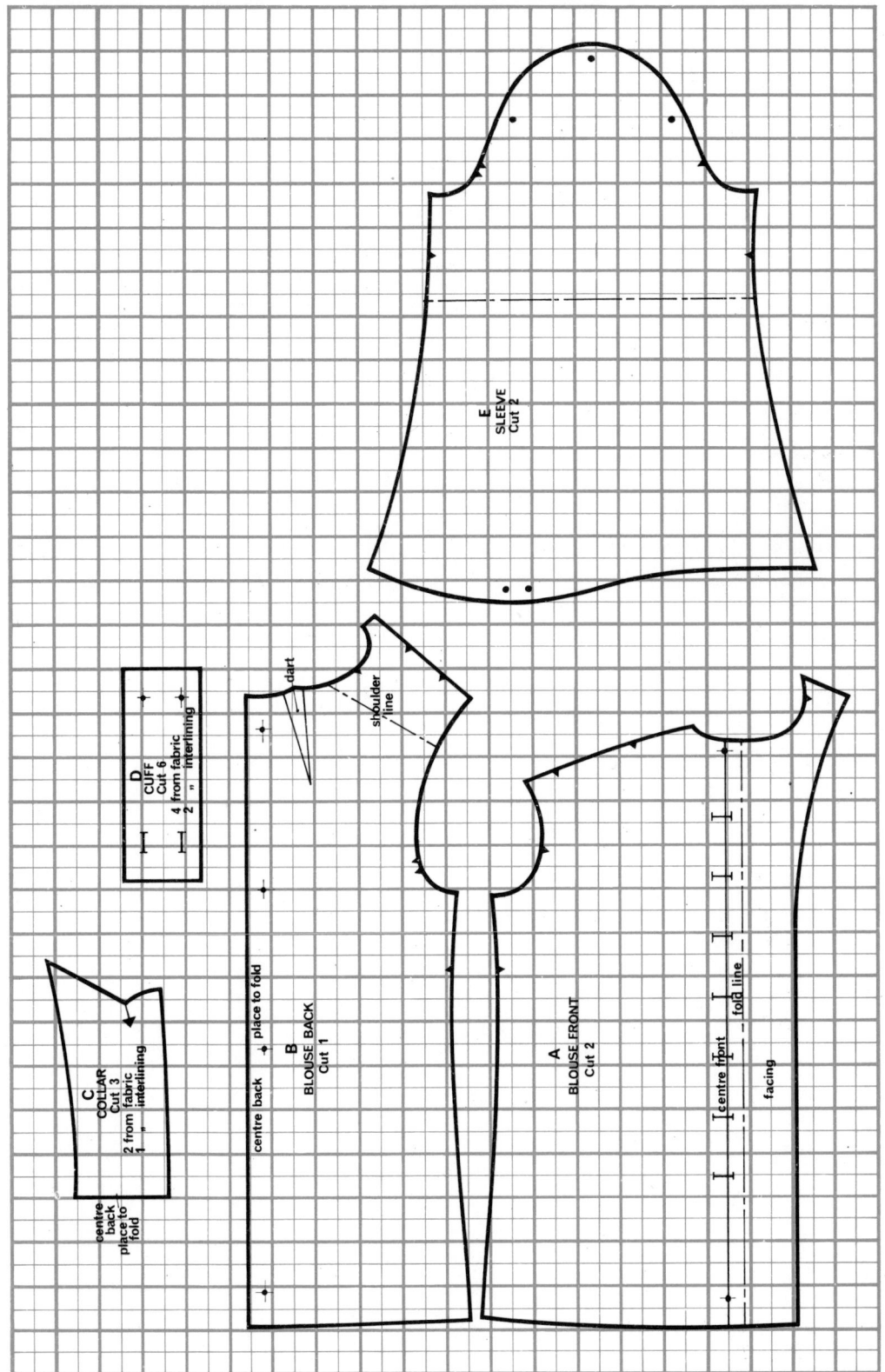

1 square = 1 inch

Shirt-style blouse

E SLEEVE Cut 2

D CUFF Cut 6 4 from fabric 2 " interlining

C COLLAR Cut 3 2 from fabric 1 " interlining

centre back place to fold

B BLOUSE BACK Cut 1

centre back · place to fold

dart

shoulder line

A BLOUSE FRONT Cut 2

centre front

fold line

facing

Classic suit

This is a suit line which is a perennial favourite and never seems to go out of fashion. It is an easy style to sew and you'll enjoy every moment of making it. The suit illustrated was made in a non-crushable woven Terylene fabric with a linen finish but most woven fabrics will do for this style. If a very loosely woven fabric is chosen, then the jacket will have to be lined.

For a distinctive look, trim the edges of the jacket with a chunky looking braid.

Materials required:

2½ yards of 54-inch wide fabric.
Interfacing for front and back neck facings.
8-inch zip fastener.
2 hooks and eyes.
1-inch Petersham ribbon, to waist measurement plus turnings.
Coats Drima thread.

Cutting directions

Make paper pattern from graph pattern 1 square = 1 inch.
⅝ inch seam allowances included.
Pattern A – Jacket front cut 2.
Pattern B – Jacket back cut 1.
Pattern C – Upper sleeve section cut 2.
Pattern D – Under sleeve section cut 2.
Pattern E – Front facing cut 4 (2 from interfacing).
Pattern F – Back neck facing cut 2 (1 from interfacing).
Pattern G – Lower pocket cut 2.
Pattern H – Upper pocket cut 2.
Pattern J – Front skirt cut 1.
Pattern K – Back skirt cut 2.

To make up

Jacket

1. Stitch darts on Front and Back sections.
2. Stitch Centre Back seam.
3. Make pockets up and stitch to jacket fronts.
4. Baste Front facing interfacing to wrong side of Front section. Baste interfacing for Back neck section to wrong side of Back neck.
5. Join shoulder seams to Back and Front.
6. Stitch shoulder seams of fabric Front facing to fabric Back neck facing.
7. Place facing to jacket, right sides together. Baste and stitch front and neck edges. Clip seams, grade and turn to right side.
8. Join side seams of Front and Back sections.
9. Stitch Upper sleeve to Lower sleeve sections.
10. Hem sleeve edges.
11. Insert sleeves in jacket armholes.
12. Hem lower edge of jacket.
13. Neaten all inside seams.

Skirt

1. Stitch darts on Front and Back sections.
2. Stitch Centre Back seam.
3. Join Front to Back at side seams, leaving left side open at top for zip.
4. Insert zip fastener.
5. Make ½ inch hems on the ends of petersham and insert petersham band in skirt waist.
6. Sew hooks and eyes at waist fastening.
7. Make hem.
8. Neaten all seams.

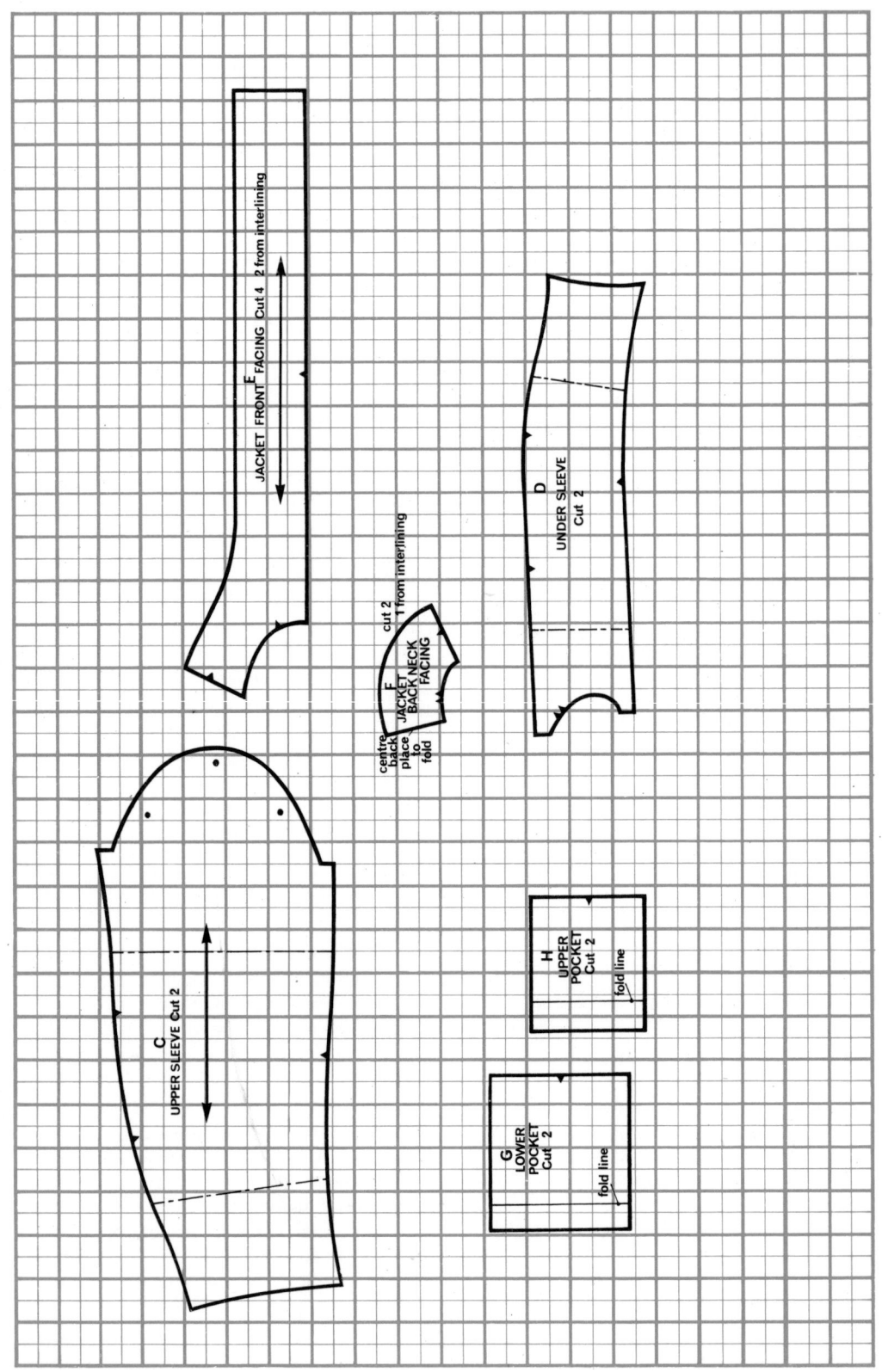

1 square = 1 inch

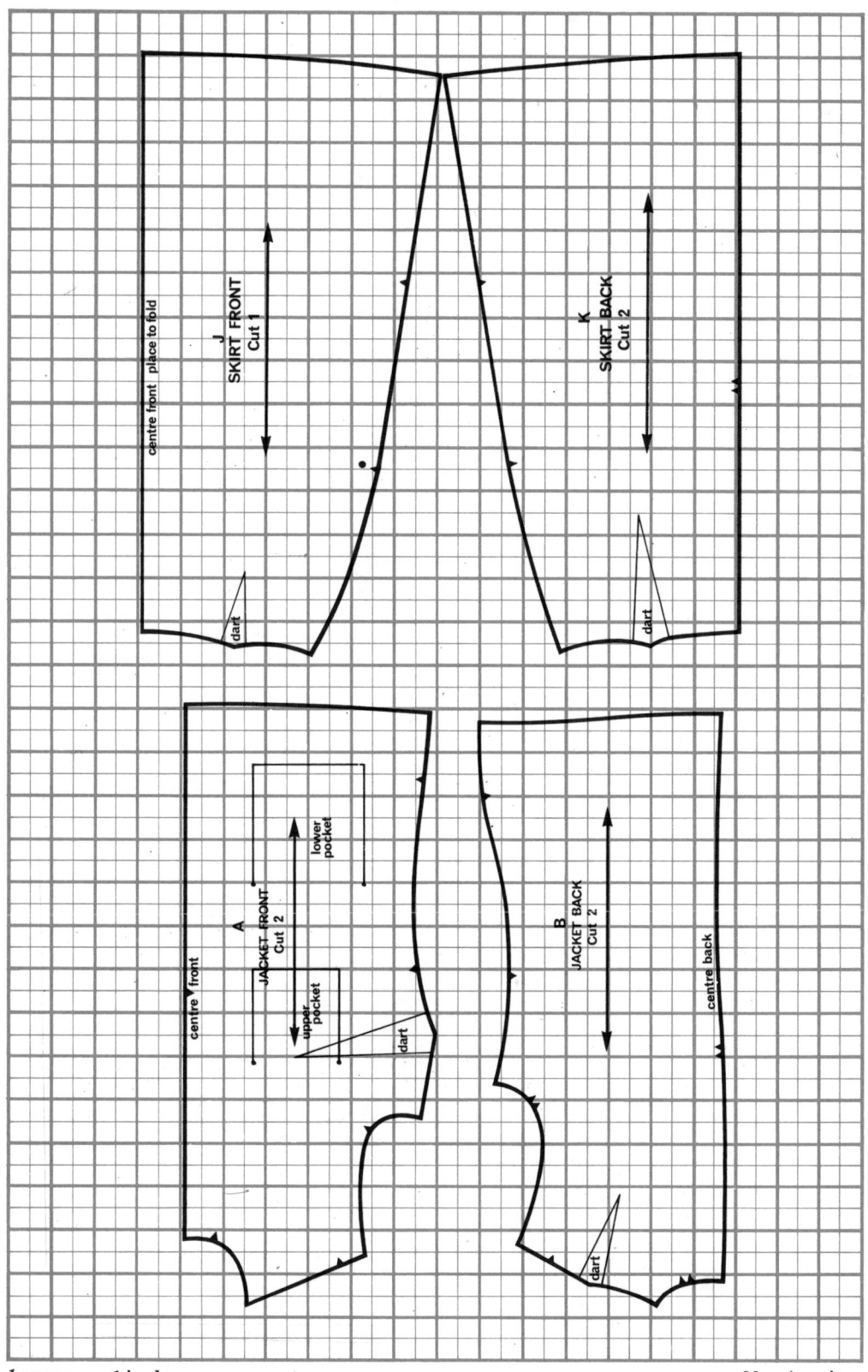

1 square = 1 inch

Classic suit

Trouser suit

A perfect suit for sports wear, for holidays and for any occasion where you want to look smart and feel comfortable.

Materials required:

Trousers
1½ yards 54-inch wide fabric.
9-inch zip fastener.
Interfacing for waist edge.
1 hook and eye.
Coats Drima thread.

Jacket
2 yards 54-inch wide fabric.
Lining for pocket.
6 × 1-inch buttons.
Interfacing for Front and neck edges.
1 snap fastener.
Coats Drima thread.

Cutting directions

Make paper pattern from the graph pattern
1 square = 1 inch.
⅝-inch seam allowance included.

Trousers
Pattern A – Front cut 2.
Pattern B – Back cut 2.
Pattern C – Front waist facing cut 2 (1 from interfacing).
Pattern D – Back waist facing cut 2 (1 from interfacing).

Jacket
Pattern E – Front cut 2.
Pattern F – Back cut 2.
Pattern G – Sleeves cut 2.
Pattern H – Back neck facing cut 4 (2 from interfacing) .
Pattern J – Pocket cut 4 (2 from interfacing).

To make up

Trousers
1. Stitch darts on Front and Back sections.

2. Stitch one Front section to one Back section at side and Inner leg seams. Repeat with other sections but leaving Left side open at top for zip.
3. Place one leg inside the other, Right sides facing. Stitch Centre seam.
4. Stitch Front interfacing to Back interfacing at short ends to form waist facing. Leave Left side open. Repeat with facing sections.
5. Baste interfacing to waist edge on wrong side of fabric.
6. Stitch facing to waist edge, right sides together. Trim, clip grade and turn to wrong side.
7. Insert zip fastener.
Make hems on trouser edges.

Jacket
Baste Front interfacings to wrong sides of Front sections along fold line. Sew lightly in position along fold line.
2. Slash along dart line as shown on pattern.
3. Stitch darts on Back and Front sections.
4. Baste Back interfacings to wrong sides of Back neck edges.
5. Stitch Centre back seam .
6. Join shoulder seams of Front and Back.
7. Stitch Centre back seams of facing.
8. Stitch Back facing to Front facing at shoulders.
9. Fold Front facing to outside of jacket, right sides together. Baste and stitch neck edge. Turn to wrong side.
10. Make hem on lower edge.
11. Stitch sleeve seams.
12. Insert sleeves in armholes.
13. Hem sleeve edges.
14. Make up pockets and stitch to jacket.
15. Make buttonholes to right side of jacket and sew buttons on left side to correspond.
16. Attach snap fastener at top edge of jacket neck to secure.

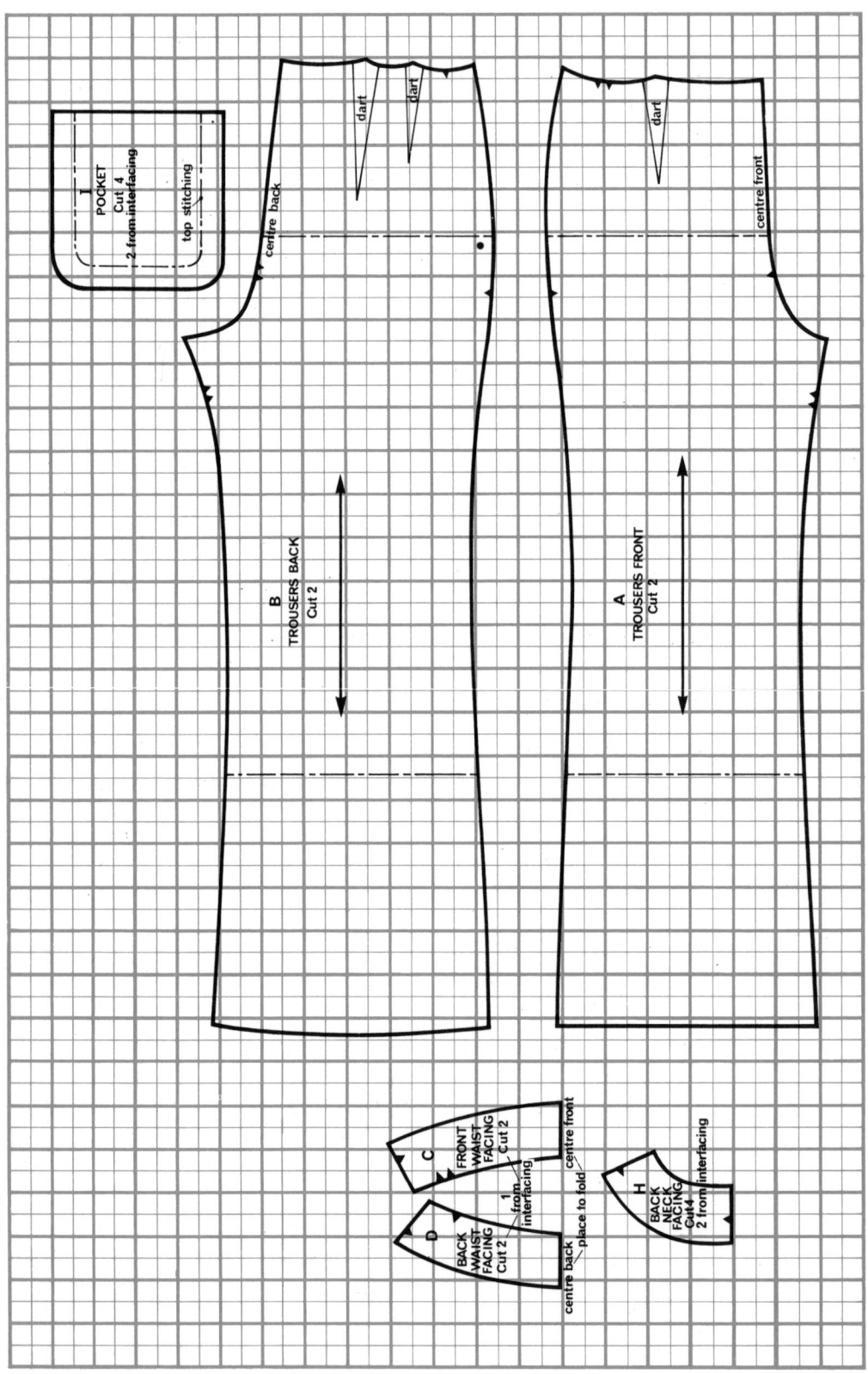

1 square = 1 inch

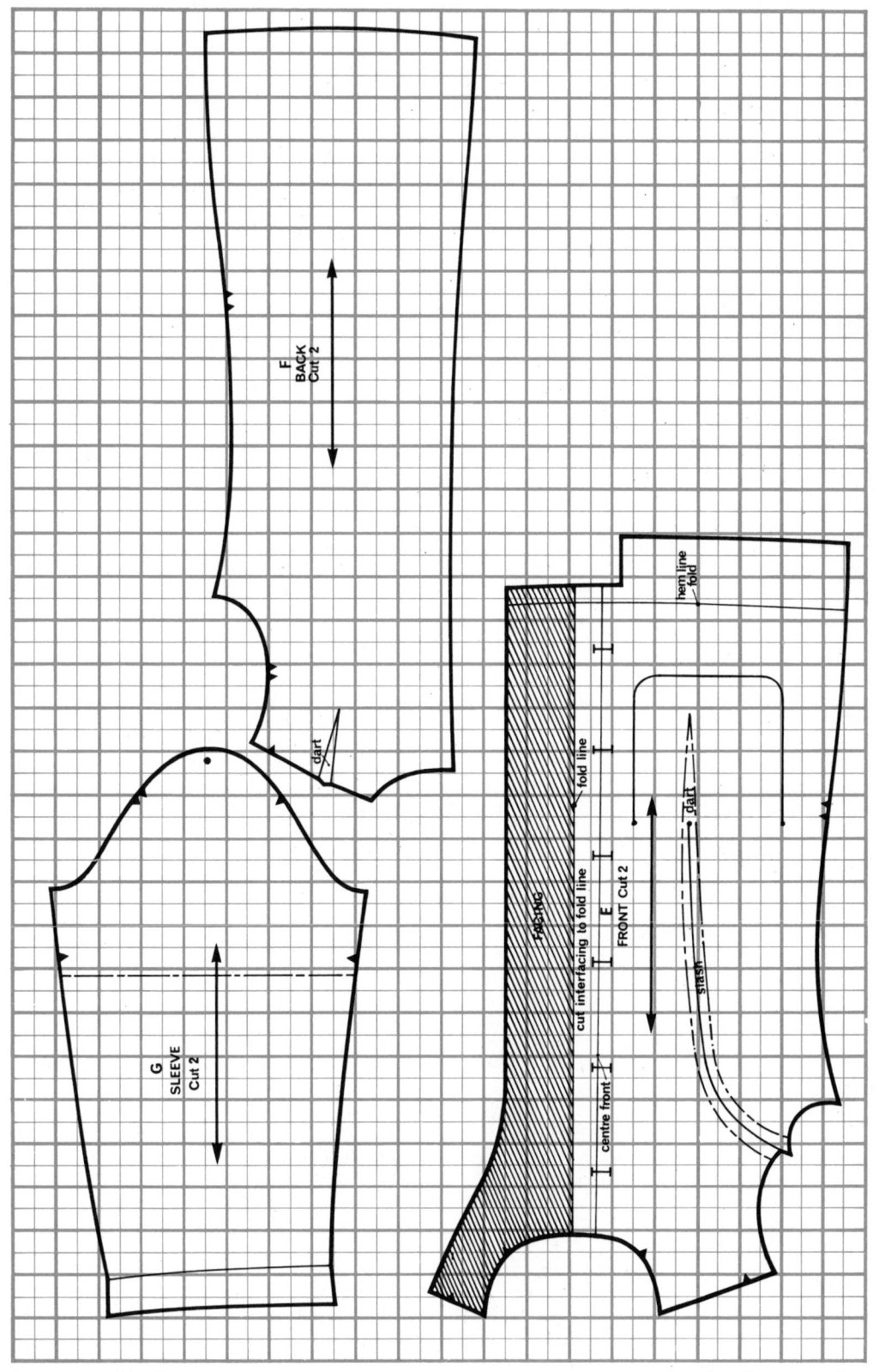

F
BACK
Cut 2

dart

G
SLEEVE
Cut 2

hem line
fold

fold line

cut interfacing to fold line

Facing

E
FRONT Cut 2

centre front

dart

slash

1 square = 1 inch

Trouser suit

Pleated skirt

Pleats are interesting to do and not as difficult as they look at first sight. The secret of success is in the pinning, pressing and basting.

Materials required

1¼ yards 54 inch wide fabric.
Interfacing for waistband.
8-inch zip fastener.

2 hooks and eyes
Coats Drima thread.

Cutting directions

Make paper pattern from graph pattern
1 square = 1 inch.
⅝ inch seam allowance has been included.
Pattern A – Front cut 1.
Pattern B – Back cut 1.
Pattern C – Side Front cut 2.
Pattern D – Side Back cut 2.
Pattern E – Waistband cut 1 plus piece from interfacing the length of the waistband by 1½ inches deep.

To make up

1. Stitch darts on Side Front sections.
2. Place Side Fronts to Front sections. Baste and stitch Side Front seams.
To make pleat nearest Side Front seam, baste and stitch Side Fronts to Front to X, matching pleat line. Press towards Centre.
3. To make pleats nearest the Centre Front; baste and stitch pleats lines together to X. Press towards Centre.
4. Baste upper edges through all thicknesses.
5. Make up Back sections in the same way stitching Side Back panels to the Back panel and pleating as above.
6. Stitch Front to Back at side seams leaving side open for zip fastener.
7. Insert zip fastener.
8. Place interfacing to the wrong side of waistband with one long edge of interfacing to one long edge of waistband. Sew interfacing to fabric at long inner edge. Press seam upwards.
9. Fold waistband in half right sides together. Baste and stitch the short ends and along Back for 2 inches. Turn to right side.
10. Attach waistband to skirt at waist edge.
11. Stitch hooks and eyes at waist opening.
12. Pin up hem. Clip Side Front and Side Back seams to top edge of hem. Press seams open below the clips. Make hem.

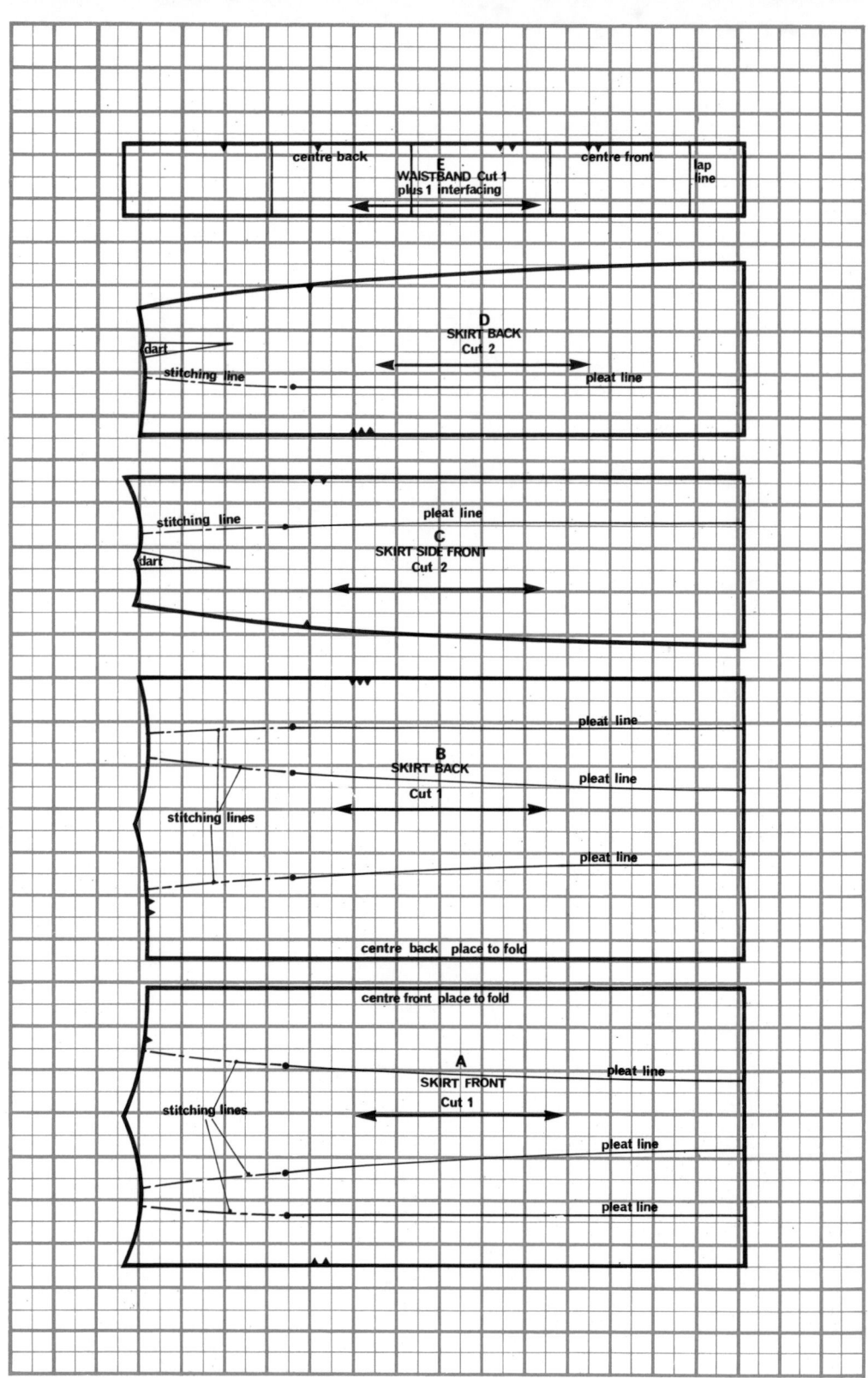

1 square = 1 inch

233

Macramé and Tatting

Macramé

Macramé–the art of creative knotting–is one of the most ancient crafts known to man. It is known to have been used by the ancient Egyptians, Chinese, Maoris and Peruvians. The tradition of magical, supernatural potency in particular knots has been handed down by sailors through the ages. The origin of the word is a mystery: the Arabic 'migramah' means 'protection, headcovering', while the Turkish 'makrama' is a decoratively fringed napkin. Whatever its origin, old-style macramé lacework was extremely delicate in materials and effect and well established in 13th century Arabia, whence it was carried to Italy via the Moors. Here it flourished during the Middle Ages, but gradually waned, to be revived in a more robust, equally attractive form in the late 19th and early 20th century in and around Turin and Genoa. It is now one of Italy's more popular traditional crafts.

Where teminology varies, an equivalent term is given in [ ].

236

Learn macramé

What to use

Any yarn can be used to work macramé, depending on the article being made and the finished result required, but the most successful are the smooth, firm yarns which knot easily and do not slip. String is one of the best – and cheapest – materials of all. If you want a crisp finish with the knotting pattern clearly defined, then it is essential you use a firm material. such as string, linen thread, nylon cord or any form of cotton. On the other hand if you prefer an all-over textural effect, then any knitting or crochet yarn, fine or thick, can be used. Rug wool is excellent for it is more substantial than ordinary knitting wools, and being thick makes up quickly.

You will need a convenient-sized board to work on for small items, and any oddment of wood – preferably a soft one which will take pins easily – can be used, or a sheet of cork, or even several thicknesses of hardboard. If using a hard wood, it is a good idea to 'pad' it first with a sheet of foam plastic, or even with a folded-up old towel. An expanse of wall makes an ideal working base for large items.

Beginning work

As well as a working surface and a suitable yarn (string is best for practice purposes) you will need some pins, scissors and a tape measure.

Before you can begin knotting, your yarn must be cut into suitable lengths, and these are mounted on to another length of yarn, known as the **holding cord**. This is called **setting [mounting] on threads.** The holding cord is sometimes used as part of the finished design – for instance, as a handle for a bag – or it can be withdrawn after knotting is complete. It is not always easy to join in new yarn in mid-knotting so it is important that working lengths are cut long enough for the complete design. As a very general guide, if setting [mounting] on each thread double (which is the usual method), then the thread should be cut to eight times the length required. For instance, if you are making a braid to measure 6 ins long, then cut each thread 48 ins. If you are setting [mounting] on threads singly, then they should be cut to four times the finished length required.

How to set on [mount] threads

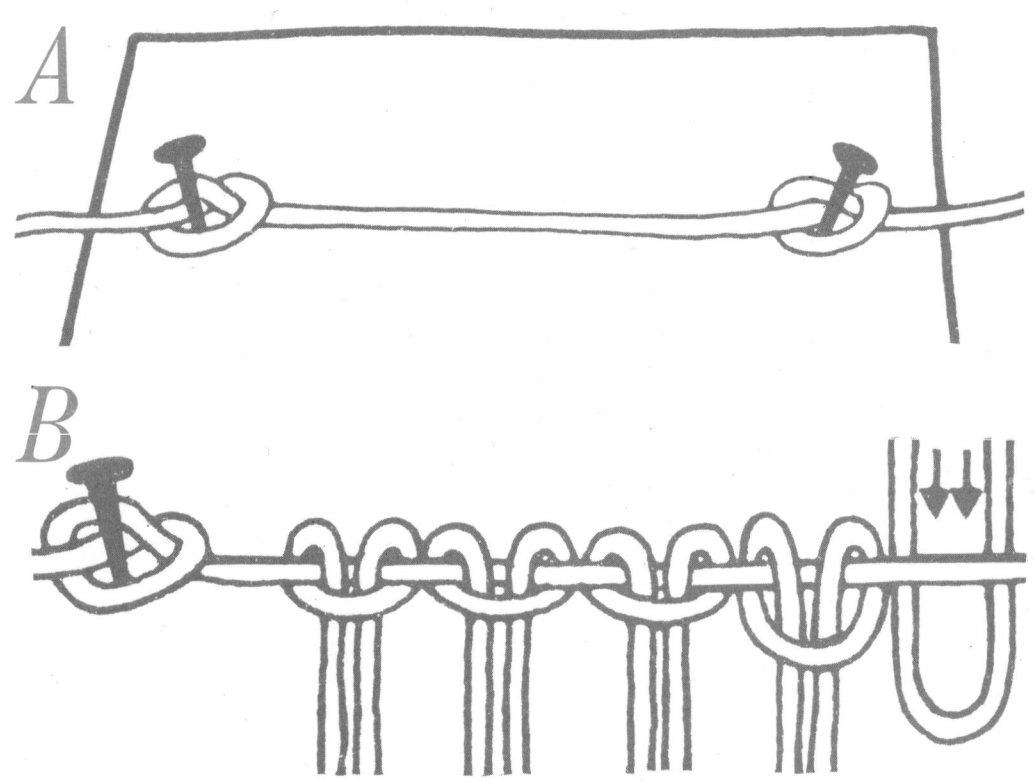

For practice purposes, cut a holding cord of about 12 ins, and 10 lengths of string, each 1 yd long. Tie a knot near one end of the holding cord by taking the end over and round itself and through the loop formed. This is known as an **overhand knot.** Pin the cord through this knot to your working surface near the top left-hand corner. Stretch the cord horizontally across your working surface, tie a similar overhand knot near the other end of the cord and pin it to your working surface. *(fig A)*

Now take the first of your working cords, double it and insert the looped end under the holding cord from top to bottom. Bring the loose ends down over the holding cord and through the loop. Draw tight. Repeat with each length of string, positioning each doubled set-on [mounted] string close to the previous one. When you have finished, you will then have 20 lengths of string hanging vertically from your holding cord, each measuring a little under 18 ins. *(fig B)*

The basic knots

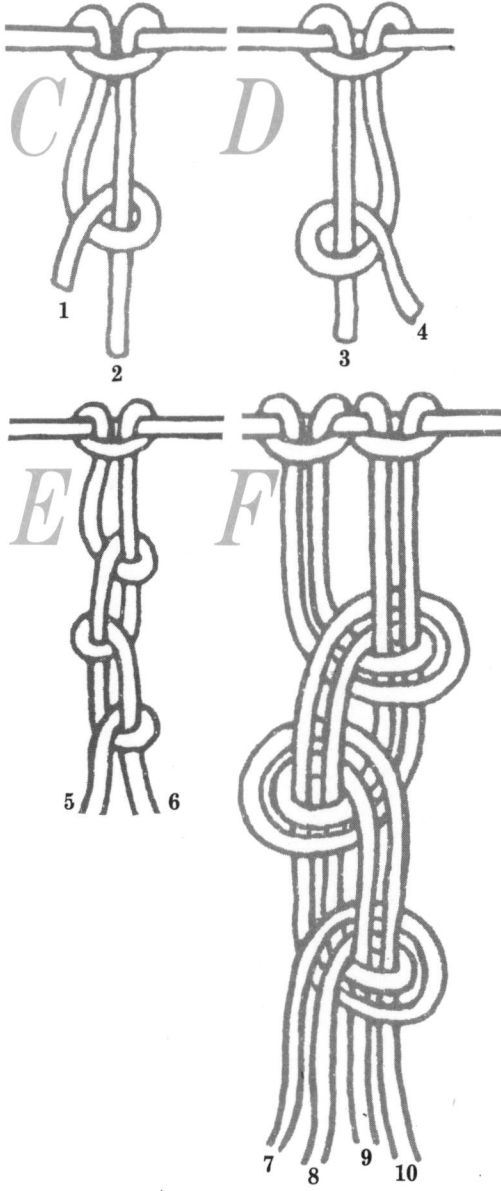

Half hitch

Work on the first 2 cords. To tie a half hitch from the left, hold right-hand cord taut, bring cord 1 in front of it then up and behind it from right to left. Bring through the loop formed. Draw tight. *(fig C)*

Work on cords 3 and 4. To tie a half hitch from the right, merely reverse the knotting procedure: hold left-hand cord taut, and bring right-hand cord in front of it, then up and under it from left to right, and down through loop formed. Draw tight. *(fig D)*

Work on cords 5 and 6: tie a half hitch from the left, then tie a half hitch from the right. Continue in this way, alternating the direction of the knot each time, and drawing each knot close to the previous one. This forms a chain of knots known as the **single alternate half hitch chain.** *(fig E)*

Work on cords 7, 8, 9 and 10. Tie half hitches alternately from the left and right, as for the single alternate half hitch chain, but this time use cords double, so first knot is tied with cords 7 and 8 over 9 and 10; the second knot is tied with cords 9 and 10 over 7 and 8. Continue in this way to form a chain of knots. This is known as the **double alternate half hitch chain**. *(fig F)*

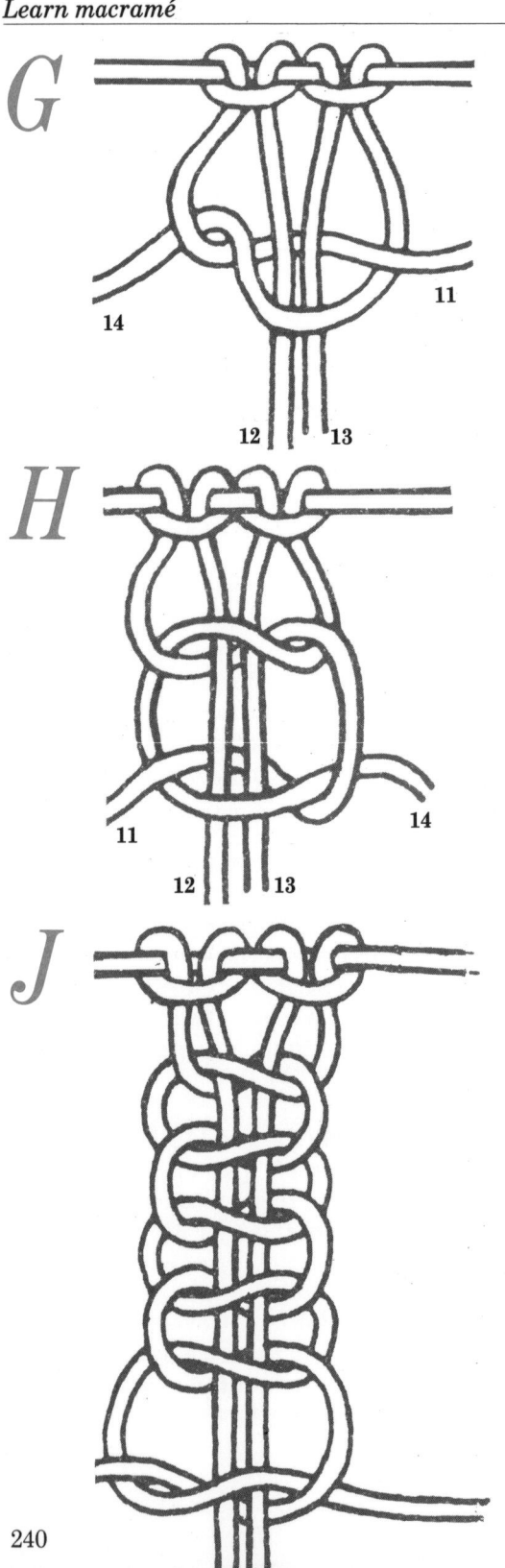

The flat [square] knot

The flat [square] knot which is the second basic knot is tied in two parts as follows: work on cords 11, 12, 13 and 14. Hold cords 12 and 13 taut, take cord 11 under them and over 14. Take cord 14 over 12 and 13 and under 11. Draw tight. This is the first half of the flat [square] knot, and is known as the **half knot.** If the half knot is tied continuously this produces an attractive twisted spiral of knots sometimes called a **sinnet** of flat [square] knots. *(fig G)*

To complete the flat [square] knot, still keeping 12 and 13 taut, bring cord 11 back under 12 and 13 and over 14. Take cord 14 over 12 and 13 and under 11. Draw tight. *(fig H)*

Continue in this way to tie flat [square] knots one below the other to form a chain. This is often known as a **Solomon's bar.** *(fig J)*

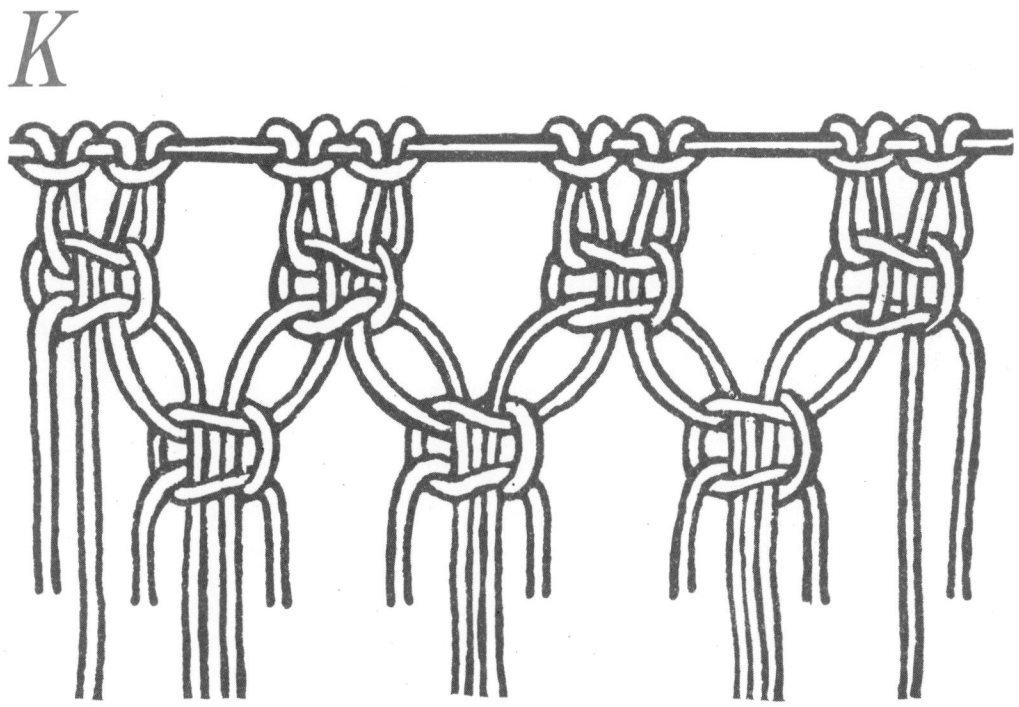

K

To work the alternate flat [square] knot pattern

This pattern occurs frequently in all forms of macramé work, and is the one most often used to form a fabric. It is worked on any number of knotting cords, provided the total number is a multiple of 4. Begin by tying flat [square] knots with each group of 4 cords to the end of the row. In the 2nd row, leave the first 2 cords unworked, then tie flat [square] knots with each group of 4 cords, to the final 2 cords in the row, leave these 2 cords unworked. The 3rd row is the same as the first, and the 4th row is the same as the 2nd. Continue in this way to build up a fabric. By tying knots and rows close together you create a dense fabric; space out knots and rows and you will achieve an open-work lacy fabric. *(fig K)*

Cording

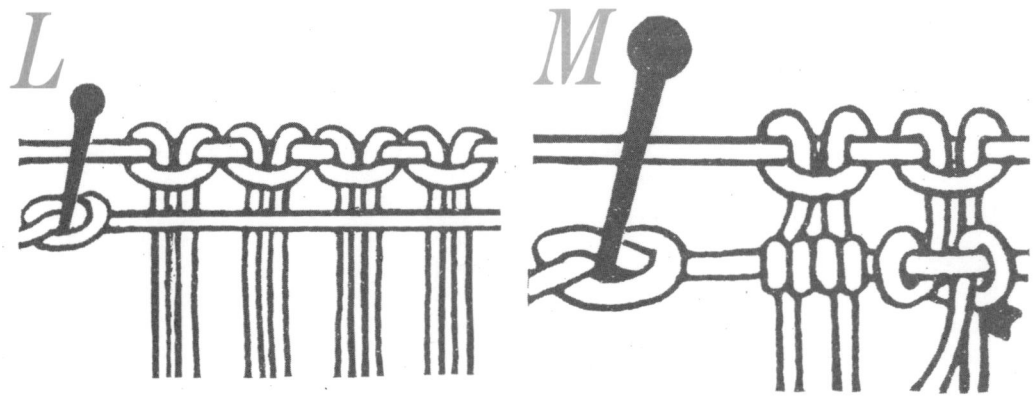

This is a useful macramé technique, for it can be used to create solid fabrics, to 'draw' outlines and figures, and to shape edges of work. It is based on the half hitch knot.

To practise cording on your set-on [mounted] strings, cut a new length of string, approximately 1 yd long. Tie an overhand knot near one end of it, and pin it to your working surface immediately to the left of working cords. Lay it horizontally across working cords. This is known as a leader cord, and as the knots are all tied on to this leader cord, it is essential that it is kept taught all the time – if necessary pin it to your working surface at the opposite side to kept it taut while you work. *(fig L)*

Now beginning with cord 1, take it up and over leader, and then down behind it, bringing end out to the left of the loop formed. Repeat sequence exactly with the same cord – this means you have tied 2 half hitches, or – as is more usually known – a double half hitch. Repeat with every cord along the row, pushing each half hitch as it is tied close to the previous one. At the end of the row you should have a row of tiny loops along the leader cord all nestling close to each other. *(fig M)*

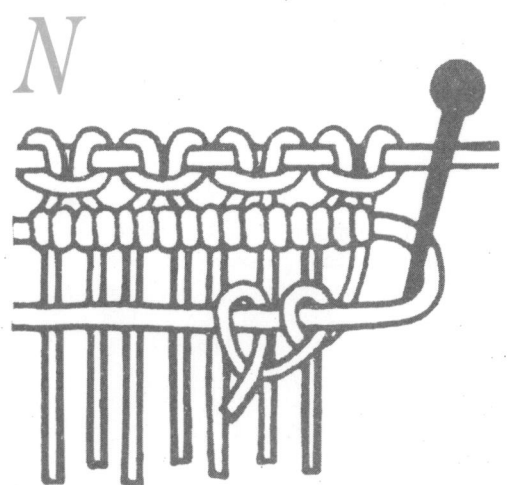

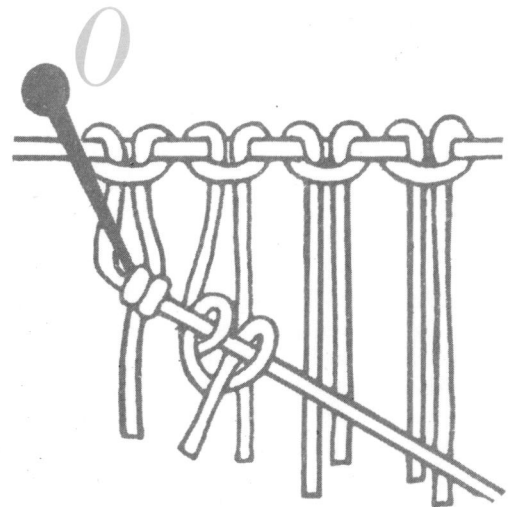

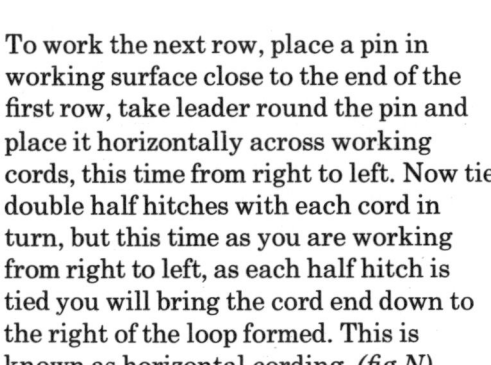

To work the next row, place a pin in working surface close to the end of the first row, take leader round the pin and place it horizontally across working cords, this time from right to left. Now tie double half hitches with each cord in turn, but this time as you are working from right to left, as each half hitch is tied you will bring the cord end down to the right of the loop formed. This is known as horizontal cording. *(fig N)*

Diagonal cording is worked in a similar way, except leader cord is placed at an angle across working cords. The leader for horizontal or diagonal cording may be a separate cord, as here, or it can be one of the set-on [mounted] cords. *(fig O)*

Tie belt

Materials: Jute, or similar mediumweight soft string; 16 oval wooden beads; long wooden beads (number will depend on size of belt required).

Measurements: Belt is intended as a loose-fitting tie belt, and can be made to any length to suit size of waist. The centre pattern section should equal size of waist plus 4 ins. Beaded tie at each end should equal approximately 9 ins.

Tension (gauge) check: Chain [sinnet] of 7 flat [square] knots measures 1 in.

Preparation: Cut 16 cords to equal 4 times the total length of belt required, including ties at each end. (*Note:* As cords are cut singly for this design, it is necessary only to cut to 4 times the total finished length required, instead of usual 8 times.)
Lay cords side by side on your working surface. Divide cords into pairs and thread an oval bead on to each pair. Tie an overhand knot close to ends of cords to prevent bead slipping off.
Leave a space of about $1\frac{1}{2}$ ins below bead then using cord on far left as leader work diagonal cording slanting down to the right with all cords.

To make
Continuing with same cord as leader work 3 more rows of diagonal cording to form a very wide zig-zag, with big areas of unworked cords between each row (*see illustration*). After the 4th row of the zig-zag has been worked, total length of work (including beads) should measure about 9 ins.

1st pattern panel
With cord on far left as leader work horizontal cording from left to right across all cords. Reverse direction of leader round a pin, and work a 2nd row of horizontal cording this time from right to left, immediately below the first. Divide cords into 4 groups of 4 cords each. With each group work a flat [square] knot chain to about $1\frac{1}{2}$ ins.
Cross first chain over 2nd, and cross 4th chain over 3rd. Pin them if necessary to hold in place so cords line up, then with cord on far left as leader work a double row of horizontal cording as before across all cords.

2nd pattern panel

With cord on far left as leader work a row of
diagonal cording slanting only slightly down
to the right with first 7 cords. In a similar way
work a row of diagonal cording slanting down
to the left, using cord on far right as leader,
and knotting over it the 7 cords on right-hand
side of work.

With cord on far left as leader work a 2nd row
of diagonal cording immediately below the
first knotting over it all the cords on this side
of work (including leader from previous row).
In a similar way work a 2nd row of diagonal
cording on right-hand side of work.

Take centre 2 cords through a long wooden
bead.

Let remaining cords curve gently round the
bead on either side – do not pull them too
tightly, or – on the other hand – allow them to
form too large curves.

With cord immediately to the left of the bead
as leader slanting down to the left, work
diagonal cording over it with all cords at left-
hand side of work. Work a 2nd row of diagonal
cording immediately below, using left-hand
cord of pair threaded through bead as leader,
and knotting over it all cords on the left,
including leader from previous row.

In a similar way work a double row of
diagonal cording slanting down to the right
with cords at right-hand side of work. * * Now
repeat from * to * * until belt is required
length, excluding tie at other end. Finish after
a first pattern panel.

To finish

Using cord on far left as leader work 4 rows of
zig-zag diagonal cording to match zig-zag at
beginning of work. Finish with an oval bead
on each pair of cords, and tie an overhand
knot beneath each bead to hold in place.

Shopping bag

Materials: Mediumweight parcel string; 2 wooden rings, each with a diameter of 3½ ins.

Measurements: Finished bag measures very approximately 12 ins deep by 13 ins wide, at widest point, but can be made to any size wished.

Tension (gauge) check: A chain [sinnet] of 5 flat [square] knots measures 1 in.

Preparation: Cut 20 cords each 16 ft (or 16 times finished length of bag required). Double these cords and pin them by their top loops, side by side on your working surface. Work chains of 2 flat [square] knots with each group of 4 cords. Unpin the chains from your working surface. Wind cords from each chain once round one of the wooden rings, having knotted sections at base of ring. Bring unworked cord ends down through centre of cords and draw tight. Repeat with each chain until all are set on [mounted] to the wooden ring. The 2-knot chains should now lie on wrong side of ring, the cord ends, ready for knotting, should be at front of work.

To make

On first 4 cords work a chain of 10 flat [square] knots; then work a 6-knot chain with each group of 4 cords to last 4 cords; work a chain of 10 flat [square] knots with these last 4 cords.

Work now continues in the alternate flat [square] knot pattern until bag is size required. However, as the bag is made 'in the round' you will not be able to work on your normal flat working surface; instead a suitable three-dimensional working base must be used.

As shaping for this bag is achieved entirely by adjusting knotting to fit the base, it is important to choose one which will give you the right finished shape and size of bag. A round glass lampshade (the globe variety) will do very well provided it is big enough; an upturned pudding basin could also be used; or a large rubber ball; or even a goldfish bowl. Padding your surface with foam plastic or a similar substance will give you a surface to pin your work to, and can also help to give you a more accurate size and shape of base. Work continues in the alternate flat [square]

for colour illustration, see page 247

knot pattern, with shaping achieved to match working base by increasing and decreasing distance between knots and rows of knots. The pattern is intended to be an open-work lacy one, so it does not matter – within reason – how big you make the distance between knots and rows. Side edges should be curved gently outwards to give shape as shown in the picture of the finished bag on page 247. To give increased strength to these edges work double knots instead of single ones on each row, and have 4 central knotbearing core cords (this will include 2 cords from the next knot along). Shaping should be such that side edges stop somewhere around the midway point of total length of bag required; main knotting continues to total depth in centre, gradually decreasing out to meet side edges.

When the first side of the bag is complete continue knotting round other side of your working base to make a 2nd side of similar size and shaping to the first. This time, of course, knotting will progress from base of bag towards the top. If knotbearing core cords along side edges are constantly pulled tight this will help to draw in side edges even more, and give better shaping to rest of bag.

When the 2 sides of the bag match up as far as the flat [square] knot chains at beginning, stop alternate flat [square] knot pattern, and end with flat [square] knot chains to match those worked at the beginning.

To finish

With right side of work face upwards, lay wooden ring over cord ends coming from flat [square] knot chains. Take the 4 cords coming from first chain and bring them down over the wooden ring, then divide in 2 pairs and take left-hand pair to back of work to left of flat [square] knot chain, take right-hand pair to back of work to right of flat [square] knot chain. Turn work over, and tie these 4 ends together in a chain of 2 flat [square] knots. Tie knots tightly against wooden ring to prevent it slipping too much. Repeat with each group of cords to end.

Trim cord ends neatly.

(*Note:* If it is preferred not to work this design three-dimensionally, the bag may be made in 2 separate sections, then the sections stitched together round side and lower edges. This will not give such a pleasing rounded and capacious bag, however. Also, there will be the problem of dealing neatly with ends along lower edge of bag – this can be solved by combining cords from each side into multiple tassels.)

String and bead choker

Materials: Mediumweight parcel string; 31 long wooden beads.

Measurements: Length from centre back fastening round to centre front drop approximately 12 ins; width at sides of choker (excluding beads) approximately 2 ins.

Tension (gauge) check: Chain [sinnet] of 7 flat [square] knots measures 1 in.

Preparation: *Note:* Each side of the choker is made separately then the 2 strips are joined at centre front.

For left-hand side strip: Cut 2 lengths of string, each 8 ft. Double these together and pin to working surface by their top loops. With cord on far left as knotting cord, begin about an inch down from the double top loop and work half hitches over the cord next to it. Work upwards to top of loop then continue down right-hand side. Finish beside point where you began, to give a complete loop of half hitches (sometimes known as a buttonhole loop).

You now have 4 knotting cords hanging down from the buttonhole loop: with these work a half knot spiral (tie the first half of the flat [square] knot continuously) for about 2 ins.

Now cut 4 new lengths of string, each 7 ft. Lay these together, and place them on your working surface so their midway point is under the 4 knotting cords from spiral just worked. Knot the new cords once round the knotting cords. Work a flat [square] knot immediately below with the 4 central knotting cords to hold the new cords in place. In a similar way introduce another 2 new cords, each cut to 7 ft on to the 4 central cords. You should now have a total of 16 cords, arranged in groups of 4, 2, 4, 2 and 4.

For right-hand side strip: Cut 2 lengths of string, each 8 ft. Place both lengths together, and thread a bead on to the double thickness, positioning it at the midway point. Tie a flat [square] knot immediately below with the 4 knotting cords to hold bead in place. Pin to your working surface through the flat [square] knot, then work a half knot spiral for about 2 ins. Complete preparation for this side strip exactly as for left-hand side strip.

To make
Work on left-hand side strip first: With cords 1–4 work a half knot spiral for about $1\frac{1}{2}$ ins. Thread cords 5 and 6 on to a bead; tie a double half hitch with cord 6 over cord 5 immediately below to hold the bead in place. Work a flat [square] knot chain with cords 7–10 for about 1 in.
(*Note:* As half knot spiral worked with first 4 cords has to be curved round slightly in order to bring its working cords into line with the others, by working the central flat [square] knot chain to only about 1 in this should bring cords into line.)
Thread cords 11 and 12 on to a bead; tie a double half hitch with cord 12 over cord 11 immediately below to hold the bead in place.

for colour illustration, see page 250

Work a half knot spiral for about 1½ ins with cords 12–16.

Begin cording pattern: With cord on the far left as leader, work horizontal cording from left to right across all cords.

Now, using cord on the far left as leader throughout, work a zig-zag of diagonal cording leaving areas of unworked cords between each row of the zig-zag. Use the same leader cord throughout – odd numbered rows will therefore be worked from left to right; even numbered rows from right to left. After you have worked the 9th row of diagonal cording (from left to right), still using the same leader, work next 2 rows of diagonal cording on 11 cords only (leaving 4 cords at left-hand side of work unworked).

Next row (right to left): Work across all cords.

Work on right-hand side strip: Work exactly as for left-hand side strip, but begin diagonal cording with cord on far right as leader. After 9th row work 2 rows of cording on 11 cords at left-hand side of work, leaving 4 right-hand cords unworked.

Link 2 side strips: Place both worked strips on your working surface side by side so working cords line up.

Now cross cord on far right of left-hand strip over cord on far left of right-hand strip. Using cord from left-hand strip as leader work diagonal cording over it with first 7 cords of right-hand strip.

In a similar way work diagonal cording over cord from right-hand side with first 6 cords of left-hand strip.

Work on the centre 12 cords (coming from cording rows just worked):

1st row: Tie 1 flat [square] knot with centre 4 cords.

2nd row: Bringing in 2 cords at either side, tie 2 flat [square] knots.

3rd row: Bring in 2 more cords at either side, and tie 3 flat [square] knots.

4th row: Leave first 2 cords unworked, tie 2 flat [square] knots, leave final 2 cords unworked.

Now cut 2 new cords each about 6 ins. Lay one of these new cords across 16 cords at left-hand side of work, and beginning 2 ins from the end of this cord, work cording over it with each of the 16 cords in turn to form lower edge. Work from left to right, and begin row at left-hand edge of final row of diagonal cording worked on left-hand strip.

In a similar way use 2nd new cord to work cording across 16 cords on right-hand side of work. Link these 2 leaders at centre of work by knotting left-hand leader over right-hand leader.

To finish

Divide cords along lower edge in pairs and thread a bead on to each pair of cords. Tie an overhand knot below each bead to hold it in place, and trim cord ends.

Cut 8 cords, each about 4 ins. Set [mount] 2 of these cords on to the 3rd 'loop' of the cording zig-zag at left-hand edge of left side strip. Set [mount] another 2 cords on to zig-zag loop immediately below. In a similar way set on [mount] remaining 4 cords to right-hand edge of right side strip.

Work on first set of 4 cords: Tie a flat [square] knot with the 4 cords, then divide cords into 2 pairs, thread a bead on to each pair, and tie an overhand knot to hold in place. Trim cords.

Repeat with each of other 3 groups of 4 cords.

Beaded sampler bag

Materials: Heavyweight parcel string. 16 oval glass beads.

Measurements: Finished bag measures approximately 11½ ins square, excluding fringe.

Tension (gauge) check: Chain [sinnet] of 4 flat [square] knots measures 1 in.

Preparation: Each side of the bag is made alike. For each side therefore cut 36 cords, each 8 ft long plus measurement of fringe required. Set [mount] these on to a holding cord of about 18 in.

To make: With cord on far left as leader work a row of horizontal cording across all all cords.

1st pattern panel

With first 4 cords, work a chain of 8 flat [square] knots. Work on next group of 12 cords: with cord 1 as leader slanting down to the right, work diagonal cording over it with cords, 2, 3, 4, 5 and 6. With cord 2 as leader work a 2nd row of diagonal cording immediately below the first with cords, 3, 4, 5, 6 and 1. In a similar way work a double row of diagonal cording slanting down to the left with cord 12 as leader for first row, cord 11 leader for 2nd row.
Link 4 central cords by tying together in a single flat [square] knot. Now let cord 2 continue as leader slanting down to the left and work diagonal cording over it with cords 1, 6, 5, 4 and 3. With cord 1 as leader slanting down to the left work a 2nd row of diagonal cording

for colour illustration, see opposite

immediately below with cords 6, 5, 4, 3 and 2. Complete right-hand side of motif by working a double row of diagonal cording slanting down to the right with cord 11 as leader for the first row, cord 12 leader for 2nd row. With next 4 cords, work a chain of 8 flat [square] knots. Work on next group of 14 cords: tie a flat [square] knot with first 4 cords, then tie a flat [square] knot with cords 3, 4, 5 and 6, then tie another flat [square] knot with cords 1, 2, 3 and 4. Tie a flat [square] knot with cords 11, 12, 13 and 14, then tie a flat [square] knot with cords 9, 10, 11 and 12 and then tie another flat (square) knot with cords 11, 12, 13 and 14. Now using cord 7 as a leader slanting down to the left work diagonal cording over it with cords, 6, 5, 4, 3, 2 and 1. Similarly with cord 8 as leader slanting to the right, work diagonal cording over it with cords 9, 10, 11, 12, 13 and 14. Weave cords in centre of motif (i.e., all cords except leaders) over and under each other to form a criss-cross lattice pattern as shown in illustration opposite. Complete diamond motif by working rows of diagonal cording beneath lattice pattern. Use cord 7 as leader for left-hand row; cord 8 leader for right-hand row.
Tie a flat [square] knot with cords 1, 2, 3 and 4, then tie a flat [square] knot with cords 3, 4, 5 and 6. Similarly tie a flat [square] knot with cords 11, 12, 13 and 14, then tie a flat [square] knot with cords 9, 10, 11 and 12. With next 4 cords work a spiral of 20 half knots (first half of the flat [square] knot tied continuously). Complete pattern panel to match section already worked: i.e., work lattice-work pattern motif with next 14 cords, then flat [square] knot chain with 4 cords, followed by criss-cross of double rows of cording with 12 cords, and finally a flat [square] knot chain with 4 cords.

Divider row: With cord on far left as leader, work a row of horizontal cording across all cords.

2nd pattern panel

Divide cords into groups of 9 cords each.
Work on first group of 9 cords: * with cord on far left as leader slanting down to the right work diagonal cording with all cords in the group.
Work on next group of 9 cords: with cord on far right as leader slanting down to the left work diagonal cording over it with all cords in group. * *
Repeat from * to * * to end of row.
Now tie a flat [square] knot at the lower point of each cording row so cording rows are linked together in pairs. Tie a flat [square] knot at the top of cording rows, again linking 2 cords from one row with the 2 cords from row next to it. Work on first linked motif only: tie a flat [square] knot with first 4 cords, then a flat [square] knot with cords 3, 4, 5 and 6, then tie a flat [square] knot with cords, 5, 6, 7 and 8.
Take cords 9 and 10 through a bead, then complete row by tying flat [square] knots in turn with cords 11, 12, 13 and 14; 13, 14, 15 and 16; 15, 16, 17 and 18.
Tie a flat [square] knot below bead with cords 8, 9, 10 and 11. Work diagonal cording down left-hand side of motif with cord 1 as leader, and cords 2–9 as knotting cords. Work diagonal cording down right-hand side of motif with cord 18 as leader, and cords 17–10 as knotting cords. Complete other motifs across row in a similar way.
Now return to first 4 cords and work a chain of 14 flat [square] knots.
On next 5 cords work a 4-row zig-zag of diagonal cording, using cord on the far right

as leader for each row.
Work on next group of 18 cords: tie cords 8, 9, 10 and 11 in a spiral of 20 half knots.
Tie cords 4, 5, 6 and 7 in a spiral of 10 half knots; tie cords 12, 13, 14 and 15 in a spiral of 10 half knots.
With cord 1 as leader slanting down to the right (leader from row of cording previously worked) work diagonal cording with cords 2–9. With cord 18 as leader slanting down to the left work diagonal cording with cords 17–10.
Now work cords on right-hand side of work to correspond with left-hand patterns worked: i.e., working from right to left, flat [square] knot chain; zig-zag of cording; diamond motif of half knot spirals.
Now work on cords at centre of work; letting cord already being used as leader for diagonal cording slanting down to the left continue as leader, continue diagonal cording at same slant knotting over the leader the cords coming from lower right-hand side of half knot spiral diamond.
In a similar way continue row of diagonal cording slanting down to the right on right of central cords.
Begin at tip of inverted 'V' of cording in centre and tie a single flat [square] knot (2 cords from each side). Work in alternate flat [square] knot pattern, bringing in 2 new cords at each end of every row until finally the row is worked using all cords and lining up with end of cording rows.
Continue in alternate flat [square] knot pattern, this time dropping 2 cords at each end of every row until finally the row is worked with only 1 flat [square] knot in it. You should now have completed a central diamond of alternate flat [square] knot pattern. Complete diamond with a cording row down each of remaining

sides, using same leaders as before. Complete remainder of pattern panel to correspond with section already worked: i.e., 2 more half knot spiral diamonds (one each side of central flat [square] knot diamond); then cording, flat [square] knot and beaded motifs.
Divider row: As first divider row.

3rd pattern panel

Work as for first pattern panel.
Divider row: As first divider row.
Work 2nd side of bag in a similar way.

To make handle

Cut 2 cords, each 16 ft, plus 8 times the length of finished handle required, plus double the measurement of fringe required (i.e., if you wish a handle of 3 ft, and a fringe round lower edge of bag of 6 in, cut handle cords to 16 + 24 + 1 ft, which equals 41 ft).
Double these cords and pin them to your working surface. Measure down from their top loops the depth of fringe you require, then begin knotting from this point. Work a chain of flat [square] knots to a depth of about $11\frac{1}{2}$ in, then continue working in half knot spirals to the measurement of handle required. Finish with a chain of flat [square] knots to $11\frac{1}{2}$ in.

To finish

Trim leader cords to about 1 in of knotting. Press to back of work and secure with a few neat stitches. Place both sides of bag together, wrong sides facing. Position handle so flat [square] knot chains form sides of bag, and spirals form handle. Stitch firmly in position. Now divide cords along lower edge of bag into groups of 8 (4 cords from back with 4 cords from front). Tie these groups into tassels, as described in To finish section of Small sampler bag (see page 261). Trim ends evenly. (*Note:* Instead of stitching final assembly of bag, handle may be worked directly in place by looping knotting cords in flat [square] knot chains round loops at row ends on main bag sections in between each flat [square] knot in the chain, thus linking side sections to main sections as you knot.)

Small sampler bag

Materials: Heavyweight parcel string.

Measurements: Length of bag (excluding fringe and handle) 9¾ ins; width 8½ ins.

Tension (gauge) check: 4 flat [square] knots measure 1 in.

Preparation: *Note:* Each side of the bag is made in the same way. For each side therefore, cut 26 cords each 88 ins. Set [mount] these on to a holding cord of about 14 ins.

To make: With cord on far left as leader, work a row of horizontal cording across all cords.

1st pattern panel

With first 4 cords, work a chain of 4 flat [square] knots. Work on next 8 cords: slant first of the 8 cords down to the right and work a row of diagonal cording with remaining 7 cords over the first cord as leader. Arrange slant of leader so cording row lines up with base of flat [square] knot chain already worked. With next 4 cords work a spiral of half knots (first half of the flat [square] knot tied continuously). Stop spiral at same depth as flat [square] knot chain and diagonal cording row already worked. With each of next 2 groups of 4 cords, work a chain of 7 flat [square] knots. With next 4 cords, work a spiral of half knots to same depth as previous spiral of half knots. With each of next 2 groups of 4 cords, work a chain of 7 flat [square] knots. With next 4 cords, work a spiral of half knots.
Work on next 8 cords: slant last of the 8 cords down to the left and use as leader for a row of diagonal cording, knotting other 7 cords over this leader cord.
With last 4 cords, work a chain of 6 flat knots. Now cross each pair of adjoining flat [square] knot chains over each other, as shown in illustration. Pin to hold in place.
Divider rows: With cord on far left as leader work a row of horizontal cording across all cords. Reverse direction of leader around a pin, and work a 2nd row of horizontal cording immediately below.

for colour illustration, see opposite

2nd pattern panel

Work on first group of 8 cords: Work a chain of 3 flat [square] knots with each group of 4 cords. Link the 2 chains by knotting right-hand 2 cords of left-hand chain with left-hand 2 cords of right-hand chain in a single flat [square] knot. Work a further 3 flat [square] knots with first 4 cords, and with 2nd 4 cords. Work on next group of 16 cords: work in alternate flat [square] knot pattern, keeping left-hand edge straight, and dropping 2 cords from right-hand edge on each row until row with only 1 flat [square] knot in it is worked.

Now work on right-hand cords to correspond with left-hand side already worked: i.e., working from right-hand side in – 2 chains of linked flat [square] knots, followed by alternate flat [square] knot pattern over 16 cords, right-hand edge kept straight, with a slanting left-hand edge.

Now work on central panel thus: with cord 17 as leader slanting to the left, work a row of diagonal cording across all cords from alternate flat [square] knot pattern section. With cord 18 as leader, work a 2nd row of diagonal cording immediately below this first one. In a similar way work a double row of diagonal cording slanting down to the right with cords 19 and 20.

Now fill in central diamond of half knot spirals. Divide cords coming from diagonal cording rows into groups of 4, so central spiral will be tied with 2 cords from the left, 2 from the right. You will then have 3 spirals on either side of this central spiral, with an odd unworked cord at either end. Central spiral will have 32 half knots tied in it (allow spiral to twist round itself after every 4th knot); first spirals on either side of central spiral will each have 28 knots; spirals either side of this will have 24 knots; and final 2 spirals at either

end will have 16 knots.

Now let cord 18 continue as leader. Reverse its direction round a pin, and let it slant down to the right. Work diagonal cording over it with all cords on left-hand side of diamond. Work a 2nd row of diagonal cording immediately below.

In a similar way work a double row of diagonal cording down right-hand side of diamond with cords 19 and 20 as leaders.

Now complete lower part of pattern panel to correspond with upper part so you have linked chains of flat [square] knots, and diamonds of alternate flat [square] knot patterns. Link the single knot of the alternate flat [square] knot triangle to the flat [square] knot chains next to it by tying a single flat [square] knot with 2 cords of each.

Divider rows: As previous divider rows.

3rd pattern panel

On first 4 cords, work a chain of 6 flat [square] knots. Work on next 8 cords: work a cross-over of diagonal cording thus – with cord 1 as leader slanting down to the right, work diagonal cording over it with cords 2, 3 and 4. Similarly with cord 8 as leader slanting down to the left, work diagonal cording over it with cords 7, 6 and 5. Now link the central point of the cross-over by tying a flat [square] knot with the 4 central cords. Renumber cords in the position in which they now lie from 1–8. With cord 4 as leader slanting down to the left work diagonal cording over it with cords 3, 2 and 1. With cord 5 as leader slanting down to the right, work diagonal cording over it with cords 6, 7 and 8. With each of next 2 groups of 4 cords, work chains of 2 flat [square] knots. Link the chains by tying 2 right-hand cords of chain 1 with 2 left hand cords of chain 2 in a single flat [square] knot. Then continue with chains as before, 2 flat [square] knots in each chain.

Work on next 6 cords: with cord 6 as leader slanting down to the left, work diagonal cording over it with cords 5, 4, 3, 2 and 1.

With cord 5 as leader slanting down to the left, work a 2nd row of diagonal cording slanting down to the left immediately below the first, knotting over it cords 4, 3, 2 and 1.

Now reverse direction of cord 5 round a pin and work diagonal cording slanting down to the right knotting over it cords 1, 2, 3 and 4. Similarly, reverse direction of cord 6 round a pin and knot over it cords 1, 2, 3, 4 and 5. Complete rest of pattern panel to correspond with first part, reversing direction of patterns as required.

Divider rows: As first divider rows. Work 2nd half of bag in a similar way.

To make handle

Cut 2 cords, each 5½ yds plus 8 times the length of finished handle required. Double these cords and pin them to your Working surface. Begin knotting about 9 ins below top loops of cords. Work a flat [square] knot chain to a depth of about 9¾ ins. Now work in half knot spirals until handle is length required. Finish with a chain of flat [square] knots to 9¾ ins.

To finish

Trim leader cords to about 1 in of knotting. Press to back of work, and secure with a few neat stitches. Place both sides of bag together, wrong sides facing. Position handle so flat [square] knot chains form sides of bag, and spirals form handle. Stitch firmly in position. Now divide cords along lower edge of bag into groups of 8 (4 cords from back with 4 cords from front). Tie these groups into tassels: take one of the cords, and form a loop in front of other cords in group. Take it round the group from left to right and them down through loop. Draw tight. Repeat 4 more times. Trim cord ends evenly.

Sampler wall hanging

Materials: Heavyweight parcel string; assorted glass and china beads.

Measurements: Hanging measures approximately 22 ins long, excluding fringe; 10 ins wide.

Tension (gauge) check: A chain [sinnet] of 3 flat [square] knots measures 1 in.

Preparation: Cut 22 cords, each 16 ft, plus length of fringe required. Set [mount] these on to a holding cord of about 24 ins.

To make: With cord on far left as leader, work a row of horizontal cording across all cords.

1st pattern panel

With first 4 cords, work a chain of 4 flat [square] knots. Work on next group of 8 cords: with cord 1 as leader slanting down to the right, work diagonal cording over it with cords 2, 3 and 4. Similarly slant cord 8 down to the left and work diagonal cording over it with cords 7, 6 and 5. Link the 2 leaders at this central point by looping one around the other. Cord 1 now continues as leader and is slanted down to the left. Work diagonal cording over it with cords 4, 3 and 2. Complete criss-cross of cording by working diagonal cording slanting down to the right with cords 5, 6 and 7 over cord 8.

With next 4 cords, work a chain of 4 flat [square] knots. Work on next group of 6 cords: work 3 rows of diagonal cording slanting down the left, each row immediately below the previous one. First row will have cord 4 as leader, and cords 3, 2 and 1 will be knotted over it. In the 2nd row, cord 5 is leader, and cords 3, 2, 1 and 4 are knotting cords. In the 3rd row, cord 6 is leader, and cords 3, 2, 1, 4 and 5 are knotting cords.

Now complete remainder of pattern panel to correspond with section already worked, reversing direction of triple row cording motif.

Divider row: With cord on far left as leader, work a row of horizontal cording across all cords.

for colour illustration, see opposite

2nd pattern panel

Work in alternate flat [square] knot pattern for 7 rows. After the first row, drop 2 cords on each row at outside edges. After the 3rd row, leave centre 4 cords unworked, then drop 4 further cords in the centre with each subsequent row, so you eventually have a 'W' shape of alternate flat [square] knot pattern. Final row should have only 2 flat [square] knots in it – one knot in each tip of the 'W'.

With cord on far left as leader slanting down to the right work diagonal cording over it with all cords coming from left-hand side of the 'W'.

Similarly work a row of diagonal cording down the right-hand side of the 'W', using cord on far right of work as leader. Work rows of diagonal cording in a similar way down each of the inside edges of the 'W', using left-hand central cord as leader for left-hand row; right-hand central cord as leader for right-hand row.

Take 4 cords now lying in centre of work (2 from left-hand cording row just worked, 2 from right-hand row). Work a spiral of 16 half knots (first half of the flat [square] knot tied continuously). With 4 cords on left of this spiral, work a spiral of 8 half knots. With 4 cords on right of centre spiral, work another spiral of 8 half knots.

Now with same leaders as before work diagonal cording beneath spirals just worked, to complete central diamond motif. Now complete pattern panel to match section already worked, working a row of diagonal cording at each side of panel first, with same leaders as before, then filling in remaining area with the alternate flat [square] knot pattern.

Divider row: As previous divider row.

3rd pattern panel

With centre 4 cords work a half knot spiral of 24 knots. Now go back to top left-hand corner of work. With cord 2nd from the left as leader slanting down to the right work a row of diagonal cording with all cords on left-hand side of work. Stop cording row at midway point of central spiral already worked (i.e. the 2 left-hand cords of spiral will be used as knotting cords for the diagonal cording).

Work a 2nd row of cording immediately below this first one, using cord on far left of work as leader. Use same knotting cords as in previous row.

In a similar way work a double row of diagonal cording down right-hand side of work.

Link the 4 cords now lying in centre of work (i.e. leaders from cording rows) by tying them in a single flat knot. Return to cords on left-hand side of work.

Work on first 6 cords: Work a 4-row zig-zag of diagonal cording, using cord 6 as leader throughout. End of 4th row of the zig-zag should line up with linked point of central 'V' of cording.

Work on next 4 cords: With central 2 cords as the knotbearing core, work a chain of reversed double half hitches from right and left alternately.

To work a reversed double half hitch: Keep central knotbearing core cords taut, as for a flat [square] knot, then tie a half hitch from the left across the knotbearing cords with cord 1.

Complete the knot by taking cord 1 under the knotbearing cords, then up and across them from right to left, then down through the loop formed. Draw tight. This completes one reversed double half hitch worked from the left.

To work the knot from the right, use cord 4 as knotting cord, and work sequence as given above, but working half hitch from the right across knotbearing cords then taking knotting cord under them, and up and across them from left to right.

A chain of reversed double half hitches tied alternately from the left and right is sometimes known as a tatted bar. Work 9 reversed double half hitches altogether, which should bring chain level with zig-zag of cording already worked.

Now work on next group of 8 cords: With first 4 cords tie a chain of 2 flat [square] knots; with 2nd group of 4 cords tie 1 flat [square] knot. Now link these 2 sets of cords by tying a multi-end flat [square] knot – i.e., you will have double knotting cords, and a central knotbearing core of 4 cords.

Divide into 2 groups of 4 cords each again, and work a single flat [square] knot with each group. Link groups as before in 1 multi-end flat [square] knot. Complete right-hand side of work to correspond with left-hand pattern.

Divider row: As first divider row.

4th pattern panel

On first 4 cords, work a tatted bar, with a total of 12 reversed double half hitches.

Work a similar tatted bar with 4 final cords in row.

Now work on central cords: Work 1 row of flat [square] knots across all cords. Now divide into 2 equal groups and continue in the alternate flat [square] knot pattern on each group, dropping 2 cords at each end of every row to form a 'V' of pattern. Work diagonal cording down each side of the 'V' shapes, using cord on far left as leader for left-hand row; cord on far right as leader for right-hand row. Complete 2nd 'V' in a similar way.

Work on cords in centre of work (coming from 2 centre rows of diagonal cording just worked). Weave these cords over and under each other to form a criss-cross lattice pattern, as shown in photograph on page 263. With same leaders as before, reverse their directions round pins and work a row of diagonal cording below lattice pattern to form a central diamond motif.

Work 2 final rows of diagonal cording to complete pattern panel, using same leaders as before to the left and right of central diamond motif, and reversing their directions round pins.

Divider row: As first divider row.

5th pattern panel

Divide cords into groups of 4 cords each. On each group work a half knot spiral with 20 half knots in each spiral.

Divider row: As first divider row.

To finish

Thread a bead on to each cord end, positioning bead where you wish on the cord, then tying an overhand knot below to secure. Trim cord ends to length required and fray out ends below beads if wished.

Untie overhand knots in holding cord, and tie ends of holding cord together so complete hanging may be hung on the wall.

(*Note:* If wished, cords for this design may be set on [mounted] directly to a length of wooden rod, to give a more substantial heading for the design.)

Tatting

Historical mention of tatting or 'purling' ('pearling') is first
made in Chaucer's 'Canterbury Tales', but tatting is known
to have been a craft of great accomplishment in Brussels and
throughout France and the Near East down the centuries.
Known as 'wrap weaving', the craft has flourished in Cam-
bodia. Many beautiful examples of tatting shuttles fashioned
in such exotic materials as abalone shell and ivory exist in
museum collections throughout Europe and Asia.

Some of the most delightful traditional designs are presented
here in their simpler, most effective forms.

Where terminology varies, an equivalent term
is given in [ ].

Tatting abbreviations

r(s) – *ring(s)*
  sr – *small ring*
  lr – *large ring*
  ds – *double stitch*
  p – *picot*
smp – *small picot*
  lp – *long picot*
  sep – *separated*
  cl – *close*
  rw – *reverse work*
  sp – *space*
ch(s) – *chain(s)*
  tog – *together*

* Asterisk
*Repeat instructions following
the asterisk as many more
times as specified in addition
to the original.*

*Repeat instructions in ( )
as many times as specified.*

For example, '(R of 8 ds, p, 8 ds, cl) twice',
means to make all that is in parentheses
twice in all.

Laundering tatting

Use a warm lather of pure soap flakes and
wash in the usual way, either by hand or
washing machine. If desired, the article
may be spin-dried until it is damp, or left
until it is half dry. Place a piece of paper,
either plain white or squared, on top of a
clean, flat board. Following the correct
measurements, draw the shape of
the finished article on to the paper,
using ruler and set-square for squares
and rectangles and a pair of compasses
for circles. Using rustless pins, pin
the tatting out to the pencilled shape,
taking care not to strain the tatting. Pin
out the general shape first, then finish by
pinning out each picot, loop or space into
position. Special points to note carefully
when pinning out are:

a When pinning loops, make sure the pin
is in the centre of each loop to form
balanced lines.

b When pinning scallops, make all the
scallops the same size and regularly
curved.

c Pull out all picots.

If the tatting requires to be slightly stif-
fened, use a solution of starch (1 dessert-
spoonful to 1 pint hot water), and dab
lightly over the article. Raise the tatting
up off the paper to prevent it sticking as
it dries. When dry, remove the pins and
press the article lightly with a hot iron.

How to tat

For left-handed pupils

The directions for each stitch apply to both the right and left-handed. The left-handed work from right to left. Place a pocket mirror to the left of each illustration and the exact working position will be reflected.

1

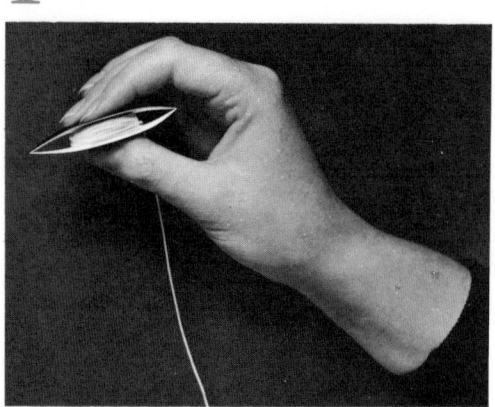

Hold the flat side of the shuttle in a horizontal position, between the thumb and the forefinger of the right hand. Allow approximately 15 ins of the shuttle thread to hang free from the back of the shuttle.

2

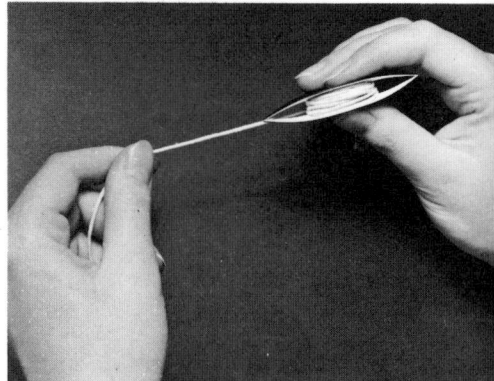

Grasp the free end of the shuttle thread between the thumb and the forefinger of the left hand.

3

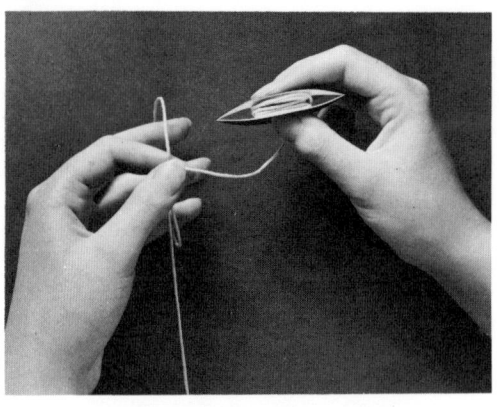

Spread out the middle, ring and little fingers of the left hand and pass the thread over them.

4

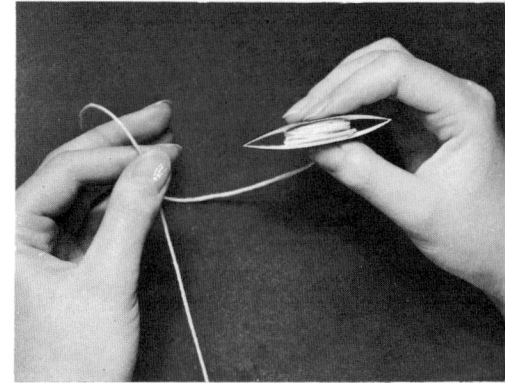

Bring the thread round the fingers of the left hand to form a circle and hold it securely between the thumb and the forefinger.

5

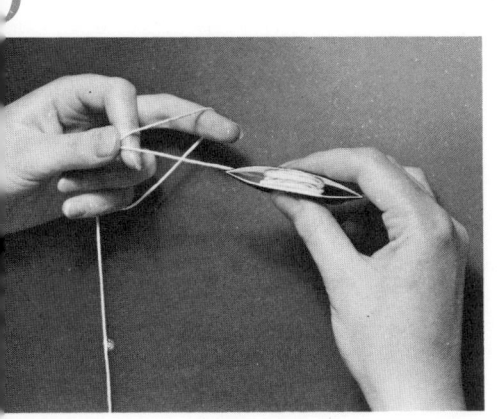

Bend the ring and the little finger of the left hand to catch the thread against the palm.

6

Raise the middle finger of the left hand to 'open' the circle.

7

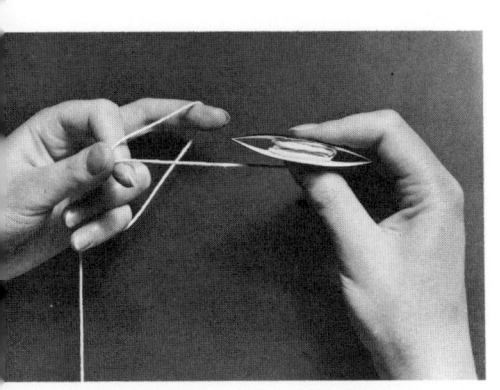

Adjust the thread so that the fingers do not feel strained and draw the shuttle thread out to its full length keeping the right and left hands at equal levels.

8

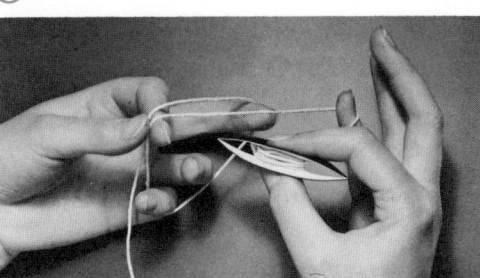

Pass the shuttle thread round the back of the little finger of the right hand. Both hands are now in position to commence the basic stitch in tatting known as the Double Stitch.

First half of double stitch

9

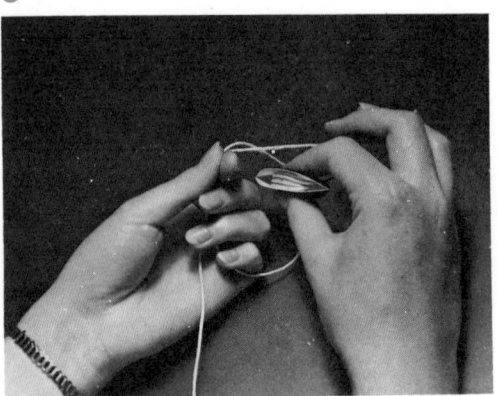

With the thread in position, drop the middle finger of the left hand and move the shuttle forward passing it under the shuttle thread and through the circle.

10

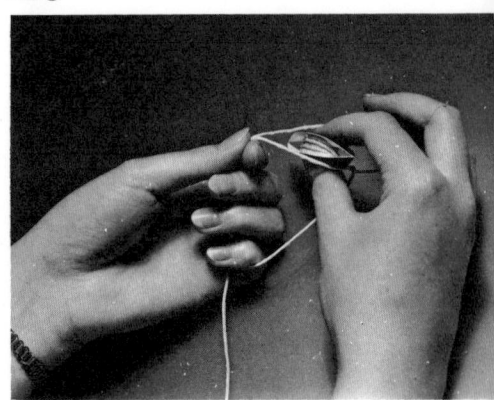

Bring the shuttle back over the circle of thread and under the shuttle thread.

11

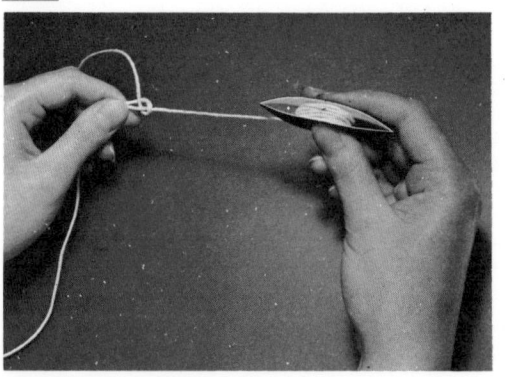

Relaxing the fingers of the left hand, drop the thread from the little finger of the right hand and draw the shuttle thread taut with a sharp jerk.

12

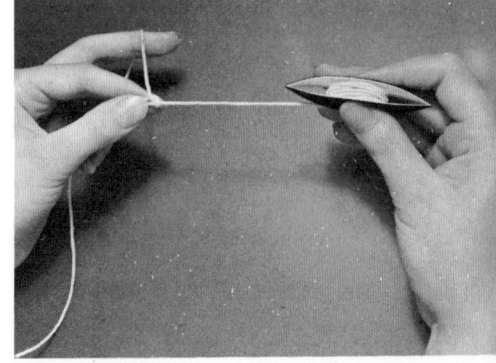

Slowly raise the middle finger of the left hand, slide the loop into position between the thumb and forefinger. This completes the first half of the double stitch.

Second half of double stitch

13

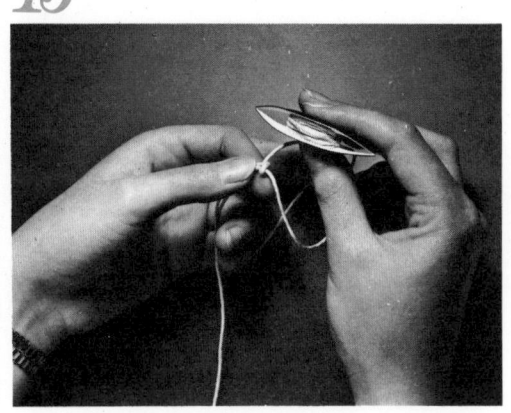

Move the shuttle forward, dropping the shuttle thread and passing the shuttle over the circle and back through between the circle and shuttle threads.

14

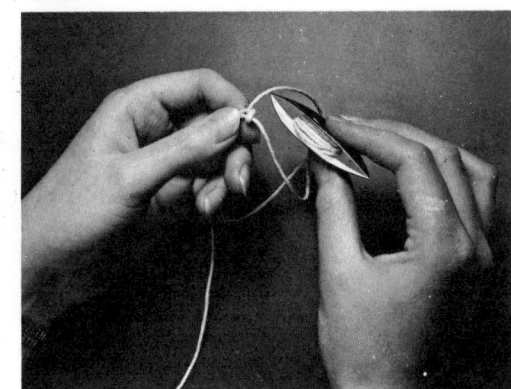

15

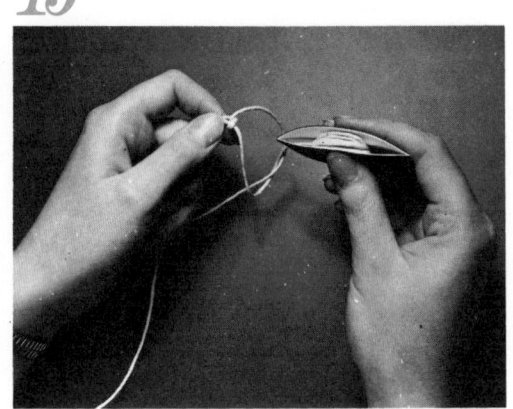

Drop the middle finger of the left hand.

16

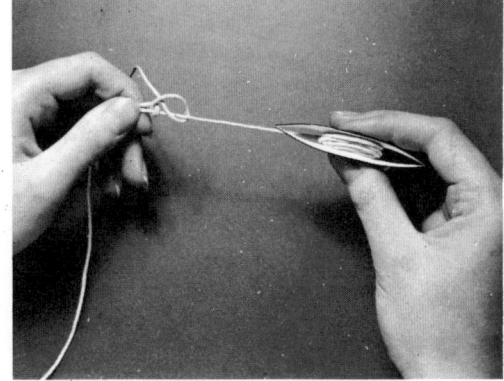

Relaxing the fingers of the left hand, draw the shuttle thread taut with a sharp jerk.

17

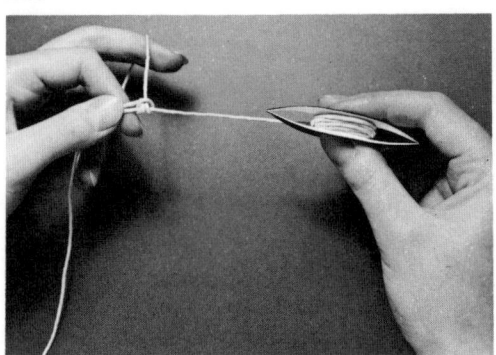

Slowly raise the middle finger of the left hand to slide the loop into position next to the first half of the stitch. This completes the second half of the double stitch.

18

This shows hands and shuttle in position to commence next double stitch.
Once this stitch has been properly mastered you should be able to work any of the designs in this book.
Practise the following directions. They give in detail the fundamentals of rings, picots and joinings.

Rings, picots and joinings

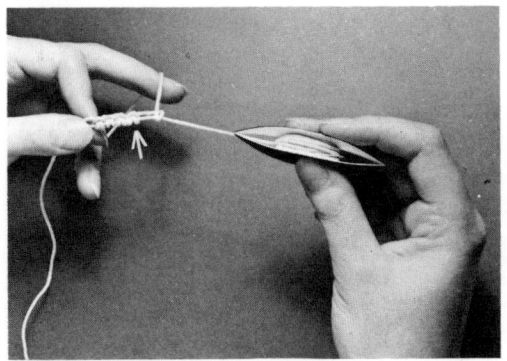

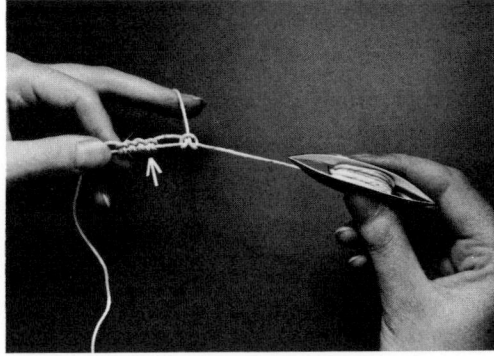

First ring

As each double stitch is formed slide it along the circle of thread to meet the preceding double stitch. Hold them securely between the thumb and forefinger. (See the arrows in *figs 19, 20 and 21.)*

Make four double stitches. Then make the first half of a double stitch sliding it to within $\frac{1}{4}$ in of the preceding stitch.

Now complete the double stitch.

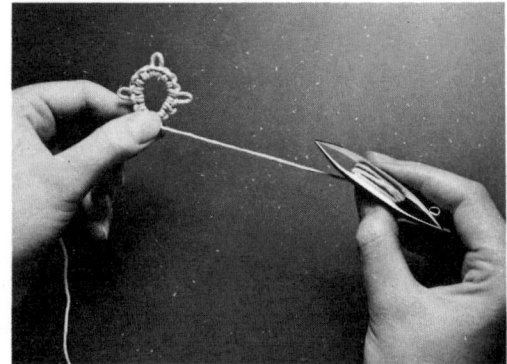

Slide the stitch along the ring to meet the first four double stitches. The small loop formed between the last two double stitches is a picot. The size of this may be altered as desired by adjusting the space left from the preceding stitch. Make three more double stitches. Make a second picot and four double stitches. Make a third picot and four double stitches.

Holding the stitches securely between the thumb and forefinger of the left hand, draw the shuttle thread tight so that the first and last stitches meet forming a ring. In general instructions the ring just completed would be written as:– R of 4 ds, 3 ps sep by 4 ds, 4 ds, cl.

Second ring and joining

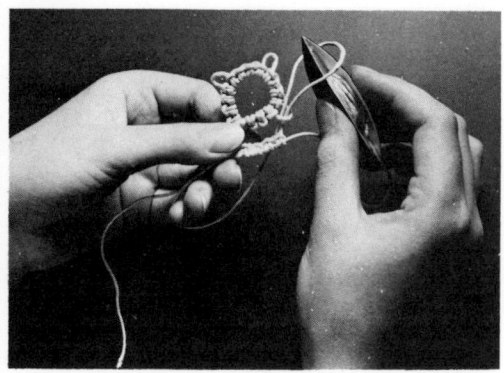

i. Wind the thread round the left hand in position for another ring. Leaving a space of ¼ in from base of previous ring, make four double stitches. **ii.** Insert the hook through the last picot of the previous ring and pull the circle thread through, being careful not to twist it as you do so.
iii. Pass the shuttle through the loop. Slowly raise the middle finger of the left hand to draw up the loop. This stands as the first half of the next double stitch.
iv. Now work the **second** half of a double stitch. (A joining and one double stitch have now been completed.) Work 3 ds, 2 ps sep by 4 ds, 4 ds, cl. (Second ring completed.)

Using ball thread and shuttle

The preceding instructions have been given in detail so that you may easily understand the various stages and their abbreviations. Now you are ready to read the same instructions as they will appear later in the chapter. When your rings are even and your picots uniform in size, proficiency should be acquired in the use of the ball thread and shuttle thread before attempting to follow a full set of instructions. The ball thread is used only in the working of chains. Rings are made with the shuttle thread.

Although some designs are made up of rings and others only contain chains, most designs consist of a combination of these two. For these it is necessary to use the shuttle thread and the ball thread. Commence by tying the ends of the two threads together. Make a ring as before.

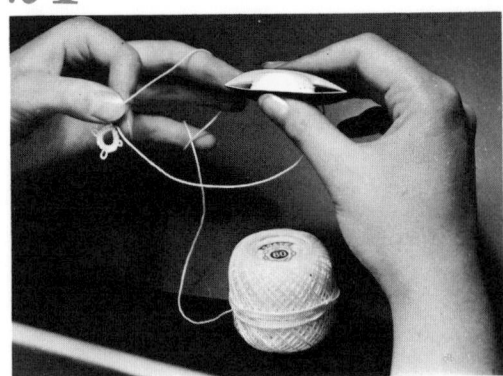

Unlike rings, chains are made with the thread held across the back of the fingers of the left hand, winding it round the little finger to control the tension.

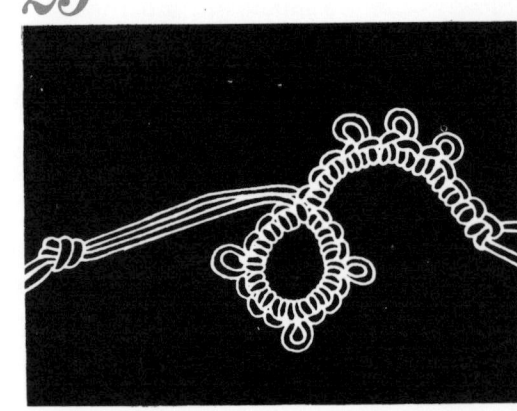

A chain consists of a given number of double stitches worked over the ball thread with the shuttle.
A chain may also include picots.

Reversing

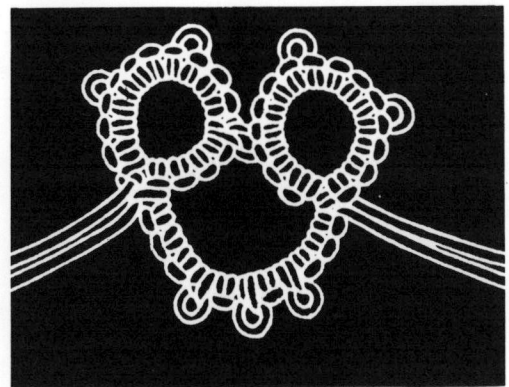

In tatting it will be noticed that the rounded end of the working ring or chain faces upwards. When working a design of rings and chains it is sometimes necessary to reverse work. *(See also fig 27.)*

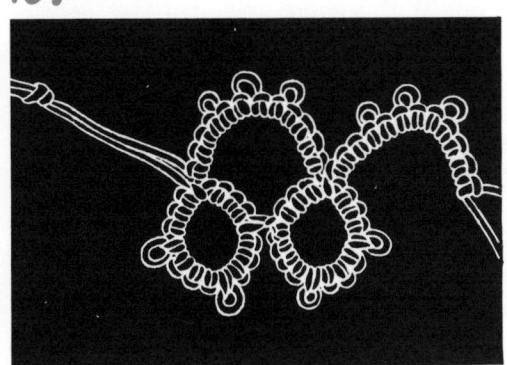

To reverse work turn the ring or chain just completed to face downwards, i.e., in the reverse position. The **next** ring or chain is then worked in the usual way having the rounded end facing upwards.

Two shuttles

When rings are to be worked in two colours two shuttles are used. The two colours (one in each shuttle) may be alternated. When this takes place the shuttle which made the preceding ring is dropped, the second shuttle is picked up and a ring is made as before. When the rings are separated by a chain, the thread of the second shuttle is held similarly to the ball thread in *fig 24.*

Josephine knot

This is an ornamental ring, consisting of the first half of a double stitch worked a specified number of times.

Finish off ends

Make flat knot, eg a Reef Knot or a Weaver's Knot close to the base of the last ring or chain. Do not cut off ends as the strain during working may loosen the knot. With a single strand of Mercer-Crochet Cotton, oversew the ends neatly to the wrong side of the work. *(See fig 28.)*

Further hints

To join threads

(a) When ball and shuttle threads are used, a knot can be avoided at the beginning of the work by filling the shuttle and commencing the ring without cutting the thread.

(b) Make a flat knot, eg, a Reef Knot or a Weaver's Knot close to the base of the last ring or chain. Do not cut off the ends, as the strain during working may loosen the knot.

Equipment

Threads

Coats Mercer-Crochet in no. 10, 20, 40 or 60. All the articles illustrated in this book can be worked in any of these four sizes. *Note:* Coats Mercer-Crochet is available in a variety of colours in the sizes mentioned above. Your retailer will be pleased to show you our shade card.

Shuttles

Shuttles are made in various materials, such as bone, tortoiseshell and plastic. Choose one that is not more than $2\frac{3}{4}$ in long. A longer shuttle is more clumsy and makes the speed of work slower. The designs in this book have been worked with a Milward tatting shuttle. These shuttles are supplied in a packet which contains a separate hook for joinings.

Winding the shuttles

Wind the thread round the centre of the shuttle. If there is a hole in the centre of the bobbin, insert the thread through the hole and tie a knot. Do not wind the thread beyond the edge of the shuttle. When making motifs it is advisable to count the number of turns of thread round the shuttle so that the amount of thread used to make one motif can be assessed. This will prevent unnecessary joining of thread.

Handkerchief edging 1

Materials: Coats Mercer-Crochet no. 40 (20 grms).
1 ball. This model is worked in Dk Jade.
Milward tatting shuttle.
Handkerchief.

Measurements: Depth of edging – $\frac{3}{4}$ in.

1st row: Tie ball and shuttle threads together. * R of 8 ds, p, 8 ds, cl, rw. Ch of 5 ds, p, 5 ds, rw. R of 8 ds, join to p of previous r, 8 ds, cl; repeat from * to next corner. (R of 8 ds, p, 8 ds, cl) twice; repeat from first * joining last r to base of first r. Tie ends, cut and oversew neatly on wrong side.

2nd row: Tie ball and shuttle threads together. Attach shuttle thread to p at join of first 2 rs, * ch of 10 ds, join by shuttle thread to p at join of next 2 rs; repeat from * to within first corner, ch of 10 ds, join by shuttle thread to next p. Ch of 8 ds, join to p of next corner r. Ch of 10 ds; repeat from first * joining last ch by shuttle thread to same place as first ch. Tie ends, cut and oversew neatly on wrong side.

3rd row: Tie ball and shuttle threads together. Working over 2nd row attach shuttle thread to p at join of first 2 rs on 1st row, * ch of 4 ds, 5 ps sep by 2 ds, 4 ds, working over 2nd row join by shuttle thread to p at join of next 2 rs on 1st row; repeat from * to p of first r at next corner. Ch of 4 ds, 5 ps sep by 2 ds, 4 ds, working over 2nd row join by shuttle thread to p of next corner r. Ch of 4 ds, 5 ps sep by 2 ds; repeat from first * joining last ch to same place as first ch. Tie ends, cut and oversew neatly on wrong side.
Sew edging to handkerchief.
Damp and pin out to measurements.

Handkerchief edging 2

Materials: Coats Mercer-Crochet no. 40 (20 grms).
1 ball. This model is worked in White.
Milward tatting shuttle.
Handkerchief.

Tension (gauge): Depth of edging – ½ in.

1st row: Tie ball and shuttle threads together. Join to handkerchief ⅛ in to right of any corner. * Ch of 4 ds, p, 4 ds, using hook join by shuttle thread to handkerchief ¼ in along; repeat from * to within ⅛ in from next corner. Ch of 5 ds, 3 ps sep by 5 ds, 5 ds, join by shuttle thread ⅛ in from corner on next side (corner ch); repeat from first * 3 times more, joining last ch to same place as first ch. Tie ends, cut and oversew neatly on wrong side.

2nd row: Tie ball and shuttle threads together, join to p of first ch on 1st row. * Ch of 2 ds, 1 smp, 1 ds, 1 p, 1 ds, 1 lp, 1 ds, 1 p, 1 ds, 1 smp, 2 ds, join by shuttle thread to next p; repeat from * to within corner ch. Ch of 5 ds, join by shuttle thread to next p. (Ch of 2 ds, 1 smp, 1 ds, 1 p, 1 ds, 1 lp, 1 ds, 1 p, 1 ds, 1 smp, 2 ds, join by shuttle thread to next p) twice. Ch of 5 ds, join by shuttle thread to next p; repeat from first * 3 times more joining last ch to same place as first ch. Tie ends, cut and oversew neatly on wrong side.
Damp and pin out to measurements.

Handkerchief edging 3

Materials: Coats Mercer-Crochet no. 40
(20 grms).
1 ball. This model is worked in White.
Milward tatting shuttle.
Handkerchief.

Measurements: Depth of edging – ½ in.

1st row: Tie ball and shuttle threads
together. Attach thread to handkerchief ⅛ in
to right of any corner. *, Ch of 4 ds, p, 4 ds,
using hook join by shuttle thread to handkerchief ¼ in along; repeat from * to within ⅛ in
from next corner. Ch of 5 ds, 3 ps sep by 5 ds,
5 ds, join by shuttle thread ⅛ in from corner on
next side (corner ch); repeat from first * 3
times more, joining last ch to same place as
first ch. Tie ends, cut and oversew neatly on
wrong side.

2nd row: Tie ball and shuttle threads
together. R of 4 ds, join to first p of first ch,
4 ds, cl, rw. * Ch of 2 ds, 1 p, 1 ds, 1 lp, 1 ds, 1 p,
2 ds, rw. R of 4 ds, join to next p of next ch, 4
ds, cl, rw; repeat from * to within corner ch,
omitting rw at end of last repeat, r of 4 ds, join
to first p of corner ch, 4 ds, cl, rw. Ch of 2 ds,
2 ps sep by 1 ds, 1 ds, 1 lp, 1 ds, 2 ps sep by 1 ds,
2 ds, rw. R of 4 ds, join to next p of corner ch,
4 ds, cl, rw. Ch of 2 ds, 2 ps sep by 1 ds, 1 ds,
1 lp, 1 ds, 2 ps sep by 1 ds, 2 ds, rw. R of 4 ds,
join to next p of corner ch, 4 ds, cl. R of 4 ds,
join to p of next ch, 4 ds, cl, rw; repeat from
first * omitting r at end of last repeat and joining last r to first r. Tie ends, cut and oversew
neatly on wrong side. Damp and pin out to
measurements.

Edging for guest towel

Materials: Coats Mercer-Crochet no. 20 (20 grms).
1 ball. This model is worked in Rose Madder.
Milward tatting shuttle.
Guest towel.
The above quantity is sufficient for 2 edgings.

Measurements:
Depth of edging – 1¾ ins.
Length of edging – 14 ins approximately.

1st row: Tie ball and shuttle threads together. R of 8 ds, p, 8 ds, cl, rw. Ch of 6 ds, p, 6 ds, 3 ps sep by 1 ds, 6 ds, p, 6 ds, rw. * R of 8 ds, join to p on previous r; 8 ds, cl. R of 8 ds, p, 8 ds, cl, rw. Ch of 6 ds, join by ball thread to last p on previous ch, 6 ds, 3 ps sep by 1 ds, 6 ds, p, 6 ds, rw; repeat from * 17 times more or length required, ending with r of 8 ds, join to p on previous r, 8 ds, cl. Tie ends, cut and oversew neatly on wrong side.

2nd row: Tie ball and shuttle threads together, attach to base of first r on previous row. * Ch of 10 ds, p, 10 ds, join by shuttle thread to base of next 2 rs; repeat from * joining last ch to base of last r on previous row. Tie ends, cut and oversew neatly on wrong side.

3rd row: Tie ball and shuttle threads together. Attach ball thread to p on first ch on previous row. Ch of 6 ds, p, 6 ds. R of 4 ds, 3 ps sep by 4 ds, 4 ds, cl. * R of 4 ds, join to last p of previous r, 2 ds, 6 ps sep by 2 ds, 4 ds, cl R of 4 ds, join to last p on previous r, 4 ds, 2 ps sep by 4 ds, 4 ds, cl. Ch of 6 ds, p, 6 ds, join by shuttle thread to next p, * * ch of 6 ds, p, 6 ds. R of 4 ds, p, 4 ds, join to centre p on previous r, 4 ds, p, 4 ds, cl; repeat from * ending last repeat at * *. Tie ends, cut and oversew neatly on wrong side.

Damp and pin out to measurements.
Sew neatly to one end of towel.

for colour illustrations, see pages 286 and 287

Motif cheval set

Materials: Coats Mercer-Crochet no. 40 (20 grms).
2 balls. This model is worked in Rose Madder.
Milward tatting shuttle.

Size of motif: 2 ins square.

Measurements: Large mat – 8 × 14 ins.
Small mat – 6 × 8 ins.

Large mat

First motif

1st row: (R of 8 ds, 2 ps sep by 4 ds, 8 ds, cl) 4 times, join to base of first r worked in group. Sp of $\frac{1}{2}$ in. R of 8 ds, join to corresponding p of adjacent r, 4 ds, p, 8 ds, cl. (R of 8 ds, 2 ps sep by 4 ds, 8 ds, cl) twice. R of 8 ds, p, 4 ds, join to first p of adjacent r in previous group, 8 ds, cl, join to base of first r worked in group. * Sp of $\frac{1}{2}$ in. R of 8 ds, join to corresponding p of 3rd r worked in previous group, 4 ds, p, 8 ds, cl. (R of 8 ds, 2 ps sep by 4 ds, 8 ds, cl) twice. R of 8 ds, p, 4 ds, join to free p of 4th r worked in previous group, 8 ds, cl, join to base of first r worked in group; repeat from * once more, joining 3rd and 4th rs to corresponding ps on previous groups. Sp of $\frac{1}{2}$ in, join to base of first group of rs worked. Tie ends, cut and oversew neatly on wrong side.

2nd row: Tie ball and shuttle threads together. Attach thread to first p on any corner r of first row. * Ch of 2 ds, 3 ps sep by 2 ds, 2 ds. R of 4 ds, 5 ps sep by 3 ds, 4 ds, cl. Ch of 2 ds, 3 ps sep by 2 ds, 2 ds, join by shuttle thread to next p on same r of first row. Ch of 8 ds, join by shuttle thread to free p on next r of first row. Ch of 4 ds. R as before. Ch of 4 ds, join by shuttle thread to next free p on first row. Ch of 8 ds, join by shuttle thread to next p; repeat from *, joining last ch by shuttle thread to same place where thread was attached. Tie ends, cut and oversew neatly on wrong side.

Second motif
Work first row as for first motif.
2nd row: Attach thread and work first ch as for first motif. R of 4 ds, 3 ps sep by 3 ds, 3 ds, join to corresponding p on any corner r of first motif, 3 ds, p, 4 ds, cl. Work to next r as for first motif. R of 4 ds, 2 ps sep by 3 ds, 3 ds, join to centre p of corresponding r on first motif, 3 ds, 2 ps sep by 3 ds, 4 ds, cl. Work to next r as for first motif. R of 4 ds, p, 3 ds, join to corresponding p on next corner r of first motif, 3 ds, 3 ps sep by 3 ds, 4 ds, cl.
Complete as for first motif.
Work 4 rows of 7 motifs, joining adjacent sides as second motif was joined to first motif.

Small mat *make 2*

Work 3 rows of 4 motifs, joining in same manner as for large mat.
Damp and press.

Edging for a chairback

Materials: Coats Chain Mercer-Crochet no. 20 (20 grms).

1 ball. This model is worked in Dk Ecru.
Piece of Old Bleach linen, Biscuit, 18 ins. square.
Milward tatting shuttle.

Depth of edging: 3¼ ins.

Measurement: 17 × 20¼ ins.
Trim linen to 17½ ins square. Make a ¼ in hem all round linen and slip stitch in position.

Edging

1st row: Tie ball and shuttle threads together. * R of 10 ds, 2 ps sep by 4 ds, 10 ds, cl, rw. Ch of 10 ds, 2 ps sep by 4 ds, 10 ds, rw. R of 10 ds, join to last p of previous r, 4 ds, p, 10 ds, cl; repeat from * for length required, having an uneven number of ch scallops. Tie ends, cut and oversew neatly on wrong side.

2nd row: Tie ball and shuttle threads together. R of 10 ds, 2 ps sep by 4 ds, 10 ds, cl, rw. Ch of 10 ds, join to first p on first ch of previous row, 4 ds, join to next p, 10 ds, rw, complete row as for first row, joining each ch to ch of first row. Tie ends, cut and oversew neatly on wrong side.

3rd row: Tie ball and shuttle threads together. R of 10 ds, join to free p on first r of previous row, 4 ds, p, 10 ds, cl, rw. * Ch of 5 ds, 2 ps sep by 12 ds, 5 ds, rw. R of 10 ds, join to last p of previous r, 4 ds, join to next free p on previous row, 10 ds, cl. R of 10 ds, join to next free p on previous row, 4 ds, p, 10 ds, cl, rw; repeat from * omitting r at end of last repeat. Tie ends, cut and oversew neatly on wrong side.

4th row: Tie ball and shuttle threads together. R of 12 ds, join to first p on first ch of previous row, 8 ds, p, 4 ds, cl, rw. * Ch of 14 ds, rw. R of 8 ds, join to last p of previous r, 8 ds, 2 ps sep by 4 ds, 4 ds, cl, rw. Ch of 4 ds, 4 ps sep by 2 ds, 4 ds, rw. R of 10 ds, join to last p of previous r, 4 ds, p, 10 ds, cl, rw. Ch of 4 ds, 4 ps sep by 2 ds, 4 ds, rw. R of 4 ds, join to last p of previous r, 4 ds, join to free p of 2nd r of group, 8 ds, p, 8 ds, cl, rw. Ch of 14 ds, rw. R of 4 ds, join to last p of previous r, 8 ds, join to next free p on previous row, 4 ds, join to next free p, 8 ds, cl, rw. Ch of 2 ds, 3 ps sep by 2 ds, 2 ds, rw. R of 8 ds, join to next free p on previous row, 4 ds, join to next free p, 8 ds, p, 4 ds, cl, rw; repeat from * omitting ch and r at end of last repeat and omitting last p of last r worked. Tie ends, cut and oversew neatly on wrong side.
Sew edging to one end of linen.
Damp and press.

for colour illustration, see page 294

Edgings for trolley cloths

Materials: Coats Mercer-Crochet no. 20 (20 grms).
3 balls. This model is worked in Coral Pink. Milward tatting shuttle.
¾ yd fine Pink linen, 36 ins wide, to match or tone.
The above quantity is sufficient for 2 trolley cloths.

Depth of edging: 1¼ ins.

Measurements: 16 × 24 ins.

Suitable fabric brand: Old Bleach linen C15 (Rose).

1st row: Tie ball and shuttle threads together. * R of 3 ds, 3 ps sep by 3 ds, 3 ds, cl, rw. Ch of 12 ds, p, 12 ds, rw. R of 3 ds, p, 3 ds, join to centre p of previous r, 3 ds, p, 3 ds, cl; repeat from * 25 times more or length required to next corner. R of 3 ds, 3 ps sep by 3 ds, 3 ds, cl, rw. Ch of 12 ds, p, 8 ds, join by shuttle thread to centre p of previous r, 8 ds, p, 12 ds, rw. R of 3 ds, p, 3 ds, join to same p as last joining, 3 ds, p, 3 ds, cl. * * R of 3 ds, 3 ps sep by 3 ds, 3 ds, cl, rw. Ch of 12 ds, p, 12 ds, rw. R of 3 ds, p, 3 ds, join to centre p of previous r, 3 ds, p, 3 ds, cl; repeat from * * 38 times more or length required to next corner. R of 3 ds, 3 ps sep by 3 ds, 3 ds, cl, rw. Ch of 12 ds, p, 8 ds, join by shuttle thread to centre p of previous r, 8 ds, p, 12 ds, rw. R of 3 ds, p, 3 ds, join to same p as last joining, 3 ds, p, 3 ds, cl; repeat from first * once more, join to base of first r. Tie ends, cut and oversew neatly on wrong side.

2nd row: Tie ball and shuttle threads together. Attach thread to p of first ch. * R of 12 ds, join to p of next ch, 12 ds, cl, rw. Ch of 6 ds, 5 ps sep by 2 ds, 6 ds, join to same p as last joining, rw; repeat from * along side. R of 8 ds, p, 8 ds, cl, rw. Ch of 4 ds, 5 ps sep by 2 ds, 4 ds, join by shuttle thread to p of previous r, rw. R of 8 ds, join to p of next ch, 8 ds, cl, rw. Ch of 4 ds, 5 ps sep by 2 ds, 4 ds, join by shuttle thread to same p as last joining, rw; repeat from first * ending with r of 12 ds, join to same p as first joining. 12 ds, cl, rw. Ch of 6 ds, 5 ps sep by 2 ds, 6 ds, join to same p as last joining. Tie ends, cut and oversew neatly on wrong side.
Damp and pin out to measurements.

To make up

Cut 2 pieces of linen 15 × 23 ins. Turn back ½ in hem, mitre corners and slip stitch in position, or mount as desired.
Sew edging neatly to edge of fabric.

for colour illustration, see page 295

Doily

Materials: Coats Mercer-Crochet no. 20 (20 grms).
1 ball.
This model is worked in Lt. French Blue.
Milward tatting shuttle.

Tension (gauge): First 2 rows = 1 in diameter.

Measurements: 9½ ins from point to point.

1st row: R of 2 ds, 6 ps sep by 4 ds, 2 ds, cl. Tie ends, cut and oversew neatly on wrong side.

2nd row: Tie ball and shuttle threads together. R of 4 ds, join to any p on previous row, 4 ds, cl, rw. * Ch of 4 ds, 2 ps sep by 4 ds, 4 ds, rw. R of 4 ds, join to next p on previous row, 4 ds, cl, rw; repeat from * omitting a r at end of last repeat and joining last ch to base of first r. Tie ends, cut and oversew neatly on wrong side.

3rd row: Tie ball and shuttle threads together. Attach thread to first p on any ch on previous row, * ch of 3 ds, p, 3 ds, join by shuttle thread to next p, ch of 3 ds, 2 ps sep by 3 ds, 3 ds, join by shuttle thread to next p; repeat from * joining last ch to same place as join. Tie ends, cut and oversew neatly on wrong side.

4th row: Tie ball and shuttle threads together. Attach thread to single p on small ch of previous row, * ch of 4 ds, p, 4 ds, join by shuttle thread to first p on next ch, ch of 4 ds, join by shuttle thread to second p on same ch, ch of 4 ds, p, 4 ds, join by shuttle thread to p on next ch; repeat from * joining last ch to same p as join. Tie ends, cut and oversew neatly on wrong side.

for detail, see page 301

5th row: Tie ball and shuttle threads together. R of 4 ds, join to first p on previous row, 4 ds, cl, rw, * Ch of 5 ds, p, 5 ds, rw. R of 4 ds, join to next p, 4 ds, cl, rw. Ch of 5 ds, 3 ps sep by 5 ds, 5 ds, rw. * * R of 4 ds, join to next p, 4 ds, cl, rw; repeat from * ending last repeat at * * joining last ch to base of first r. Tie ends, cut and oversew neatly on wrong side.

6th row: Tie ball and shuttle threads together. Attach thread to first p on previous row. * Ch of 3 ds, 2 ps sep by 3 ds, 3 ds, join by shuttle thread to next p, (ch of 3 ds, p, 3 ds, join by shuttle thread to next p) twice, ch of 3 ds, 2 ps sep by 3 ds, 3 ds, join by shuttle thread to next p; repeat from * joining last ch to same place as join. Tie ends, cut and oversew neatly on wrong side.

7th row: Tie ball and shuttle threads together. Attach thread to first p on previous row. * Ch of 2 ds, p, 2 ds, join by shuttle thread to next p, ch of 3 ds, p, 3 ds, join by shuttle thread to next p, ch of 4 ds, p, 4 ds, join by shuttle thread to next p, ch of 3 ds, p, 3 ds, join by shuttle thread to next p, ch of 2 ds, p, 2 ds, join by shuttle thread to next p, ch of 3 ds, p, 3 ds, join by shuttle thread to next p; repeat from * joining last ch to first p. Tie ends, cut and oversew neatly on wrong side.

8th row: Tie ball and shuttle threads together. R of 4 ds, p, 4 ds, join to p of large ch on previous row, 4 ds, p, 4 ds, cl, rw. * Ch of 3 ds, 4 ps sep by 3 ds, 3 ds, rw. (R of 4 ds, join to next p, 4 ds, cl, rw. Ch of 3 ds, p, 3 ds, rw) 4 times. R of 4 ds, join to next p, 4 ds, cl, rw. Ch of 3 ds, 4 ps sep by 3 ds, 3 ds, * * rw. R of 4 ds, p, 4 ds, join to next p, 4 ds, p, 4 ds, cl, rw; repeat from * ending last repeat at * * and joining last ch by shuttle thread to base of first r. Tie ends, cut and oversew neatly on wrong side.

9th row: Tie ball and shuttle threads together. R of 4 ds, join to second p on first large ch on previous row, 4 ds, cl, rw. * Ch of 3 ds, 3 ps sep by 3 ds, 3 ds, rw. R of 4 ds, miss 1 p, join to next p, 4 ds, join to next p, 4 ds, cl, rw. Ch of 3 ds, 7 ps sep by 3 ds, 3 ds, rw. R of 4 ds, miss 2 ps, join to next p, 4 ds, join to next p, 4 ds, cl, rw. Ch of 3 ds, 3 ps sep by 3 ds, 3 ds, rw. R of 4 ds, miss 1 p, join to next p, 4 ds, cl, rw. Ch of 3 ds, 3 ps sep by 3 ds, 3 ds, rw. * * R of 4 ds, miss 2 ps, join to next p, 4 ds, cl, rw; repeat from * ending last repeat at * * and joining last ch to base of first r. Tie ends, cut and oversew neatly on wrong side.

10th row: Tie ball and shuttle threads together. Attach thread to first p on large ch of previous row. * Ch of 2 ds, p, 4 ds, p, 2 ds, miss 1 p, join by shuttle thread to next p; repeat from * joining last ch to same place as join. Tie ends, cut and oversew ends neatly on wrong side.

11th row: Tie ball and shuttle threads together. Attach thread to first and last p of previous row. * (Ch of 2 ds, p, 2 ds, join by shuttle thread to next p) 4 times, ch of 2 ds, p, 2 ds, join by shuttle thread to next 2 ps, (ch of 2 ds, p, 2 ds, join by shuttle thread to next p) 8 times, ch of 2 ds, p, 2 ds, * * join by shuttle thread to next 2 ps; repeat from * ending last repeat at * * and joining last ch to same place as first ch. Tie ends, cut and oversew neatly on wrong side.

12th row: Tie ball and shuttle threads together. Attach thread to first and last p of previous row. * (Ch of 3 ds, p, 3 ds, join by shuttle thread to next p) 3 times, ch of 3 ds, p, 3 ds, join by shuttle thread to next 2 ps, (ch of 3 ds, p, 3 ds, join by shuttle thread to next p) 7 times, ch of 3 ds, p, 3 ds, * * join by shuttle thread to next 2 ps; repeat from * ending last repeat at * * and joining last ch to first ch. Tie ends, cut and oversew neatly on wrong side.

13th row: Tie ball and shuttle threads together. R of 4 ds, p, 4 ds, join to first p on previous row, 4 ds, join to next p, 4 ds, p, 4 ds, cl, rw. * Ch of 3 ds, 9 ps sep by 3 ds, 3 ds, rw. * * R of 4 ds, p, 4 ds, miss 2 ps, join to next p, 4 ds, join to next p, 4 ds, p, 4 ds, cl, rw; repeat from * ending last repeat at * * and joining last ch to base of first r. Tie ends, cut and oversew neatly on wrong side.

14th row: Tie ball and shuttle threads together. Attach thread to second p on first ch of previous row. * (Ch of 4 ds, 2 ps sep by 4 ds, 4 ds, miss 2 ps, join by shuttle thread to next p) twice, ch of 4 ds, p, 4 ds, miss 2 ps, join by shuttle thread to next p; repeat from * joining last ch by shuttle thread to first ch. Tie ends, cut and oversew neatly on wrong side.

15th row: Tie ball and shuttle threads together. R of 4 ds, p, 4 ds, join to first single p on first small ch of previous row, 4 ds, p, 4 ds, cl, rw. * Ch of 4 ds, 3 ps sep by 4 ds, 4 ds, join by shuttle thread to next p, (ch of 2 ds, p, 2 ds, join by shuttle thread to next p, ch of 3 ds, p, 3 ds, join by shuttle thread to next p) 6 times, ch of 2 ds, p, 2 ds, join by shuttle thread to next p, ch of 4 ds, 3 ps sep by 4 ds, 4 ds, rw. * * R of 4 ds, p, 4 ds, join to next p, 4 ds, p, 4 ds, cl, rw; repeat from * ending last repeat at * * joining

last ch to base of first r. Tie ends, cut and oversew neatly on wrong side.

16th row: Tie ball and shuttle threads together. R of 4 ds, join to first p on first ch of previous row, 4 ds, cl, rw. (Ch of 4 ds, p, 4 ds, rw. R of 4 ds, join to next p, 4 ds, cl, rw) twice. * Ch of 4 ds, p, 4 ds, rw. R of 4 ds, miss next p, join to next p, 4 ds, cl, rw. (Ch of 2 ds, p, 2 ds, rw. R of 4 ds, join to next p, 4 ds, cl, rw) 10 times. Ch of 4 ds, p, 4 ds, rw. R of 4 ds, miss next p, join to next p, 4 ds, cl, rw. (Ch of 4 ds, p, 4 ds, rw. R of 4 ds, join to next p, 4 ds, cl, rw) 5 times; repeat from * ending last repeat with (ch of 4 ds, p, 4 ds, rw. R of 4 ds, join to next p, 4 ds, cl, rw) twice. Ch of 4 ds, p, 4 ds, join by shuttle thread to base of first r. Tie ends, cut and oversew neatly on wrong side.

17th row: Tie ball and shuttle threads together. Attach thread to p on first ch of previous row. (Ch of 5 ds, p, 5 ds, join by shuttle thread to next p) twice. * (Ch of 2 ds, p, 2 ds, join by shuttle thread to next p) 3 times. (Ch of 3 ds, p, 3 ds, join by shuttle thread to next p) 5 times. (Ch of 2 ds, p, 2 ds, join by shuttle thread to next p) 3 times. * * (Ch of 5 ds, p, 5 ds, join by shuttle thread to next p) 6 times; repeat from * ending last repeat at * *. (Ch of 5 ds, p, 5 ds, join by shuttle thread to next p) 4 times, joining last ch to same place as first ch. Tie ends, cut and oversew neatly on wrong side.

Damp and pin out to measurements.

Runner

Materials: Coats Mercer-Crochet no. 10
(20 grms).
3 balls. This model is worked in Spring Green.
Milward tatting shuttle.

Measurements: $36 \times 8\frac{1}{2}$ ins.

1st row: Tie ball and shuttle threads together. Lr of 4 ds, 8 ps sep by 3 ds, 4 ds, cl. Rw,
ch of 6 ds, p, 6 ds. Rw, r of 10 ds, p, 3 ds, p, 7 ds,
cl. Rw, ch of 6 ds, 5 ps sep by 3 ds, 4 ds. Rw, r of
9 ds, join to last p of previous r, 9 ds, p, 3 ds, cl.
* Lr of 3 ds, join to p of previous r, 6 ds, 3 ps
sep by 3 ds, 2 ds, 3 ps sep by 3 ds, 6 ds, p, 3 ds, cl.
R of 3 ds, join to last p of lr, 9 ds, p, 9 ds, cl. Rw,
ch of 4 ds, 8 ps sep by 3 ds, 4 ds. Rw, r of 9 ds,
join to p of last r, 9 ds, p, 3 ds, cl; repeat from *
23 times more, lr of 3 ds, join to p of previous r,
6 ds, 3 ps sep by 3 ds, 2 ds, 3 ps sep by 3 ds, 6 ds,
p, 3 ds, cl. R of 3 ds, join to last p of lr, 9 ds, p, 9
ds, cl. Rw, ch of 4 ds, 5 ps sep by 3 ds, 6 ds. Rw,
r of 7 ds, join to p of previous r, 3 ds, p, 10 ds,
cl. Rw, ch of 6 ds, p, 6 ds. Rw, lr of 4 ds, 8 ps sep
by 3 ds, 4 ds, cl. Rw, ch of 6 ds, join to p of previous ch, 6 ds. Rw, r of 10 ds, p, 3 ds, p, 7 ds, cl.
Rw, ch of 6 ds, join to first p of adjoining ch,
(3 ds, join to next p of same ch) twice, 3 ds,
2 ps sep by 3 ds, 4 ds. Rw, r of 9 ds, join to last p
of previous r, 9 ds, p, 3 ds, cl. * Lr of 3 ds, join
to p of previous r, 6 ds, 3 ps sep by 3 ds, 2 ds, 3
ps sep by 3 ds, 6 ds, p, 3 ds, cl. R of 3 ds, join to
last p of lr, 9 ds, p, 9 ds, cl. Rw, ch of 4 ds, 2 ps
sep by 3 ds, 3 ds, join to 3rd p of adjacent ch,
(3 ds, join to next p of same ch 3 times, 3 ds,
2 ps sep by 3 ds, 4 ds. Rw, r of 9 ds, join to p of
previous r, 9 ds, p, 3 ds, cl; repeat from last * 23
times more, lr of 3 ds, join to p of previous r,
6 ds, 3 ps sep by 3 ds, 2 ds, 3 ps sep by 3 ds, 6 ds,
p, 3 ds, cl. R of 3 ds, join to last p of lr, 9 ds, p,
9 ds, cl. Rw, ch of 4 ds, 2 ps sep by 3 ds, 3 ds,
join to 3rd p of adjacent ch, (3 ds, join to next p
of same ch) twice, 6 ds. Rw, r of 7 ds, join to p

for colour illustration, see page 303

of previous r, 3 ds, p, 10 ds, cl. Rw, ch of 6 ds, join to p of adjacent ch, 6 ds, join to base of first lr. Tie ends, cut and oversew neatly on wrong side.

2nd row: Tie ball and shuttle threads together. R of 11 ds, 2 ps sep by 11 ds, 3 ds, cl. Lr of 3 ds, join to last p of previous r, 3 ds, 3 ps sep by 3 ds, 3 ds, join to 5th p of first lr of first row, 3 ds, 3 ps sep by 3 ds, 3 ds, cl. R of 3 ds, join to last p of lr, 11 ds, p, 11 ds, cl. Rw, ch of 4 ds, 8 ps sep by 3 ds, 4 ds. Rw, r of 11 ds, join to p of previous r, 11 ds, p, 3 ds, cl. Lr of 3 ds, join to p of previous r, 6 ds, 2 ps sep by 3 ds, 3 ds, join to p of next r on first row, 3 ds, 2 ps sep by 3 ds, 6 ds, p, 3 ds, cl. R of 3 ds, join to last p of last lr, 11 ds, p, 11 ds, cl. * Rw, ch of 4 ds, 8 ps sep by 3 ds, 4 ds. Rw, r of 11 ds, join to p of previous r, 11 ds, p, 3 ds, cl. Lr of 3 ds, join to p of previous r, 6 ds, 2 ps sep by 3 ds, 3 ds, join to 3rd p of lr of first row, 2 ds, join to next p of same lr, 3 ds, 2 ps sep by 3 ds, 6 ds, p, 3 ds, cl. R of 3 ds, join to last p of lr, 11 ds, p, 11 ds, cl; repeat from * 24 times more. Rw, ch of 4 ds, 8 ps sep by 3 ds, 4 ds. Rw, r of 11 ds, join to p of previous r, 11 ds, p, 3 ds, cl. Lr of 3 ds, join to p of previous r, 6 ds, 2 ps sep by 3 ds, 3 ds, join to p of single r on first row, 3 ds, 2 ps sep by 3 ds, 6 ds, p, 3 ds, cl. R of 3 ds, join to last p of last lr, 11 ds, p, 11 ds, cl. Rw, ch of 4 ds, 8 ps sep by 3 ds, 4 ds. Rw, r of 11 ds, join to p of last r, 11 ds, p, 3 ds, cl. Lr of 3 ds, join to p of last r, 3 ds, 2 ps sep by 3 ds, 3 ds, join to 4th p of end r, 3 ds, 4 ps sep by 3 ds, 3 ds, cl. R of 3 ds, join to last p of lr, 11 ds, p, 11 ds, cl. Rw, ch of 4 ds, 8 ps sep by 3 ds, 4 ds, Rw, r of 9 ds, join to p of last r, 9 ds, p, 3 ds, cl. R of 3 ds, join to p of last r, 9 ds, p, 9 ds, cl. Rw, ch of 4 ds, 8 ps sep by 3 ds, 4 ds. Rw, r of 11 ds, join to p of last r, 11 ds, p, 3 ds, cl. Lr of 3 ds, join to p of last r, 3 ds, 2 ps sep by 3 ds, 3 ds, miss 2 ps on last lr, join to next p, 3 ds, join to next p on end r, 3 ds, 3 ps sep by 3 ds, 3 ds, cl. R of 3 ds, join to last p of lr, 11 ds, p, 11 ds, cl. Now work along other side to correspond, joining last lr and last r to adjacent ps and last ch to base of first lr. Tie ends, cut and oversew neatly on wrong side.

3rd row: Tie ball and shuttle threads together. R of 6 ds, join to last p of ch before double rings at one end of runner, 4 ds, join to first p of next ch, 6 ds, cl. Rw, ch of 4 ds, 6 ps sep by 4 ds, 4 ds, join by shuttle thread to next p of same ch, ch of 4 ds, join to first p of adjacent ch, 4 ds, join to next p of same ch, 4 ds, 5 ps sep by 4 ds, 4 ds, miss 2 ps of ch on second row, join by shuttle thread to next p of same ch, * ch of 4 ds, join to first p of adjacent ch, 4 ds, join to next p of same ch, 4 ds, 6 ps sep by 4 ds, 4 ds, join by shuttle thread to last p of ch on second row, ch of 3 ds, join by shuttle thread to first p of next ch on second row, 4 ds, join to first p of adjacent ch, (4 ds, join to next p on same ch) twice, 4 ds, 5 ps sep by 4 ds, 4 ds, miss 2 ps of ch on second row, join by shuttle thread to next p on same ch, 3 ds, join by shuttle thread to next p of same ch; repeat from * until 2 centre ps of second last ch of this side have been joined, 4 ds, join to first p of adjacent ch, 4 ds, join to next p of same ch, 4 ds, 6 ps sep by 4 ds, miss 2 ps of ch on second row, join by shuttle thread to next p of same ch, 3 ds, join by shuttle thread to first p of next ch on second row, 4 ds, join to first p of adjacent ch, (4 ds, join to next p on same ch) twice, (4 ds, 5 ps sep by 4 ds, 4 ds, miss 2 ps of ch on second row, join by shuttle thread to next p on same ch, 4 ds, join to first p of adjacent ch, 4 ds, join to next p on same ch) twice, 4 ds, 4 ps sep by 4 ds, 4 ds. Rw, r of 6 ds, join to last p of same ch on second row, 4 ds, join to first p of next ch, 6 ds, cl. Rw, ch of 4 ds, join to first p of adjacent ch, 4 ds, 5 ps sep by 4 ds, 4 ds. Now continue to work other side to correspond joining last ch to first p of first ch and last ch to base of first r. Tie ends, cut and oversew neatly on wrong side.

4th row: Tie ball and shuttle threads to centre p of any ch on third row, ch of 3 ds, 6 ps sep by 3 ds, 3 ds, * join by shuttle thread to centre p of next ch, 3 ds, join to first p of adjacent ch, 3 ds, 5 ps sep by 3 ds, 3 ds; repeat from * all round, joining last ch to first p of first ch and joining last ch to same p as threads were joined. Tie ends, cut and oversew neatly on wrong side.

Damp and pin out to measurements.

Lemonade set

Materials: Coats Mercer-Crochet no. 20
(20 grms).
2 balls. This model is worked in Jade.
Milward tatting shuttle.
1 piece of glass 6½ ins diameter.
4 pieces of glass 4 ins diameter.
The above quantity is sufficient for 1 large mat
and 4 glass mats.

Measurements:
Large mat – 6½ ins diameter approximately.
Glass mat – 4 ins diameter approximately.

Large mat

1st row: Tie ball and shuttle threads together. R of 3 ds, 5 ps sep by 3 ds, 3 ds, cl, rw. *
Ch of 4 ds, 3 ps sep by 4 ds, 4 ds, rw. R of 3 ds, p,
3 ds, join to second last p on previous r, 3 ds,
3 ps sep by 3 ds, 3 ds, cl, rw; repeat from * 8
times more, joining second last p on last r to
second p on first r. Ch of 4 ds, 3 ps sep by 4 ds,
4 ds, join by shuttle thread to base of first r.
Tie ends, cut and oversew neatly on wrong
side.

2nd row: Tie ball and shuttle threads
together. Attach thread to centre p of any ch
on previous row. * Ch of 8 ds, p, 8 ds, join by
shuttle thread to centre p on next ch; repeat
from * joining last ch to same place as first ch.
Tie ends, cut and oversew neatly on wrong
side.

3rd row: Tie ball and shuttle threads
together. R of 12 ds, join to p of any ch on previous row, 12 ds, cl, rw. * Ch of 12 ds, p, 5 ds,
join by shuttle thread to same place as chs on
previous row. Ch of 5 ds, join by ball thread to
p on previous ch, 12 ds, * * rw. R of 12 ds, join
to next p on previous row, 12 ds, cl, rw; repeat
from * ending last repeat at * *, join last ch by
ball thread to base of first r. Do not tie ends.

4th row: Ch of 8 ds, 5 ps sep by 4 ds, 6 ds, p,
8 ds, join by shuttle thread to joining of chs on
previous row. Ch of 8 ds, join by ball thread to
adjacent p on previous ch, 6 ds, join by ball
thread to adjacent p on previous ch, 4 ds, 4 ps
sep by 4 ds, 8 ds, join by shuttle thread to base
of next r. * * Ch of 8 ds, join by ball thread to
last p on previous ch, 4 ds, 4 ps sep by 4 ds,
6 ds, p, 8 ds, join by shuttle thread to joining of
chs on previous row; repeat from * ending last
repeat at * * joining p of last ch to p of first ch
to correspond and last ch to base of first ch.

for colour illustration, see page 307

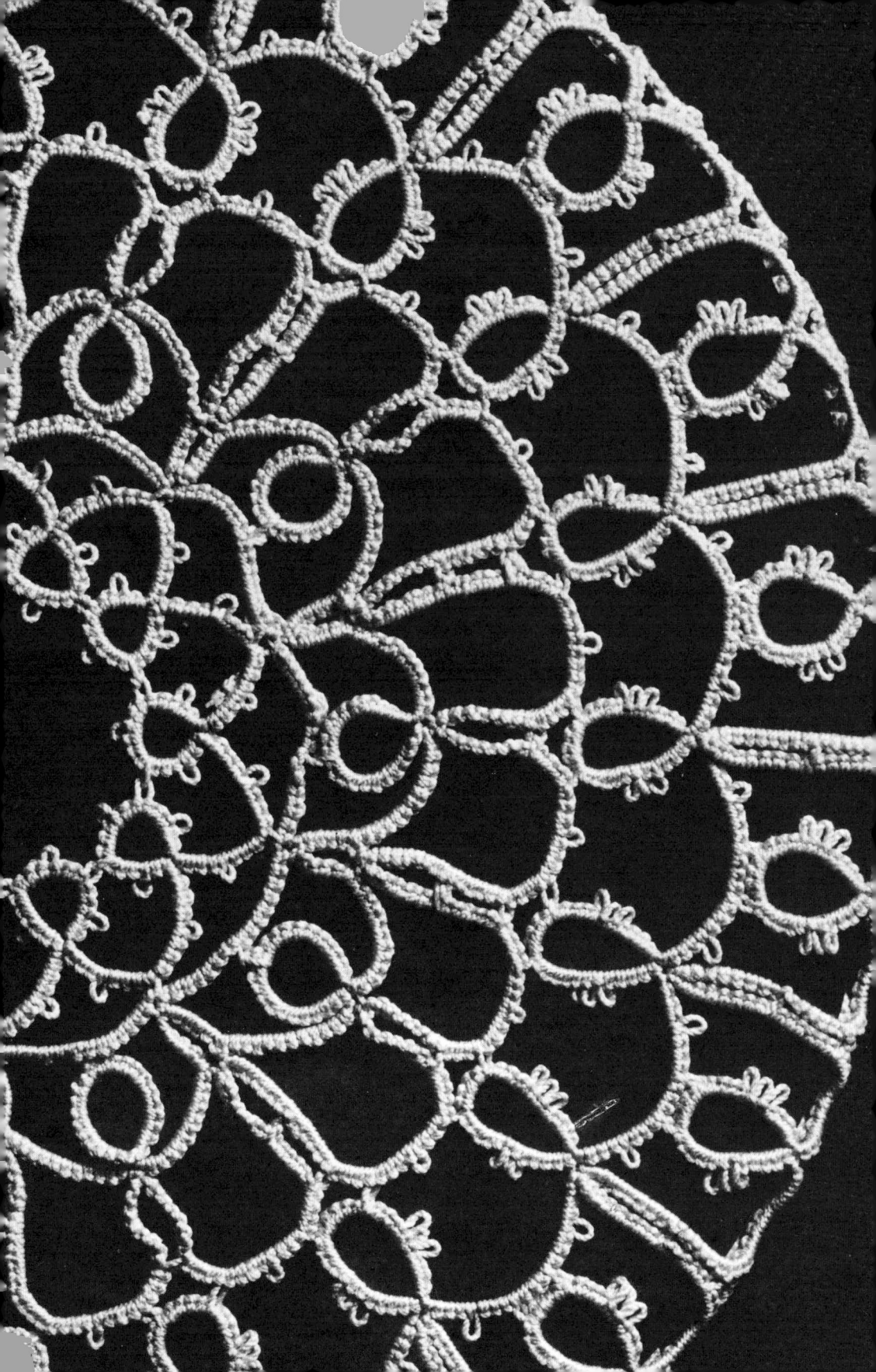

Tie ends, cut and oversew neatly on wrong side.

5th row: Tie ball and shuttle threads together. R of 5 ds, 3 ps sep by 1 ds, 5 ds, join to any p to left of any join, 5 ds, join to next p on next ch, 5 ds, 3 ps sep by 1 ds, 5 ds, cl, rw. * Ch of 4 ds, 4 ps sep by 4 ds, 4 ds, rw. R of 5 ds, 3 ps sep by 1 ds, 5 ds, miss next p on same ch, join to next p, 5 ds, join to next p on next ch, 5 ds, 3 ps sep by 1 ds, 5 ds, cl, rw; repeat from * omitting r at end of last repeat and joining last ch by shuttle thread to base of first r. Do not tie ends.

6th row: Ch of 8 ds, p, 6 ds, 3 ps sep by 4 ds, 4 ds, rw. R of 5 ds, 3 ps sep by 1 ds, 5 ds, join to second p on next ch, 5 ds, join to next p on same ch, 5 ds, 3 ps sep by 1 ds, 5 ds, cl, rw. * Ch of 4 ds, 3 ps sep by 4 ds, 6 ds, p, 8 ds, join by shuttle thread to base of next r. Ch of 8 ds, join by ball thread to last p on previous ch, 6 ds, join by ball thread to adjacent p on previous ch, 4 ds, 2 ps sep by 4 ds, 4 ds, rw. R of 5 ds, 3 ps sep by 1 ds, 5 ds, miss 1 p of next ch, join to next p, 5 ds, join to next p, 5 ds, 3 ps sep by 1 ds, 5 ds, cl, rw; repeat from * ending with ch of 4 ds, 2 ps sep by 4 ds, 4 ds, join to next p on first ch, 6 ds, join to next p on first ch, 8 ds, join to base of next r. Tie ends, cut and oversew neatly on wrong side.

7th row: Lr of 8 ds, p, 8 ds, join to p at left of any join, 5 ds, join to next p, 8 ds, p, 8 ds, cl, rw. Leave a sp of $\frac{3}{8}$ in. R of 4 ds, 3 ps sep by 4 ds, 4 ds, cl, rw. * Leave a sp of $\frac{3}{8}$ in. Lr of 8 ds, join to last p on previous lr, 8 ds, join to next p on previous row, 5 ds, join to next p, 8 ds, p, 8 ds, cl, rw. Leave a sp of $\frac{3}{8}$ in. R of 4 ds, join to last p on previous r, 4 ds, 2 ps sep by 4 ds, 4 ds, cl, rw; repeat from * joining last lr to first lr and

last r to first r. Tie ends, cut and oversew neatly on wrong side.

Glass mat *make 4*

Work as large mat for 3 rows. Do not tie ends.

4th row: * Ch of 4 ds, 3 ps sep by 4 ds, 4 ds, join by shuttle thread to joining of chs on previous row. Ch of 4 ds, 3 ps sep by 4 ds, 4 ds, join by shuttle thread to base of next r; repeat from * joining last ch to base of first ch. Tie ends, cut and oversew neatly on wrong side.

5th row: Lr of 8 ds, p, 8 ds, join to centre p of any ch on previous row, 8 ds, p, 8 ds, cl, rw. Leave a sp of $\frac{3}{8}$ in. R of 4 ds, 3 ps sep by 4 ds, 4 ds, cl, rw. * Leave a sp of $\frac{3}{8}$ in. Lr of 8 ds, join to last p on previous lr, 8 ds, join to centre p of next ch on previous row, 8 ds, p, 8 ds, cl, rw. Leave a sp of $\frac{3}{8}$ in. R of 4 ds, join to last p on previous r, 4 ds, 2 ps sep by 4 ds, 4 ds, cl, rw; repeat from * joining last p of last lr to first p of first lr and last p of last r to first p of first r. Tie ends, cut and oversew neatly on wrong side.

Damp and pin out to measurements. Slip over glass.

Motif coffee table mat

Materials: Coats Mercer-Crochet no. 20 (20 grms).
3 balls. This model is worked in Emerald Green.
Milward tatting shuttle.

Size of motif: 3 ins.

Measurements: 21 × 18 ins.

First motif

1st row: R of 3 ds, 3 ps sep by 3 ds, 3 ds, cl.
* Sp of ¼ in. R of 3 ds, join to last p of previous r, 3 ds, 2 ps sep by 3 ds, 3 ds, cl; repeat from * 4 times more, joining last p of last r to first p of first r. Tie ends, cut and oversew neatly on wrong side.

2nd row: Tie ball and shuttle threads together. Sr of 4 ds, 2 ps sep by 4 ds, 4 ds, cl, rw. Ch of 9 ds, join to any p on previous row, 9 ds, rw. * Sr of 4 ds, join to last p on previous sr, 4 ds, p, 4 ds, cl, rw. Ch of 5 ds, p, 5 ds, rw. R of 3 ds, join to last p on previous sr, 3 ds, 2 ps sep by 3 ds, 3 ds, cl, rw. Ch of 3 ds, rw. Lr of 3 ds, join to last p on previous r, 2 ds, 2 ps sep by 2 ds, 2 ds, lp, 2 ds, 3 ps sep by 2 ds, 3 ds, cl, rw. Ch of 3 ds, rw. R of 3 ds, join to last p on previous lr, 3 ds, 2 ps sep by 3 ds, 3 ds, cl, rw. Ch of 5 ds, join to p on corresponding ch, 5 ds, rw. * * Sr of 4 ds, join to last p on previous r, 4 ds, p, 4 ds, cl, rw. Ch of 9 ds, join to next p on previous row, 9 ds, rw; repeat from * ending last repeat at * * joining last r to first sr, p of last ch to p of first ch and last ch to base of first r. Tie ends, cut and oversew neatly on wrong side.

Second motif

Work as first motif for 1 row.

2nd row: Tie ball and shuttle threads together. Sr of 4 ds, 2 ps sep by 4 ds, 4 ds, cl, rw. Ch of 9 ds, join to any p on previous row, 9 ds, rw. Sr of 4 ds, join to last p on previous sr, 4 ds, p, 4 ds, cl, rw. Ch of 5 ds, p, 5 ds, rw. R of 3 ds, join to last p on previous sr, 3 ds, 2 ps sep by 3 ds, 3 ds, cl, rw. Ch of 3 ds, rw. Lr of 3 ds, join to last p on previous r, 2 ds, 2 ps sep by 2 ds, 2 ds, join to corresponding p on first motif, 2 ds, 3 ps sep by 2 ds, 3 ds, cl, rw. Ch of 3 ds, rw. R of 3 ds, join to last p on previous lr, 3 ds, 2 ps sep by 3 ds, 3 ds, cl, rw. Ch of 5 ds, join to p on corresponding ch, 5 ds, rw. Sr of 4 ds, join to last p on previous r, 4 ds, p, 4 ds, cl, rw. Ch of 9 ds, join to next p on previous row, 9 ds, rw; repeat from * once more and complete as first motif. Make 35 more motifs joining each as second motif was joined to first, placing as shown on diagram. Where 3 corners meet, join 3rd corner to joining of previous motifs. Damp and pin out to measurements.

for colour illustration, see page 311
for diagram, see page 314

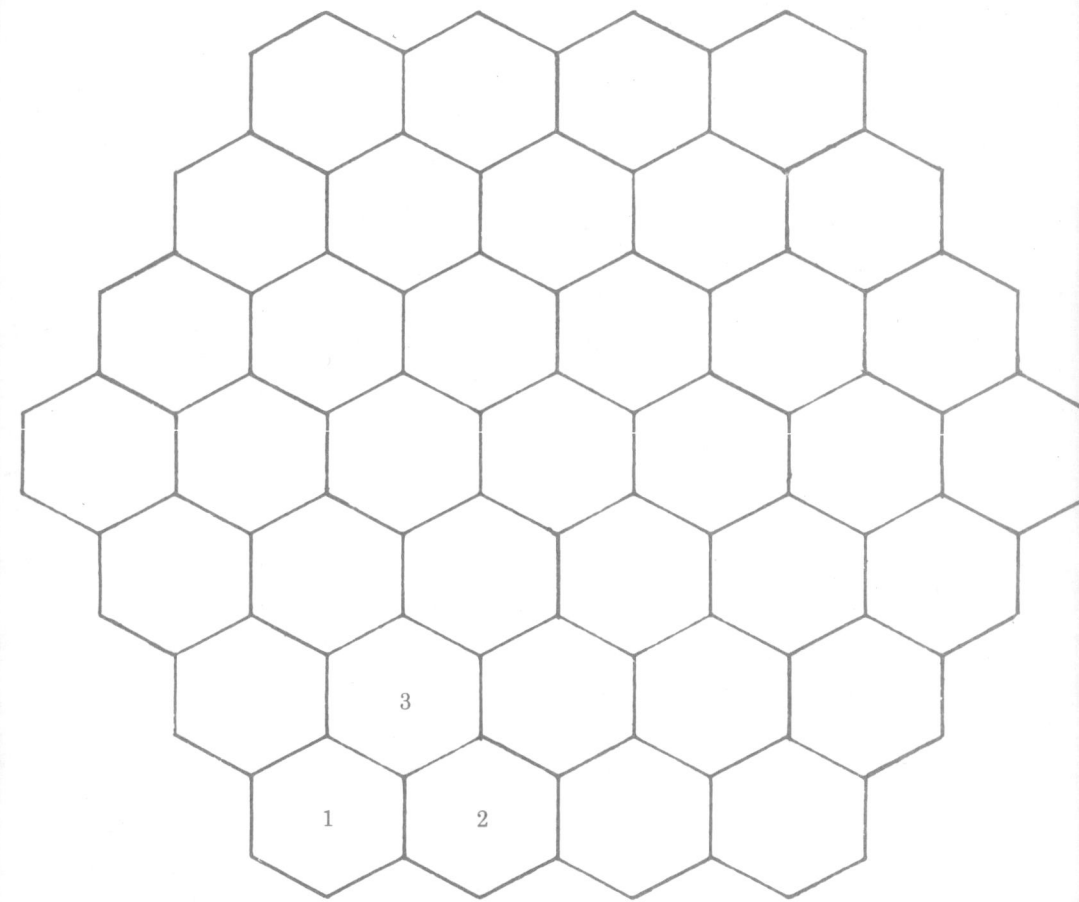

Traycloth with insertion

Materials: Coats Mercer–Crochet no. 40
(20 grms).
1 ball. This model is worked in Ecru.
Piece of Old Bleach linen, Biscuit, 15 × 21 ins.
Milward tatting shuttle.

Width of insertion: 1 in.

Measurements: 14½ × 20½ ins.

Mark 2 ins in from edge all round linen. Cut
out this rectangle 11 × 17 ins. (linen centre).
Turn back ¼ in for hems on inside and outside
edges of linen border. Trim linen centre to
measure 10 × 16 ins.
Turn back ¼ in for hems all round linen centre.
Slip stitch hems.

Insertion

1st row: Tie ball and shuttle threads together. R of 6 ds, 3 ps sep by 6 ds, 6 ds, cl, rw.
* Ch of 4 ds, 2 ps sep by 3 ds, 3 ds, rw. Sr of 3 ds,
join to last p of previous r, 3 ds, 2 ps sep by
3 ds, 3 ds, cl, * * rw. Ch of 3 ds, join to adjacent
p on previous ch, 3 ds, p, 4 ds, rw. R of 6 ds,
join to last p of previous sr, 6 ds, 2 ps sep by
6 ds, 6 ds, cl, rw; repeat from * for length
required to corner of linen centre, ending last
repeat at * *. Sr of 3 ds, join to last p of previous sr, 3 ds, 2 ps sep by 3 ds, 3 ds, cl; repeat
from first * * joining last p of last sr to first p
of first r and last ch to base of first r. Tie ends,
cut and oversew neatly on wrong side.

2nd row: Tie ball and shuttle threads together. R of 6 ds, p, 6 ds, join to p of first sr on
previous row, 6 ds, p, 6 ds, cl, rw. * Ch of 4 ds,
2 ps sep by 3 ds, 3 ds, rw. Sr of 3 ds, join to p of
previous r, 3 ds, join to p of next r on previous
row, 3 ds, p, 3·ds, cl, rw. Ch of 3 ds, join to
adjacent p on previous ch, 3 ds, p, 4 ds, * * rw.
R of 6 ds, join to p of previous sr, 6 ds, join to p
of next sr on previous row, 6 ds, p, 6 ds, cl, rw;
repeat from * to corner. Ch of 6 ds, 2 ps sep by
6 ds, 6 ds, rw. R of 6 ds, join to p of previous r,
6 ds, 2 ps sep by 6 ds, 6 ds, cl, rw. Ch as previous ch. R of 6 ds, join to p of previous r, 6 ds,
join to p of next sr on previous row, 6 ds, p, 6
ds, cl, rw; repeat from first * ending last repeat
at * *, joining last p of last sr to first p of first r
and last ch to base of first r. Tie ends, cut and
oversew neatly on wrong side.
Sew insertion neatly in place *(see illustration)*.
Damp and press.

for colour illustration, see page 315

Pillowcase edging and insertion

Materials: Coats Mercer-Crochet no. 20 (20 grms).
2 balls. This model is worked in White.
1 pillowcase.
Milward tatting shuttle.

Width of insertion: $1\frac{7}{8}$ in.

Depth of edging: $\frac{7}{8}$ in.

Insertion

1st row: Tie ball and shuttle threads together. * R of 8 ds, 2 ps sep by 4 ds, 8 ds, cl. Ch of 8 ds; repeat from * for length required, having an even number of chs between rs and joining last ch to base of first r, without twisting work, rw. * * R of 8 ds, 2 ps sep by 4 ds, 8 ds, cl. Ch of 8 ds, join by shuttle thread to base of next r; repeat from * *, joining last ch to base of first r. Tie ends, cut and oversew neatly on wrong side.

2nd row: Tie ball and shuttle threads together. R of 5 ds, join to p at right of any r on lower edge of previous row, 5 ds, join to next p of next r, 5 ds, cl, rw. * Ch of 3 ds, 4 ps sep by 3 ds, 6 ds, join by shuttle thread to next p. Ch of 3 ds, join by shuttle thread to next p. Ch of 6 ds, join to last p of adjacent ch, 3 ds, 3 ps sep by 3 ds, 3 ds, rw. R of 5 ds, join to next p, 5 ds, join to next p, 5 ds, cl, rw; repeat from * omitting r at end of last repeat and joining last ch to base of first r. Tie ends, cut and oversew neatly on wrong side.
Work other side to correspond.

Edging

1st row: Work as for first side of first row for length required. Tie ends, cut and oversew neatly on wrong side.

2nd row: Work as for first side of 2nd row. Tie ends, cut and oversew neatly on wrong side.

To make up

Pin insertion in place $3\frac{1}{2}$ ins from edge of pillowcase. Cut away surplus material at back of insertion, leaving $\frac{1}{4}$ in for hem on each side. Sew hems and insertion neatly in place, attaching 2 ps of each ch, as in illustration. Sew on edging, attaching at base of each r. Damp and press.

for colour illustrations, see pages 318 and 319

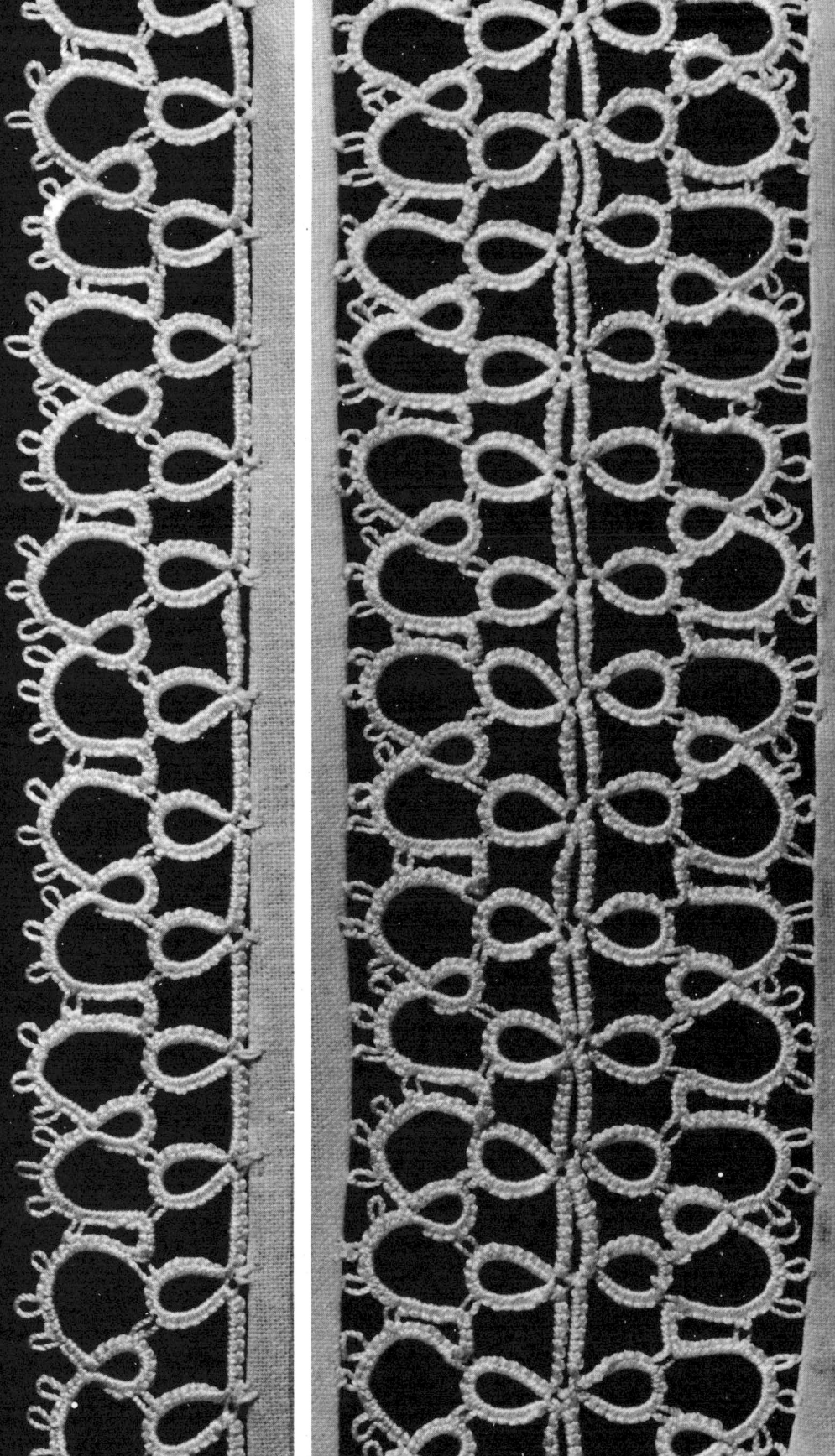

Long john runner

Materials: Coats Mercer-Crochet no. 20
(20 grms).
2 balls Cream and 3 balls Brown.
2 Milward tatting shuttles.

Size of motif: 2¾ ins square.

Measurement: 11× 35¾ ins.

First motif

1st row: Using shuttle with Cream, r of 5 ds,
5 ps sep by 2 ds, 5 ds, cl. (R of 5 ds, join to corresponding p of adjacent r, 2 ds, 4 ps sep by 2
ds, 5 ds, cl) twice. R of 5 ds, join to corresponding p of adjacent r, 2 ds, 3 ps sep by 2 ds, 2 ds,
join to corresponding p on first r, 5 ds, cl. Tie
ends, cut and oversew neatly on wrong side.

2nd row: Using shuttle with Brown and ball
of Cream, tie ball and shuttle threads together. R of 5 ds, join to first free p of any r, 5 ds,
cl. Ch of 5 ds, rw. R of 5 ds, p, 5 ds, cl, rw. *
Ch of 6 ds, rw. R of 5 ds, p, 5 ds, rw (corner r
made). Ch of 6 ds, rw. R of 5 ds, p, 5 ds, cl, rw.
Ch of 5 ds. R of 5 ds, join to last free p on same
r of previous row, 5 ds, cl. Ch of 5 ds, rw. R of 5
ds, join to p of adjacent r, 5 ds, cl, rw. Ch of 4
ds, rw. R of 5 ds, p, 5 ds, cl, rw. Ch of 4 ds, rw.
R of 5 ds, p, 5 ds, cl, rw. Ch of 5 ds. * * R of 5 ds,
join to first free p on next r of previous row,
5 ds, cl. Ch of 5 ds, rw. R of 5 ds, join to p of
adjacent r, 5 ds, cl, rw; repeat from * 3 times
more ending last repeat at * *, joining last r to
second r correspond and joining last ch to
base of first r. Tie ends, cut and oversew
neatly on wrong side.

for detail, see page 325

3rd row: Using shuttle with Brown and ball of Cream, tie ball and shuttle threads together. R of 5 ds, join to any corner p, 5 ds, cl, rw. * Ch of 3 ds, p, 3 ds, rw. R of 5 ds, join to same p as last r, 5 ds, cl, rw. Ch of 3 ds, 3 ps sep by 3 ds, 3 ds, rw. R of 5 ds, join to same p as last r, 5 ds, cl, rw. Ch of 3 ds, p, 3 ds, rw. R of 5 ds, join to same p as last r, 5 ds, cl, rw. Ch of 3 ds, p, 3 ds, join by shuttle thread to p at joining of next 2 rs. Ch of 3 ds, p, 3 ds, rw. R of 5 ds, join to p of next r, 5 ds, cl, rw. Ch of 3 ds, 3 ps sep by 3 ds, 3 ds, rw. R of 5 ds, join to same p as last r, 5 ds, cl, rw. Ch of 3 ds, p, 3 ds, join by shuttle thread to p at joining of next 2 rs. Ch of 3 ds, p, 3 ds, rw. * * R of 5 ds, join to next corner p. 5 ds, cl, rw; repeat from * 3 times more, ending last repeat at * * joining last ch to base of first r. Tie ends, cut and oversew neatly on wrong side.

Second motif

Work as first motif for 2 rows.

3rd row: Using shuttle with Brown and ball of Cream, tie ball and shuttle threads together. R of 5 ds, join to any corner p, 5 ds, cl, rw. Ch of 3 ds, p, 3 ds, rw. R of 5 ds, join to same p as last r, 5 ds, cl, rw. Ch of 3 ds, 2 ps sep by 3 ds, 3 ds, join to corresponding p on first motif, 3 ds, rw. R of 5 ds, join to same p as last r, 5 ds, cl, rw. Ch of 3 ds, p, 3 ds, rw. R of 5 ds, join to same p as last r, 5 ds, cl, rw. Ch of 3 ds, p, 3 ds, join by shuttle thread to p at joining of next 2 rs. Ch of 3 ds, p, 3 ds, rw. R of 5 ds, join to p of next r, 5 ds, cl, rw. Ch of 3 ds, p 3 ds, join to corresponding p on first motif, 3 ds, p, 3 ds, rw. R of 5 ds, join to same p as last r, 5 ds, cl, rw. Ch of 3 ds, p, 3 ds, join by shuttle thread to p at joining of next 2 rs. Ch of 3 ds, p, 3 ds, rw. R of 5 ds, join to next corner p, 5 ds, cl, rw. Ch of 3 ds, p, 3 ds, rw. R of 5 ds, join to same p as last r, 5 ds, cl, rw. Ch of 3 ds, join to corresponding p on first motif, 3 ds, 2 ps sep by 3 ds, 3 ds, rw and complete as first motif.

Make 4 rows of 13 motifs, joining adjacent sides as second motif was joined to first motif. Damp and pin out to measurements.

Motif cheval set

Materials: Coats Mercer-Crochet no. 20 (20 grms).
4 balls. This model is worked in Amber Gold. Milward tatting shuttle.

Size of motif: 2 ins from point to point.

Measurements:
Centrepiece – 20 × 10 ins.
Small mat – 6 ins square.

Centrepiece
First motif

1st row: R of 2 ds, 8 ps sep by 3 ds, 1 ds, cl. Tie ends, cut and oversew neatly on wrong side.

2nd row: Tie ball and shuttle threads together. Attach thread to any p on previous row. Ch of 8 ds. (R of 6 ds, p, 6 ds, cl) 3 times. * Ch of 8 ds, join by shuttle thread to same p on previous row. Ch of 3 ds, join by shuttle thread to next p on previous row. * * Ch of 8 ds. R of 6 ds, join to p of last r, 6 ds, cl. (R of 6 ds, p, 6 ds, cl) twice; repeat from * ending last repeat at * *, joining last r to first r and last ch to same place as first ch. Tie ends, cut and oversew neatly on wrong side.

Second motif

Work as first motif for 1 row.

2nd row: Tie ball and shuttle threads together. Attach thread to any p on previous row. Ch of 8 ds. R of 6 ds, p, 6 ds, cl. * R of 6 ds, join to corresponding p on first motif, 6 ds, cl. R of 6 ds, p, 6 ds, cl. Ch of 8 ds, join by shuttle thread to same p on previous row. Ch of 3 ds, join by shuttle thread to next p on previous row. Ch of 8 ds. R of 6 ds, join to p of last r, 6 ds, cl; repeat from * once more and complete as first motif.
Make 10 rows of 5 motifs, joining adjacent sides as second motif was joined to first.

Filling

1st row: R of 1 ds, 8 ps sep by 2 ds, 1 ds, cl. Tie ends, cut and oversew neatly on wrong side.

2nd row: Tie ball and shuttle threads together. Attach thread to any p on previous row. Ch of 8 ds, join to p at joining of any 2 motifs, 8 ds, join by shuttle thread to same p on previous row. * Ch of 2 ds, join by shuttle thread to next p on previous row. Ch of 8 ds, join to p at joining of next 2 rs, 8 ds, join by shuttle thread to same p on previous row. Ch of 2 ds, join by shuttle thread to next p on previous row. * * Ch of 8 ds, join to p at joining of next 2 motifs, 8 ds, join by shuttle thread to same p on previous row; repeat from * ending last repeat at * * and joining last ch to same place as first ch. Tie ends, cut and oversew neatly on wrong side.

Small mat *make 2*

Make 3 rows of 3 motifs joining as before, having 4 filling motifs.
Damp and pin out to measurements.

for detail, see page 326
for colour illustration, see page 327

Motif luncheon set

Materials: Coats Mercer-Crochet no. 10
(20 grms).
8 balls. This model is worked in Lt French
Blue.
The above quantity is sufficient for one centrepiece and one place mat.
Milward tatting shuttle.

Size of motif: 1¾ in diameter.

Measurements:
Centrepiece – 14¾ × 19½ ins approximately.
Place mat – 14¾ × 16½ ins approximately.

Centrepiece

First motif
R of 10 ds, 3 ps sep by 4 ds, 10 ds, cl. * R of 10
ds, join to last p of previous r, 4 ds, 2 ps sep by
4 ds, 10 ds, cl; repeat from * 10 times more,
joining last p of last r to first p of first r. Tie
ends, cut and oversew neatly on wrong side.

Second motif
R of 10 ds, p, 4 ds, join to centre p of any r on
first motif, 4 ds, p, 10 ds, cl. R of 10 ds, join to
last p of previous r, 4 ds, join to p of next r on
first motif, 4 ds, p, 10 ds, cl.
Complete as for first motif.
Work 7 rows of 10 motifs, joining adjacent
sides as second motif was joined to first motif
leaving one free p between joins.

for colour illustration, see page 331

Border

1st row: Tie ball and shuttle threads together. Attach thread to free p to right of centre free p on any corner. * Ch of 3 ds, 2 ps sep by 3 ds, 3 ds, join by shuttle thread to next p. Ch of 4 ds, 5 ps sep by 4 ds, 4 ds, join by shuttle thread to 2nd free p on next motif; repeat from * to next corner motif. Ch of 3 ds, 2 ps sep by 3 ds, 3 ds, join by shuttle thread to next p. Ch of 4 ds, 5 ps sep by 4 ds, 4 ds, miss 1 p, join by shuttle thread to next p; repeat from first * joining last ch to same place as first ch. Tie ends, cut and oversew neatly on wrong side.

2nd row: Tie ball and shuttle threads together. Work 5 rs as for first motif. Ch of 3 ds, 2 ps sep by 3 ds, 4 ds, join by shuttle thread to 5th p of second ch on previous row. * Ch of 4 ds, 2 ps sep by 3 ds, 3 ds, join to last p of previous r, 3 ds, 4 ps sep by 3 ds, 4 ds, miss 2 ps on previous row, join by shuttle thread to next p. Ch of 4 ds, 2 ps sep by 3 ds, 3 ds. * * R of 10 ds, join to 3rd p of 2nd last ch, 4 ds, 2 ps sep by 4 ds, 10 ds, cl. Work 4 rs as for first motif. Ch of 3 ds, 2 ps sep by 3 ds, 4 ds, miss 3 ps on previous row, join by shuttle thread to next p; repeat from * to next corner but only miss 1 p on corner ch at end of last repeat. Ch of 4 ds, 2 ps sep by 3 ds, 3 ds. R of 10 ds, join to last p of previous r, 4 ds, 2 ps sep by 4 ds, 10 ds, cl. Work 4 rs as for first motif. Ch of 3 ds, 2 ps sep by 3 ds, 4 ds, miss 1 p on previous row, join by shuttle thread to next p; repeat from first * ending last repeat at * * joining second last ch to first p of first r and last ch to base of same r. Tie ends, cut and oversew neatly on wrong side.

Place mat

Work 7 rows of 8 motifs joining as before.
Work border as for centrepiece.
Damp and press.

Coffee table mat

Materials: Coats Mercer-Crochet no. 10
(20 grms).
3 balls. This model is worked in Ecru.
Milward tatting shuttle.

Tension (gauge): First row $1\frac{7}{8}$ in diameter.

Measurement: 19 ins diameter, approximately.

1st row: Tie ball and shuttle threads together. R of 3 ds, 5 ps sep by 3 ds, 3 ds, cl, rw.
* Ch of 3 ds, 3 ps sep by 3 ds, 3 ds, rw. R of 3 ds,
p, 3 ds, join to 2nd last p on previous r, 3 ds,
3 ps sep by 3 ds, 3 ds, cl, rw; repeat from * 8
times more joining 2nd last p of last r to 2nd p
on first r. Ch of 3 ds, 3 ps sep by 3 ds, 3 ds, join
to base of first r. Tie ends, cut and oversew
neatly on wrong side.

for colour illustration, see page 335

2nd row: Tie ball and shuttle threads together. Attach thread to centre p of any ch on
previous row. Ch of 4 ds, p, * 6 ds, 2 ps sep by
4 ds, 6 ds, * * p, 4 ds, join by shuttle thread to
centre p of next ch on previous row, 4 ds, join
to last p on adjacent ch; repeat from * ending
last repeat at * *, join to first p on first ch,
4 ds, join to same p as first ch was attached.
Tie ends, cut and oversew neatly on wrong
side.

3rd row: Tie ball and shuttle threads together. R of 3 ds, 5 ps sep by 3 ds, 3 ds, cl, rw.
Ch of 6 ds, join to first free p of ch on previous
row, 3 ds, p, 6 ds. [R of 3 ds, 5 ps sep by 3 ds,
3 ds, cl, rw. Ch of 4 ds, join to 2nd last p on
adjacent r, 3 ds, 2 ps sep by 3 ds, 4 ds, rw. * (R
of 3 ds, p, 3 ds, join to 2nd last p on previous r,
3 ds, 3 ps sep by 3 ds, 3 ds, cl, rw]. Ch of 4 ds,
3 ps sep by 3 ds, 4 ds, rw) 7 times. R of 3 ds, p,
3 ds, join to 2nd last p on previous r, 3 ds, p,
3 ds, join to 2nd p on adjacent r, 3 ds, p, 3 ds, cl.
Ch of 6 ds, join to p on adjacent ch, 3 ds, join to
next p of ch on previous row, 6 ds, rw. R of 3
ds, p, 3 ds, join to first p on adjacent ch, 3 ds,
3 ps sep by 3 ds, 3 ds, cl, rw. Ch of 6 ds, join to
first p of next ch on previous row, 3 ds, p, 6 ds.
Repeat within [ ] once. Ch of 4 ds, p, 3 ds, join
to corresponding p on adjacent ch, 3 ds, p, 4 ds,
rw; * * repeat from * working within ( ) 6 times
and ending last repeat at * *. Repeat within
( ) 4 times. R as before, rw. Ch of 4 ds, p, 3 ds,
join to corresponding p on adjacent ch, 3 ds, p,
4 ds, rw. R as before, rw. Ch of 4 ds, 2 ps sep by
3 ds, 3 ds, join to 2nd p of first r, 4 ds, rw. R of 3
ds, p, 3 ds, join to 2nd p on previous r, 3 ds, p,
3 ds, join to 2nd p on adjacent r, 3 ds, p, 3 ds, cl,
rw. Ch of 6 ds, join to p on adjacent ch, 3 ds,
join to next p on previous row, 6 ds, join to
base of first r. Tie ends, cut and oversew
neatly on wrong side.

4th row: Tie ball and shuttle threads together. R of 2 ds, 3 ps sep by 3 ds, 3 ds, join to centre p of 6th 3 p ch on previous row, 4 ds, p, 4 ds, join to centre p on adjacent ch, 3 ds, 3 ps sep by 3 ds, 2 ds, cl, rw. * Ch of 4 ds, 6 ps sep by 2 ds, 4 ds, join by shuttle thread to centre p on next ch, 4 ds, 5 ps sep by 2 ds, 4 ds, join by shuttle thread to centre p on next ch, 4 ds, 6 ps sep by 2 ds, 4 ds, * * rw. R of 2 ds, 3 ps sep by 3 ds, 3 ds, join to centre p on next ch, 4 ds, p, 4 ds, join to centre p on next ch, 3 ds, 3 ps sep by 3 ds, 2 ds, cl, rw; repeat from * ending last repeat at * *, join to base of first r. Tie ends, cut and oversew neatly on wrong side.

5th row: Tie ball and shuttle threads together. R of 8 ds, join to last p of last ch on previous row, 3 ds, join to first p on next ch, 8 ds, cl, rw. Ch of 4 ds, p, * 7 ds, p, 9 ds, p, 4 ds, miss 2 ps on previous row, join by shuttle thread to next p, 4 ds, join to corresponding p on adjacent ch, 9 ds, p, 7 ds, p, 4 ds, rw. R of 8 ds, miss 4 ps on previous row, join to next p, 8 ds, cl, rw. Ch of 4 ds, join to corresponding p on adjacent ch, 7 ds, p, 9 ds, p, 4 ds, miss 4 ps on previous row, join by shuttle thread to next p, 4 ds, join to corresponding p on adjacent ch, 9 ds, p, 7 ds, * * p, 4 ds, rw. R of 8 ds, miss 2 ps, join to next p, 3 ds, join to next p, 8 ds, cl, rw. Ch of 4 ds, join to corresponding p on adjacent ch; repeat from * ending last repeat at * *, join to first p on first ch, 4 ds, join to base of first r. Tie ends, cut and oversew neatly on wrong side.

6th row: Tie ball and shuttle threads together. R of 2 ds, 7 ps sep by 3 ds, 2 ds, cl, rw. Ch of 6 ds, p, 3 ds, join to free p of first ch on previous row, 3 ds, p, 6 ds. * R of 3 ds, 5 ps sep by 3 ds, 3 ds, cl, rw. Ch of 4 ds, 2 ps sep by 3 ds, 3 ds, join to 3rd p of adjacent r, 4 ds, rw. (R of

3 ds, p, 3 ds, join to 2nd last p of last r, 3 ds, 3 ps sep by 3 ds, 3 ds, cl, rw. * Ch of 4 ds, 3 ps sep by 3 ds, 4 ds, rw) 7 times. * * R of 3 ds, p, 3 ds, join to 2nd last p of previous r, 3 ds, p, 3 ds, join to 2nd p of adjacent r, 3 ds, p, 3 ds, cl. Ch of 6 ds, p, 3 ds, join to p of next ch on previous row, 3 ds, p, 6 ds, rw. R of 2 ds, 2 ps sep by 3 ds, 3 ds, join to 3rd p on adjacent ch, 3 ds, 4 ps sep by 3 ds, 2 ds, cl, rw. Ch of 6 ds, p, 3 ds, join to p of next ch on previous row, 3 ds, p, 6 ds. Repeat from * to * once. Ch of 4 ds, p, 3 ds, join to corresponding p of adjacent ch, 3 ds, p, 4 ds, rw. * * * Repeat within ( ) 6 times; repeat from * * ending last repeat at * * *. Repeat within ( ) 4 times. R as before, rw. Ch of 4 ds, p, 3 ds, join to corresponding p of adjacent ch, 3 ds, p, 4 ds, rw. R as before, rw. Ch of 4 ds, join to 2nd p of adjacent r, 3 ds, 2 ps sep by 3 ds, 4 ds, rw. R of 3 ds, p, 3 ds, join to 2nd last p of previous r, 3 ds, p, 3 ds, join to 2nd p of adjacent r, 3 ds, p, 3 ds, cl. Ch of 6 ds, p, 3 ds, join to p of next ch on previous row, 3 ds, p, 6 ds, join to base of first r. Tie ends, cut and oversew neatly on wrong side.

7th row: As 4th row.

8th row: Tie ball and shuttle threads together. R of 8 ds, miss 2 ps on first ch on previous row, join to next p, 2 ds, join to next p, 8 ds, cl, rw. * Ch of (10 ds, p) twice, 4 ds, miss 4 ps on previous row, join by shuttle thread to next p, 4 ds, join to corresponding p on adjacent ch, (10 ds, p, 10 ds, rw. R of 8 ds, miss 4 ps on previous row, join to next p, 2 ds, join to next p, 8 ds, cl, rw) twice; repeat from * omitting r at end of last repeat, join to base of first r. Tie ends, cut and oversew neatly on wrong side.

9th row: As 6th row.
Damp and pin out to measurements.

Cheval set

Materials: Coats Mercer-Crochet no. 20
(20 grms).
2 balls. This model is worked in Blush Pink.
Milward tatting shuttle.

Measurements:
Centrepiece – 16 × 10½ ins approximately.
Small mat – 6¾ ins from point to point.

for colour illustration, see page 339
for detail. see page 341

Centrepiece

Tie ball and shuttle threads together.

1st row: *1st ring* – R of 12 ds, p, 12 ds, cl. *2nd ring* – R of 10 ds, 2 ps sep by 3 ds, 10 ds, cl, rw. *1st p chain* – Ch of 5 ds, p, 8 ds, 2 ps sep by 8 ds, 8 ds, rw. *3rd ring* – R of 12 ds, join to base of last r, 12 ds, cl. Repeat 2nd ring. *2nd p chain* – Ch of 8 ds, join to corresponding p on adjacent ch, 8 ds, 2 ps sep by 8 ds, 5 ds, p, 5 ds, rw. Repeat 3rd and 2nd rings once more, rw. *3rd p chain* – (Ch of 5 ds, join to corresponding p on adjacent ch) twice, 8 ds, 2 ps sep by 8 ds, 5 ds, p, 5 ds, rw. Repeat 3rd ring, rw. * Ch of 5 ds, rw. Repeat 2nd ring, rw. Ch of 5 ds, join to base of adjacent r. Repeat 3rd p chain, rw. *9th ring* – R of 12 ds, join to base of same r as ch was joined, 12 ds, cl, * rw. Ch of 8 ds, rw. Repeat 2nd ring, rw. Ch of 8 ds, join to base of adjacent r. Repeat 3rd p chain, rw. Repeat 9th ring, rw. Repeat from * to * once more. Repeat 2nd ring, rw. (Ch of 5 ds, join to corresponding p on adjacent ch) twice, 8 ds, 2 ps sep by 8 ds, 8 ds, rw. Repeat 3rd and 2nd rings, rw. Ch of 8 ds, join to corresponding p on adjacent ch, 8 ds, 2 ps sep by 8 ds, 5 ds, rw. Repeat 3rd and 2nd rings, rw. Ch of 5 ds, join to corresponding p on adjacent ch, 8 ds, p, 8 ds, rw. Repeat 3rd ring. Sr of 4 ds, 2 ps sep by 3 ds, 4 ds, cl, rw. Ch of 8 ds, rw. R of 12 ds, 2 ps sep by 3 ds, 12 ds, cl, rw. Ch of 8 ds, rw. Sr as before, rw. Ch of 8 ds, join to p on corresponding ch, 8 ds, p, 5 ds, rw. R of 12 ds, join to base of last sr, 12 ds, cl. Repeat 2nd ring, rw. *11th p chain* – Ch of 5 ds, join to corresponding p on adjacent ch, 8 ds, join to free p on corresponding ch, 8 ds, p, 8 ds, rw. Repeat 3rd and 2nd rings, rw. *12th p chain* – Ch of 8 ds, join to corresponding p on adjacent ch, 8 ds, join to p on corresponding ch, 8 ds, 2 ps sep by 5 ds, 5 ds, rw. Repeat 3rd and 2nd rings, rw. *13th p chain* – (Ch of 5 ds, join to corresponding p on adjacent ch) twice, 8 ds, join to p on corresponding ch, 8 ds, 2 ps sep by 5 ds, 5 ds, rw. Repeat 3rd ring, rw. * * Ch of 5 ds, rw. Repeat 2nd ring, rw. Ch of 5 ds, join to base of adjacent r. Repeat 13th p chain, rw. Repeat 9th ring, * * rw. Ch of 8 ds, rw. Repeat 2nd ring rw. Ch of 8 ds, join to base of adjacent r. Repeat 13th p chain, rw. Repeat 9th ring, rw. Repeat from * * to * * once more. Repeat 2nd ring, rw. (Ch of 5 ds, join to corresponding p on adjacent ch) twice, 8 ds, join to p on corresponding ch, 8 ds, p, 8 ds, rw. Repeat 3rd and 2nd rings, rw. Ch of 8 ds, join to p on adjacent ch, 8 ds, join to p on corresponding ch, 8 ds, p, 5 ds, rw. Repeat 3rd and 2nd rings, rw. Ch of 5 ds, join to p on adjacent ch, 8 ds, p, 8 ds, rw. Repeat 3rd ring. Sr of 4 ds, 2 ps sep by 3 ds, 4 ds, cl, rw. Ch of 8 ds, rw. R of 12 ds, 2 ps sep by 3 ds, 12 ds, cl, rw. Ch of 8 ds, rw. Sr of 4 ds, 2 ps sep by 3 ds, 4 ds, join to p on first r worked, cl, rw. Ch of 8 ds, join to p on corresponding ch, 8 ds, join to adjacent p on first ch worked, 5 ds, join to base of first r. Tie ends, cut and oversew neatly on wrong side.

2nd row: Tie ball and shuttle threads together. R of 12 ds, join to first free p on 2nd last sr, 3 ds, join to next p, 8 ds, p, 12 ds, cl, rw. Ch of 12 ds, 2 ps sep by 12 ds, 12 ds, join by shuttle thread to p on last r, rw. * R of 12 ds, join to first p of next r on previous row, 3 ds, p, 12 ds, cl, rw. Chain as before, rw. (R of 3 ds, join to next p on previous row, 12 ds, join to first p of next r on previous row, 3 ds, p, 15 ds, cl, rw. Chain as before, rw) 8 times. R of 3 ds, join to next p on previous row, 12 ds, p, 15 ds, cl, rw. Chain as before, rw. R of 12 ds, join to first p of next sr, 3 ds, join to next p, 8 ds, p, 12 ds, cl, rw. Chain as before, rw. R of 8 ds, join to first p of next r on previous row, 8 ds, p, 12 ds, cl, rw. Chain as before, rw. * * R of 8 ds, join to

p of r on previous row, 8 ds, p, 12 ds, cl, rw. Chain as before, rw. R of 12 ds, join to first p on next sr, 3 ds, join to next p, 8 ds, p, 12 ds, cl, rw. Chain as before, rw; repeat from * to * * once more. R of 8 ds, join to next p on previous row, 8 ds, join to base of first r, 12 ds, cl, rw. Chain as before, join to base of first r. Tie ends, cut and oversew neatly on wrong side.

3rd row: Tie ball and shuttle threads together. R of 3 ds, 4 ps sep by 3 ds, 3 ds, join to first p of last ch on previous row, 3 ds, 3 ps sep by 3 ds, 3 ds, cl, rw. * Ch of 4 ds, 5 ps sep by 2 ds, 4 ds, rw. R of 3 ds, 3 ps sep by 3 ds, 3 ds, join to next p of same ch on previous row, 3 ds, join to first p of next ch on previous row, 3 ds, 3 ps sep by 3 ds, 3 ds, cl, rw; repeat from * 12 times more. Chain as before, rw. R of 3 ds, 3 ps sep by 3 ds, 3 ds, join to next p of same ch on previous row, 3 ds, 4 ps sep by 3 ds, 3 ds, cl, rw. Chain as before, rw. R of 3 ds, 2 ps sep by 3 ds, 3 ds, join to corresponding p on last r, 3 ds, 5 ps sep by 3 ds, 3 ds, cl, rw. Ch of 4 ds, 8 ps sep by 2 ds, 4 ds, rw. * * R of 3 ds, 2 ps sep by 3 ds, 3 ds, join to corresponding p on last r, 3 ds, 5 ps sep by 3 ds, cl, rw. Ch of 4 ds, 5 ps sep by 2 ds, 4 ds, rw. R of 3 ds, 2 ps sep by 3 ds, 3 ds, join to corresponding p on last r, 3 ds, p, 3 ds, join to first p of next ch on previous row, 3 ds, 3 ps sep by 3 ds, 3 ds, cl, rw; repeat from first * to * * once more. R of 3 ds, 2 ps sep by 3 ds, join to corresponding p on last r, 3 ds, 2 ps sep by 3 ds, 3 ds, join to corresponding p on first r, 3 ds, 2 ps sep by 3 ds, 3 ds, cl rw. Ch of 4 ds, 5 ps sep by 2 ds, 4 ds, join to base of first r. Tie ends, cut and oversew neatly on wrong side.

4th row: Tie ball and shuttle threads together. R of 2 ds, 3 ps sep by 2 ds, 2 ds, join to last p of last ch on previous row, 3 ds, join to first p on next ch, 2 ds, 3 ps sep by 2 ds, 2 ds, cl, rw. * Ch of 3 ds, 7 ps sep by 2 ds, 3 ds, p, 8 ds, miss 3 ps on previous row, join by shuttle thread to next p, 2 ds, join by shuttle thread to first p on next ch, 8 ds, join to corresponding p on adjacent ch, * * 3 ds, 7 ps sep by 2 ds, 3 ds, rw. R of 2 ds, 3 ps sep by 2 ds, 2 ds, miss 3 ps on previous row, join to next p, 3 ds, join to first p on next ch, 2 ds, 3 ps sep by 2 ds, 2 ds, cl, rw; * * * repeat from * 6 times more and from * to * * once. Ch of 3 ds, 8 ps sep by 2 ds, 3 ds, rw. R of 2 ds, 3 ps sep by 2 ds, 2 ds, miss 2 ps in previous row, join to next p, 3 ds, join to next p, 2 ds, 3 ps sep by 2 ds, 2 ds, cl, rw. Ch of 3 ds, 8 ps sep by 2 ds, 3 ds, p, 8 ds, miss 2 ps on previous row, join by shuttle thread to next p, 2 ds, join by shuttle thread to first p on next ch, 8 ds, join to corrsponding p on adjacent ch, 3 ds, 7 ps sep by 2 ds, 3 ds, rw. R of 2 ds, 3 ps sep by 2 ds, 2 ds, miss 3 ps on previous row, join to next p, 3 ds, join to first p on next ch, 2 ds, 3 ps sep by 2 ds, 2 ds, cl, rw. Repeat from * to * * * 7 times and from * to * * once. Ch of 3 ds, 8 ps sep by 2 ds, 3 ds, rw. R of 2 ds, 3 ps sep by 2 ds, 2 ds, miss 2 ps on previous row, join to next p, 3 ds, join to next p, 2 ds, 3 ps sep by 2 ds, 2 ds, cl, rw. Ch of 3 ds, 8 ps sep by 2 ds, 3 ds, p, 8 ds, miss 2 ps on previous row, join by shuttle thread to next p, 2 ds, join by shuttle thread to first p on next ch, 8 ds, join to corresponding p on adjacent ch, 3 ds, 7 ps sep by 2 ds, 3 ds, join to base of first r. Tie ends, cut and oversew neatly on wrong side.

5th row: Tie ball and shuttle threads together. R of 2 ds, 3 ps sep by 2 ds, 2 ds, join to last free p of 2nd last ch on previous row, 3 ds, join to first p on next ch, 2 ds, 3 ps sep by 2 ds, 2 ds, cl, rw. * Ch of 3 ds, 7 ps sep by 2 ds, 3 ds, p, 8 ds, miss 5 ps on previous row, join by shuttle thread to next p, 2 ds, join by shuttle thread to first p on next ch, 8 ds, join to corres-

ponding p on adjacent ch, 3 ds, 7 ps sep by 2 ds, 3 ds, rw. R of 2 ds, 3 ps sep by 2 ds; 2 ds, miss 5 ps on previous row, join to next p, 3 ds, join to first p on next ch, 2 ds, 3 ps sep by 2 ds, 2 ds, cl, rw; * * repeat from * 7 times more. Ch of 3 ds, 10 ps sep by 2 ds, 3 ds, p, 8 ds, miss 6 ps on previous row, join by shuttle thread to next p, 2 ds, join by shuttle thread to first p on next ch, 8 ds, join to corresponding p on adjacent ch, 3 ds, 10 ps sep by 2 ds, 3 ds, rw. R of 2 ds, 3 ps sep by 2 ds, 2 ds, miss 6 ps on previous row, join to next p, 3 ds, join to first p on next ch, 2 ds, 3 ps sep by 2 ds, 2 ds, cl, rw; repeat from * to * * 8 times. Ch of 3 ds, 10 ps sep by 2 ds, 3 ds, p, 8 ds, miss 6 ps on previous row, join by shuttle thread to next p, 2 ds, join to first p on next ch, 8 ds, join to corresponding p on adjacent ch, 3 ds, 10 ps sep by 2 ds, 3 ds, join to base of first r. Tie ends, cut and oversew neatly on wrong side.

6th row: Tie ball and shuttle threads together. R of 2 ds, 3 ps sep by 2 ds, 2 ds, join to last free p of first ch on previous row, 3 ds, join to first p on next ch, 2 ds, 3 ps sep by 2 ds, 2 ds, cl, rw. * Ch of 3 ds, 8 ps sep by 2 ds, 3 ds, p, 8 ds, miss 5 ps on previous row, join by shuttle thread to next p, 2 ds, join by shuttle thread to first p on next ch, 8 ds, join to corresponding p on adjacent ch, 3 ds, 8 ps sep by 2 ds, 3 ds, rw. * * R of 2 ds, 3 ps sep by 2 ds, 2 ds, miss 5 ps on previous row, join to next p, 3 ds, join to first p on next ch, 2 ds, 3 ps sep by 2 ds, 2 ds, cl, rw; * * * repeat from * 6 times more and from * to * * once. R of 2 ds, 3 ps sep by 2 ds, 2 ds, miss 5 ps on previous row, join to next p, 3 ds, 4 ps sep by 2 ds, 2 ds, cl, rw. Ch of 3 ds, 10 ps sep by 2 ds, 3 ds, rw. R of 2 ds, 3 ps sep by 2 ds, 2 ds, join to corresponding p on last r, 3 ds, miss 3 ps on next ch, join to next p, 2 ds, 3 ps sep by 2 ds, cl, rw; repeat from first * to * * * 8

times and from * to * * once. R of 2 ds, 3 ps sep by 2 ds, 2 ds, miss 5 ps on previous row, join to next p, 3 ds, 4 ps sep by 2 ds, 2 ds, cl, rw. Ch of 3 ds, 10 ps sep by 2 ds, 3 ds, rw. R of 2 ds, 3 ps sep by 2 ds, join to corresponding p on previous r, 3 ds, miss 3 ps on next ch, join to next p, 2 ds, 3 ps sep by 2 ds, 2 ds, cl, rw; repeat from * to * * joining last ch to base of first r. Tie ends, cut and oversew neatly on wrong side.

7th row: Tie ball and shuttle threads to-gether. R of 3 ds, p, 3 ds, join to last p of last ch on previous row, 3 ds, join to first p on next ch, 3 ds, 3 ps sep by 3 ds, 3 ds, cl, rw. (Ch of 3 ds, 4 ps sep by 3 ds, 3 ds, rw. R of 3 ds, p, 3 ds, join to corresponding p on last r, 3 ds, 4 ps sep by 3 ds, 3 ds, cl, rw) 5 times. [Ch of 3 ds, 4 ps sep by 3 ds, 3 ds, rw. R of 3 ds, p, 3 ds, join to corres-ponding p on last r, 3 ds, p, 3 ds, join to last p of next ch on previous row, 3 ds, join to first p on next ch, 3 ds, p, 3 ds, cl, rw. Ch of 3 ds, join to corresponding p on adjacent ch, 3 ds, 3 ps sep by 3 ds, 3 ds, rw. R of 3 ds, p, 3 ds, miss 6 ps on previous row, join to next p, 3 ds, join to first p on next ch, 3 ds, 3 ps sep by 3 ds, 3 ds, cl, rw]. * Ch of 3 ds, join to corresponding p on adjacent ch, 3 ds, 3 ps sep by 3 ds, 3 ds, rw. R of 3 ds, p, 3 ds, join to corresponding p on last r, 3 ds, 4 ps sep by 3 ds, 3 ds, cl, rw. * * * (Ch of 3 ds, 4 ps sep by 3 ds, 3 ds, rw. R of 3 ds, p, 3 ds, join to corresponding p on last r, 3 ds, 4 ps sep by 3 ds, 3 ds, cl, rw) 4 times. * * Repeat within [ ] once more. * * * Repeat from * 4 times more ending at * * at end of last repeat. * * * * Ch of 3 ds, 4 ps sep by 3 ds, 3 ds, join by shuttle thread to second p on last r, rw. Lr of 3 ds, join to next p on last r, 3 ds, 3 ps sep by 3 ds, 3 ds, join to 5th p of corner ch on previous row, 3 ds, join to next p, 3 ds, 4 ps sep by 3 ds, 3 ds, cl, rw. Ch of 3 ds, join to corresponding p on adjacent ch, 3 ds, 3 ps sep by 3 ds, 3 ds, rw.

R of 3 ds, p, 3 ds, join to base of lr, 3 ds, join to last p on lr, 3 ds, 3 ps sep by 3 ds, 3 ds, cl, rw. * * * * Repeat from * * * to * * * once more then from first * to second * * * 6 times more ending last repeat at * *. Repeat from * * * * to * * * * once more. Repeat from * * * to * * * once more omitting last r at end of last repeat and joining last p of last ch to first p of first ch, join to base of first r. Tie ends, cut and oversew neatly on wrong side.

Small mat *make 2*

1st row: Tie ball and shuttle threads together. R of 14 ds, p, 12 ds, cl, rw. * Ch of 12 ds, 2 ps sep by 12 ds, 12 ds, join by shuttle thread to p on last r, rw. * * R of 14 ds, p, 12 ds, cl, rw; repeat from * 4 times more and from * to * * once joining last ch to base of first r. Tie ends, cut and oversew neatly on wrong side.

2nd row: Tie ball and shuttle threads together. R of 3 ds, 3 ps sep by 3 ds, 3 ds, join to first p of first ch on previous row, 3 ds, 4 ps sep by 3 ds, 3 ds, cl, rw. * Ch of 4 ds, 6 ps sep by 2 ds, 4 ds, rw. R of 3 ds, 2 ps sep by 3 ds, 3 ds, join to corresponding p on last r, 3 ds, p, 3 ds, join to next p on previous row, 3 ds, 3 ps sep by 3 ds, 3 ds, cl, rw. Ch as before. R of 3 ds, 2 ps sep by 3 ds, 3 ds, join to corresponding p on last r, 3 ds, 5 ps sep by 3 ds, 3 ds, cl, rw. Ch as before. * * R of 3 ds, 2 ps sep by 3 ds, 3 ds, join to corresponding p on last r, 3 ds, join to first p of next ch on previous row, 3 ds, 4 ps sep by 3 ds, 3 ds, cl, rw; repeat from * ending last repeat at * * joining corresponding p of last r to 3rd p of first r. Tie ends, cut and oversew neatly on wrong side.

3rd row: Tie ball and shuttle threads together. R of 2 ds, 3 ps sep by 2 ds, 2 ds, join to last p of last ch on previous row, 4 ds, join to first p on next ch, 2 ds, 3 ps sep by 2 ds, 2 ds, cl, rw. * Ch of 3 ds, 8 ps sep by 3 ds, 8 ds, miss 4 ps on previous row, join by shuttle thread to next p, 2 ds, join by shuttle thread to first p on next ch, 8 ds, join to corresponding p on adjacent ch, 3 ds, 7 ps sep by 3 ds, 3 ds, * * rw. R of 2 ds, 3 ps sep by 2 ds, 2 ds, miss 4 ps on previous row, join to next p, 4 ds, join to first p on next ch, 2 ds, 3 ps sep by 2 ds, 2 ds, cl, rw; repeat from * ending last repeat at * * and joining last ch to base of first r. Tie ends, cut and oversew neatly on wrong side.

4th row: Tie ball and shuttle threads together. R of 2 ds, p, 3 ds, join to last p before any r on previous row, 3 ds, join to first p on next ch, 3 ds, 3 ps sep by 3 ds, 2 ds, cl, rw. * (Ch of 3 ds, 4 ps sep by 3 ds, 3 ds, rw. R of 2 ds, p, 3 ds, join to corresponding p on last r, 3 ds, 4 ps sep by 3 ds, 2 ds, cl, rw) 5 times. Ch as before. R of 2 ds, p, 3 ds, join to corresponding p on last r, 3 ds, p, 3 ds, join to last p of next ch on previous row, 3 ds, join to first p on next ch, 3 ds, p, 2 ds, cl, rw. Ch of 3 ds, 6 ps sep by 3 ds, 3 ds, * * rw. R of 2 ds, p, 3 ds, miss 5 ps on previous row, join to next p, 3 ds, join to first p on next ch, 3 ds, 3 ps sep by 3 ds, 2 ds, cl, rw; repeat from * ending last repeat at * * and joining last ch to base of first r. Tie ends, cut and oversew neatly on wrong side. Damp and pin out to measurements.

Four edgings

Materials: Coats Mercer-Crochet no. 10, 20, 40, or 60.
Milward tatting shuttle.
Milward steel crochet hook.

Edging 1

Tie ball and shuttle threads together. R of 3 ds, 5 ps sep by 2 ds, 3 ds, cl. (R of 3 ds, join to last p of previous r, 2 ds, 4 ps sep by 2 ds, 3 ds, cl) twice, rw. Ch of 4 ds, 6 ps sep by 3 ds, 4 ds, rw. * Ch of 4 ds, join to 3rd p of last r, 3 ds, 5 ps sep by 3 ds, 4 ds, rw. R of 3 ds, 2 ps sep by 2 ds, 2 ds, join to last p of adjacent ch, 2 ds, 2 ps sep by 2 ds, 3 ds, cl. (R of 3 ds, join to last p of previous r, 2 ds, 4 ps sep by 2 ds, 3 ds, cl) twice, rw. Ch of 4 ds, join to corresponding p of adjacent ch, 3 ds, 5 ps sep by 3 ds, 4 ds, row; repeat from * for length required, ending to correspond with beginning. Tie ends, cut and oversew neatly on wrong side.

Crochet heading

Attach thread to centre p of second r worked, 1 dc into same place as join, * (6 ch, 1 dc into second p of next ch, 1 ch, 1 dc into next p on same ch) twice, 6 ch, 1 dc into centre p of next r; repeat from * to end. Fasten off.

for colour illustration, see page 343

Edging 2

Tie ball and shuttle threads together. Ch of 3 ds, 5 ps sep by 3 ds, 3 ds, rw. * Ch of 3 ds, 5 ps sep by 3 ds, 3 ds, miss 1 p on previous ch, join by shuttle thread to next p, rw; repeat from * for length required. Tie ends, cut and oversew neatly on wrong side.

Crochet heading
Attach thread to centre p of last ch of edging, 1 dc into same place as join, * 6 ch, 1 dc into centre free p of next ch; repeat from * to end. Fasten off.

Edging 3

1st row: Tie ball and shuttle threads together. R of 6 ds, p, 6 ds, lp, 6 ds, p, 6 ds, cl, rw. Ch of 6 ds, p, 6 ds, rw. * R of 6 ds, join to last p of previous r, 6 ds, join to lp of previous r, 6 ds, p, 6 ds, cl, rw. Ch of 6 ds, p, 6 ds, rw. R of 6 ds, join to last p of previous r, 6 ds, join to same lp as last r was joined, 6 ds, p, 6ds, cl, rw. Ch of 6 ds, p, 6 ds, rw. R of 6 ds, join to last p of previous r, 6 ds, join to same lp as previous r was joined, 6 ds, p, 6 ds, cl. R of 6 ds, p, 6 ds, lp, 6 ds, p, 6 ds, cl, rw. Ch of 6 ds, join to p of adjacent ch, 6 ds, rw; repeat from * for length required, ending to correspond with beginning. Tie ends, cut and oversew neatly on wrong side.

2nd row: Tie ball and shuttle threads to p of first r of previous row, * 10 ds, join by shuttle thread to p of next r of previous row; repeat from * to end. Tie ends, cut and oversew neatly on wrong side.

Edging 4

Tie ball and shuttle threads together. R of 5 ds, 3 ps sep by 5 ds, 5 ds, cl. * (R of 5 ds, join to last p of previous r, 5 ds, 2 ps sep by 5 ds, 5 ds, cl) twice, rw. Ch of 3 ds, 5 ps sep by 3 ds, 3 ds, rw. R of 6 ds, join to last p of previous r, 6 ds, cl. R of 6 ds, p, 6 ds, cl, rw. Ch of 3 ds, 5 ps sep by 3 ds, 3 ds, rw. R of 5 ds, join to p of previous r, 5 ds, 2 ps sep by 5 ds, 5 ds, cl; repeat from * for length required, ending to correspond with beginning. Tie ends, cut and oversew neatly on wrong side.

Crochet heading
Attach thread to first p of first r, 8 ch, miss one p of first ch, 1 ss into next p, * (1 ch, 1 ss into next p) twice, 5 ch, miss next 2 ps, 1 ss into next p; repeat from * ending last repeat with 5 ch, miss next p, 1 tr into next p, Fasten off.

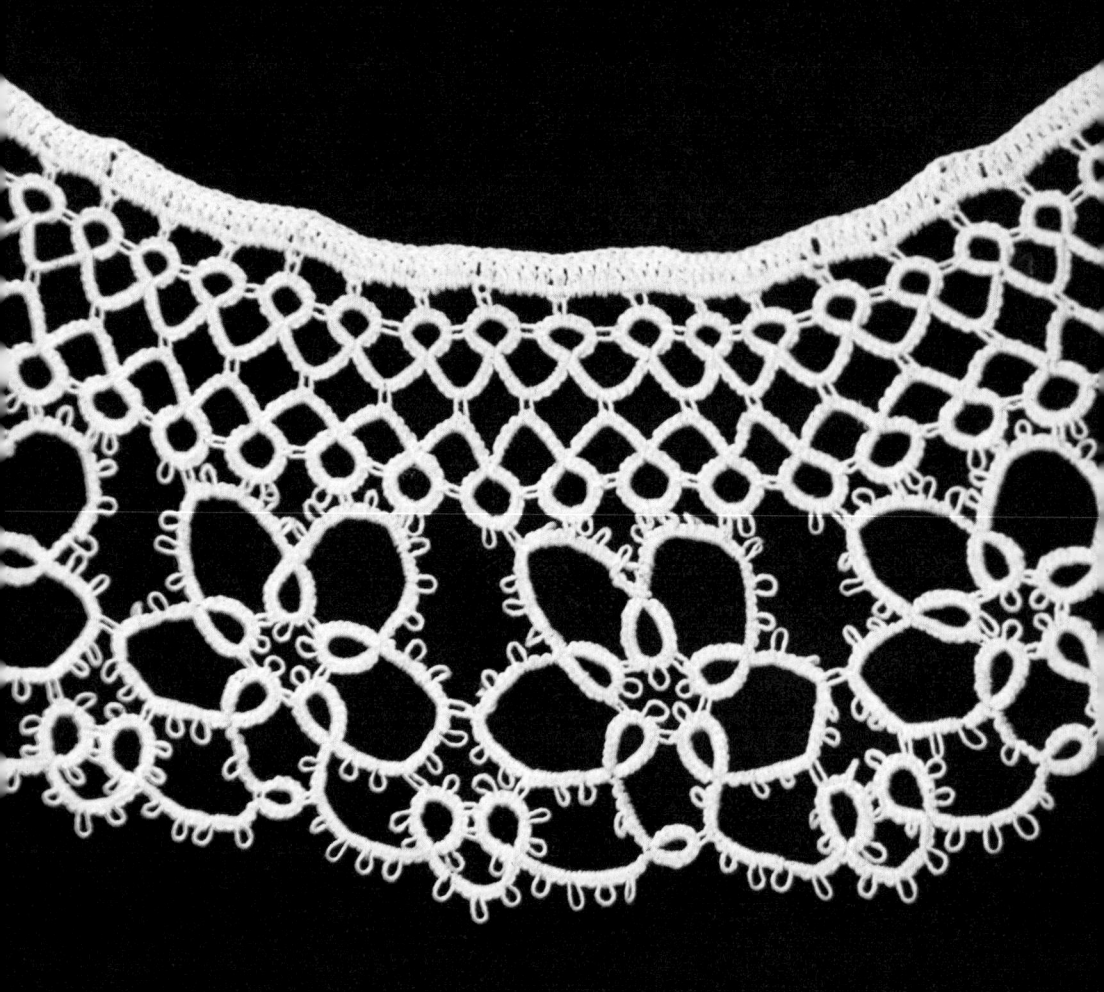

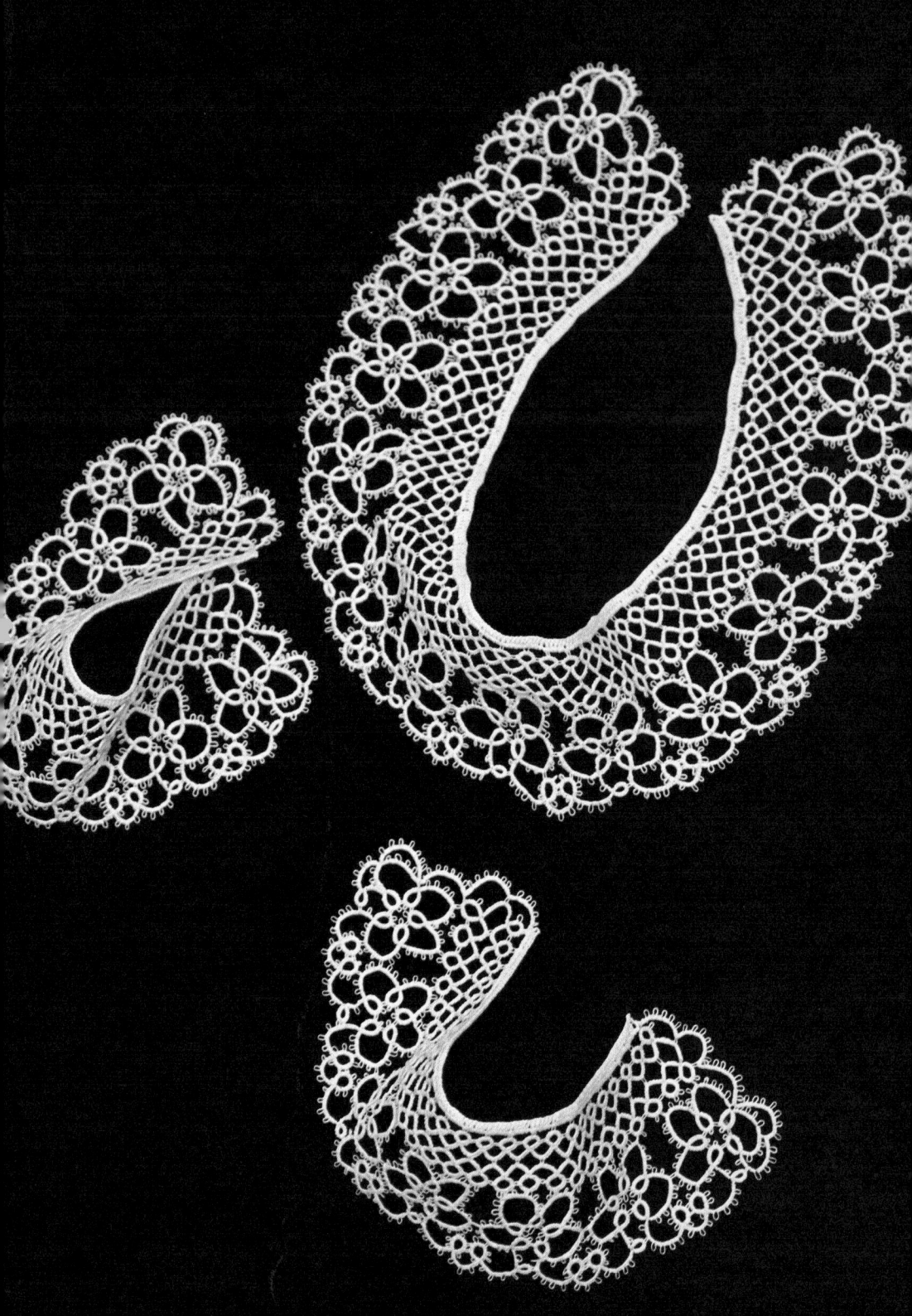

Collar and cuff set

Materials: Coats Mercer-Crochet no. 40 (20 grms).
1 ball. This model is worked in White.
Milward steel crochet hook 1·00 (no. 4).
Milward tatting shuttle.

Depth of edging: 2½ ins.

Collar

1st row: Tie ball and shuttle threads together. R of 4 ds, 3 ps sep by 4 ds, 4 ds, cl. * Rw, ch of 5 ds, p, 5 ds, rw. R of 4 ds, join to last p of previous r, 4 ds, 2 ps sep by 4 ds, 4 ds, cl; repeat from * 56 times more. (58 rings.)

2nd row: Ch of 8 ds, p, 8 ds. R of 5 ds, p, 5 ds, p, 2 ds, p, 5 ds, p, 5 ds, cl. * Rw, ch of 5 ds, join to p of ch on previous row, 5 ds, rw. R of 5 ds, join to last p of previous r, 5 ds, p, 2 ds, p, 5 ds, p, 5 ds, cl; repeat from * to end, ch of 8 ds, p, 8 ds, join to base of first r on previous row. Tie ends, cut and oversew neatly on wrong side.

3rd row: Tie ball and shuttle threads together. Attach thread to centre p of last r on first row. Ch of 3 ds, 5 ps sep by 3 ds, 3 ds, join by shuttle thread to p of next ch on previous row, 3 ds, 6 ps sep by 3 ds, 3 ds, join by shuttle thread to 2nd free p of first r on previous row, 3 ds, 7 ps sep by 3 ds, 3 ds, leave small sp, 3 ds, 7 ps sep by 3 ds, 3 ds, leave small sp, 3 ds, 4 ps sep by 3 ds, 3 ds. Sr of 6 ds, p, 6 ds, cl. Ch of 3 ds, p, 3 ds. R of 8 ds, 3 ps sep by 2 ds, 8 ds, cl, rw. Ch of 3 ds, 3 ps sep by 3 ds, 3 ds, join to small sp, 3 ds, 4 ps sep by 3 ds, 3 ds, join to next small sp, rw. R of 8 ds, join to last p on previous r, 2 ds, p, 2 ds, p, 8 ds, cl, rw. Ch of 3 ds, 4 ps sep by 3 ds, 3 ds, join to next free p on last r on previous row, 3 ds, 3 ps sep by 3 ds, 3 ds, rw. R of 8 ds, join to last free p on previous r, 2 ds, p, 2 ds, p, 8 ds, cl, rw. Ch of 3 ds, 3 ps sep by 3 ds, 3 ds, miss 1 r on previous row, join to first free p on next r, 3 ds, 4 ps sep by 3 ds, 3 ds, rw. R of 8 ds, join to last p on previous r, 2 ds, p, 2 ds, p, 8 ds, cl, rw. Ch of 3 ds, 8 ps sep by 3 ds, 3 ds, rw. R of 8 ds, join to last p on previous r, 2 ds, p, 2 ds, join to first p on first r, 8 ds, cl. * Ch of 3 ds, p, 3 ds, join to p on sr, 3 ds, 4 ps sep by 3 ds, 3 ds, rw. R of 2 ds, p,

for detail, see page 348
for colour illustration, see page 349

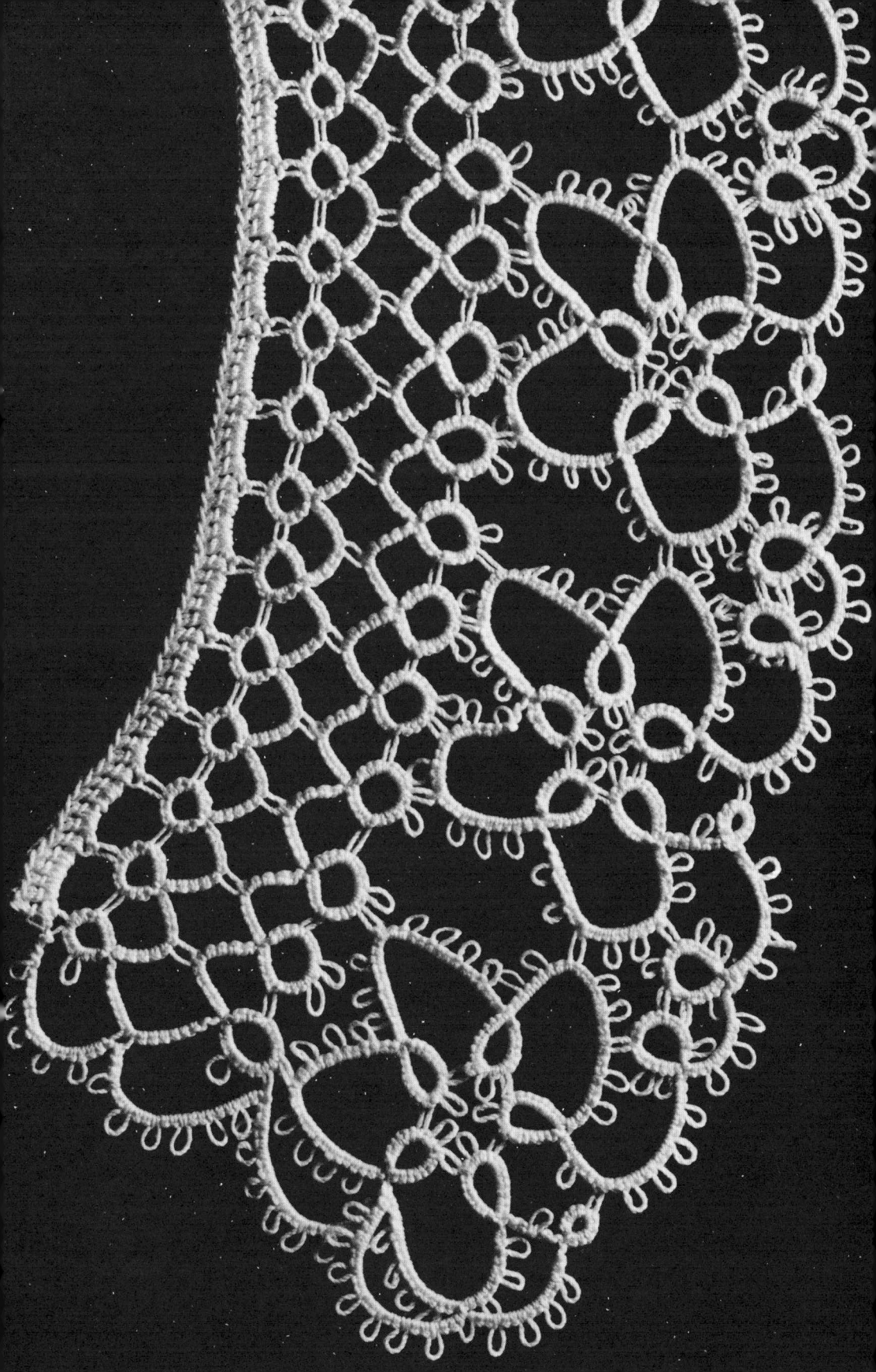

3 ds, p, 3 ds, miss 2 ps on last 8 p ch, join to next p, 3 ds, 4 ps sep by 3 ds, 2 ds, cl, rw. Ch of 3 ds, 3 ps sep by 3 ds, 3 ds, rw. R of 2 ds, p, 3 ds, join to 2nd p of last r, 3 ds, join to next p of last r, 3 ds, 4 ps sep by 3 ds, 2 ds, cl, rw. Ch of 3 ds, 4 ps sep by 3 ds, 3 ds. Sr of 6 ds, p, 6 ds, cl. Ch of 3 ds, p, 3 ds. * * R of 8 ds, 3 ps sep by 2 ds, 8 ds, cl, rw. Ch of 3 ds, 2 ps sep by 3 ds, 3 ds, join to 3rd p of adjacent r, 3 ds, 2 ps sep by 3 ds, 3 ds, join to corresponding p on adjacent ch, 3 ds, 2 ps sep by 3 ds, 3 ds, rw. R of 8 ds, join to last p of previous r, 2 ds, p, 2 ds, p, 8 ds, cl, rw. Ch of 3 ds, 3 ps sep by 3 ds, 3 ds, join to 2nd free p of next r on previous row, 3 ds, p, 3 ds, join to first free p of next r on previous row, 3 ds, 2 ps sep by 3 ds, 3 ds, rw. R of 8 ds, join to last p on previous r, 2 ds, p, 2 ds, p, 8 ds, cl, rw. Ch of 3 ds, 2 ps sep by 3 ds, 3 ds, miss 1 p on next r on previous row, join to next p, 3 ds, p, 3 ds, join to first free p on next r on previous row, 3 ds, 3 ps sep by 3 ds, 3 ds, rw. R of 8 ds, join to last p on previous r, 2 ds, p, 2 ds, p, 8 ds, cl, rw. Ch of 3 ds, 8 ps sep by 3 ds, 3 ds. R of 8 ds, join to last p of previous r, 2 ds, p, 2 ds, join to first p of adjacent r, 8 ds, cl; repeat from * until 3 rs remain on previous row then repeat from * to * * once. R of 8 ds, 3 ps sep by 2 ds, 8 ds, cl, rw. Ch of 3 ds, 2 ps sep by 3 ds, 3 ds, join to 3rd p of adjacent r, 3 ds, 2 ps sep by 3 ds, 3 ds, miss 2 ps on adjacent ch, join to next p, 3 ds, 2 ps sep by 3 ds, 3 ds, rw. R of 8 ds, join to last p on previous r, 2 ds, p, 2 ds, p, 8 ds, cl, rw. Ch of 3 ds, 4 ps sep by 3 ds, 3 ds, miss 1 p on next r on previous row, join to next p, 3 ds, 3 ps sep by 3 ds, 3 ds, rw. R of 8 ds, join to last p on previous r, 2 ds, p, 2 ds, p, 8 ds, cl, rw. Ch of 3 ds, 3 ps sep by 3 ds, miss 1 r on previous row, join to p on next r, 3 ds, 4 ps sep by 3 ds, 3 ds, rw. R of 8 ds join to last p of previous r, 2 ds, 2 ps sep by 2 ds, 8 ds, cl, rw. Ch of 3 ds, 8 ps sep by 3 ds, 3 ds, rw. R of 8 ds, join to last p of previous r,

2 ds, p, 2 ds, join to first p of adjacent r, 8 ds, cl. Ch of 3 ds, p, 3 ds, join to p of sr, 3 ds, 4 ps sep by 3 ds, 3 ds, miss 3 ps on last 8 p ch, join by shuttle thread to next p, 3 ds, 7 ps sep by 3 ds, 3 ds, join by shuttle thread to base of second last r worked, 3 ds, 7 ps sep by 3 ds, 3 ds, join by shuttle thread to first free p of next r on 2nd row, 3 ds, 6 ps sep by 3 ds, 3 ds, join by shuttle thread to p on next ch on last row, 3 ds, 5 ps sep by 3 ds, 3 ds, join to centre p on first r on first row. Tie ends, cut and oversew neatly on wrong side.

Cuffs *make 2*

1st row: Tie ball and shuttle threads together. R of 4 ds, 3 ps sep by 4 ds, 4 ds, cl. * Rw, ch of 5 ds, p, 5 ds, rw. R of 4 ds, join to last p of previous r, 4 ds, 2 ps sep by 4 ds, 4 ds, cl; repeat from * 24 times more. (26 rings.)

2nd row: Ch of 8 ds, p, 8 ds. R of 5 ds, p, 5 ds, p, 2 ds, p, 5 ds, p, 5 ds, cl. * Rw, ch of 5 ds, join to p of ch on previous row, 5 ds, rw. R of 5 ds, join to last p of previous r, 5 ds, p, 2 ds, p, 5 ds, p, 5 ds, cl; repeat from * to end, ch of 8 ds, p, 8 ds, join to base of first r on previous row. Tie ends, cut and oversew neatly on wrong side.

3rd row: As 3rd row of collar.

Crochet heading for collars and cuffs.
1st row: Join thread to same p as last ch on last row, 1 dc into p, * 4 ch, 1 dc into next p; repeat from * ending with 3 ch, turn.

2nd row: * 4 tr into next sp, 1 tr into next dc; repeat from * to end of row. Fasten off. Damp and pin out to measurements.

Cheval set in two colours

Materials: Coats Mercer-Crochet no. 20 (20 grms).
2 balls each Buttercup and Dk Ecru.
Milward tatting shuttle.

Size of motif: 2 ins square.

Measurements: Centrepiece – 10 × 18 ins.
Small mat – 8 × 12 ins.

Centrepiece

First motif
Wind approximately ¾ yd of Dk Ecru on to shuttle. Work a centre r of 2 ds, 8 ps sep by 3 ds, 1 ds, cl. Tie ends, cut and oversew neatly on wrong side.

Wind shuttle with Buttercup and, using Dk Ecru ball, tie ball and shuttle threads together. R of 4 ds, 2 ps sep by 4 ds, 2 ds, join to any p of centre r, 2 ds, 2 ps sep by 4 ds, 4 ds, cl, rw. * Ch of 5 ds, 3 ps sep by 5 ds, 5 ds, rw. R of 4 ds, p, 4 ds, join to 2nd last p of previous r, 2 ds, join to next p on centre r, 2 ds, 2 ps sep by 4 ds, 4 ds, cl, rw. Ch of 5 ds, rw. Sr of 4 ds, p, 4 ds, cl, rw. Ch of 10 ds, p, 10 ds, rw. Sr of 4 ds, join to p of previous sr, 4 ds, cl, rw. Ch of 5 ds, rw. R of 4 ds, p, 4 ds, join to 2nd last p of previous r, 2 ds, join to next p on centre r, 2 ds, 2 ps sep by 4 ds, 4 ds, cl, rw; repeat from * 3 times more, omitting r at end of last repeat, joining last r worked to first r and last ch to base of first r. Tie ends, cut and oversew neatly on wrong side.

Second motif
Work as for first motif to end of first sr, rw. Ch of 10 ds, join to p of any corresponding ch on first motif, 10 ds, rw. Work as before to end of next r, rw. Ch of 5 ds, p, 5 ds, join to centre p of next corresponding ch on first motif, 5 ds, p, 5 ds, rw. Work as before to end of next sr, rw. Ch of 10 ds, join to p of next corresponding ch on first motif, 10 ds, rw. Complete motif as before. Tie ends, cut and oversew neatly on wrong side.
Work 5 rows of 9 motifs, joining adjacent sides as second motif was joined to first motif.

Small mat *make 2*
Work 4 rows of 6 motifs, joining as before.
Damp and press.

for colour illustration, see page 351

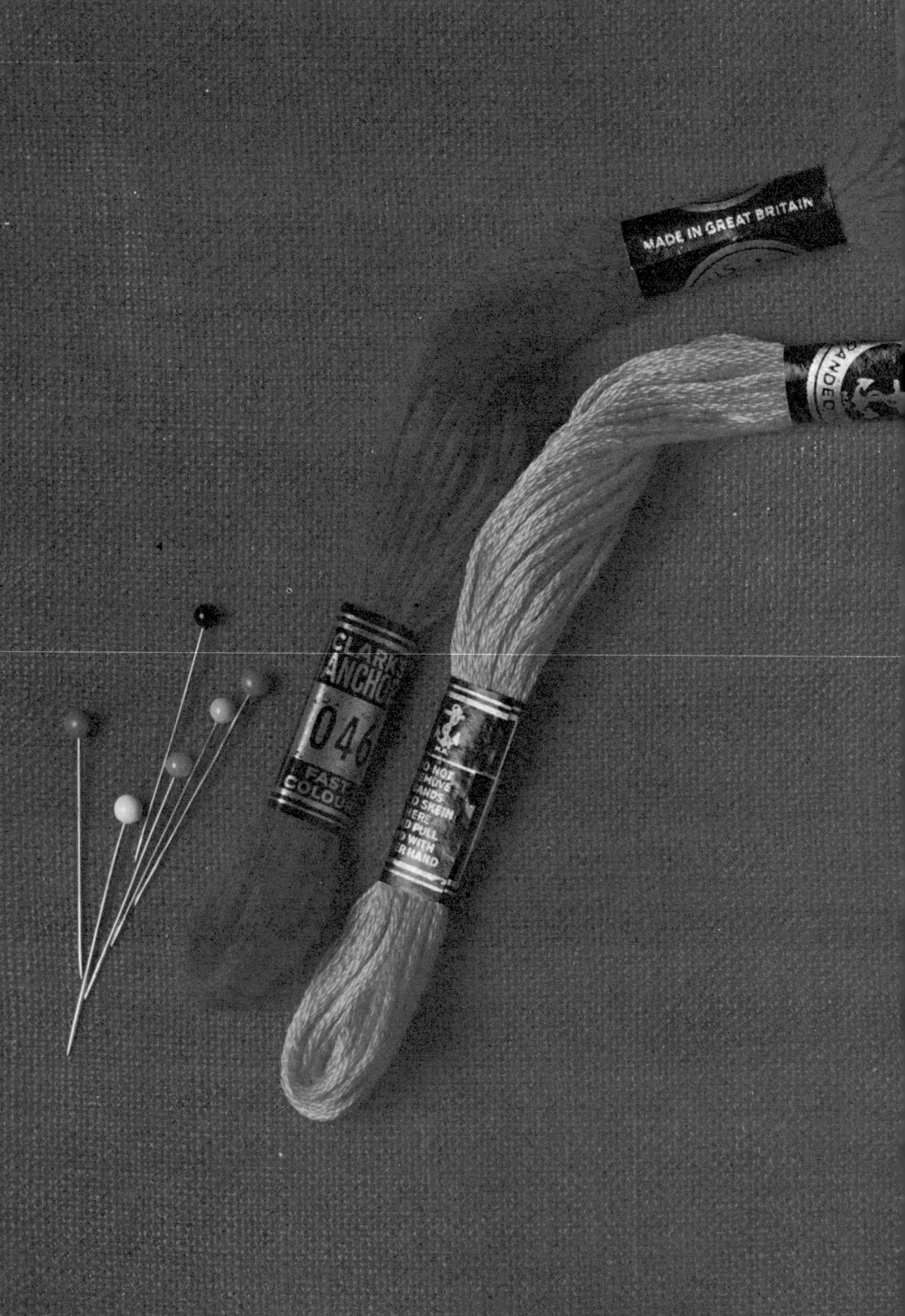